THE SACK OF DETROIT

THE SACK OF DETROIT

GENERAL MOTORS AND THE
END OF AMERICAN ENTERPRISE

Kenneth Whyte

ALFRED A. KNOPF   NEW YORK   2021

THIS IS A BORZOI BOOK
PUBLISHED BY ALFRED A. KNOPF

www.aaknopf.com

Knopf, Borzoi Books, and the colophon are
registered trademarks of Penguin Random House LLC.

Library of Congress Cataloging-in-Publication Data
Names: Whyte, Kenneth, author.
Title: The sack of Detroit: General Motors and the end of
American enterprise / Kenneth Whyte.
Description: First edition. | New York: Alfred A. Knopf, [2021] |
Includes bibliographical references and index.
Identifiers: LCCN 2020042695 (print) | LCCN 2020042696 (ebook) |
ISBN 9780525521679 (hardcover) | ISBN 9780525563426 (paperback) |
ISBN 9780525521686 (ebook)
Subjects: LCSH: General Motors Corporation—History. |
Automobile industry and trade—
United States—History. | Detroit (Mich.)—History—20th century.
Classification: LCC HD.U52 G388 2021 (print) |
LCC HD9710.U52 (ebook) | DDC 338.7/629222097309046—dc23
LC record available at https://lccn.loc.gov/2020042695
LC ebook record available at https://lccn.loc.gov/2020042696

Jacket photograph by Steven Bennett / Alamy
Jacket design by Chip Kidd

Manufactured in the United States of America
First Edition

for Thea Whyte

CONTENTS

THE SACK OF DETROIT

Prologue

AMERICAN BERSERKS

This is a book about America in the 1960s, a notoriously hectic time, and it felt that way in the living. The pace of events, the pace of change, seemed to have sped up to a point where, as Norman Cousins famously said, "the metabolism of history has gone berserk." It was the era of John F. Kennedy, Lyndon Baines Johnson, and Richard Nixon; of the civil rights movement and landmark decisions from Earl Warren's Supreme Court; of nuclear standoffs and the Vietnam War and student-led antiwar protests; of political violence, assassinations, domestic terrorism, and urban riots; of the women's movement and the birth control pill; of the counterculture, its veneration of youth, and its challenges to authority. It was the era of the moon shot. These were the stories that captured headlines throughout the decade, and they remain the focus of most historical treatments. They deserve the attention they receive but they were not all that happened in the 1960s.[1]

With more than a half century's perspective, we can now recognize that certain developments considered of moderate to low significance in the moment were, in fact, the stirrings of profound movements that would transform the United States and, indeed, the world. Jill Lepore's recent survey of American history, *These Truths*, does a masterful job of teasing out the development of digital technology in mid-twentieth-century America and how it was almost immediately exploited by opportunistic political operatives determined to segment and divide the citizenry for partisan gain, sowing seeds of the vicious polarization that plagues us today.[2]

Finding in a historical landscape the seeds of later issues or incidents is one way that we improve our perspective on the past. Another is to consider not what grew from that period but what failed to grow, or grew more slowly, or declined. It has become painfully evident over the last half century that America itself ceased to grow at its accustomed pace in the late 1960s. Between 1920 and 1970, despite stretches of world war and depression, Gross Domestic Product (GDP) per American citizen per hour increased at 2.86 percent annually. Since, it has grown far slower, at an average of 1.62 percent a year, a decline of 43 percent, notwithstanding a substantial boost from the personal computer and the digital economy. This collapse in the dynamism of American business, perhaps the greatest mystery in economic history today, was invisible at its start. It was well known that the economy, having grown spectacularly through most of the 1960s, slowed at the end of the decade and fell into a brief recession at the start of the 1970s but there was no sense that anything epochal had occurred. That only became evident with the passage of time.[3]

This book is neither a history of that economic decline nor a quantitative analysis of it. It is an inquiry into the course of American business in the 1960s, a topic largely ignored in the decade's record, in part because there was so much else going on but also because American historiography, on the whole, is light on business. It may have been recognized from Benjamin Franklin through Alexis de Tocqueville to Calvin Coolidge that the business of America is business, but historical literature is overwhelmingly concerned with politics, governance, military conflict, and sociology.

More particularly, this book takes as its subject the automobile industry and its leading company, General Motors. As Robert Gordon demonstrates in *The Rise and Fall of American Growth*, the internal combustion engine shares with electricity the title of most economically important invention of all time. Gas-powered automobiles, trucks, and buses revolutionized transportation in the twentieth century, and the rise of motor vehicle registrations from

2.3 percent of households in 1910 to 140.8 percent in 1970 was a crucial element in producing the world-beating standard of living enjoyed by Americans over this time. At its peak, in the 1960s, the automobile accounted for one in six of the nation's jobs, and one in five retail dollars.[4]

Because of the automobile's centrality to American life, General Motors, to an extent almost inconceivable today, *was* American business in the mid-twentieth century. In the 1950s and 1960s, General Motors produced almost half of the vehicles sold in the United States. It was the largest and most admired corporation in the land and, indeed, in the world. Both Wall Street and Washington recognized G.M. as the engine of American prosperity. In 1953, former company president Charles E. Wilson, nominated as secretary of defense by President Dwight Eisenhower, told his confirmation hearing before the Senate Armed Services Committee: "For years I thought what was good for our country was good for General Motors, and vice versa. The difference did not exist. Our company is too big. It goes with the welfare of the country. Our contribution to the nation is quite considerable." While much has been written about the implications of those words, it goes unnoticed that none of the senators challenged them as a statement of fact.[5]

Given General Motors' vast scale and the automobile's importance to American prosperity, it should not be controversial to suggest that a study of G.M. in the 1960s will enhance our understanding of American business in this period, and perhaps yield clues as to why the nation's commerce has been grinding its gears ever since.

Where the narrative gets more challenging is my contention that the fortunes of General Motors turned on a series of incidents in 1965 and 1966, when the corporation was charged with responsibility for the carnage on American roads, and was subsequently found to be spying on its chief critic, Ralph Nader, whose book *Unsafe at Any Speed* had damned G.M.'s record on vehicle safety and indicted its Chevrolet Corvair as a particular danger, a "one-car accident." Nader further accused the company of trying to entrap him with attractive women and intimidate him with anonymous threatening phone calls.[6]

At the time, the Nader affair was viewed as something of a farce and a massive embarrassment for General Motors. The largest corporation in the world was caught in an amateurish plot to discredit a critic and the whole thing blew up in its face. "There may be a Ford in your future," wrote a newspaper columnist, riffing on a popular television advertisement, "but there's a Chevrolet on your tail." At the same time, the incident was recognized as more than a joke. It was widely believed that G.M.'s determination to find dirt on Nader supported or proved his claim that the company and other Detroit automakers were foisting unsafe vehicles on the public. Before the year was out, Washington had passed bills that put car manufacturers under direct federal regulation for the first time in history. That legislation has since been credited with forcing heedless auto executives to address the built-in dangers of their product, saving tens of thousands of lives a year, ushering in a new era of consumer protection in the nation's legislatures, and permanently tempering America's trust in its corporate sector.[7]

This book began as an effort to explain how the world's most successful company could get something so spectacularly wrong. A few years as head of public policy for a multibillion-dollar communications company had awakened me to the innumerable ways in which large, thriving businesses can grow blind to their best interests, to say nothing of the public interest, and I thought it would be instructive to trace G.M.'s trail of arrogance, indifference, and error. That approach did not survive the evidence. It was true that G.M. and other automakers were arrogant, and that they made some boneheaded decisions, contributing to their own misfortunes. It was true that the Nader affair was a crucial moment in the history of General Motors, the automobile industry, and maybe even American commerce, but it was not what it seemed.

Rather, the Nader affair was a visible manifestation of a shift in American attitudes toward business that occurred among a significant portion of the citizenry and its political and intellectual leadership in the 1960s. During the 1950s, the Eisenhower years, the country had been preoccupied with economic growth and its handmaiden, consumer spending. This produced a backlash among certain critics who began voicing grave concerns about the consequences of unbridled growth and materialism in American life. Some of the dissenters were sincere, and their issues urgent: there was no disputing, for instance, that a shocking number of people were dying on U.S. roads every year and that automobiles—those totems of American affluence and corporate achievement—were somehow involved. But others, including activists, trial lawyers, and high-ranking politicians, were less sincere. They were opportunistic, and by the 1960s they were seeing in such causes as vehicle safety a chance to assail the wealth, power, and esteem of corporate America, and to seize some of that for the state, the people, or themselves.

General Motors and the city of Detroit were sacked in 1966 by a well-educated, well-placed, suit-and-tie-wearing band of crusaders united by a determination to knock automakers and the whole of corporate America down a peg and make them pay for perceived sins. Often self-righteous, uncompromising, reckless, and in important ways irrational, these men succeeded marvelously. Preaching new theories and belittling the ideas, evidence, and experience of others, they brought to its knees the greatest industrial enterprise in human history. The harm they inflicted on G.M. and Detroit's autoworkers was severe and lasting. America's confidence in its corporate sector was permanently impaired. The cause of traffic safety, contrary to expectations, was set back for generations. The careers of the marauders were enormously enhanced.

The whole affair had about it the whiff of what Philip Roth identified as another berserk—the "indigenous American berserk," a furious, destructive force, a ruthless determination of a nation to self-harm, unleashed in the 1960s as in no other decade, although our times are proving competitive.[8]

CHAPTER 1

ALL ROADS LEAD TO DETROIT

In 2001, French paleoanthropologists working in Chad dug up the skull and teeth of a *Sahelathropus tchadensis,* the oldest known species in the human family tree. They discovered that its foramen magnum, the large opening where the spinal cord enters the cranium, was forward of those of earlier hominids. The location of the opening indicated an upright posture, which suggests that our ancestors first learned to amble on two feet some seven million years ago. Evolution being a slow process, it required another 5.2 million years for *Homo erectus* to stretch its longer legs and abjure the tree in favor of a bipedal terrestrial lifestyle. For a long while after that, it was common for human males to awake in the morning and depart the cave or some similar place of protection to wander in search of sustenance, returning as the sun lowered to share the spoils of the forage or the hunt with other members of the tribe. Given the limits of human mobility, the males usually confined their hunts well within an area of twelve square miles. Apart from the occasional migration from one twelve-square-mile area to another in search of better food or more security, that constitutes the history of transportation for the vast majority of human existence.[1]

A mere eight to ten thousand years ago, mankind learned to

canoe. A few thousand years after that, the horse was domesticated somewhere north of the Black Sea. About 3500 BC, the wheel was invented and large animals were trained to pull people in carts. The Egyptians gave us sailing boats in 3100 BC, and not long after that the sailing ship. Only the fortunate, however, had access to these alternate modes of transportation, which is why so much of the action in Chaucer's *Canterbury Tales* (1387–1400), arguably the world's first road novel, occurs on foot. The stagecoach was invented in the sixteenth century and the steamboat in the eighteenth, while the steam locomotive and the first omnibuses, early forms of public transit, made their debuts in the more advanced parts of the globe in the nineteenth century. Still, the vast majority of people got around each day one step at a time, and they continued to do so into the twentieth century even in North America where horseflesh and bicycles were relatively cheap and abundant.[2]

In 1885, Karl Benz built his first Motorwagen powered by an internal combustion engine. He received a patent for it a year later. Many other French, German, and American automobile pioneers built similar vehicles in the 1890s and some sold hundreds of units, but it was not until December 1913 when Henry Ford began mass-producing his Model T on an assembly line in Highland Park, Michigan, that the automobile ceased to be a toy for affluent adventurers and instead became a new means of transport for the masses. Cars remained an expensive proposition (the Model T cost $525 in 1913 when 50 cents an hour was a good wage) but between that year and 1930, a mere 0.0000023 percent of human existence, the mobility of the species was revolutionized, particularly in the United States where all but the poorest households acquired a car. In that blink of time, reported the President's Research Committee on Social Trends in 1933, the automobile had become "a dominant influence" in the life of individual Americans. By their own choice, they had become in a very real sense "dependent on it."[3]

Between 1913 and 1930, manufacturers, the largest of them clustered around Detroit, sold motor vehicles into nine of every ten households in the land, the fastest rate of adoption of any technology to that time (only four in a thousand urban households owned horses in 1900). Vast numbers of people were now able to travel far beyond their traditional twelve-square-mile perimeter, covering far more ground than could ever have been imagined on foot or even on horseback, and in a fraction of the time. The travel was almost effortless and comfortable even for small groups with large loads. It was inexpensive (once the vehicle had been purchased) and so it could be accomplished again and again. It enhanced the ability of people to do things they needed to do, whether driving to work or running errands, and to enjoy what they wanted to enjoy, whether visiting a friend or seeing the country. By improving the drivers' opportunities for action at every moment and in every direction, automobiles gave people unprecedented control over time and space and, with that, a personal freedom denied the previous seven million years of hominids.[4]

Of course, there has never been an invention universally beloved of humanity, and the automobile was no exception. Right from the start, a small minority of motoring critics were appalled to find cars roaring along public thoroughfares at high speeds, horns blaring, engines backfiring, trailing dust and fumes as they knocked carriages into the ditch, mangled dogs and chickens, and stampeded defenseless pedestrians. These critics declared cars a public menace and denounced motorists as "a reckless, blood-thirsty, villainous lot of purse-proud, crazy trespassers upon the legitimate avenues of trade."[5]

Before the Model T made cars ubiquitous, jurisdictions in South Dakota and West Virginia sought to ban the automobile outright. Farmers in Minnesota and Sacramento plowed up roads to block cars from invading their countryside. Stories appeared in Western newspapers suggesting the use of guns against motorists and, while that advice appears to have passed unheeded, stone throwing was common, as was the practice of strewing nails or glass on routes favored by autos and the more dangerous tactic of stringing ropes or wires across roads. Demonstrating their relative civility were Vermonters, who directed cars to approach a town at a crawl preceded by a man waving a red flag, and Iowans, who required drivers to telephone ahead to warn a community of an impending approach. None of these efforts were effective in braking the nation's headlong rush to motorize itself.[6]

. . .

From the moment they began transforming individual lives, automobiles began transforming America. Farm and town were brought closer together. Rural life was relieved of much of its isolation and, with internal combustion engines now powering tractors, much of its drudgery. Cities were liberated, at great benefit to public health, from narrow, crowded streets ankle deep in horse dung. Millions were able to wave off their cramped rental apartments in sooty urban neighborhoods to achieve a dream of home ownership that had long been reserved for their social betters. They commuted to and from affordable, healthful suburbs with single-family homes on plots of grass with gardens and trees. Regardless of where people lived, they were no longer dependent on their family and neighbors for community and support. The young were able to escape the overbearing supervision of parents, neighbors, and clergy, motoring into the city to take advantage of its amenities and entertainments, or out to the seclusion of a quiet country lane. Pre-automobile proprieties and pre-automobile parochialism were everywhere in retreat.[7]

The effects of the automobile on American commerce were equally profound. The demand for steel, rubber, glass, gasoline, and industrial chemicals skyrocketed. Horsepower replaced horses for the transportation of both goods in trucks and people in taxis, and sprawling fields once devoted to equine silage were converted to more marketable crops. Myriad new industries sprung up to serve the motorist including new and used car dealerships, repair shops, parts and accessory suppliers, automobile insurers, roadside motels, and fast food restaurants (White Castle in 1921 and A&W in 1923). Automobiles enabled factories to leave urban cores and expand in industrial districts. They permitted supermarkets to supplant corner groceries. Retail activity in general was redirected from the vicinity of train stations to highways and commuter routes, a modification that, together with the accommodation of 121,000 fueling stations and innumerable parking lots, played havoc with land values. The auto industry's methods of mass production and mass marketing were imitated not only by manufacturers of other durable goods such as radios and refrigerators but by makers of cosmetics, tobacco, footwear, and many other consumer products.[8]

All of this disruption strained the resources of local governments, which had to deal with the dizzying problems of high-speed traffic, the decline in demand for urban transit, the consolidation of schools and churches, and the explosion of signage, both commercial and directional, at roadside. New patterns of urban and suburban living, the expansion of towns and cities beyond their traditional borders, caused complicated jurisdictional issues. Tens of billions of dollars in public money was needed to upgrade old roads, build new roads, control traffic, protect pedestrians, provide emergency services, and police delinquent drivers. Courthouses were crowded with motor vehicle cases. Prosecutors, defenders, and judges could not keep up. A whole other set of problems, including the licensing of drivers and the regulation of automobiles, their use, their size, and their equipment, beset state governments which were constitutionally responsible for commerce within their borders.

Critics of the automobile had shifted their arguments by the 1920s. The complaint that cars were an assault on the senses and the public peace, while long-lived, had been overtaken by a more sophisticated claim that they were a catalyst of regrettable social change. Motorization was loosening the bonds of community by making people less dependent on their neighbors, local businesses, and civic organizations. It was hollowing out towns and cities as residents migrated to suburbs or larger urban centers. Family time, serious cultural pursuits, and churchgoing were seen to be taking a backseat to joyriding. Links were made between cars and the crime rate, cars and delinquent teens, cars and sexual promiscuity. There was an aura of vice about the innumerable roadhouses and motels that had sprung up in service to the automobile. Some intellectuals were repulsed at the sight of the common man jacked up on four wheels, racing around, loose of all restraints, reveling in his freedom, putting on airs. The Sinclair Lewis character George Babbitt was a pathetic businessman and a devotee "of the Great God Motor." He thought himself a pirate in his automobile and the simple act of parking became "a virile adventure masterfully executed." This critique was developed and disseminated by the automobile's detractors in the same blink of an eye that saw it embraced as an indispensable feature of American life. The broader public remained unpersuaded.[9]

The authors of the President's Committee report in 1933 were astonished at how transformative and liberating a force the automobile had been, how it had quickened change in every corner of the nation to such an extent that it seemed the whole of history could be divided into pre-auto and post-auto phases. This was a common sentiment at the time. Not long after the commission filed its report, James Truslow Adams, the esteemed historian who coined the term "American Dream," cited the advent of the automobile as "the most important turning-point and change of direction for the common man in all history."[10]

Adams's identification of the common man as the prime beneficiary of the automotive age is crucial. This was not a top-down revolution. It was not foisted on Americans by wealthy automakers or government or anyone else. Car owners decided that vehicles would be used for pleasure, convenience, and work. The advantages of motorization were so profound and clear to them that there was minimal public resistance to the comprehensive reordering of life driving required, and none that seriously hampered the automobile's accommodation and development. The very shape of the automobile was influenced by an informal dialogue between manufacturers and drivers, who, especially in the early decades of motoring, took it upon themselves to tinker with their vehicles, making them faster, more durable, more comfortable, and more versatile. While certain auto executives and government figures would from time to time exert important influence over the industry, most of the time they were struggling to keep up with a burgeoning automobile culture that consistently exhibited a life of its own.[11]

It was a point of pride to American commentators that the automobile came to life in their country, even if it had been conceived overseas. Left in the hands of the Europeans, some said, the car would have remained a rich man's toy. It was the inventive, mechanical, and commercial genius of free men in a democratic society that had engineered the mass production of automobiles for a mass market.

There was some truth to this jingoism. The American automobile industry was led by risk-taking entrepreneurs such as Henry Ford, Billy Durant, and Walter Chrysler, men who with their own money had placed huge bets on the production of cars and made fortunes (and sometimes lost them and made them again) while rising to dominance in a highly competitive field. Between 1900 and 1908 there were 502 American companies launched to build cars, most using the internal combustion engine (a few relied on steam or battery power). The auto industry was far more entrepreneurial than the rail industry before it, or the commercial aviation industry after it. The former had been dependent on heavy government grants and subsidies while the latter was goosed by government air mail contracts and the development of publicly owned airfields. Government helped the automobile by building and improving roads, but roads were always catching up to public demand, not leading it.[12]

The founders of the automotive industry shared with other great entrepreneurs qualities of strong will and commercial vision. They also possessed a deep appreciation for how the public related to their product, which set them apart from earlier tycoons in railways, oil, and steel, who did most of their business with other businesses. Automobiles were a consumer business, and an ability to speak directly and persuasively to customers was a critical part of the game. Henry Ford led the way in producing a durable, utilitarian, inexpensive car for the masses, meeting in the simplest manner their desire for motorized personal transportation. "No man making a good salary will be unable to own one," said Ford, "and enjoy the blessings of hours of pleasure in God's open spaces."[13]

General Motors was founded in 1908 by the visionary financier William Crapo "Billy" Durant, who in a brilliant fifteen-year streak of stock-swapping acquisitiveness rolled thirteen carmakers and associated parts manufacturers into a combine that he hoped would one day rival John D. Rockefeller's oil interests and J. P. Morgan's banks for monopolization of its field. Durant was well on his way to realizing his ambitions before losing control of the company first in 1910 and again, for good, in 1918 due to extreme indebtedness. To the anti-Durant, Alfred P. Sloan, cool, rational, and disciplined, installed as president of General Motors in 1923, fell the challenge and the honor of assembling the company's diverse parts into a brilliantly engineered corporate machine that would not only dominate its field but the whole of American industry deep into the twentieth century. Adopting Durant's quest for dominance, Sloan combined many of Ford's production innovations with the further insight that drivers saw their cars as expressions of themselves. Rather than hew to Ford's insistence on one identical compact black car for every owner—the Model T was smaller than a Volkswagen Beetle—G.M. offered a suite of vehicles differentiated by style, size, and price. Pontiac was for the "poor but proud," Chevrolet for Everyman, Oldsmobile for the "comfortable but discreet," Buick for the striver, and Cadillac for those who had made it. Differing colors and trims offered further opportunity for drivers to assert their individuality. G.M. models were restyled annually like fashionable clothes, growing ever sleeker and flashier and sprouting new features such as balloon tires, hydraulic shock absorbers, plush seats, glistening dashboards, interior lights, and side windows that rolled up and down. Massive national advertising campaigns informed the public of the attributes of each brand of vehicle, from entry level to elite, and prodded buyers to always be in the market and trading up.[14]

General Motors was hardly alone in its realization that the automobile had infiltrated the American psyche. F. Scott Fitzgerald published *The Great Gatsby* in 1925, a novel in which driving is as critical to the story as walking is to *Canterbury Tales*. Indeed, the novel can be read as a treatise on automobiles and the new American culture they had wrought. Cars carry the action and serve as symbols of freedom and carelessness. They are social delineators, measuring the distance between sad George B. Wilson's "dust-covered wreck of a Ford" crouched in a dim corner of his garage, to Gatsby's gorgeous chariot, "rich cream color, bright with nickel, swollen here and there in its monstrous length with triumphant hatboxes and supper-boxes and tool-boxes, and terraced with a labyrinth of windshields that mirrored a dozen suns."[15]

Less than a decade into the age of mass-produced automobiles, Fitzgerald, who began writing *Gatsby* in 1923, could already count on his readers to understand the nuances of character and status that adhered to different automotive brands. This suggests that the symbolism of the automobile was established long before General Motors began elaborating it in its marketing, which was, in fact, the case. Humans have always invested material possessions with larger meaning. Previous to the internal combustion engine, horses and carriages communicated an owner's power, virility, and success, or lack thereof. Many of the first cars to venture beyond such functional names as Locomobile and Runabout borrowed snobbish horse-and-buggy nomenclature: Brougham, Coupe, and Cabriolet. Car owners needed no prodding from manufacturers and their marketers to decide that vehicles would convey prestige and personality.[16]

The great automakers continued to improve the mechanics, ease of use, comfort, and style of their vehicles through the 1930s and 1940s, although the Great Depression and Second World War somewhat crimped the advance of the motorized society. Gasoline was rationed and civilian vehicle production was temporarily halted and people held back on major purchases despite high employment and a doubling of personal disposable income between 1936 and 1945. The average automobile on the road was seven years old at the end of the war. Once the fighting stopped and the economy readjusted to peace, all restraint was abandoned and car lots were swamped with buyers. Americans burst out of the 1940s into one of the greatest spending sprees in history, led by a middle class much enlarged through expansion at its top and bottom ends. The golden age of American automobile and consumer culture had dawned.[17]

The anticipated household dividend from the triumph of democratic capitalism in World War II was a ranch-style three-bedroom with central heating, indoor plumbing, a refrigerator, stove, washer and dryer. Their owners filled those homes with TV dinners and Tupperware, joined the Diners Club, and took holidays on commercial air flights to Disneyland or Florida. And they bought cars, millions upon millions of long, gleaming, chrome-lined wagons with power steering and automatic transmissions, smooth-riding sedans on whitewall tires, and jaunty convertibles with radios and leather seats. Total sales of new cars jumped from 70,000 in 1945 to 2.1 million in 1946, 5.1 million in 1949, all the way to 7.9 million in 1955, a year in which there were 47 million American households.[18]

Cars were now the first major purchase in most people's lives, and often their first experience of indebtedness, a development that would help open the door to many other forms of consumer debt, including the credit card. The number of American households owning a vehicle passed the number of households owning their own homes soon after the war. By 1950, the average household for the first time owned more than one vehicle, with the second used primarily by a spouse and/or teenaged children. The whole family was now enjoying the time-and-space-conquering freedoms and convenience of the automobile. By the late 1950s, the number of miles traveled by Americans had tripled from wartime lows to 75 billion a year. Ninety percent of family vacations now involved a car.[19]

Once more, there were critics, a new generation of intellectuals who cited the automobile as Exhibit A in a general indictment of America's burgeoning commercial culture. The age of mass production and mass distribution, of super brands and chain stores and national advertising campaigns, had introduced an unprecedented degree of conformity and materialism to national life. The auto industry was said to be forcing upon the great mass of consumers a worship of sheet metal and horsepower. Drivers were crazy for new models of cars with nothing to recommend them beyond "needless variations in external fashion—variations not demanded by consumers but thrust upon them by snobbish and expensive advertising and salesmanship." That salesmanship might appeal to the basest motives of the buyer by advertising a car as a "beast," a "brute" with a "monster" engine that would "leave your neighbor in the dust." All of this was denounced as frivolous, wasteful, and degrading of humane values. It underlined the emptiness of both consumer and automobile culture.[20]

Lewis Mumford was one of a small number of social critics who had hoped the martial disciplines of the Second World War would purify the American people, persuade them to curtail their consumption, lower their standard of living, and adopt a less materialistic existence with the peace. The basics of life were already well distributed in the United States, Mumford argued, so it was time to accept culture rather than comfort as the highest social good. A true community valued love, freedom, justice, poetry, disinterested thought, and the free use of the imagination over profitmaking and material consumption. Cosmetics, candy, pulp fiction, glossy magazines, electric refrigerators, mechanical gadgets, and "sleek motor cars" should be abandoned in favor of schools, galleries, and theaters. Mumford prayed that the "deceptive orgy of economic expansion" would give way to "a hundred years of heroic, unremitting effort, poor in physical comforts but rich in political inventiveness, spiritual audacity, and human meaning." He and his ilk were sorely disappointed. Instead of a New Jerusalem came automatic transmissions, television sets, and McDonald's.[21]

With the assistance of Madison Avenue, automakers continued to improve their understanding of how people felt about their cars and created brands that better advertised an owner's worldly success and notions of the good life. The results were evident in new frontiers of automotive nomenclature: Cadillac's Biarritz and Pontiac's Catalina sang of exotic locales; the Studebaker Commander and Sky Hawk denoted military prowess; the Dodge Coronet Diplomat and the Packard Patrician reached new heights of four-wheel dignity; the Nash Rambler cast a romantic spell. As befit a nouveau riche nation, vehicle design trends were exuberant, featuring bulbous curves, two-tone paint, fake portholes, tailfins, and front seats like overstuffed sofas. Excessive as this styling looked to some, it was clear that Detroit was not so much leading the parade as struggling to keep up with the imaginations of its customers, who were simultaneously supporting a billion-dollar industry in after-market accessories, performance enhancers, and custom paint jobs.

The young were especially ardent about cars, cruising in them, preening at drive-in restaurants with radios blaring Chuck Berry's "Maybellene" and "No Particular Place to Go" and countless other car-themed hits. Hot rodding and stock car racing developed into popular subcultures celebrated in magazines and movies (including the original *The Fast and the Furious* in 1954), not to mention informal and organized competitions that made national icons of drivers Junior Johnson and Lee Petty. That popular youth culture and automobile culture were inextricably linked can make the whole scene seem frivolous and ephemeral, but high culture was no less obsessed with the car. Some of the finest novels of the era, including Robert Penn Warren's *All the King's Men*, Vladimir Nabokov's *Lolita*, Jack Kerouac's *On the Road*, were loaded with scenes on wheels and meditations on the role of cars and driving in modern life. The automobile was such an object of desire, so freighted with meaning, and so deeply ingrained in American culture it was easy to forget that its fundamental appeal was its utility. Had it been a stationary, two-ton pile of gleaming metal sitting outside the house to advertise its owner's virility or prosperity, car buyers would have been scarce and American streets would still have been paved with horseshit.[22]

Detroit was the capital of automania. It was home to General Motors, Ford, and Chrysler—the Big Three—a fact owed to an accident of birth. The city's strategic location on the shores of a Great Lakes shipping route stretching from Duluth, Minnesota, to the Atlantic Ocean, along with its ready access to timber and iron, and its history as a manufacturing and shipbuilding hub, had given it certain advantages in the race to host a nascent automobile industry, but what mattered most was that Henry Ford was raised on a farm just outside of town. He apprenticed as a machinist in the city and built his empire in nearby Dearborn. The Ford Motor Company served as a magnet for suppliers, engineering talent, labor, and everything else necessary to work with Ford and compete with Ford, and Detroit won the title of Motor City.

Its ascent was stunning. In 1900, Detroit had been less than half the size of Boston and St. Louis, smaller than Buffalo, Cleveland, and New Orleans. By 1940, it had grown by a factor of five while the population of the major East Coast centers had merely doubled. It emerged from the Second World War the fourth-largest city in the nation, with a population of just under two million. It was glittering, fast moving, and filthy rich, celebrated internationally as a cradle of entrepreneurship and the pinnacle of manufacturing genius. Detroit shared in and capitalized on all of the power wielded by the automobile over American life. The raw economic power of the industry required no explaining: its $65 billion in 1955 sales were almost one sixth of the Gross National Product. Political power was amassed by virtue of the city's contributions to the nation's unexampled standard of living and high rates of employment, and its service in the Second World War and the Cold War as the Arsenal of Democracy, churning out stupendous volumes of military hardware. And Motor City enjoyed a powerful cultural influence by virtue of its standing as the most dynamic commercial center on earth, the producer of highly coveted products, and the repository of the largest advertising budgets capitalism had ever known. In these and many other ways, Detroit was setting the pace for America throughout the twentieth century.[23]

It was nevertheless a parvenu by the standards of New York, Washington, Boston, Philadelphia, Chicago, St. Louis, and San Francisco. As such, it was suspect and sometimes resented in those quarters, not to mention feared. With forty more years of sustained growth—no one expected its expansion to stop—Detroit would be rivaled only by New York. And think how rich it would be then. How powerful. How untouchable, way out in the Midwest, a bridge away from Canada, beholden only to a customer base astonished and grateful for having been miraculously freed from the old twelve-mile ambit. All of America, in its lifestyle, its values, its aspirations, was becoming a suburb of Motor City, and nothing, it seemed, could stand in its way. Until 1958.

Elected premier of the Union of Soviet Socialist Republics on March 27, 1958, Nikita Khrushchev devoted his first speech in that role to a promise of communism's ultimate victory over the exploitive and unjust system of Western enterprise. "We shall conquer capitalism with a high level of work and a higher standard of living," he said, predicting the USSR would surpass American economic performance in "the shortest possible historical period of time." This was not a new line from the Kremlin. For almost half a century, its promises of burying capitalism had been as routine as Soviet milk and meat shortages. Nevertheless, the squat, bald, routinely inebriated figure of Khrushchev brought to his nation's economic war against the West a legitimacy that had eluded his predecessors.* In the previous year, he had launched the world's largest particle accelerator, turned the switch on the world's largest hydroelectric project, and, most impressively, inaugurated the space race

---

* "Not since Alexander the Great had mankind seen a despot so willingly, so frequently, and so publicly drunk. Not since Adolf Hitler had the world known a braggard so arrogantly able to make good his own boasts." *Time*, January 8, 1958.

by launching two Sputnik satellites into orbit. The Sputniks had shifted the Cold War's balance of military and technological power so decisively that the whole world could feel it in its knees. Khrushchev was *Time* magazine's Man of the Year two months prior to his elevation to premier.[24]

One month after Khrushchev's speech, the director of the Central Intelligence Agency, Allen W. Dulles, opened the annual meeting of the United States Chamber of Commerce in Washington, D.C., with a bracing speech of his own. Educated at Princeton and leaping back and forth throughout his life between legal practice and the espionage game, Dulles was a Cold Warrior par excellence, renowned for his ability to peer all the way through his wire-rimmed glasses, his clouds of pipe smoke, and the cloak of secrecy behind which communist Russia operated, to divine the real state of American-Soviet competition. He informed business leaders that the Soviets were bent on expansion and that their economic growth was far outpacing the United States, presenting "the most serious challenge this country has ever faced in time of peace."[25]

To underline his point that the challenge of saving the world from a totalitarian future rested with American business, Dulles noted that the Soviets were having "a field day" with the recession in which the States had been mired since mid-1957: "Every Soviet speech, magazine article, or radio broadcast beamed to underdeveloped nations plays up and exaggerates our economic difficulties. The uncommitted millions are being told by the Communists— 'see, we told you so. Crises and unemployment are inevitable under capitalism. Communism is the only true road to social progress.'"

The state of the American economy in March 1958 was indeed dispiriting, rather like the first U.S. attempt to match the achievement of the Sputniks, the internationally televised launch of the Vanguard TV3 satellite at Cape Canaveral on December 6, 1957. Its booster rocket rose four feet from the ground before losing thrust, falling back to earth, exploding, and destroying its launchpad. "Kaputnik," groaned the newspapers.[26]

U.S. unemployment was up sharply and its Gross National Product had been slipping for six months, leaving the economy in recession. The man elected to lead the nation through the Cold War and its challenges, President Dwight D. Eisenhower, seemed as listless as his economy. Now sixty-seven years old, he had won two landslide elections, wrestled with the Soviets globally and with red-baiting Senator Joseph McCarthy at home, and the strains of office were showing. A 1955 heart attack had been followed by surgery for Crohn's disease in 1956 and a stroke in 1957. Although still popular, he had been scolded in the press for golfing as unemployment surged. His legendary good humor wilting, he showed an edge in his formerly cordial press conferences and seemed exhausted by the contortions forced upon him by the recession. The downturn was mild and required no hasty action, he said in one breath, yet with the next he announced new congressional stimulus bills. It was at one of these press conferences that Eisenhower pointed a testy finger at Detroit.[27]

On the morning of April 9, 1958, before 235 journalists in the Executive Office Building, the president was bombarded with questions on the economy. Every time it seemed the conversation was veering in another direction, to foreign affairs or judicial appointments, the next query would return to the recession. Eisenhower endured an hour of hectoring before a question on why American consumers were not spending caused him to snap. "I personally think our people are just being a little bit disenchanted about a few items that have been chucked down their throats, they are getting tired of them; and I think it will be a very good thing when the manufacturers wake up—I am not going to name names—and begin to give us the things we want instead of the things they think we want. That is what I think."[28]

Despite his pledge to not name names, it was clear to the press gallery, to Washington, and to Detroit that the president had singled out the automotive industry as a cause of the recession. He had been known to lament the garish products of American automakers in conversations with visitors to the White House. The syndicated columnist Doris Fleeson recalled Eisenhower telling the story of "a Texas millionaire friend" who had turned in his bloated Cadillac for a smaller, more manageable car.[29]

Detroit's response to the president's charge was immediate and injured. General Motors complained that it was a victim of the recession, not its cause. One auto executive called the notion that automakers were chucking anything down consumers' throats absurd:

"Our normal position is one of abject prostration at the feet of our customers." The industry found consolation in a National Industrial Conference Board analysis that showed car sales were slumping primarily in states suffering the most unemployment and not across the board, which would have been the case if Americans hated the current automotive styles. It was only in the quiet of Detroit's boardrooms that the executives admitted the president had a point.[30]

When asked during his April 1958 press conference what Americans could do to counter the Russian "propaganda noise" about the U.S. recession, President Eisenhower said they should start buying.

"Buy what?" asked a reporter.

"Anything," said the president.[31]

His response was a perfect encapsulation of an informal doctrine known as the Cold War Consensus. It held that an ever-expanding consumer economy was the key to American greatness. People worked hard, earned money, spent that money in pursuit of the good life, however they defined it, and then worked harder to earn and spend still more. Through all this striving and spending Americans lifted themselves and others out of poverty, broadened the middle class, funded health care and education, and created a world-leading standard of living. Consumption was fundamental to the success of democratic capitalism. It made the United States a beacon of freedom, prosperity, and hope in the eyes of a world that might otherwise be tempted by the Soviet model, and it covered the enormous costs of building an insuperable nuclear arsenal and fighting communism around the globe. Consume, consume, consume, and the world would be a better, safer place. By the same logic, the failure of citizens to consume, or the failure of the business community to stimulate consumption, weakened the economy and, in doing so, posed a security risk.

The Cold War Consensus held sway in the 1950s: Eisenhower believed it, his fellow Republicans believed it, most Democrats believed it, Rotary Clubs, chambers of commerce, and editorialists preached it. Every red-blooded American, it was said, owed it to his countrymen to double what he ate, double what he smoked, and wear three shoes. The consensus informed Allen Dulles's lecture on

the Khrushchev challenge as well as President Eisenhower's indictment of Detroit. By chucking inferior product down the throats of
consumers, automakers were scoring points for the Reds.[32]

Another conviction evident in the president's comments was
that Detroit, on its own, was powerful enough to drive the world's
largest economy off the road. In fact, it was. The top ten firms in
the Fortune 500 list of America's richest corporations for 1958 were
either car manufacturers or producers of steel or fuel for cars. G.M.,
Ford, and Chrysler, together with the two leading tire manufacturers, Goodyear and Firestone, had as much combined revenue as the
entire bottom half of the five hundred. More than half a million
businesses directly supplied the auto industry. There may have been
disagreement on whether the industry was hampering the economy
or vice versa but there was no denying the centrality of automobiles
to America's economic performance. Said A. H. Raskin of *The New
York Times:* "Detroit leads the economy and it is chained to it."[33]

It was worrying, then, that Detroit was struggling in the recession of 1958, its factories quiet, many of its employee parking lots
empty. By one estimate, a third of the city's productive capacity was
idle. A quarter million autoworkers were sitting at home watching
television or fishing for perch on the banks of the Detroit River.
Michigan's unemployment rate led the nation, and Detroit's led
Michigan at 16.3 percent. The backload of unsold vehicles was stag-
gering, and behind it lay enormous, wasting inventories of steel,
tires, glass, and auto parts.[34]

Detroit executives kept up their courage by telling the usual
recession jokes about driving last year's Cadillacs and their wives
wearing last year's minks but many were quietly concerned that their
product indeed was missing the mark. Off the record, they admitted they had made no fundamental changes to their vehicle lineups
in the last several years, choosing instead to add more brightwork,
larger tailfins, and more bloat to the point where their vehicles were
"chromed up like brewery horses." In that time, the standard Chevrolet, the nation's best-seller, had grown eighteen inches in length
and six in width while putting on 400 pounds and $600 in extra
costs. It was now seventeen and a half feet long and 3,750 pounds.
German automakers, enjoying the worldwide success of their
thirteen-foot, 1,600-pound Volkswagen Beetle, called U.S. cars

"Strassenkreuzers," or street battleships. Walter Reuther, president of the United Automobile Workers, who might have been expected to countenance the product of his membership, complained that "the auto industry should make a car which at least could be parked in a single block."[35]

The criticisms would not have mattered if the buying public was entirely satisfied with the size, chrome, and ostentatious trimmings on offer, but a consumer survey in *Fortune* magazine suggested that a significant minority of American drivers was disaffected. This minority was absconding to a small-car market that had scarcely existed five years earlier. Total sales of small cars in the United States in 1954 were 32,403 (22,064 were foreign). By 1957, the total was 206,827. Projections for the full year of 1958 were 500,000-plus, exceeding 10 percent of the American automobile market. Some of the small cars were produced by American Motors and Studebaker but most were imported, an estimated 377,000 for 1958. These trends received little notice until the recession hit and the Sputniks were launched.[36]

"America," said the press, "is in the midst of a peaceful invasion on wheels." France, Germany, England, Italy, Sweden, and Japan were all in the market with "perky little economy models" and "racy sports jobs." Saab, the Swedish manufacturer, was selling four thousand units a year of a vehicle with an engine only slightly more powerful than a riding mower. The humble Volkswagen Beetle, with nothing new for 1958 but an ashtray, had a waiting list of six months. A spokesman for the European industry claimed that sales of imports in 1958 could have far surpassed the 500,000 mark in America but for shortages of inventory and a lack of dealerships. *Ward's*, the official scorekeeper of U.S. auto sales, called the foreign performance "spectacular." Almost all of the imports were inexpensive, cheap to operate thanks to good gas mileage, and reasonably dependable. That their styling changed little year to year made for a strong resale value. The Volkswagen today, said one Detroit executive, "is no uglier today than it was in 1947."[37]

Executives at the Big Three were sniffy about the imports in public. Small cars, said one, would never represent more than a "respectable trickle" in the market. Agreed another: "If the public wants to lower its standard of living by driving a cheap, crowded car, we'll make it. But we still don't believe that's what they want." Better for an economy-minded buyer to pick up a good used car rather than a foreign "shitbox," as Henry Ford II dubbed the Volkswagen. One particular school of thought saw the imports as appealing only to "misfits and masochistic snobs," to the "automotively bohemian," to the 5 percent of the car market "made up of individualists and nonconformists who cannot permit themselves to choose a car" built in the United States. "It's just a fad," said a Detroit-area dealer. "Like pizza pie."[38]

Those inclined to see the imports as a passing fancy noted that they sold best in California where manias were always coming and going. Others were not so sure. There was research indicating that foreign car buyers tended to be better-educated, more self-assured, and better-paid than the average American. And many long-lasting cultural and commercial trends had emerged from California. Its drivers, with fifteen thousand miles of good highways and beautiful weather at their disposal, were known to be serious about their cars. The state supported four hundred import dealers. A reporter on the scene said sales of foreign vehicles were not a fad but "an epidemic."[39]

Never mind its dismissals of foreign vehicles, Detroit was spooked. Rushing to get into the import game, G.M. announced that it would stock its dealerships with small cars built by its foreign subsidiaries, the Vauxhall Victor from Britain and the Opel Rekord from Germany. Ford began shipping in its German-made Taunus, and Chrysler struck an arrangement with France's Simca. The automakers said these moves were ploys to lure import and small-car buyers into their showrooms where they could be upsold to a proper American vehicle, but this was posturing. A Big Three consumer analyst admitted that "we are in midst of a consumer revolution. . . . We kind of left people behind by upgrading our cars through size and luxury year after year. We left a vacuum that the imports preempted."[40]

There was speculation in late 1957 that the Big Three might build their own compacts but it was not clear that it made economic sense for them to try to beat the imports at their own game. Small cars were popular in Europe in part because streets were narrow and distances short. Incomes were lower and gasoline more expensive. An American small car would require roughly the same number of parts and the same amount of labor as a standard car, yet it would have to be sold at a price competitive with the imports, which meant a slim profit margin for American automakers. Reduced profits were especially unappetizing because some experts were predicting domestic small cars were as likely to cannibalize the market for highly profitable standard domestics as they were to kill the market for imports. Finally, Detroit, unlike the Europeans, operated at so vast a scale that even a fast-growing market for 600,000 small vehicles in the United States might not be worth the effort for the Big Three.

All of these factors suggested it would be a huge risk for the Detroit colossi to abandon the automotive game they had invented and mastered to compete with imports. Big cars, with all their frippery and horsepower, had been good to the city. They were what Detroit's production facilities were geared to produce, what its labor was trained to assemble, and what its dealer networks knew how to sell. They were also what most Americans wanted to drive. No executive wanted to be responsible for investing hundreds of millions of dollars and the two or three years necessary to design, plan, and retool for small-car production only to find that compacts were indeed a fad, or that a foreign badge was a big part of the attraction, or that small cars did indeed cannibalize standard car sales, or that the best answer would have been to build a better standard car.[41]

There things stood, or seemed to stand, in the spring of 1958 in the city of Detroit, its "somber streets," according to the *Times*'s Raskin, full of "somber homes and somber people wondering whether we know as much about keeping our economy from causing wholesale human suffering as we think we do." The greatest industrial complex ever created by mankind was shaken, dishonored by Washington, its customers aloof, its executives apparently years from answering a foreign competitive threat that if left unchecked was on pace to devour 20 percent of the domestic market in twenty-four months, less time than it would take to produce an American small car from scratch. In that same amount of time, the imports could ramp up production and marketing and expand their dealer networks, enabling them to threaten more of the U.S. auto industry's revenue, not to mention millions of jobs, decades of national productivity growth, America's high standard of living, its reputation for genius in economic organization, and its military security. This was the "front line in the battleground Khrushchev has picked for the contest between totalitarianism and freedom," wrote Raskin. "How well we do in Detroit will be a large measure of our ability to stay ahead—and to stay alive."[42]

CHAPTER 2

BURSTS OF UNTAMED IDEALISM

Nathra Nader had left Lebanon for the New World at age nineteen with six years of education. He worked at a variety of jobs and made enough money to return home thirteen years later, in 1925, to enter into an arranged marriage with Rose Bouziane, the daughter of a sheep broker who was raising a large family under a sod roof. The couple returned to America and eventually settled in the foothills of the Berkshires in Winsted, Connecticut, where Nathra prospered as owner of the Highland Arms, a lunch counter and dining room on Main Street. The Highland Arms catered to mill workers during the day and traveling salesmen in the evenings. The Naders had four children; the youngest, born in a blizzard on February 27, 1934, was named Ralph.[1]

Nathra was the type of man who not only presided over his restaurant but much of the talk within it. "For a nickel," it was said, "you get a cup of coffee and an hour's conversation." Shrewd, stubborn, self-reliant, enterprising, and community-minded in what some resented as a meddling, holier-than-thou manner, he seemed to delight in out-Yankeeing the Yankees. He was keenly aware of his democratic rights, obstreperous in the face of perceived injustice, and given to what one acquaintance called "bursts of untamed idealism." A regular at town hall meetings, he would give free vent to his singular notions of egalitarianism and the public good. The local establishment regarded him as a nuisance. "He didn't leave anybody alone," admitted Ralph's sister Claire. "Not his customers, his siblings, his wife, his children. He wanted to talk and he wanted to talk about the problems of the day."[2]

The Naders spoke English and Arabic at home. Meals in the household were conducted by Nathra as seminars on the outrages perpetrated by civic authorities on the local population, or on the evils of large corporations, their exploitation of workers and customers. Ralph remembered that his father "used to tell us about the tricks big business used. He told us about how large grocery stores would shave one ounce off each five-pound bag of potatoes," which added up to big savings when the bags were sold by the thousands. Every member of the family was expected to participate in the exchanges at table, the more vehemently the better. "We were never allowed to run under fire," said Claire. "You know how you can get mad or frustrated and just want to run out of the room crying? We were never allowed to do that. You had to stand your ground and talk it out."[3]

The youngest and the most precocious of the children, Ralph was considered by his siblings to be somewhat spoiled. He was allowed a bicycle and participation in sports. His father would occasionally take him on field trips, including an outing to the local courthouse where they sat listening to the lawyers argue, Nathra describing the action for Ralph and interpreting even the most mundane cases as heroic contests between good and evil, between haves and have-nots. It was not long before Ralph decided he would be a lawyer.

Rose Nader, although dwarfed by her tall, rangy husband, was at least his match for strength of character. She had grown up in an Eastern Orthodox Christian family surrounded by Lebanese Muslims and she knew how to stand her ground. Presiding over the family's rambling ten-room home on the hillside one block up from the Highland Arms, Rose demanded that her children keep busy and work hard. She reinforced her husband's insistence on the value of education and community involvement and added emphases of her own on stamina, resilience, and personal responsibility. Ralph was made to wear short pants until the age of eight. When he complained, Rose asked him if he was a leader or a follower. Her Greek

Orthodox children were sent to Methodist Sunday schools and on a number of occasions she took them to Lebanon to visit her family.[4]

Ethnicity, Nathra's politics, and short pants were just a few of the ways that the Nader household stood apart from mainstream American experience in the middle years of the century. The family lived in a small town within walking distance of work, school, and all amenities when the general societal trend was toward cities and suburbs and long commutes. Nathra was a sole proprietor, with his entire family involved in his business, at a time when the male American workforce was migrating in droves to large corporations, massive factories, and national chains. As other shoppers were loading up on packaged foods at the new supermarkets, Rose raised Ralph and his siblings on Middle Eastern staples, fava beans, lamb kaftas, baba ghanoush, tabbouleh, and hummus. She refused to serve canned or processed foods and she was critical of the American appetite for bread and sugar. She was known to present a child with a frosted birthday cake and then scrape off the frosting before serving it. The family was comfortable, even prosperous by the standards of its community, yet its habits and values remained rooted in some combination of Lebanese village life and nineteenth-century America even as the Second World War ended and a restless, mass-produced consumer culture swept the rest of the nation. Materialism was anathema to Nathra Nader. "We tried to show the children that the wealth of the nation was people, not the dollar, so if you want a rich nation, you should love and help each other."[5]

Some of their neighbors respected the family's self-sufficiency and cohesiveness. "The Naders," said one Winstedite, "were free-standing." Others considered them a "noisy immigrant family," uppity newcomers with too many opinions. The latter crowd steered clear of the Highland Arms and neglected to invite Nathra and Rose to their parties. The author David Halberstam, a native of Winsted and Ralph's contemporary, said "there was a certain amount of tension between the Arabs and the Jews in Winsted when we were kids." The two communities took opposed views of the establishment of a Jewish homeland in the Middle East. Halberstam remembered as a significant occasion a social gathering hosted by a Jewish family that ran a dry-cleaning business in town. The Naders were not welcome. Meanwhile, Halberstam said he and Ralph were excluded from the New England establishment and the town's large Italian immigrant community. They were both "aware of the prejudices of the country, that all was not as it was said to be. You grew up a little tougher, a little more skeptical about the ideal and the reality of the situation."[6]

By the time he attended the local high school, the Gilbert School, Ralph was a gangly six-foot-three with thick black hair, round brown eyes, large ears, hollow cheeks, and a complexion darker than most kids in town. Among the top students in his class, he was one of those effortless learners who seemed to absorb information by osmosis. He was vocal in the classroom but respectful of his teachers. A fan of the New York Yankees, he liked to think of himself as a budding Lou Gehrig but, Halbertstam said, "Ralph was the kind of kid who if you threw a ball at him, he couldn't catch it." Nader was better verbally. He had been argumentative, even pedantic, for as long as Halberstam could remember: "[Ralph] would make you define your terms outside the windows of the fourth grade." The two of them had once debated Franklin Roosevelt's politics in the playground with snow blowing in their faces, Nader insisting that FDR's liberalism had been insufficiently bold, a radical proposition for the times.[7]

None of these qualities, nor his mildly pretentious habit of combing the unbroken columns of seven-point-type in the *Congressional Record* in the presence of other students, made Nader especially popular in high school. He had a small circle of studious friends, most of them college bound. He did not go to parties or dances. A female classmate considered him a social nonentity. "I don't recall Ralph ever dating," she said. "He never showed any interest. I think the girls in the class saw him as sort of different." His only extracurricular in high school was the drama club, for which he toiled in the wings. The Gilbert yearbook describes him as "quiet-smart—can be found either at home or at the restaurant—woman hater." The latter designation is said to have referred to his indifference to girls.[8]

Whatever his schoolmates thought of him, Ralph possessed a powerful sense of his own capacities, and confidence in his destiny. He spent a great deal of time alone, walking through the town's leafy streets to school, the Highland Arms, and the public library. He was a strong reader, attracted to the great journalistic crusaders

Ida Tarbell, Lincoln Steffens, and Upton Sinclair, social reformers with a keen sense of justice, a commitment to the underdog, and suspicion of concentrated wealth and authority. He reveled in their shaming of corrupt institutions and public eminences as other students piled into cars and headed out for football games and sock hops, or double features at the Pleasant Valley Drive-In a couple of miles up Highway 44. An outsider by virtue of his birthright, his upbringing, his intellect, and his own inclinations, Nader graduated and headed for college.

There had never been a doubt that Ralph Nader would attend university. "The children were made to understand that the family was a bank," said Nathra. "They put in work, duty, trust. Then they could take out what a child must have—education." He took pride in paying full freight for his son, whose marks were good enough to qualify for a scholarship. Ralph chose Princeton University, majoring in Far Eastern politics and languages at the Woodrow Wilson School of Public and International Affairs.[9]

Having stayed up too late reading, Nader overslept and missed classes his first college morning. When he did eventually meet his classmates, the modest sense of privilege he had enjoyed in Winsted was instantly negated. The big men on campus, products of the nation's finest preparatory schools, swaggered about in informal uniforms of scuffed white bucks, khakis, and blazer. Most were athletes content to slide through class with the gentleman's C. Once again, Nader did not fit. He studied hard and lived in the least expensive rooms he could find on campus. He took his meals at the least prestigious of Princeton's eating clubs, one of only two without servants, and even there he was something of a loner. An acquaintance recalled their dinner conversations: "We were fascinated by the ethnic quality of our lives. I was a Jewish boy from the Bronx, and Ralph was Lebanese, and very much Lebanese. We would trade long stories about our ethnic background."[10]

On one occasion, Nader attempted a minor rebellion against what he considered to be the conformity of his fellow undergraduates by wearing his bathrobe to class. On another he was bullied by a fellow student who threw empty beer bottles at him as he was taking a shower. "He terrorized me for about two hours," said Nader. "The idea that he had a naked, dripping person in a room with broken glass all over the floor did something for him. He kept going to get more bottles. Crash against the wall."[11]

One of Ralph Nader's professors at Princeton was H. H. Wilson, a cranky yet magnetic figure who taught the politics of power from the perspective of a profound skeptic. Wilson tried to instill in his students a passion for social criticism: "Be shunned, be hated, be ridiculed, be scared, be in doubt," he told them, "but don't be gagged."[12]

Wilson was an original: a professed anarchist and a socialist with conservative tendencies. He viewed Congress as a corrupt institution that undermined public trust by refusing to discipline its own members. He kept up a twenty-year feud with J. Edgar Hoover over the Federal Bureau of Investigation's treatment of civil libertarians, and made it his mission in life to tell the world "how destructive, how stupid and how ridiculous the FBI really is." His targets extended beyond the state. He could not say enough about the irresponsibility of corporate America. Once, on finding for sale at the edge of campus a can of hairspray that had supposedly been discontinued for its flammability, he purchased it, brought it to class, took out his lighter, and demonstrated its problem. As an early consumer advocate, Wilson was also among the first to speak of regulatory capture, the theory that government regulatory agencies care more for the welfare of the businesses they oversee than for the public interest. Ralph Nader acknowledged Wilson as a deep and lasting influence on his thinking.[13*]

The mid-1950s were a perfect time for a student of Nader's inclinations to be in university and looking for intellectual guidance. A new school of criticism of America's corporations and commercial culture was taking shape. H. H. Wilson was one academic manifes-

---

* Harper Hubert Wilson was found dead in his home swimming pool in 1977. Apparently, he had entered the pool to escape swarms of bees or hornets he had agitated with his lawn mower. He was sixty-eight years old. *New York Times*, August 17, 1977.

tation of it. Columbia sociologist C. Wright Mills, whose work was taught in Wilson's courses, was another. At Harvard, where Nader would head next, the economist John Kenneth Galbraith and the historian Arthur Schlesinger Jr. were promoting similar ideas in print and through Americans for Democratic Action, a pressure group seeking to move the Democratic Party in a progressive direction. Galbraith and the journalist Vance Packard elaborated the same themes in best-selling books. Together they fostered an intellectual milieu attractive not only to Nader but a generation of rebellious thinkers, journalists, and activists to whom the Cold War Consensus and its dedication to an ever-expanding consumer economy seemed a hollow mission.*

C. Wright Mills did not look like most sociologists. He had a cleft chin, a thick neck, large powerful hands, and a way of leaning into conversations, tense and focused, that bordered on belligerent. He was photographed riding his BMW motorcycle, bent forward over the handlebars, the wind dragging his hairline still further back on his large head, dressed in the same outfit of work boots, work shirt, and thigh-length leather jacket that he often wore to class. He did not so much teach at Columbia as thump his desk and exhort his students to think for themselves before mass society turned them into robots. He was hard on his colleagues, hard on his several wives (he divorced one twice), and hard on America. Out of Waco, Texas, by way of graduate school at the University of Wisconsin–Madison, he was promoted at age forty to the rank of full professor at Columbia. That was the same year, 1956, that he published *The Power Elite*, a study of the nation's organization of corporate, military, and political power.[14]

In Mills's view, America in the 1950s, with its massive corporate oligopolies, its swollen federal government and globe-spanning armed forces, had strayed light-years from the old Jeffersonian ideal of a limited government of independent yeoman farmers and self-sufficient entrepreneurs. The country was run by an elite of corporate, political, and military leaders, scions of socially prominent families who had all attended the same preparatory schools and Ivy

---

* Nader was introduced to both Mills and Galbraith as an undergraduate at Princeton. He would later write of his admiration for Packard.

League colleges and graduated to wear the same Brooks Brothers suits in the highest offices of the country's critical institutions. They lived in the same neighborhoods, belonged to the same clubs, holidayed at the same resorts, and shared an "upper class character" that permitted each to exude "a confidence in his own ability to judge, to decide, and in this confidence he is supported by his ready access to the experience and sensibility of those who are his social peers." These elites, most of them White Anglo-Saxon Protestants, all of them philistines, had usurped the traditional authority of family, church, and the academy and acquired a monopoly over the nation's power, money, and prestige. Having perfected the means of protecting their private interests and those of the institutions they represented, they ensured their self-perpetuation and comprised a "system" that controlled the destinies of their countrymen.[15]

The place in which the elite, this "homogenous social type," most naturally converged was the corporate boardroom. There one found a heavy "overlapping" of "the warlords, the corporation chieftains, the political directorate," wrote Mills. And it was in the boardroom that these highly compensated men proclaimed ceaseless economic growth as America's highest priority while divvying up the nation's abundant resources among themselves and securing their markets against competitive threats. They determined what consumers would buy and at what price. They decided what to demand of "compliant political authority." They encouraged massive defense spending, and rigged the system to their advantage by inventing shelters and loopholes to avoid paying their share of taxes.[16]

Mills harped incessantly on the system, "the American system of power," and how it was maintained and operated by unaccountable elites to the detriment of the average citizen. He absolved the elites somewhat by supposing that they were only vaguely aware of what they were doing, limited as they were by their narrow personal experience. For all their advantages, they were mediocrities, smug and comfortable conformists doing what the system demanded, heedless of morality and any true notion of the public good. They did what they did because they were bred to it. They got away with it because the booming postwar economy had created a material contentment that enabled people "to accept public depravity without any private sense of outrage."[17]

Mills was not writing about the automobile industry per se in *The Power Elite* but General Motors was his primary illustration of the workings of the system. The automaker was its hub. The company's executives, directors, and leading shareholders, Mills asserted, were well connected in political and diplomatic circles. Mills offered no supporting evidence on this point, nor did he see a need to validate empirically his contention of social homogeneity among the depersonalized elites. To him, it was self-evident. Hunter S. Thompson would salute him as "one of the few people around with the simple guts" to go after "the boobs with a chain mace."[18]

Mills's arguments, peppered with current sociological jargon and theory, struck many as plausible. *The Power Elite* would find a small but avid audience among the alienated left in the age of Eisenhower. It took to heart Mills's skepticism of authority and conformity, his elucidation of a closed, corrupt system manipulating America to its own advantage. Those influenced by him would have no problem mustering the sense of outrage Mills found lacking in the public at large. For General Motors, being cast as a kingpin in an exploitative, quasi-conspiratorial cabal working against the interests of its customers, employees, and the general public was a new experience, but one to which it would grow accustomed before long.

In 1957, magazine writer Vance Packard published *The Hidden Persuaders*, the first of his three books in four years that would climb best-seller lists and make him one of the most famous journalists of his day. *The Hidden Persuaders* was an investigation of a "strange and rather exotic new area of modern life," the use by advertisers of psychological insights and social science methodology to influence the purchases of consumers. It would not have been news to most of Packard's readers that Noxzema was marketed as a promise of beauty rather than as skin cream, or Cadillac cars as prestige rather than as transportation. Advertising had always played upon feelings. What Packard revealed was the ingenious methods of motivational research that postwar advertisers employed in their attempts to engineer consent among consumers. Madison Avenue was studying the subconscious mind to understand how a consumer's "hidden weaknesses and frailties" might be exploited to make them more susceptible to a product pitch. It deliberately preyed on people's loneliness and doubts, their feelings of sexual inadequacy and social anxiety, in order to open their minds to a message. It preached self-indulgence, ego gratification, or a sense of security to overcome any lingering puritanical objections to spending money on nonessentials. Packard viewed all of this as a campaign by capitalists to reach into the minds of Americans and enslave them as consumers.[19]

Not all of Packard's evidence was psychologically sound. He put weight on Rorschach testing, now largely discredited, as well as subliminal advertising, the claims for which were overstated. Moreover, some of what he presented as devious was merely improved research technique, for instance, the use of representative samples of opinion, demographic profiles, and unbiased survey questions, all of which permitted a better understanding of consumer behavior and a sharpening of commercial rhetoric. He nevertheless found enough that was new and disconcerting in the methods of marketers—most Americans had never before heard such phrases as subliminal messaging and planned obsolescence—that his book became a sensation.

When it required an illustration for an argument, *The Hidden Persuaders* frequently turned to the automobile industry, the world's largest advertiser. Packard maintained that America's obsession with big cars was driven by the impression, hammered home by advertisements, that small cars were for small, inferior people. He reported that automakers had been known to raise prices on a vehicle simply because some buyers could be convinced to drive a high-priced car to prove that they could afford it. Packard used the work of Dr. Ernest Dichter, a consumer researcher who had worked with Chrysler, to show how sexual psychology was employed on the dealer's lot. It was Dichter who gave Detroit an answer to the puzzle of why married men tended to buy sedans despite a stated preference for convertibles. Dichter held that the convertible represented the man's "symbolic mistress," a romantic adventure that he fantasized about but never acted upon, ultimately making the safe choice to "marry the sedan" just as he had once married the plain, practical girl from the old neighborhood. This notion led car dealers to put their convertibles at the front of their lots where they would play on their customers' sexual vulnerabilities and lure them into the showroom.[20]

While the journalist in Packard reported much of this detail with bemused detachment, there was a message in his book. He grew up on a Pennsylvania farm, the son of Methodist parents who instilled in him values of sturdy individualism, self-restraint, and concern for his fellow man. Looking out at postwar America with these values in mind, he was appalled by what he saw. Like Mills, he viewed corporations as oversized and untrustworthy, manipulative, and generally detrimental to the public good. Abetted by advertising agencies, they were playing people for fools, taking advantage of the nonrational sides of their nature and pushing them to consume against their better judgment. The constant bombardment of individuals with ads designed to upset their psychological equilibriums had "seriously anti-humanistic implications." It prevented people from acting as "rational and self-guiding being[s]." Like Mumford, Packard believed the triumph of large corporations and mass consumption had been achieved at the expense of individual liberty and freedom of choice, indeed by subverting the meaning and sanctity of human existence. Under pressure of multimillion-dollar marketing campaigns, people were losing confidence in their self-directed lives and adopting a status-driven, hedonistic morality created by Madison Avenue. A nation of producers had become a nation of brittle, compulsive, unthinking consumers, so voraciously materialistic, said Packard in another work, as to "look a bit fatuous in the eyes of the world."[21]

The Hidden Persuaders took more than a year after publication to reach the *New York Times* best-seller list. It then steadily rose to number one and remained near the top for fifty weeks. The end of that remarkable run coincided with the debut on the *Times* list of John Kenneth Galbraith's *The Affluent Society*. Unlike Mills and Packard, who wrote from the perspective of an outsider peering into the consumer economy, Galbraith had a more complicated relationship with his subject. A Canadian agricultural economist who did postgraduate work at Berkeley and Harvard, he had spent the war in Washington rationing consumer goods at the Office of Price Administration and, occasionally, writing speeches for President Franklin Roosevelt. After a brief spell on the staff of *Fortune* maga-

zine, he returned to Harvard, gained tenure, and tutored Democratic presidential nominee Adlai Stevenson on economics prior to
the 1952 and 1956 elections. He was very much an insider, and an
imposing one at that, standing six-foot-eight with a long patrician
nose and a confident, sardonic manner.[22]

Notwithstanding his privileged position, Galbraith was a stern
critic of American culture and economics, and he shared with C.
Wright Mills a disdain for authority, particularly in the worlds of
business and politics. Whereas Mills chose as his bête noire a like-
minded elite, Galbraith targeted "conventional wisdom," by which
he meant ideas and values that had long outlived their usefulness yet
remained lodged in the uncritical, unchanging minds of people in
positions of influence. His prime examples of conventional wisdom
were two ideas that had been foundational to economics since the
birth of the discipline: that economies were driven by scarcity and
insecurity, and that the answer to every problem of public policy was
continued economic growth.[23]

How, asked Galbraith, could anyone credit the old teachings
on the importance of scarcity when America had achieved a level
of affluence unprecedented in human history? Virtually all people,
he said, had access to the basic requirements of life, even if those
requirements were expanded to include an automobile and an electric toaster. Material goods for private consumption had never been
more abundant or affordable. These facts, together with the wide
availability of jobs paying decent incomes and the availability of
unemployment insurance and old age pensions, all but guaranteed
that a person could acquire without undo struggle what was needed
to live. The historic problems of scarcity and insecurity had been
conquered and nothing was likely to reverse this happy outcome.

That large amounts of advertising were necessary to convince
Americans to spend their cash was proof to Galbraith that the
nation was awash with goods, and that there was little real demand
for much of what was marketed. Galbraith, too, drew examples from
the automotive industry: "To create the demand for new automobiles, we must contrive elaborate and functionless changes each year
and then subject the consumer to ruthless psychological pressures to
persuade him of their importance." That decisions to buy new vehi-

cles must be "synthesized by advertising, catalyzed by salesmanship, and shaped by the discreet manipulations of the persuaders shows that they are not very urgent. A man who is hungry need never be told of his need for food."[24]

It followed in Galbraith's mind that if scarcity was a myth, so was the need for higher volumes of production of consumer goods, especially when those goods were no longer food, clothing, and shelter but items that satisfied "a craving for more elegant automobiles, more exotic food, more erotic clothing, more elaborate entertainment—indeed for the entire modern range of sensuous, edifying and lethal desires." These products were incidental if not meretricious, he said. Their utility to social well-being and contentment was inversely proportional to the urgency with which they were flogged in television ads. That the production of so much trash exhausted people's lives in the making and acquisition was to Galbraith "foolish." Better to have no growth, he ventured, than growth on these terms. Improvements in the standard of living through the consumption of un-necessaries were not real improvements at all. The frantic pursuit of still more economic growth was an unworthy goal for an already affluent nation, and unlikely to improve America's security against the communist threat as so many in Washington believed. Despite a relatively weak consumer economy, the Soviets had managed to put a satellite in space before the United States.[25]

Here Galbraith was dismissing the Cold War Consensus as conventional wisdom. The notion that greater production of consumer goods was the central problem in American life was a self-serving invention of businessmen hungry for profit and anxious to keep their social prestige from leaking to others who might be more worthy, including public servants, professors, writers, and artists. Again like Mills, Galbraith saw conspiracy at work in the "system" or "mechanism" that business leaders and their cheerleaders in government had developed to protect their interests. While encouraging an overinvestment in consumer goods, they starved public goods such as education. "Simple minds, presumably, are the easiest to manage," wrote Galbraith. Better education might lead people to appreciate music and the fine arts, literature and science, whereas dull people can be convinced through mass advertising to engage in a relentless pursuit of the simple physical objects of consumption, "and hence it is on these things that we find concentrated the main weight of modern want creation."[26]

Galbraith's solution was to curtail advertising, slow the production of goods, slow consumption, and let economic growth flatten. People did not dread flat law and order, or flat security of life and property, he said, so why should they fear flat incomes or flat growth? American corporations did not need more growth: they were now so large and so successful at forming oligopolies to avoid competition that they showed "marked indications of immortality" and could be considered permanent features of the economic landscape. "Almost no large industrial corporation in the United States, which is also large in its industry, has failed or been seriously in danger of insolvency in many years," wrote Galbraith. "Where there has been danger, the government has come to the rescue."[27]

Galbraith wanted government to step in and steer investment from commercial production of alcohol, comic books, mouthwash, narcotics, pornography, and automobiles to public goods such as schools, hospitals, urban redevelopment, sanitation, parks, and playgrounds. Unless America wanted to be a nation of "private opulence and public squalor," it needed to strike a new balance between quantity of goods and quality of life. He returned, again and again, to the automobile by way of illustration:

> The family which takes its mauve and cerise, air-conditioned, power-steered and power-braked automobile out for a tour passes through cities that are badly paved, made hideous by litter, blighted buildings, billboards, and posts for wires that should long since have been put underground. . . . They picnic on exquisitely packaged food from a portable icebox by a polluted stream and go on to spend the night at a park which is a menace to public health and morals. Just before dozing off on an air mattress, beneath a nylon tent, amid the stench of decaying refuse, they may reflect vaguely on the curious unevenness of their blessings.[28]

Galbraith, like Mills and Packard, was making a fundamentally moral argument against what he perceived to be the prevailing values of the times. All three authors asked questions about consumer capitalism that remain valid today, even if their presentation of themselves as protectors of benighted consumers under attack by predatory corporations and their political handmaidens was at times tendentious. Like previous generations of critics of the automobile and consumer culture, they were a minority, distinctly so judging by the fact that America, with 6 percent of the world's population, was consuming roughly half of its goods and automobiles. Nonetheless, they were an increasingly influential minority: articulate, persuasive, backed by academic affiliations and best-seller status, and, in Galbraith's case, direct connections to the highest reaches of the Democratic Party. Directly or indirectly, they would win many converts in the years after their publication, among them young Ralph Nader.[29]

After graduating from Princeton magna cum laude, Nader traveled west in the summer of 1955. "I wanted a real change of pace, a change of scene," he said. He picked apricots among the migrant workers in orchards north of Los Angeles and wandered up to San Francisco and Yosemite, taking odd jobs along the way to pay his keep. He returned east in the autumn to Cambridge, Massachusetts, where he attended Harvard Law School.[30]

Nader fit Harvard no better than Princeton. Ill at ease on campus, he blamed the university, starting with its design. "Everything was towers, vertical, cramped," he said. The noise and grime of Boston seeped over the campus's walls and blanketed everything. "It was very uncomfortable."[31]

His fellow students Nader scorned as compliant grunts grateful for "the freedom to roam in their cages." Worse were the faculty, who seemed to Nader pleased with themselves and unperturbed by the world outside their doors. They were "blind to the social injustices of the last half century." Their heroes, including the progressive Supreme Court justices Louis Brandeis and Benjamin Cardozo, and Learned Hand, who ran one of the great appeals courts in U.S. history, were in Nader's estimation "the staid, the dry, those who were respected by the power structure. Who the hell says a lawyer has to be like that?" Rather than teach law as an instrument of justice, Harvard's lecturers, in Nader's estimation, were preparing students for corporate life and conventional government service, never suggesting to them that they might sacrifice their time or their incomes to the public good. "And that turned me off," he said. "I was not going to become sharp by becoming narrow, which is the way they taught."[32]

Seeking a more fulfilling life, Nader rebelled at Harvard, this time with idleness, skipping classes and disappearing for days at a time. He lived off campus and was viewed by those who bothered to notice him as a shy, awkward person, one with secrets, never explaining his comings or goings, never saying exactly where he lived. "He always acted in mysterious ways," said an acquaintance, "I didn't know whether it was a Lebanese thing, might be a family thing."[33]

Among his other unusual habits, Nader would read or work through the night, eat a dinner of ham and eggs at dawn, sleep all morning, and wake to an afternoon breakfast of roast beef. His appetite was a thing of wonder to those who knew him. He once won a bet by disposing of two twelve-inch strawberry shortcakes at a sitting. Notably frugal, he typed term papers and managed a bowling alley to earn what little cash he required to get by.

One place at Harvard where Nader did apply himself was the law school's student newspaper, the *Record*. He began as a correspondent, writing not on the usual campus affairs but on capital punishment, Boston's blue laws, and the plight of American Indians, who he believed deserved better from the European invader after having bestowed upon him a range of gifts from corn flakes to American federalism. He was promoted to section editor and eventually became president of the publication, or managing editor, until his penchant for running his own lengthy crusading articles, including a piece on Puerto Rico's commonwealth status that took over most of a six-page issue, prompted an insurrection among his staff. He was ousted. "He was never really a person who was inclined to make a practical compromise," said Robert Oliver, his replacement. "He could rationalize issues easily to suit his own views."[34]

CHAPTER 3

THE PLAGUE OF
THE TWENTIETH CENTURY

The single issue that seemed to appeal to Nader more than any other at law school was traffic safety. He was not a car guy. He had briefly owned a 1949 Studebaker while attending Princeton. By his own report, he had almost run over Albert Einstein one day while leaving campus. He sold the car, preferring to hitchhike, which he rationalized as a favor to the drivers who picked him up—he kept them alert with his conversation.[1]

Nader would later cite two principal spurs to his thinking on traffic safety. The first was an undocumented collision he saw somewhere between Winsted and Cambridge in 1954 or 1955, in which a young girl was nearly decapitated by the door of a glove compartment that had sprung open in the crash. The second was a 1956 article by Harold Katz in the *Harvard Law Review*.[2]

The chess-playing son of a Russian emigrant, Katz had grown up in Tennessee and graduated from the University of Chicago Law School in the spring of 1948. He initially practiced in Chicago as a labor lawyer, but in the early 1950s became embroiled in an automobile crash case. This experience prompted him to reconsider some of the fundamentals of torts, the branch of law dealing with personal injuries resulting from wrongful acts that do not necessarily amount to crimes.[3]

It was striking to Katz how little the law concerned itself with the bloodbath on America's highways. Forty thousand people were killed annually in traffic crashes, a horrifying toll that kept increasing, decade after decade. A whole industry had developed in America to respond to crashes, mopping them up and treating victims. Laws had been passed to better manage traffic. Engineering expertise had been developed to make highways less dangerous. Nationwide campaigns had been launched to impress upon the public the need for safe driving habits. Yet the gross number of fatalities continued to mount. It occurred to Katz that maybe the nation's traffic safety advocates were approaching the problem the wrong way.

His ideas were not entirely his own. Katz had been following the work of police and safety researchers who were studying the dynamics of traffic crashes and asking what else might be done to mitigate the damage. The U.S. armed forces were also involved in this work in a bid to combat an alarming rate of personnel loss behind the wheel. Even more useful to Katz was a growing medical literature produced by doctors and surgeons frustrated by the heavy flow of maimed, crippled, paralyzed, brain-damaged, and dead victims of automobile crashes through their emergency rooms and operating theaters. Radicalized by their frontline experience and the stubborn refusal of annual fatality totals to fall, the physicians were asking questions and making arguments of their own. All of this fed into Katz's analysis of the situation and the 1956 article that would captivate Ralph Nader with its bold new strategy for traffic safety.

The death toll on American roads traces back to September 13, 1899, a cool, blustery Manhattan evening when Henry Hale Bliss alighted from a trolley car at 74th Street and Central Park West. Bliss was a stout, dapper Wall Street real estate broker who for many of his sixty-nine years had done a brisk trade in New York apartment buildings. Stepping from the trolley to the pavement, he turned to help a female companion with her descent. An automobile driven by a man named Arthur Smith at that same moment was attempting to thread the needle between the trolley and a large truck on the opposite side of the road. Smith's car struck Bliss and ran him over, crushing his head and chest. With his female companion hysterical on the street and Smith in police custody, Bliss was carried by ambulance to Roosevelt Hospital where the house surgeon declared him beyond hope. He died the next day, the nation's first known automobile fatality.[4]

Before long, auto fatalities were a weekly occurrence in America. In 1902, *The New York Times* worked up a feature on what it called "The Automobile Terror." That year alone, the wife of a Nevada senator had been struck down and killed by a car; a young man had died after driving his vehicle into a large boulder in upstate New York; a Manhattan pedestrian had been run over by a taxicab; a boy had been left for dead by an unknown chauffeur in Central Park; an attempt to break a land speed record in Staten Island had left one dead and nine injured; and an automobile had spooked horses pulling a mower near Newark, killing one man by knocking him into the road and injuring another by throwing him into the revolving blades of the mower.[5]

It might have been anticipated that the introduction of large, heavy, fast-moving machines into well-trafficked thoroughfares would produce gore. Streets in the pre-automobile era were public spaces where people strolled, friends gathered, children played, and vendors sold their wares. There were few sidewalks and no crosswalks, stop signs, stoplights, traffic lanes, speed limits, or traffic cops, indeed, no rules at all to govern automobiles. The vehicles themselves had little in the way of safety equipment beyond rudimentary brakes and loud horns, and their unlicensed drivers seldom had more training behind the wheel than the salesmen supplied to get them off the lot. In 1902, New York City recorded an incredible 8.32 fatalities for every 1,000 autos registered, a majority of the victims being pedestrians.[6]

Improvements in the handling of cars, the competence of drivers, the wariness of pedestrians, and some crude traffic controls brought the New York fatality rate down to 1.28 per 1,000 cars by 1916, but the enormous increase in the number of vehicles on the road drove the annual death total to new heights. Twenty years after the *Times* had proclaimed the automobile terror on the basis of a handful of fatalities, 858 people were killed in one year by cars in the city, and almost 15,000 nationwide. While data on nonfatal crashes was difficult to gather, it was estimated that an additional half million people were injured in crashes. Traffic safety was on the verge of becoming a major public health issue.[7]

It is curious that it took so many fatalities to spark a national conversation on traffic safety, one that Katz and Nader and the American medical community would eventually join. Manhattan's infamous 1911 Triangle Shirtwaist Factory Fire killed at least 141 people and led immediately to new social and workplace legislation. By comparison, the 423 lives lost in New York vehicular collisions (including automobiles, wagons, trains, and streetcars) that same year were of no great consequence. Several factors were at play, starting with the horse.[8]

At the dawn of the century, horses and horse-drawn vehicles did far more damage to people than cars, killing 200 in New York City annually while automobiles killed 36 nationwide. It took motor vehicles until 1912 to kill over 200 New Yorkers a year, by which time animal-drawn wagons were still killing just under 200 people in the city per annum. As late as 1916, the horse was still competitive: Chicago recorded 16.9 horse-related deaths for every 10,000 horse-drawn vehicles; a year later, Detroit posted 26 fatalities per 10,000 registered automobiles. Horses also added to the fatality rolls indirectly by dropping at their peak more than 2.25 million pounds of manure (and 40,000 gallons of urine) on the streets of New York each day, leading to 20,000 human deaths annually, according to one contemporary magazine.[9]

Another important factor in acceptance of automotive mayhem was that Americans were accustomed to perilous travel. The nation's railroads killed 11,800 people in a twelve-month period between 1906 and 1907, a number that automobiles would not catch until 1920. New York State recorded 58 deaths by rail and 15 by streetcar in April 1914, compared to 25 by automobile.[10*]

More generally, untimely and accidental deaths were routine

---

* On top of this was an astonishing equine fatality rate. The dead horse was a staple of urban street life in the late nineteenth and early twentieth centuries. In one year, New York removed an average of 41 per day from its streets, or 15,000 in total. *New York Times*, June 9, 2009.

in the early twentieth century. Average life expectancy in 1910 was fifty years. Infectious diseases such as influenzas, pneumonia, and tuberculosis took millions to early graves. The 12,155 traffic fatalities in 1920 were one quarter the number of nontraffic accidental deaths, including falls, drownings, burns, poisonings, inadvertent shootings, and farm and workplace mishaps. All of these figures were dwarfed, moreover, by such deadly phenomena as the Great War, which killed seventeen million soldiers and civilians globally, including 117,465 Americans, and the Spanish Flu pandemic of 1918–1920, which claimed at least fifty million lives, 675,000 of them American. Life, in these years, was a precarious business.[11]

The recognition of traffic fatalities as a public health issue was further inhibited by the pace at which they occurred: steadily over time rather than all at once like a factory fire. They were geographically dispersed, as well. And it did not help that most people believed management of road risks was primarily the personal responsibility of pedestrians and drivers, an attitude that would have militated against public action even if the dangers of automobiles had been better appreciated. Finally, and perhaps most importantly, auto fatalities were a complicated problem. Each road death was unique. The number of ways in which drivers, pedestrians, automobiles, and roads could conspire to snuff a human life was incalculable. There was no agreement among the few people interested in tackling the problem on how to proceed.

The disagreement did not stop some from trying. Katz and Nader were hardly the first legal minds to consider traffic safety. There were early attempts by the courts to define the vehicle itself as the problem. "Automobiles," wrote a Georgia Court of Appeals judge in the early 1900s, "are to be classed with ferocious animals and . . . the law relating to the duty of owners of such animals is to be applied." This approach did not stick. By 1905, when Xenophon P. Huddy published the first serious treatment of the legal status of the automobile in the *Yale Law Journal*, the courts had decided that the car had as much right to the avenues of travel as any person or vehicle. It was clear to Huddy that it is "the manner of driving the machine, and that alone, which threatens the public safety." The automobile's ability to respond to guidance and stop quickly made it "one of the least dangerous of conveyances if properly driven."[12]

This identification of drivers, rather than cars or their manufacturers, as culpable for crashes accorded with the public's view
of the situation. "Any time an automobile collides with a post, a
pedestrian, or other obstacle," reported the Philadelphia *Public Led-
ger*, "the crowd that gathers always displays prejudice against the
driver . . . though the latter's very middle name may be Caution."
These attitudes persisted into the 1920s as the automobile found
its way into almost every household and the American economy
became increasingly dependent upon it.[13]

While highway safety was a state and local responsibility,
Secretary of Commerce Herbert Hoover, an unusually progressive Republican, believed Washington could use its influence to
force the issue of traffic safety on behalf of the people. In 1924,
he invited state highway commissioners, transportation engineers,
police chiefs, safety advocates, and auto industry representatives to
a National Conference on Street and Highway Safety. His confer-
ees analyzed the problem from a variety of angles and ultimately
recommended the universal licensing and examination of motorists,
a minimum driving age of sixteen years (many urban truck drivers
were younger), the hiring of more traffic patrolmen, crackdowns
on reckless and drunk driving, the imposition and enforcement of
uniform speed limits, new laws against passing vehicles on curves
and hills, the establishment of crosswalks and controlled railway
crossings, and the construction of playgrounds to get children off
the streets, among many other measures. Hoover's initiative was
followed in 1926 by a Detroit conference bringing state and local
government safety officials together to operationalize many of those
recommendations.[14]

Hoover's gathering, twenty-five years after Henry Hale Bliss's
last breath, was a watershed in the history of traffic safety. At least
in official circles, the shame-the-driver school of road management
was augmented with a constructive approach emphasizing the education of drivers, the development and enforcement of laws, and the
engineering of roadways. This so-called Triple-E strategy would
undergird the consensus on traffic safety until Katz and Nader
entered the picture.

Hoover's conference forced acknowledgment of the automobile
as a permanent and central feature of American life, one that soci-

ety needed to accommodate. The old notion of pedestrians, horses, and cars having equal right to the street was reversed.* By 1928, the New York Police Department's Safety Bureau was reprimanding pedestrians for leaving the sidewalk, crossing against traffic lights, or otherwise intruding on the automobile's space. At the same time, drivers were coming under pressure to fix defective equipment on their vehicles. One Michigan report found 38 percent of cars did not comply with state-legislated standards for brakes, lamps, steering, and so forth. And the new emphasis on engineering concerned itself with the frequency with which drivers faced sharp curves, narrow pavements, short sightlines, and other perils (there was also attention to the braking and steering capabilities of automobiles but most engineering concerns focused on the driving environment).[15]

The emergence of an official consensus on how to tackle traffic fatalities did not solve the problem of traffic fatalities. Rather, its major contribution was to highlight the many ways in which the problem was out of control. One of the more amusing illustrations of the manifold nature of automobile risk is found in the 1937 movie *Topper*. It features Cary Grant and Constance Bennett as a devil-may-care couple destined to die in an auto wreck in the film's first minutes. Grant's character is seen behind the wheel, drunk, driving at unconscionable speeds, steering with his feet, and blithely disobeying the police. His car is a customized Buick Roadmaster convertible with a dorsal fin over its trunk and a windshield too low to keep dust and bugs out of his eyes, as he learns in the moment of his fatal crash. The road on which he dies is a commuter strip between suburb and city, a winding and uneven affair, scarcely more than one lane wide with no shoulders and many large trees impinging on the grade. The behavioral and material hazards on display were an accurate reflection of contemporary traffic realities. They would require an abundance of education, enforcement, and engineering to solve.

As the years passed, new research identified still more ways in which the safety consensus might be reinforced. Some researchers

---

* The question of who had right to the road is reflected in an exasperated comment in the Bureau of Census's 1920 report on mortality statistics: "Each year it becomes more and more dangerous for a person to walk the streets." W. M. Steuart, *Mortality Statistics 1920* (Washington: U.S. Government Printing Office, 1922), p. 63.

emphasized driver fatigue, others the psychology of drivers, traffic spacing, lane markings, passing zones, school zones, illumination of roads, tire failure, brake pedal placement, the optimal height of car hoods, headlight glare, and so on. A concentration on the dangerous problem of entering and exiting high-speed thoroughfares led to the proliferation of divided highways and restricted-access freeways.

Progress was impressive. Traffic fatalities per 1,000 registered vehicles dropped from 2.0 in 1917 to 0.9 in 1942 to 0.5 in the late 1950s. These gains came even as Americans were using their cars more. Total yearly miles driven by vehicles in the United States increased from under 100 billion in 1920 to more than 750 billion by the late 1950s. In that time, annual fatalities per billion miles driven plunged from 240 to less than 50, an improvement of 80 percent, largely attributable to the Triple-E regime. The absolute number of traffic fatalities peaked at around 39,000 in 1937, declined in the war years, and stabilized in the range of 34,000 to 39,000 through the 1950s.[16]

The avidity with which Americans thrust themselves behind the wheel suggests that the vast majority, rightly or wrongly, believed driving to be safe, or safe enough. Two thirds of adults were licensed to drive in the late 1950s, and virtually everyone traveled by car at least on occasion. More women were driving, often with their children in the car. It was no secret to anyone that traffic crashes occurred and that some were lethal, yet these incidents were rare enough, representing just 2 percent of annual deaths in the United States, that drivers cheerfully put themselves and their loved ones in cars even for nonessential purposes. The nation had considered the risks of injury and death from automobiles against the utility and pleasure they afforded, and come down firmly on the side of more driving, preferably, if their buying habits were any indication, in larger cars with stronger engines.[17]

Russell Brown, the commissioner of the Iowa Department of Public Safety, found in his state little evidence of a public desire for improved safety: "If we had it, there would be constant aggressive demands for action at every level of government. There would be in every community a voluntary organization of citizens prepared to set a good example and to sacrifice time and money for greater traffic safety." Instead, he found "a marked apathy in many states and communities toward efforts to come to grips with the problem."[18]

To the extent that there was concern it was most frequently top down, voiced by public officials and community leaders like Commissioner Brown who were creatures of the Triple-E consensus. They were disinclined to declare the roads safe with close to forty thousand people still dying annually in traffic. The head of the National Safety Council complained that road fatalities were met with "a tidal wave of carelessness, selfishness and cold indifference . . . that should shame any civilized nation." His organization made headlines with its announcement in late 1951 of America's millionth traffic fatality, which came weeks after its millionth soldier was lost in battle since the founding of the Republic. The president of the American Association of Motor Vehicle Administrators proclaimed road deaths "the Black Death of the twentieth century." Police chiefs, traffic engineers, academics, the National Congress of Parents and Teachers, and the American Motorist Association all applied pressure on the issue. President Truman held a Highway Safety Conference in 1946 and President Eisenhower established a President's Committee for Traffic Safety in 1954. These initiatives amounted to a doubling down on the Triple-E agenda just as other observers, including Katz, the medical profession, and crash injury researchers, were beginning to doubt the wisdom of the strategy.[19]

For its part, the automobile industry agreed with public officials that driving was not yet safe enough. A routine concern voiced at gatherings of auto dealers was that road fatalities were bad for business and might dissuade people from driving. Dealers supported the Triple-E, as did manufacturers. As early as 1926, Studebaker endowed a bureau of street traffic research at Harvard University, and a decade later the Automobile Manufacturers Association sponsored fifteen fellowships at the bureau. The industry also funded the Yale University Bureau for Street Traffic Research and supported the Traffic Safety Institute at Northwestern University, which served as the operating arm of the first Traffic Safety Committee of the International Association of Chiefs of Police. Automakers funded the training of 120 police officers in the scientific investigation of crashes and G.M.'s Alfred P. Sloan personally financed the creation of the organization that in 1937 became the Automotive Safety Foundation. Regardless of whether its motive was self-preservation or the public good, Detroit was an easy touch for safety researchers.[20]

The major criticisms of Detroit were that it built fast cars and marketed speed and aggression. Between 1948 and 1955, the average horsepower of an automobile had increased by 66 percent and its top speed by 14 percent. The so-called horsepower race and advertisements such as the Oldsmobile 88's "Drive the 'Rocket'" campaign were knocked as inducements to thrill-seeking and reckless driving. Manufacturers defended the power increases as leading to improved responsiveness for such purposes as pulling into the flow of freeway traffic and passing farm vehicles on rural roads. They also argued that the vast majority of their advertisements emphasized modern or futuristic design, smooth rides, and dependability, and that their more provocative messages simply responded to preexisting public appetites. The latter, while not wrong, was a poor defense, especially with the car company's claiming a commitment to safety education.[21]

Automakers seldom mentioned safety in their advertisements. It did not matter to their customers as much as styling, performance, and brand prestige. Raising the specter of a crash, moreover, was not great salesmanship. Marketers preferred to emphasize handling, traction, visibility, reliability, comfort, ease of operation, and other factors that contributed to a secure driving experience. The possibility of a crash was thus recognized but not dwelt upon, which seemed to suit both parties to a new car transaction.

Apart from their encouragement of speed and racing, automakers were doing their part in the eyes of the traffic safety community. That remained the case until safety experts and advocates began to question the Triple-E regime in the 1950s. Despite decades of education, enforcement, and engineering, and great improvement in the number of fatalities per automobile registered and the number of fatalities per millions of miles driven, America's annual road death total remained stubbornly above thirty thousand. Frustration crept in. This was the beginning of Katz's opportunity.

While the consensus held on the need for better road engineering, critics questioned the utility of education. It was fine in principle but every year brought new data on where and how crashes happened, and new disagreement on what drivers most needed to be taught. Drilling drivers in caution and the simple rules of the road was beginning to seem insufficient in light of new insights on the roles played by age, fatigue, drinking, medications, anger, and hormones in crashes. It was noticed that well-funded safe-driving campaigns often landed to little discernible effect. Drivers always believed it was the other guy who needed educating.

Enforcement was still more controversial. The National Safety Council, among many other agencies, was calling for uniformly lower speed limits across the land, more policing of the highways, and the abolition of advertisements that referenced speed. Yet it was supposed that most fatalities occurred at speeds of less than forty miles per hour and that the most rigorous efforts at enforcement had delivered weak results.* More discouraging, the marked increases in traffic citations and fines that accompanied stern enforcement proved a public irritant. Too much policing, explained Yale's Frederick W. Hurd, was turning otherwise model citizens into outlaws. There was a growing sense that speed traps were a local government revenue grab, which discredited them as a public health measure.[22]

The Triple-E consensus was fraying. Some experts saw driver aggression as the most important problem, others public apathy. Some wanted stricter licensing and vehicle maintenance requirements, others mandatory seat belts or court reforms. Each specialist tended to view his specialization as the key to improving safety, and other approaches as distractions. This compounded frustration and confusion and demonstrated to some authorities that traffic safety research, despite all the work that had been done, was still in its infancy.

Harold Katz's search for fresh ideas on safety brought him to a body of research into the biomechanics of automobile injury and death, much of it conducted at Cornell University's medical college. A world leader in this new field, Cornell was home to the Automotive Crash Injury Research Project. Hugh DeHaven, cofounder and director of the project, had survived a crash as a Canadian Royal Flying Corps pilot in the Great War, leading to a lifelong interest

---

* To this day, reports on the speeds at which crashes occur are estimates.

in how properly packaging pilots and drivers within their cockpits could save lives. His project collected data and experimented with means to make car interiors more crashworthy.[23]

DeHaven and like-minded researchers were taking the novel approach of dividing every auto crash into two parts, a first collision, when a vehicle hits the ditch or a tree or another vehicle, and a second collision, when the occupants of the crashing vehicle are thrown into its dashboard, windshield, steering wheel, or some other part of its unforgiving interior, or flung into the road.* From this perspective, it was not the driver's initial mistake or misfortune that caused injury or death; it was the so-called second collision of human against steel, glass, or pavement. It followed that if vehicle interiors could be designed to better protect people in crashes, much road carnage could be eliminated.

The Cornell research, partially funded by the automakers, hit home with Katz. It had also hit home with physicians on the front lines of traffic injury who had noticed that while the precariousness of life was generally receding in America—workplaces were safer, the menace of infectious diseases was lessened, life expectancy was sixty-nine years by the late 1950s, 40 percent longer than at the start of the century—the absolute number of traffic deaths continued to climb.[24]

Second-collision research made intuitive sense to the doctors. When faced with a body on a stretcher, they usually had no idea what had happened on the road, and they did not much care. They dealt entirely with the consequences of the second collision. It made sense to them that a more crashworthy automobile interior be required of car manufacturers. This effectively reversed Xenophon P. Huddy's view that driver behavior was the main problem in traffic safety and put the onus on the vehicle itself. It harked back to the earlier Georgia Court of Appeals justice who had described the car

---

* Other early movers in the field were Air Force colonel John Stapp, a surgeon and biophysicist who strapped himself onto rocket sleds to prove that the human body could withstand strong forces if properly protected; Dr. Claire Straith, a Detroit plastic surgeon whose exposure to facial and head injuries prompted him to advocate for padded dashboards and safety belts; Elmer Paul of the Indiana State Police, who documented skull fractures in the accidents he investigated in order to identify automobile interiors most likely to cause head injuries.

as a ferocious animal. The traffic safety problem, and estimations of Detroit's culpability for road casualties, would never be the same.

Of special interest to Katz was the work of Dr. C. Hunter Shelden, a Pasadena neurosurgeon of impressive pedigree. He had studied at the University of Wisconsin, the Albert-Ludwigs-Universität in Freiburg, Germany, and the University of Pennsylvania before developing his surgical skills at the Mayo Clinic and serving four years as head of the Neurosurgical Service at the U.S. Naval Medical Center in Bethesda, Maryland. It was in Bethesda during the Second World War that he established his expertise on the movement of the brain in response to sudden acceleration and deceleration, and in Pasadena that he began to research and publish on traffic safety. His November 1955 article in *The Journal of the American Medical Association*, titled "Prevention, the Only Cure for Head Injuries Resulting from Automobile Accidents," galvanized his colleagues and the small but growing band of dissenters from the Triple-E consensus.[25]

A vigorous and practical man who built his own putter to improve his golf game, Dr. Shelden disputed the very notion that automobile crashes were accidental. Yes, he acknowledged, the initial crash might come as an unintentional result of poor judgment, reckless driving, or mechanical failure but once that error has been made, and, realistically, such errors were always being made, the injuries that followed in the so-called second collision of body against automobile interior or road surface were predictable, indeed inevitable. Nor, wrote Dr. Shelden, was the harm accidental when "faulty interior design features" had been installed in automobiles, and enhancements that might have provided for the safety of passengers had been omitted. He considered vehicles so poorly constructed from a safety standpoint that it was surprising to him that anyone escaped a crash without serious injury. He estimated that 75 percent of fatalities could be avoided if interiors were redesigned with safety in mind, and he asserted that automakers knew how to improve their product to save lives but could not be bothered to do so.[26]

Dr. Shelden had recommendations for automobile design improvements. With 25 to 35 percent of fatalities resulting from people being thrown from vehicles, stronger door latches were essential. Car seats, he said, were "a disgrace." They needed to be bolted down firmly so that they did not rip from the floor in a crash, and they needed headrests to prevent whiplash in the event of a rear collision. Dashboards needed to be padded and cleared of project-ing knobs and buttons. Dr. Shelden took particular exception to "a prominent knife-like projection" just above the instrument panel in Cadillacs that was designed to prevent light from the instruments from projecting onto the windshield but in actuality was "as lethal a device as is seen on any American passenger car." He favored large and deep steering wheels that would absorb the force of a collision with a driver's chest rather than crush him or her against the steer-ing column. He asked for more roll resistance in car roofs.[27]

Dr. Shelden also had a lot to say about seat belts. "There is no doubt that seat belts in passenger cars will prevent many injuries and fatalities," he wrote, "if only the public will fasten them." He was not optimistic that the public would do any such thing, largely because a two-piece seat belt that fastened in the middle was, to his mind, as complicated as surgery: "The free ends when not in use lie across the seat, and frequently the outside strap falls out the door as one leaves the car, or falls onto the floor of the front seat. If the free ends lie on the seat and one enters the car in a hurry, he is likely to sit on the straps and drive off before remembering to fasten them. While driving, he must find the two ends and place them across his lap. Then in order to fasten the seat belt he must take both hands off the wheel, and, unless he is very dexterous, he must also take his eyes off the road for a split second. More likely than not, he will decide to forego the use of the safety belt for a short trip." He wanted the auto industry to invent a seat belt that would require minimal human intervention, or none whatsoever.[28]

Uninterested in scourging Detroit, Dr. Shelden's aim was to call attention to the safety problem and recommend design changes based on his clinical experience. He maintained that the industry had continually added to the safety of the automobile by developing and adopting mechanical and design improvements. He mentioned stronger frames, power brakes, power steering, more reliable and responsible engines, and the automatic transmission, all of which permitted greater driving efficiency and safety. Detroit had not done enough, however, and it seemed reluctant to do more because it would cost money and reduce profits. Dr. Shelden wanted business considerations to take a backseat to safety. Automakers failing to eliminate "known hazards" in the designs of their vehicles was comparable to doctors withholding "known methods of live-saving value" from patients. It was unethical. Skeptical of the industry's willingness to move briskly on safety, he called for automobiles to be federally regulated in the same manner as food, drugs, airlines, and railroads.[29]

Harold Katz, in his 1956 *Harvard Law Review* article, built on Dr. Shelden's discussion of second-collision theory, and elaborated its legal implications, which struck him as immense. He quoted a medical professional who said that putting humans in cars was like shipping teacups loose in a barrel. On impact, heads were bashed against unyielding instrumental panels, chests were crushed on unforgiving steering wheels, and bodies were launched through jagged windshields. Auto engineers and designers—people who ought to know better—were making no real effort to protect occupants in the event of crashes. Rather, they "concentrated their efforts for years on styling, power, and effortless driving, to the exclusion of any real interest in occupant safety." They plied consumers with cosmetic innovations such as tinted windshields which obscured vision and made collisions more likely. Katz cited a Cornell report that found in the last fifteen years of automobile design "no improvement as far as their injury potential is concerned."[30]

Surely, argued Katz, manufacturers had a legal duty to warn the public of the dangers of their products and to refrain from making cars that exposed people to unreasonable risks. "Lawyers, who as a group have given little attention to this important area of negligence, will, when they think in those terms, undoubtedly discover other respects in which manufacturers have not exercised reasonable care in design, and it is to be hoped that manufacturers, aware of their potential liability and legal duty, may make additional important contributions to safety through improvements in design." Here was something new in the annals of torts.[31]

Torts generally turn on demonstrations of negligence, such as a manufacturer failing to use reasonable care to ensure the safety of people using its product. In the early twentieth century, a manufacturer's legal duty of care to anyone injured by a product was strictly limited. That a driver broke his neck after the wheels fell off his car was insufficient to secure an award for damages from a manufacturer: the driver's legal counsel had to convince a court that the wheels had fallen off because the vehicle had been negligently manufactured as opposed to, say, negligently driven or maintained. What's more, a privity requirement shielded manufacturers from the consequences of their own negligence by limiting their duty of care to consumers who had purchased products directly from the manufacturer. If a defective and dangerous automobile was sold through a dealer, the manufacturer was in the clear. But torts evolve.[32]

The privity requirement was set aside in the famous 1916 case of *MacPherson v. Buick Motor Company*. Judge Benjamin N. Cardozo ruled that privity was outdated in an age of independent retailers and dealerships when consumers seldom purchased goods directly from manufacturers. His ruling opened the door for more individuals to sue large corporations for harms resulting from negligently made products, among other expansions of the notion of duty of care. Not long after, courts relaxed other legal burdens on victims and increased demands on manufacturers. Some embraced the concept of strict liability, which held that a company could be liable for injuries to people using its products even if those products were flawlessly manufactured, so long as they were used as intended. Katz used the example of a forklift operator who had lost two limbs when it overturned on him and sued its manufacturer claiming that the vehicle had been negligently designed. Its center of gravity was too high, according to the claim, rendering it an unnecessary hazard to human life. The driver had received an award of $165,000.[33]

The courts believed this new approach would be a deterrent to corporate recklessness. The elaboration of the manufacturers' duty of care also reflected a desire to manage the costs of crashes. It seemed to make sense that those choosing to engage in a business and earning a profit from it ought to pay for any harms associated with it. *Someone* in the community had to cover the cost of harms, and businesses were generally better positioned to do so than crash victims. In practical terms, and Harold Katz thought in practical terms, courts were recognizing that manufacturers were obligated to build the safest practicable products for their customers, and allowing plaintiffs to pursue damages against some of the biggest, richest companies in America.

Applying all this directly to automobiles, Katz accused their manufacturers of blaming drivers for auto crashes in order to deflect from their own culpability. The public was largely ignorant of the relationships between car design and injury potential, he argued, so people drove recklessly and drunkenly. They were offered seat belts and other safety equipment and refused them, heedless of the risks because they were not experts. Manufacturers, with their near monopoly on automotive engineering and design expertise, owed their customers a greater duty of care. They knew the realities and risks of driving yet failed to employ the knowledge and technology they possessed to build crashworthy cars. That, in itself, was evidence of negligent design and courts should be holding automakers liable for the injuries and deaths that followed.

"Tort liability arises from the creation of unreasonable risks," he argued. "Nothing in law or logic insulates manufacturers from liability for deficiencies in design any more than for defects in construction." The public deserved safely designed, crashworthy vehicles, and the law, Katz insisted, should be used to force change.[34]

Katz's article, implicating the largest, richest companies in America in thousands of deaths and millions of injuries annually, was catnip to the personal injury bar and also to the law student Ralph Nader. "I got a call from this fellow, I'd never heard of him, but he was quite ecstatic," said Katz of Nader. "He told me that he was utterly astonished and absolutely delighted by my article. He didn't have any prior notion of using tort law to reform the auto industry. The idea captivated him."[35]

In his final year of law school, Nader rallied himself for a spurt of academic engagement, writing a paper on traffic safety that reflected his excitement about Katz's ideas. He received an A and shortly after his graduation arranged his arguments for publication. He placed an article in *The Nation*, a small-circulation, money-losing weekly of admirable lineage that was having a difficult time in the 1950s. It had been banned from libraries for its criticisms of Senator Joseph McCarthy's attempts to ferret Reds out of American public life, and it was routinely attacked as pro-communist because of its calls for friendly accommodation of the Soviet Union. H. H. Wilson and C. Wright Mills also published in *The Nation*.[36]

Nader's piece echoed Katz in absolving drivers of responsibility for road casualties, and by indicting Detroit for negligent product design. He, too, referenced that small but salient base of academic literature suggesting occupants of a crashing automobile suffered less from the initial impact of vehicle against tree, or moose, or guardrail than from the second collision of unrestrained human bodies against car interiors or concrete. Nader, like Katz, suggested that automakers had the knowledge and technological means to "make accidents safe," and that failing to do so was akin to medical practitioners withholding lifesaving medical procedures. Nader outpaced Katz by suggesting that automobiles "are so designed as to be dangerous at any speed":

> It is clear that Detroit today is designing automobiles for style, cost, performance and calculated obsolescence, but not for safety. Doors that fly open on impact, inadequately secured seats, the sharp-edged rearview mirror, pointed knobs on instrument panel and doors, flying glass, the overhead structure—all illustrate the lethal potential of poor design. A sudden deceleration turns a steering wheel or a sharp-edged dashboard into a bone- and chest-crushing agent. Penetration of the shatterproof windshield can chisel one's head into fractions. The apparently harmless glove-compartment door has been known to unlatch under impact and guillotine a child.[37]

Nader also exceeded Katz by suggesting a conspiracy of silence around the fact that forty thousand people were dying annually on American roads. Newspapers and broadcasters dared not discuss this "national health emergency" for fear of losing their lucrative car advertising. Universities were uninterested in researching the subject due to "widespread amorality among our scholarly elite." Politicians were timid, and the people needed to be protected from the "indiscretion and vanity" which made them susceptible to Detroit's sparkling, roaring "death-traps." Whereas Katz wanted the legal profession to sue automakers into a proper respect for safety, Nader was skeptical of success given "the limited authority and resources of the judiciary." He wanted new federal laws and a new Washington-based traffic safety administration to enforce them. Only federal regulation of automakers would strike at "the heart of the malady— the blueprint on the Detroit drawing board."[38]

Echoes of Mills, Galbraith, and Packard are obvious in Nader's article: his concern for the welfare of consumers; his portrayal of those same consumers as ignorant and easily distracted from their own interests by styling and packaging; his description of corporations as powerful, unaccountable, even venal entities conspiring with other institutions and authorities against the public welfare; his dismissal of the Triple-E consensus as conventional wisdom. But while Mills et al. had found much to criticize in automobiles, it was Nader's inspiration to focus entirely on the discrete and actionable problem of road carnage and, taking Katz's cue, holding Detroit responsible. He also brought an uncompromising urgency to safety issues, underlined by his graphic anecdotes of traffic gore and his advocacy of concrete solutions.

Nader graduated in the bottom 20 percent of his class in the spring of 1958 with no firm plans or promising opportunities, which was unusual among Harvard Law students. He did some casual research work for a Harvard professor for six months before enlisting in the army under a reserve program that brought less onerous terms of service than if he had waited to be drafted. At Fort Dix, New Jersey, he learned to fire an M1 rifle during basic training and afterward cooked banana bread for thousands of soldiers at a time. Once discharged, he set off on a series of educational adventures.[39]

Cuba was not a popular destination for Americans in 1959. It had just come through several years of civil war by the end of which a revolutionary socialist, Fidel Castro, was living in the penthouse of the Havana Hilton in his new capacity as the island's prime minister. Intrigued by Castro's politics, Nader found his way across the Straits of Florida and attended an interview given by the new leader to a foreign press delegation. He wrote a dispatch for the *Harvard Law Record* claiming that the revolution offered Cuba's first real hope for progress in a half century and that Americans doubtful of the situation were misguided. It was true that the new regime was dispatching its enemies with alacrity through hastily convened military tribunals, wrote Nader, and there was no denying that the tribunals had "no real substance" and were designed for "retaliation" rather than due process, but the revolutionaries were eager to get on with their important domestic reforms and "justice delayed means justice denied." Nader was among the first of a large coterie of American liberals and socialists to defend the Cuban revolution, beating C. Wright Mills and his best-selling polemic *Listen, Yankee* by more than a year.[40]

Nader returned from visiting Cuba to work briefly in a part-time capacity for George Athanson, whose one-man legal firm operated out of a single room on Church Street in Hartford. Athanson did the usual trade in bankruptcy, personal injury, and divorce. Nader helped with paperwork, never bringing in or taking on cases of his own. He was soon off traveling again, visiting Scandinavia and the ombudsman offices of Denmark and Sweden to learn how they worked on behalf of individual citizens to hold governments accountable. Here, too, Nader was ahead of his time: the model of the ombudsman as a bureaucratic control and advocate for the common man would be adopted by the United Kingdom, France, Canada, Australia, and in a limited way in the United States, in the 1960s and 1970s.[41]

He next skipped over to the Soviet Union for two weeks and came away impressed by the lack of automobiles and the quality of food in its cities, if disappointed at the interest of the Russian people in American popular culture, a subject that had never held much appeal for Nader. In 1963, he headed to South America, this time following in the footsteps of Mills, who had visited three years earlier. Nader spent time in Recife in northeastern Brazil where unrest among the sugar farmers promised another revolution, and in Santiago, Chile, where he met Salvador Allende, then in the midst of successive and ultimately successful efforts to become the first Marxist head of a Latin American government.

Articles Nader wrote based on his travels, as well as his interest in Indigenous issues and Alaska's bid for statehood, appeared occasionally in *The Atlantic*, *The Christian Science Monitor*, and other publications. The fees for these pieces together with his light work for Athanson were Nader's only apparent means of support in the years after law school. His old friend David Halberstam wondered exactly how he was getting by. Now writing for *The New York Times* and recently returned from Vietnam, where he had distinguished himself as a critic of America's military leadership, Halberstam was not bothered by Nader's leftish politics or his skepticism about powerful institutions. It disturbed him that Nader spoke in a furtive, even clandestine manner about his activities. He had a lot of knowledge, facts and figures, about the political hot spots he'd visited, but he was oddly evasive about what he was doing in these places and whom he was working for. "Jesus Christ," Halberstam told his brother, Michael. "He's a C.I.A. man." While the reporter would later back away from this assertion, Nader's unorthodox ways would continue to baffle those who knew him.[42]

Late into his twenties, Nader drifted, writing infrequent articles, helping out at Athanson's office, and testifying occasionally before state legislatures in Connecticut, Maine, and New York on traffic safety. He headed to Washington for a short time to lobby for statehood on behalf of Alaska and Hawaii. He was going nowhere until another traffic safety enthusiast, Daniel Patrick Moynihan, a rising star in the Department of Labor, telephoned him with a proposition.

CHAPTER 4

THE RISE OF THE HONKERS

The former Talladega lawyer Kenneth Roberts was in his third year of representing the Fourth Congressional District of Alabama when four Puerto Rican nationalists in the visitor's gallery of the House of Representatives shouted "Viva Puerto Rico Libre" and opened fire on the congressmen below. As one of five wounded representatives, Roberts, a Democrat, spent a good part of 1954 convalescing in hospitals and thinking about his life. In particular, he wondered "what I could do to save some lives, since my own life had been so miraculously spared." He turned his mind to traffic safety.[1]

That is one account of Roberts's 1956 decision, sandwiched between Dr. Shelden's influential article in *The Journal of the American Medical Association* and Harold Katz's piece in the *Harvard Law Review*, to propose in the House the creation of a new subcommittee to study traffic safety. Another account claims that Roberts was motivated by his memory of an auto crash on his honeymoon during which carefully wrapped dishes and crystal in his car came through undamaged while he was bruised and battered. Either way, traffic safety was right up Roberts's alley, and consistent with his long-standing involvement in consumer affairs. He had championed legislation requiring that poisonous household substances be labeled, and that refrigerators be manufactured with safety locks that could be opened from the inside for the protection of children. Although from Alabama, the left-leaning Roberts also advocated for public television and health care for migrant workers.[2]

Roberts was granted his subcommittee by a House Rules Committee dominated by his powerful southern Democratic pals, much to the displeasure of many congressional colleagues, the Eisenhower administration, and Detroit, all of which opposed the initiative as meddlesome. He opened hearings in June 1956 and to the relief of his opponents focused on learning what was then known of traffic safety. Manufacturers, whom he treated courteously, testified that more information was needed before design changes to their product might be warranted. Nothing came of the hearings, which the press largely ignored, although Roberts did manage to build a strong record of fact that included evidence from second-collision experts Hugh DeHaven, Dr. C. Hunter Shelden, and the Cornell researchers among others. Their points of view were allowed to stand shoulder to shoulder with those of Triple-E proponents.[3]

Once the hearings had closed, Representative Roberts could not interest his fellow Democrats in any sort of legislation on road safety. Unperturbed, he opened hearings into seat belts months later. These were long in data and arguments supporting the second-collision theory but, again, no legislation followed. In fairness, it was not yet clear how effective seat belts might be in saving lives. Dr. John O. Moore of Cornell University medical college said he and his colleagues had high hopes but were still working on statistical proof that seat belts would reduce fatalities in real-world circumstances.[4]

In 1958, the indefatigable "Seat Belt Roberts," as he had become known, held hearings into a resolution brought by a fellow congressman urging states to do more for traffic safety. His congressional colleagues, loath to interfere in a voter's relationship with his automobile, did not mind advising state politicians to do so. The resolution was passed and roundly ignored by the states.[5]

Roberts's efforts were not fruitless, however. He had caught the attention of a Harvard law student, Ralph Nader, who avidly followed the hearings in the *Congressional Record*. When he eventually published his article in *The Nation*, Nader scorched the Washington press gallery for having ignored Roberts. He simultaneously berated the congressmen for moving "too cautiously for so urgent a matter." Roberts had been "too solicitous of recommendations for delay advanced by some academicians who see automotive design from the viewpoint of engineering perfection rather than as a national health emergency requiring immediate, even if not perfect, engineering remedy. Better techniques will be developed but at least for the present, there will be added protection from remedying known design hazards. This has been the point that many safety engineers and physicians have vainly been urging."[6]

But Roberts was moving. As the years passed, his belief in the importance of the second-collision school of road safety deepened and his attitude toward Triple-E advocates hardened. "I, frankly, am tired of hearing that our drivers are delinquents, alcoholics, and incompetents," he said. His attitude toward Detroit also toughened. He had hoped to see some sort of voluntary action from the industry. His optimism on this score waned as he heard auto executives defend more powerful engines as useful in evading collisions, which seemed to him a self-interested rationalization for a desire to market speed. It further dwindled when they gave him what would become a standard General Motors line attributing the dangers of the road to the nut behind the wheel: "If the drivers do everything they should, there wouldn't be accidents, would there?" With his reams of testimony and growing expertise in the field of traffic safety, Roberts, to the delight of the medical community, attempted a more aggressive tactic.[7]

Each year, the federal government's General Services Administration bought 36,000 vehicles from Detroit. In other words, it had purchasing power. If those cars and trucks were required to have padded dashboards, seat belts, safer steering columns, stronger door latches, and other safety equipment, automakers might be convinced to build crashworthy vehicles for everyone. If Washington did not have enough clout on its own, other institutions and levels of government—anyone who bought vehicles in bulk—might be persuaded to follow Washington's example. Roberts was now speaking a language he was certain automakers understood. He was also pushing the federal government deep into the operations of the automobile industry, one of several unwelcome and unprecedented incursions that rattled Detroit in the postwar years.[8]

. . .

From a certain perspective, and certainly from its own point of view, the automotive industry in the 1950s was a model of free enterprise. Out of the more than two thousand American manufacturers that had attempted to sell automobiles to consumers, the surviving handful were at liberty to allocate capital as they pleased, free to build their own plant, develop their own product lines, make as many vehicles as they wanted, set their own prices, and forge their own relationships with consumers. Those consumers made up their own minds about the full range of product available to them and while there were no longer hundreds of automakers barking for their attention, there were three major companies, two lesser firms (American Motors and Studebaker-Packard), and plenty of foreign manufacturers that in combination offered an overwhelming array of brands, models, drive train configurations, and optional features, from the entry-level AMC Rambler to the Cadillac Eldorado with extra rear cigarette lighter and gold-finished radiator grille. Buyers could choose between these myriad alternatives, trade up, trade down, dicker on price, buy used, keep what they owned for another year, take a bus, or walk. In short, they had options, which kept automakers on their toes.[9]

In the early years of the automobile, the role of government in this close relationship between automakers and drivers had been limited to that of facilitator and road builder. At the start of the Great War, it was said, there was scarcely enough pavement in America to fill a tooth, a mere 750 miles of concrete highway leaving Ford's Model T to travel for the most part on dirt roads and old horse paths. When municipalities could not meet the demand for new roads, states stepped up with new funds derived from gasoline taxes, and by 1916 when states, too, were struggling to keep up, Washington recognized highways as a national problem and gave matching grants to states for road construction and the establishment of highway departments. There was much work to be done, as Major Dwight Eisenhower discovered in 1919 when he led a convoy of army vehicles 3,242 miles across the continent as a test of the national road system and the durability of the army's trucks and ambulances. His journey took two months. In the 1920s, Congress appropriated approximately $600 million to build a network of paved highways connecting every American community with at least fifty thousand inhabitants.[10]

Even as Washington funded roads, the regulation of automobiles and traffic remained a local responsibility, a fact that initially annoyed automakers. They worried about the potential for varying and conflicting requirements in different parts of the country, which would disrupt their national production and marketing strategies. As a consequence, they repeatedly invited federal regulation. Congress demurred, unwilling to step between Americans and their cars even in the earliest stages of automotive history. Over time, the states developed mechanisms to coordinate their rules and activities and the manufacturers shelved their federal objective. The feds were content to leave the auto industry alone until 1924 when Hoover held his national conference on highway safety, but even this was an advisory rather than a legislative initiative. Washington saw its role as cheering the automobile industry along, leaving the states to manage the minimum of necessary regulation.[11]

The Great Depression of the 1930s changed the auto industry's relations with the federal government significantly and permanently. Coming to power in 1932, President Franklin Roosevelt read the Depression as proof of the inequities and instability of American capitalism, and imposed a new regulatory state. Federal agencies were granted the authority to involve themselves in commercial affairs at the expense of the free operations of capital and the historic role of the states in commercial regulation. Roosevelt's reforms, popular with Democratic voters, were considered unwise and provocative by the business community, including the leadership of General Motors.

Roosevelt's rhetoric, too, offended capitalists. In a famous 1936 campaign speech at Madison Square Garden, he railed against the "forces of selfishness" that abused workers, cheated consumers, and denied opportunity to the young. Organized money, he said, was as dangerous as organized crime. Only an expanded and militant federal government, said the president, could deliver the people from "privileged princes" seeking to "regiment the people, their labor, and their property."[12]

These assaults on capital and capitalists were central to Roosevelt's political strategy. They galvanized a New Deal electoral coalition heavy with labor and farmers. They also drove a wedge between consumers, a new constituency emerging from the blossoming consumer economy, and the far less populous and mostly Republican corporate sector.

From time to time, the president backed his rhetoric with a chain mace. After limiting competition and establishing cartels in his first term, he switched gears in his second and pursued business on antitrust grounds, bringing ninety-nine criminal actions and a bevy of civil suits against the tobacco, railroad, pharmaceutical, and fertilizer industries, among others. He roused the Treasury and the Justice Department to investigate a list of "economic royalists" for tax evasion, including Andrew Mellon, the former Republican treasury secretary and, in FDR's estimation, the "master mind among the malefactors of great wealth." With FDR's knowledge and active support, the government pursued Mellon relentlessly and well beyond the limits of the law and, despite an absence of incriminating evidence, charged him with tax evasion. The former secretary was chased to his grave, only to be exonerated by the Board of Tax Appeals three months after his death in 1937.[13]

Roosevelt's regulations and attacks on business did little to stall the Depression, which was a global phenomenon owing much to monetary policy and the gold standard. His expansion of the federal role in the economy was nevertheless popular. It outlived his presidency. So, too, at least among Democrats, did his conviction that the state rather than the market is the arbiter of equity in American life.

The auto industry felt itself injured by many of Roosevelt's policies but it was on the specific issue of labor reform that tensions between Washington and Detroit became acute. When the Depression caused auto production to plummet, G.M. slashed its labor force by 40 percent. Remaining autoworkers sought the protection of organized labor, an objective that suddenly seemed within reach in 1933 due to Roosevelt's legislation granting employees the right to organize and bargain collectively. The American Liberty League, a pro-business lobby group with strong ties to the management and shareholders of General Motors, including Alfred Sloan and the du Pont family, owners of the largest single block of G.M. shares, considered the legislation a step toward a "Sovietized America" and challenged it in the courts, to no avail.[14]

Automakers were as hostile to unions as any other industrialists. They sometimes fought them with generous pay and improved working conditions and, at other times, with contemptible methods. In the early 1930s, G.M. fired employees suspected of union activity and spent a million a year on fifteen security agencies that spied on workers. By 1936, having watched as management in shipyards and steel mills failed to placate workers radicalized by hard times, and having seen picket line confrontations lead to broken heads and expensive production shutdowns, G.M. laid in $24,000 worth of tear gas in preparation for trouble at its own plants.[15]

Trouble was not long in coming, albeit in an unexpectedly nonviolent form. On December 30, 1936, shortly after Roosevelt's reelection and just as Michigan's new governor, Frank Murphy, a labor-friendly Democrat, was sworn into office, laborers at G.M.'s Fisher Body Plant Number One in Flint declared a sit-down strike, occupying the premises and refusing to work until the company recognized the United Auto Workers as their bargaining agent. Management denounced the strike as an illegal act, which it was, and acquired a court injunction ordering the workers removed from the plant. Governor Murphy and FDR, however, refused to enforce the injunction, insisting instead that General Motors negotiate with the workers.

The Flint location had been carefully chosen by strike organizers as a choke point in G.M.'s production. As a result, the automaker's output swiftly declined from 12,500 to 125 cars a week. The company capitulated after forty-four days and recognized the UAW. The Flint strike represented a major government-sanctioned transfer of power from capital to labor and touched off a nationwide expansion of union membership. Wages and benefits in the auto sector would for decades grow faster than in unorganized parts of the economy. The strike also set a precedent for Washington's intercession on behalf of labor in future conflicts at auto plants.[16]

Something of a truce between Detroit and Washington was necessitated by the Second World War. Automakers converted their production facilities to military purposes, with G.M. producing

$12.3 billion worth of machine guns, artillery shells, tanks, anti-aircraft guns, and other matériel. Its employee count edged back up toward a half million and, crucially for its long-term fortunes, its total productive capacity was increased by almost half thanks to prodigious government investment. When the guns were silenced, management and labor both claimed, rightly, to have done their part to win the war, and G.M. looked forward to a rapid reconversion to peacetime markets and to fulfilling the pent-up demand for new automobiles.[17]

Before G.M. could capitalize on its postwar opportunity, however, its employees walked out again in late 1945, this time demanding increases to their already generous wages and benefits. Following FDR's lead, President Harry S. Truman placed the onus on G.M. to settle on grounds that the work stoppage was delaying the reestablishment of a peacetime economy. He appointed a fact-finding commission to increase pressure for a resolution. General Motors capitulated once again, this time after 113 days.[18]

While Truman was less overtly hostile than Roosevelt to big business, he took the remarkable measure of nationalizing the steel industry to avoid a strike, only to be told by the Supreme Court that he lacked the authority to do so. He also went beyond meddling in Detroit's labor issues to take an interest in the pricing of automobiles. In December 1950 his Economic Stabilization Agency, backed by Congress, asked Ford and G.M. to rescind their annual price increases in service of the Korean War effort. The automakers had little choice but to comply, at least for that year, and G.M. felt compelled to ask permission for a price increase the following summer.[19]

By 1950, the long-promised return to economic growth was well under way, fueled by strong employment, a high savings rate, a growing population, and, not incidentally, high levels of defense spending and federal mortgage lending programs. General Motors' profits lagged the overall economy in the 1950s due to labor pressure but still grew by a third.

In some respects, the decade was a golden age for the firm in its relations with Washington. Despite President Eisenhower's later complaints about the kind of cars G.M. was producing, he was generally friendly toward industry. He appointed what was called a "businessman's cabinet," or what might have been better termed a

General Motors cabinet. The company's CEO, Charles E. Wilson, was sworn in as secretary of defense. Michigan Chevrolet dealer Arthur Summerfield became postmaster general. Former Oregon Chevrolet dealer Douglas McKay was secretary of the interior.[20]

All of these choices reflected Eisenhower's adherence to the Cold War Consensus and its prescription of relentless consumer spending and economic growth. The auto sector continued to be a direct beneficiary of Washington's large military expenditures[*] and received the additional gift of a massive road-building project: $25 billion in 1956 for the 41,000-mile system of interstate highways to accommodate the 50 percent increase in road traffic recorded in the 1950s and the greater volumes anticipated in decades ahead.[21]

It may seem that Detroit was playing with a stacked deck in the Eisenhower years, and Democrats certainly thought so, but the reality was more complicated. Even with Republicans in the White House, Congress asked tough questions and made new demands of the automakers. The New Deal's transfer of power from the private sector to the public sector, together with the full-scale mobilization of industry in World War II and persistently high levels of military spending in the Cold War, was in this sense permanent. Congress had become habituated to dictating to business, and was less inclined to allow private actors a long leash.

In March 1954 Republican congressman Shepard J. Crumpacker of Indiana asked the Federal Trade Commission to investigate Ford and General Motors for attempting to monopolize the auto industry. They had 86.7 percent of the market between them, with G.M.'s share hovering around 50 percent. Crumpacker might have been dismissed as a partisan of Indiana-based Studebaker-Packard, one of the few remaining independent automakers, but the anticompetitive charges leveled at Detroit were only beginning.[22]

The sheer size of General Motors was making Washington

---

* General Motors remained a favored defense contractor during the Cold War, producing trucks, turret lathes, and M-16 rifles in great quantities. As the largest industrial firm in the nation, it received many non-tendered contracts, the government finding it faster and easier to work with a single source of supply.

uneasy, never mind that its size was partly enabled by military contracts. The Department of Justice's antitrust division launched an investigation into competition in the auto industry in 1954. The Senate held its own hearings on the same topic in 1955 and recommended that General Motors divest itself of its financing arm, General Motors Acceptance Corporation. In 1956, the Department of Justice filed suit against G.M. for monopolizing the manufacture and sale of transit buses (it produced 85 percent of the nation's supply out of a single factory). Another set of Senate hearings alleged that G.M. and Ford were so dominant that they could set prices for their industry. There were calls for G.M. to sell off its earthmover business, to dispose of all of its nonautomotive operations, to divest itself of its auto parts subsidiaries, and to divide its main divisions—Chevrolet, Pontiac, Cadillac, etc.—into separate and independent companies. Those who would break up G.M. were buoyed by a report of the Senate subcommittee on antitrust laws that declared big business was harming the national economy by undermining competition. The document claimed General Motors' size all but guaranteed "success and domination" in every field it entered.[23]

There is no doubt that General Motors leveraged its scale in an anticompetitive manner. Its dealers were forced to finance the cars they sold through GMAC and to use G.M. parts in their repair shops. Corporate managers routinely strong-armed suppliers, as when General Motors bolstered its diesel-electric engine market by shipping its cars only with rail lines that bought its engines. Minor divestitures were forced on G.M. in the course of the decade. As well, Congress passed the Automobile Information Disclosure Act, which made it mandatory for car lots to put a price tag on new passenger cars, and President Eisenhower signed a law protecting the nation's 25,000 auto dealers from summary cancellations of their dealership contracts by manufacturers.[24]

By far the most significant measure taken by Washington against G.M. was a federal suit alleging that E. I. du Pont de Nemours & Co., with a controlling 23 percent stake in General Motors, was insulated from having to compete to sell paint, varnish, and fabric to the automaker. Begun in the Truman era, the suit was appealed to the Supreme Court during the Eisenhower administration. The court ruled for the government on June 3, 1957. The du Pont family's shares were eventually put on the open market and for the first time in its history, General Motors, absent a majority shareholder, was in the hands of its management. This development would have a profound effect on the behavior of the company in the years ahead.[25]

Few had expected the Republican Eisenhower administration to pursue the Democrats' suit against du Pont, or to intervene in the auto industry in other ways. That it did so is further evidence of the new complexity in Detroit's relationship with the federal government. While still facilitating the romance between Americans and their cars, building interstates and feeding automakers defense contracts, Washington was increasingly asserting itself as a mediator between Detroit and its workers, Detroit and its suppliers, Detroit and its competitors, and, most strikingly, Detroit and its customers. General Motors might still be "the biggest enterprise ever developed by the freedom, ingenuity and ambition of private enterprise," as James Truslow Adams said, but beneath the Eisenhower era's pro-business veneer was a move against the autonomy of American industry, one felt acutely in Detroit even before the recession of 1958. Whether it was likely to intensify or relax in the years ahead was an open question.[26]

Arthur M. Schlesinger Jr. was a young bow-tied Harvard historian and a close friend of John Kenneth Galbraith. They shared leadership of Americans for Democratic Action and dedicated the organization in the 1950s to keeping the liberal flame alive in what seemed to them the dark ages of the Eisenhower era. Crucial to this project was a recasting of liberalism. Schlesinger had written an essay titled "The Future of Liberalism: The Challenge of Abundance," which adumbrated many of the themes Galbraith brought to greater notice in *The Affluent Society*. It denounced the old liberalism for its obsession with economic growth and labor issues, and called for the establishment of a new liberalism concerned with economic and social justice and the quality of life in American homes and communities:

> Our gross national product rises; our shops overflow with gadgets and gimmicks; consumer goods of ever-increasing

ingenuity and luxuriance pour out of our ears. But our schools become more crowded and dilapidated, our teachers more weary and underpaid, our playgrounds more crowded, our cities dirtier, our roads more teeming and filthy, our national parks more unkempt, our law enforcement more overworked and inadequate.[27]

Having failed to vault the Democrat Adlai Stevenson to victory over Eisenhower in the contests of 1952 and 1956, Schlesinger and Galbraith swung their support to John F. Kennedy in 1960. They plied the candidate with advice and speeches and were duly rewarded on his election, Galbraith as United States ambassador to India, and Schlesinger as special assistant to the president, a role that involved advising, speechwriting, and serving as "court historian."[28]

It was a heady time for Schlesinger. He took enormous pride in his access to Kennedy and the president's willingness to staff his offices with other bright minds from elite universities, principally Harvard and Oxford. Of the new administration's first two hundred appointments, 18 percent came from universities and think tanks and just 6 percent from the business community. Serving in addition to himself and Galbraith were Walt Whitman Rostow, MIT professor and Rhodes Scholar; James Tobin, Sterling Professor of Economics at Yale; McGeorge Bundy, the youngest dean in the history of Harvard University; Daniel Patrick Moynihan, history PhD and Fulbright Fellow; and Robert McNamara, the defense secretary who had worked at Ford Motor Company but at least had a Harvard MBA. "Intelligence at last was being applied to public affairs," wrote Schlesinger. "We felt an excitement which comes from an injection of new men and new ideas, the release of energy which occurs when men with ideas have a chance to put them into practice."[29]

Schlesinger drew sharp lines between the "New Frontier," as the Kennedy Democrats fashioned themselves, and the old Eisenhower order in which 42 percent of initial appointees had been drawn from business. He detested Eisenhower's crowd as "God-anointed apostles of free enterprise" and accused them of practicing a "complaisant," anti-intellectual "politics of boredom." They had talked in slogans, spread public apathy, and ignored "the needs and potentialities of the nation." This, broadly, was Schlesinger's view of businessmen in American history: political incompetents with narrow class interests who inevitably needed to be rescued from their mishaps by popular Democratic heroes such as Andrew Jackson, Franklin Roosevelt, and John Kennedy. His liberalism was founded on opposition to the influence of business in American life, and to redressing what he saw as an imbalance of power between business and the federal state as representative of the people.[30]

The ideas that Galbraith and Schlesinger had promoted to little effect in the 1950s gained currency in the Kennedy era. Official heads nodded approvingly when the historian declared that America "had achieved abundance," as though all economic targets had been met. His claims that "quantitative" liberalism had been superseded by a new "qualitative" liberalism devoted to social services and civil rights were answered with choruses of approval in *The New York Times*. His old friend Adlai Stevenson was permitted to plagiarize Galbraith in the pages of *Life* magazine and *The New York Times:* "The contrast between private opulence and public squalor on most of our panorama is now too obvious to be denied."[31]

Schlesinger and his cohort insisted that the new president shared their ideas and they did manage, from time to time, to get Jack Kennedy to sound like them. He had been heard to say that the minds of businessmen were "clogged by illusion and platitude." He had echoed Galbraith's disdain for conventional wisdom, accusing the Eisenhower men of having indulged in "the comfort of opinion without the discomfort of thought." Better still:

> The great trouble with American politics today, is that we talk in slogans too often and symbols and we fight old battles. The Sixties are going to be entirely different. . . . We are a new generation which science and technology, and the change in world forces are going to require to face entirely new problems which will require new solutions.[32]

In the eyes of the court historian, who had spent the 1950s writing an acclaimed three-volume history of the Franklin Roosevelt years, Kennedy was a modernized second coming of that earlier liberal icon: "both were patrician, urbane, playful, cultivated, inquisitive, gallant; both were detached from the business ethos, both skeptical of the received wisdom, both devoted to politics but never enslaved by it, both serene in the exercise of power, both committed to the use of power for the ends of human welfare and freedom; both too had more than their share of physical suffering."[33]

Interestingly, Schlesinger had the same blind spot about both presidents. It had required of him a highly selective use of evidence and a tireless manufacture of alibis to bring a liberal coherence to FDR's crucial and notoriously opportunistic 1932 campaign. The sober reality was that FDR, while sympathetic to liberalism, subordinated all ideological concerns to his primary mission of winning office. There were no liberal shibboleths that he would not strangle to further his purposes, and few conservative bromides that he would not cheerfully recite for the appropriate audience. FDR was consumed by politics, as was JFK.

When not paying lip service to the Schlesinger-Galbraith program, Kennedy sounded like a holdover from the Eisenhower administration, preoccupied with America's arms race with the Soviet Union. He retained a number of Eisenhower hawks, including Allen Dulles as his CIA chief, and he sang the tenets of the Cold War Consensus in harmony with them. "Our way of life is under attack," he said. "We are opposed around the world by a monolithic and ruthless conspiracy that relies primarily on covert means for expanding its sphere of influence."[34]

Kennedy presented the problem in starkly quantitative terms, citing Russia's rate of economic expansion and the need for America to grow its GNP by 5 percent a year to maintain its lead. He worried over intelligence estimates indicating that the enemy's economy would be three times larger than America's by the year 2000 if current trends held. "We have to get this country moving again," he said, by which he meant that consumer demand required a boost, whether or not abundance had been achieved.[35]

Throughout his three years in office, Kennedy concentrated almost exclusively on international matters, his attention bouncing from one Cold War front to another—Havana, Berlin, Hanoi. There was a half sentence about human rights in his inaugural address, the only domestic content it contained, and even that had been insisted upon by his staff. "It really is true that foreign affairs is the only important issue for a President to handle, isn't it?" Kennedy asked of Richard Nixon in a rare conversation between them shortly after the election. "I mean who gives a shit if the minimum wage is $1.15 or $1.25 in comparison to something like this?" He dismissed reform-minded liberals as "honkers."[36]

Kennedy's remove from domestic matters was so thorough that he resented the media attention given to busloads of young activists or "Freedom Riders" traveling through the South to test enforcement of a 1960 Supreme Court ruling on racial segregation. Kennedy saw their confrontations with gangs of angry whites as an embarrassment for America and a propaganda win for the Soviets. To the extent that he had a plan for solving racial tensions and social ills, it conformed with the Eisenhower-era method of advising patience. Capitalism was the best system in the world and the less fortunate would gain over time from the benefits of steady economic growth. Confrontation would only set the country back.[37]

It follows that Kennedy gave no thought to General Motors or the broader automobile industry during his time in office. He was uninterested in business or businessmen, finance, or labor, and contemptuous of those who spent their lives "chasing the dollar." He was the beneficiary of a $10 million trust fund, a gift from his father, Joseph P. Kennedy, who was worth about $200 million. The only paychecks Jack Kennedy had ever received, from the U.S. Navy during the war and from the U.S. Congress afterward, he had donated to charity. He rarely carried cash and spent the princely sum of $50,000 a year (about twelve times the average national income) on incidentals, forwarding his bills to a family office in New York.[38]

In addition to his ignorance of the commercial world, Kennedy had a tenuous grasp of economics. Well into his presidency, he was asking his advisors to remind him of the difference between fiscal and monetary policy. What he understood best about economics was its implications for politics and international affairs. Federal budget deficits made him look like an irresponsible Democratic spender. Growth was good, strong growth was better, and 5 percent growth would keep him ahead of the Soviets. When U.S. GNP soared toward the end of 1961, Kennedy was quick to boast that an "economy which Mr. Khrushchev once called 'a stumbling horse' was racing to new records in consumer spending."[39]

On the infrequent occasions that Kennedy was brought face-to-face with the business community, he was cautious. Financiers and industrialists, generally aligned with the Republicans, were considered unfriendly, but he did not want trouble with them, and he did not want to be seen as hostile to them, an impression that would rile the conservative elements of his own party. He counseled wage restraint and price stability to weaken inflation, which he knew would undermine growth.

With Detroit keeping a lid on prices, Kennedy's inflation anxieties fixed on its major supplier, the steel industry and, particularly, the mammoth United States Steel Corporation. U.S. Steel was due for a new contract with the United Steelworkers union. Kennedy personally pressured both sides to moderate their demands. He was elated when his labor secretary, Arthur Goldberg, reported on March 31, 1962, that a new contract had been signed allowing for wage increases of less than 2.5 percent. "Terrific Arthur," said Kennedy. "Terrific job!" He put out a statement congratulating the negotiating parties on a "forward looking and responsible" settlement. "It is obviously non-inflationary and should provide a solid base for continued price stability."[40]

It appears to have escaped the president that U.S. Steel, which represented a quarter of the industry's production, had made no commitment to hold its prices, whatever the outcome of the contract talks. He was shocked when the company's chairman, Roger Blough, walked into the White House at 5:45 p.m. on April 10 and handed him a mimeographed copy of a four-page announcement that had already been released to the press. "For the first time in nearly four years," it read, "United States Steel today announced an increase in the general level of its steel prices. The 'catch-up' adjustment, effective at 12:01 a.m. tomorrow, will raise the price of the company's steel products by an average of about 3.5 percent."[41]

"You have made a terrible mistake," said Kennedy. "You double-crossed me."

Blough answered that he had made no promises on prices. After he was shown out, the president fumed at Secretary Goldberg: "They fucked us and we've got to try to fuck them."

Goldberg, deflated, concerned for his reputation in the labor community, spoke of resigning. Kennedy was not finished with his rant. "My father told me businessmen were all pricks but I didn't really believe he was right until now. . . . God I hate the bastards. . . . They kicked us right in the balls."[42]

Five steel companies followed U.S. Steel's lead and raised prices the next day. Kennedy considered asking Congress for special legislation to freeze prices and a draft of the Steel Price Emergency Act of 1962 was promptly prepared. Instead of acting on it, the president held a news conference and called the price increases a "wholly unjustifiable and irresponsible defiance of the public interest."[43]

> In this serious hour in our nation's history, when we are confronted with grave crises in Berlin and Southeast Asia, when we are devoting our energies to economic recovery and stability, when we are asking Reservists to leave their homes and families for months on end and servicemen to risk their lives—and four were killed in the last two days in Vietnam—and asking union members to hold down their wage requests; at a time when restraint and sacrifice are being asked of every citizen, the American people will find it hard, as I do, to accept a situation in which a tiny handful of steel executives whose pursuit of private power and profit exceeds their sense of public responsibility can show utter contempt for the interests of one hundred eighty-five million Americans.[44]

There were audible gasps from reporters in the room. The nation's chief executive had implied that one of the nation's leading industries was an enemy of the public good. By the time he was finished, Kennedy had also claimed that the price increases would add a billion dollars to the cost of national defense, undermine national security, and make American goods less competitive in foreign markets, sinking the U.S. dollar.

Kennedy personally led a campaign from the White House to force U.S. Steel to capitulate. Cabinet members were assigned to complain about the effects of price increases in their portfolios. The Justice Department, where JFK's younger brother Robert F. Kennedy was attorney general, discussed grand jury investigations of steel executives. The Defense Department canceled orders with U.S. Steel and transferred them to smaller competitors that had not increased prices. Senators and congressmen were urged to hold antitrust hearings and investigations into steel pricing policies.

Steel company executives tried to justify the price hikes as necessary to fund new investments that would create jobs and build plants that could better compete with new steel mills in Western Europe and Japan. The increases, they said, would add just 65 cents to the price of a refrigerator, or 0.3 percent to the price of a new car, amounts too low to spike inflation. They complained that their prices were not keeping pace with the costs of their inputs. The more they protested, the higher the administration turned up the heat. Robert Kennedy ordered the FBI and CIA to initiate dozens of wiretaps and spying operations on steel executives. He summoned a grand jury on price-fixing and sent FBI agents to the offices and homes of steel executives to gather records. "We're going for broke," he said. "Their expense accounts and where they'd been and what they were doing. . . . I told the FBI to interview them all—march into their offices . . . subpoena for their personal records . . . subpoena for their company records." The president was fully on board, telling an ally:

> I don't think U.S. Steel or any other of the major steel companies wants to have Internal Revenue Agents checking all the expense accounts of their top executives. Do you want the government to go back to hotel bills that time you were in Schenectady to find who was with you? Too many hotel bills and night club expenses would be hard to get by the weekly wives' bridge group out at the country club.[45]

The White House fed stories to the media to stoke public outrage at the behavior of the steel companies and were outraged in turn when the media did not play ball. After watching Chet Huntley of NBC play the story straight, President Kennedy called the chairman of the Federal Communications Commission: "Did you see that goddamn thing on *Huntley-Brinkley*. I thought they were supposed to be our friends. I want you to do something about that. You do something about that."[46]

Amid all the fireworks, the federal Bureau of the Budget presented the administration with an estimation of the effects of a steel price increase on the economy. It found that Gross National Product would rise by as much as $2.85 billion, and that federal budget receipts would increase by $900 million in fiscal 1963, more than offsetting increased budgetary costs of $600 million. This was all consistent with the president's objective of stoking economic growth yet it did nothing to assuage Kennedy's sense of political embarrassment, nor to slow his attacks on Big Steel. The executives, led by Blough at U.S. Steel, surrendered, first rolling back half of the price increase and then, at Kennedy's insistence, eliminating it entirely. The president called off the dogs and publicly congratulated himself on his moral courage.[47]

Republican congressional leaders called the steel fight "a display of naked political power never seen before in this nation. . . . We have passed within the shadow of police-state methods." The *Los Angeles Times* compared Kennedy to Mussolini and the *New York Herald Tribune* ran a cartoon showing the president being briefed by an envoy: "Khrushchev said he liked your style in the steel crisis."[48]

Kennedy promptly canceled all White House subscriptions to the *Herald Tribune*, which only brought him more ridicule from cartoonists and comedians. "I understand better every day, why Roosevelt who started out such a mild fellow, ended up so ferociously anti-business," he said. "It is hard as hell to be friendly with people who keep trying to cut your legs off. . . . There are about ten thousand people in the country involved in this—bankers, industrialists, lawyers, publishers, politicians—a small group, but doing everything they can to say we are going into a depression because business has no confidence in the administration."[49]

There was folly, bad faith, and hysteria on both sides of the steel price conflict. In the ensuing months, steel companies introduced their price increases in stages, which they should have done in the first place. Inflation remained low throughout Kennedy's term and the president would later admit the existence of "a cost-profit squeeze on American business." Schlesinger, the court historian, would eventually write his history of the Kennedy years without mention of the administration's abuses of power against the steel industry.[50]

Kennedy's political attack was nevertheless thrilling to Schlesinger, Galbraith, and like-minded liberals. By going after industrialists with a chain mace, the president had lent credence to their representation of the corporate sector as greedy, conscienceless, and a threat to true American values. With his assertion that "ten thousand people" were trying to thwart his work on behalf of the people, Kennedy had also posited a smug conspiracy of the power elites. By asserting national priorities contrary to the interests of business, the president seemed to endorse their view that abundance had been achieved and it was time to focus on public interests and social reform. All this was in addition to the service Kennedy had already provided liberal intellectuals by including them in the highest counsels of government and leaving business, for the most part, on the periphery. That he differed from his advisors in still seeing an urgent need for economic production, and that he cut corporate taxes to smooth things over with the business community after the steel dispute, were subtleties lost in the ruckus. Galbraith's ambition of a "major wrench in our attitudes," one that would demote to second-class citizenship the forces of "materialism and philistinism" and elevate in their place the writers, scientists, professors, and authors more worthy of public esteem, seemed on its way to realization. Schlesinger's new generation, with its finer feelings, higher ideals, and bigger brains, could feel its foot on the gas and the steering wheel in its hands. "We thought for a moment," he said, "that the world was plastic and the future unlimited."[51]

Meanwhile, Dwight Eisenhower, having watched the steel debacle at a distance, warned industry that the world was changing: "Businessmen can no longer be sure that there are well designed and well observed limits beyond which government will not go."[52]

Several years before John F. Kennedy arrived at the White House, another Democratic playboy of patrician lineage had set himself up in an executive manse. In 1956, Governor Averell Harriman inaugurated an ambitious reform administration in Albany, New York, or "Albania," as the jaded cosmopolitan Marie Norton, Harriman's middle wife, called it.* The governor promised New Yorkers

* The son of a railway baron, Averell Harriman had attended Groton and Yale before turning to banking. He served as U.S. ambassador to the Soviet Union,

a "bold, adventurous" administration, and he surrounded himself with platoons of exiled New Dealers and well-educated young progressives to make it come about. They would fight for equality and social justice, for labor, for children, for the aged, the mentally ill, and for consumers. They would confront the problems of juvenile delinquency and organize an "attack on poverty." The adventure was short-lived, in no small part because the governor's predecessor had spent New York's purse, but Harriman was not without accomplishments. Among his greatest was to launch the long public career of Daniel Patrick Moynihan.[53]

Moynihan's background was not remotely patrician. He was the son of a hard-drinking journalist and inveterate gambler who skipped out during the Great Depression, leaving his wife and three children to years of insecurity and genteel poverty in the East Harlem district of New York City. Daniel Patrick, or Pat, as he was known, attended Benjamin Franklin High School, hated his stepfather, and shined shoes in Times Square for pocket money. Tall and awkward in movement and manner, he was bullied by classmates at Benjamin Franklin. He was nevertheless an honor student and, eventually, class valedictorian. He escaped his circumstances through academics, progressing from City College of New York to Tufts to the London School of Economics with time out in the last years of the Second World War for service in the U.S. Navy. He managed two undergraduate degrees, a master's, and a PhD in history. He was buoyed by the G.I. Bill and a Fulbright Scholarship during his time in London, allowing him to live relatively well. He developed tastes for Savile Row suits, classical music, and Labour Party politics. On his return to New York in the mid-1950s, he found his way into Harriman's orbit, starting as a researcher and ending as acting secretary and the administration's official historian.[54]

Among Moynihan's bright young colleagues in the Harriman

U.S. ambassador to the United Kingdom, secretary of commerce in the Truman administration, director of the Mutual Security Agency, one-term governor of New York, and under secretary of state for political affairs in the Kennedy administration. Marie Norton abandoned her marriage into the Whitney-Vanderbilt fortunes to become the second Mrs. Harriman. Rudy Abramson, *Spanning the Century: The Life of W. Averell Harriman, 1891–1986* (New York: William Morrow, 1992).

ranks was William Haddon Jr., a graduate of MIT and the Harvard Medical School, where he earned an MD and a master's in public health. Employed at the New York State Department of Health, the jumpy and brush-cut Haddon had a wide range of interests but one public health problem in particular captured his imagination: traffic safety. Passionate and convincing, he found a ready convert to his views in Moynihan, who liked bold ideas. They would get nowhere on the subject during their time in Albany but both men would leave their marks on the issue.

Haddon was a disciple of Hugh DeHaven, a believer in the importance of the second-collision school of traffic safety, as well as a protégé of Professor Ross McFarland of the Harvard School of Public Health, who had bolstered the second-collision approach with the insights of epidemiology. What this meant, as Haddon explained to Moynihan, was that road injuries and deaths should be understood as a noncontagious disease of epidemic proportions. Every epidemic has an environment (the highway), an agent through which the disease is transmitted (the automobile), and a host who gets the disease (the driver or passenger). An epidemiologist studies the interrelationships of environment, agent, and host with an eye to controlling one or another so as to limit the exposure of the host. It seemed logical to McFarland, Haddon, and, in due course, Moynihan that trying to control the behavior of eighty million potential hosts in the highway environment was futile: people were fallible in their judgment and physical abilities, prone to rage and recklessness and drunkenness, and nothing would ever change that. Far easier to alter the agents of the automobile crash epidemic, the vast majority of which were manufactured by three companies in Detroit. By applying pressure to a handful of executives at those companies who had final say over the interior designs of their product, automobiles could be made safer and the lives of many hosts saved.[55]

On Harriman's expulsion from Albany in 1958, Moynihan returned to the academy and took up journalism to further his intellectual interests and maintain his profile. Thirty-two years old, he wrote the first substantial article of his career for *The Reporter*, a small newsmagazine edited by Irving Kristol and highly influential among American liberals. "Epidemic on the Highways" hit the newsstands several days before its official publication date of April 30, 1959, and roughly two weeks after Ralph Nader had published his article on traffic safety in *The Nation*.

There are many similarities between the pieces: abundant data on highway deaths and injuries, inventories of the design deficiencies of American automobiles, recitations of arguments from *The Journal of the American Medical Association* (with better attribution by Moynihan), and a heavy reliance on the work of Hugh DeHaven and his fellow Cornell researchers. Moynihan, like Nader, believed that the Triple-E advocates had failed: "Something more effective than simply urging people to stop killing each other must be done." Both authors dismissed government officials as unscientific bunglers and captives of the automobile industry. "No first-class officials" are interested in vehicle safety, wrote Moynihan. Rather, the problem had been managed by "an innocent but ineffective" alliance of politicians and police. Motor vehicle bureaus were staffed with "deservedly low-paid clerks and run by an assortment of genial 'pols' with utterly no training or interest in traffic safety except to do small favors . . . lifting a suspension, restoring a license here or there."[56]

Moynihan agreed with Nader that safety campaigns aimed at motorists were a waste of time. Drivers were incorrigible. That an eight-year study of single-car crash fatalities in Westchester County, New York, found 49 percent of the victims to have been legally drunk (with at least 0.15 percent blood alcohol level), and another 20 percent to have been almost drunk (0.08 per cent), was to Moynihan proof that a better approach to safety would be to shift the focus from hosts to agents and force automakers to do a better job of protecting passengers from their inevitable crashes. His prescriptions for safer vehicles were consistent with the second-collision consensus on padded dashes, stronger door latches, recessed steering wheels, seat belts, and so on.[57]

While Nader and Moynihan, writing independently, neither of them drivers, were in lockstep on the fundamentals, Moynihan was a PhD rather than a crusading lawyer and felt compelled from time to time to consider facts that did not neatly fit his case. He acknowledged that the rate of deaths per hundred million miles of travel had been declining steadily for decades. He attributed the improvement, without supporting evidence, to gains in lifesaving medicine rather than to the efforts of Triple-E adherents. He admitted that Detroit had occasionally and voluntarily made safety items available to consumers as options, and sometimes even as standard features (the safety steering wheel, for instance, and improved door locks). Whereas Nader tended to latch on to the most alarming statistics he could find, Moynihan identified a huge discrepancy in crash injury numbers between the National Safety Council (1.5 million injuries per year) and the U.S. Public Health Service (5.0 million injuries per year). The National Safety Council only recognized injuries "disabling beyond the day of accident." Moynihan, like Nader, preferred the higher number but nevertheless presented both while lamenting the lack of rigor in traffic safety studies and highlighting the need for an authoritative base of facts. "Very little is actually known about accidents," he wrote. Police crash reports in particular were "hopelessly inadequate—and often inaccurate as well."[58]

Moynihan's misgivings about the data were not so strong as to frustrate his conclusions. Again like Nader, he found Detroit grossly irresponsible on the safety file and claimed that its executives knew how to stop the epidemic of traffic deaths yet stubbornly refused to do so. He, too, wanted federal regulation that would compel Detroit to install more safety equipment in automobiles, rendering them crashworthy. He, too, was inspired by the muckrakers of old, making direct reference to Upton Sinclair's *The Jungle* (1906), a novelistic exposé of unsanitary practices and other evils in the meatpacking industry:

> If the industry cannot rise to its responsibilities, the entire matter should be removed from its jurisdiction and be solved by methods employed in any other urgent public-health problem. . . . If any automobile magnate wonders what that can mean, he would do well to run over to Chicago to watch government officials in white coats giving their safety ratings to the sides of beef as they roll off the packing house production lines.[59]

Unlike Nader's article, which came and went without a trace, Moynihan's caused what he called "a respectable little stir" in the right circles. He was delighted:

Thousands on thousands of reprints have been ordered, from all over the world. The insurance industry has sent copies to a mailing list of ten thousand executives. The Cornell people have sent two thousand to physicians and public health officials around the country. It is going into Congressional Record, and will be used as a discussion paper at a forthcoming meeting of the Council of Europe.[60]

Moynihan promptly signed a contract with Knopf to write a book about traffic safety. In his correspondence with the publisher he set as his goal descriptions of pain and loss so powerful as to not only advance vehicle safety but "impair if not in fact destroy the personal and social symbolism of the American automobile which is as precious to those who manufacture them as to those who buy them." Moynihan, in short, was gunning for Detroit.[61]

Another outcome of his article was the start of a friendly correspondence with Ralph Nader.

CHAPTER 5

SAVIOR SANS TAILFINS

General Motors in the 1950s and 1960s produced cars, trucks, tanks, aircraft engines, bicycles, earthmovers, school buses, a full selection of home appliances, and executives. Of all these things, none was more purely a product of General Motors than the executive. Cars carried a General Motors nameplate, whether Chevrolet, Plymouth, Buick, Oldsmobile, or Cadillac. They were advertised on television as being made by one of these divisions, and they were sold in the General Motors dealer network and financed by General Motors Acceptance Corporation, but they were not so much manufactured in G.M. plants as they were assembled from thousands of parts, many of which were purchased from external suppliers. Executives, by contrast, were often head-to-toe General Motors, raised in the company almost from the cradle, like Ed Cole.

He was born Edward Nicholas Cole on September 17, 1909, and grew up on a farm a dozen miles northwest of Grand Rapids, Michigan, near the town of Marne (known as Berlin until the end of the Great War). At age five, he crawled into the driver's seat of his family's 1908 Buick and figured out which levers to pull in order to propel the vehicle into a tree. He developed a strong work ethic and a gift for things mechanical, building and selling radios while in high school, milking twenty cows and delivering fresh bottles to neighbors by car before class, selling Fordson tractors in his summers after having mastered the art of the on-field demonstration. He was consumed by automobiles, driving them, tinkering with them, and, especially, improving them. He souped up old Model T Fords and made a hot rod out of a two-seat, four-cylinder Saxon. At age sixteen he was one of only a handful of two-car owners in the Grand Rapids region.

Cole had originally intended to go to law school but chose instead to follow his genius and study automotive engineering at the General Motors Institute of Technology. GMI was a degree-granting college founded as the School of Automotive Trades in 1919 and acquired by the automaker in 1926 as a means to attract and train talent to fill its swelling managerial ranks. By Cole's time, it was well on its way to earning its later reputation as the "West Point" of American industry. The corporation was proud of the college. Ford had only a high school.[1]

Most students at GMI were drawn, like Cole, from small midwestern towns and sponsored in their educations by a division of General Motors. They would work and study in six-week shifts, forty-eight weeks a year, for four years. They learned the theoretical and practical aspects of automotive engineering, design production, and marketing, and they were steeped in the disciplines and hierarchies of the General Motors corporate leviathan. Cole thrived at the institute. He joined the Phi Kappa Epsilon fraternity and married his blue-eyed hometown sweetheart, Esther Engman. He performed well enough that his sponsor, Cadillac, plucked him out of school and applied him to special projects before his graduation. He was a full-time engineer at Cadillac at age twenty-four, the first big step in what would be an unbroken run up the organizational chart.[2]

During his long tenure as head of General Motors (1923–56), Alfred Sloan had imbued G.M. with a culture requiring of its executives a commitment to long days at the office, fierce loyalty, and team play, meaning the subjugation of large parts of their individuality to the good of the organization. Rising men of Cole's generation worked together, ate meals together, lived in the same leafy Detroit suburbs of Bloomfield Hills and Grosse Pointe, joined the same country clubs, golfed together, bought cottages on the same lakes in northern Michigan, and cheered for the University of

Michigan football team and the Detroit Tigers. They were white, mostly Protestant, and occasionally Catholic individuals who talked in a forthright manner and kept good eye contact. Their suits, their neckties, their haircuts, and their homes were uniformly conservative. Only the cars they drove were ostentatious. It was said that the smart ones "never say or do anything that might separate him from his peer group." The social protocol was for an executive to invite to a dinner party at his home one guest from above him in the hierarchy, and one from below, and the rest from his own level. "It's like entering the priesthood," said one observer. "They get out of college and go into the system. . . . From then on, the corporation takes care of everything. It sells their houses when they move, invests their incomes, provides them with new cars every few thousand miles, gets them memberships in the right clubs and so on. They even retire together in G.M. colonies in the South and Southwest. . . . The farther they advance, the more monastic they become."[3]

G.M.'s culture as perceived by outsiders was a mix of truth and mythology. Some of Cole's colleagues did have similar backgrounds and some were conformist in their lifestyles. Most of them internalized certain General Motors attitudes and ways of looking at the market and the world, and many would spend the whole of their working lives in the comfortable, lucrative womb of the company. At the same time, they were generally intelligent, ambitious, and highly motivated men capable of innovative, even daring work, and a significant number of them were able to protect a strong sense of self even while locked in the G.M. orbit. It was the company's combination of individual talent, entrepreneurial zeal, and corporate discipline that made it great.[*]

* The notion that G.M. was overrun by accountants and conformists emerged in the 1950s despite the fact that the senior ranks of the company included Ed Cole; the flamboyant G.M. designer Harley Earl; the Japanese American designer Larry Shinoda, who had grown up in a U.S. government internment camp and who went on to design the Corvette Stingray; the Belgian-Jewish former race car driver Zora Arkus-Duntov, who would make a performance vehicle out of the Corvette; the team of Bunkie Knudsen and Pete Estes, who more or less invented the muscle car and established Pontiac as a force in stock car racing; and Knudsen's protégé, the legendary John DeLorean, whose personal flair, talent, and misadventures as a cocaine dealer speak for themselves.

A well-built man with a low center of gravity and a long, friendly face, Ed Cole advanced steadily through the ranks of Cadillac during the Depression, moving jobs every couple of years as promising young managers were expected to do. On the eve of Pearl Harbor, he was assigned to apply his knowledge of Cadillac V8 engines to improve the army's light tanks, and given ninety days to do so. He made the deadline and Cadillac produced more than ten thousand tanks and another ten thousand engines for other armored vehicles, a major contribution to the war effort. When the Cadillac production facilities were reconverted to peaceful purposes, Cole and the division's general manager, John Gordon, developed a sensational new short-stroke V8 engine with high compression, high power, less weight, and 15 percent better fuel economy than its predecessor. Cole loved that Cadillac engine. He would sneak out to his garage from his own dinner parties to play with its tuning, reducing noise, adjusting its temperature.[4]

In his spare time, Cole designed a tank with an air-cooled, horizontally opposed engine that was rushed into production as the T-41 Walker Bulldog at Cadillac's massive plant in Cleveland during the Korean War. Plagued with technical issues and subjected to massive design corrections by the military, the T-41 was not Cole's best work. What is interesting about it is that it was entirely his initiative. No one, not his company or the military, had asked him for a new tank design. Cole was brimming with initiative. During his Cadillac years, he had proposed some change to some engine and was told that "they" would not allow it—"they" being the front office. He went from executive suite to executive suite looking for someone to argue with and not finding anyone who admitted to having a problem with his idea went ahead and executed it. The incident became a Cole parable about the need to push for change and test limits. He told his associates to "kick the hell out of the status quo."[5]

Extending these attitudes to his personal life, Cole would eventually divorce his first wife, Esther, and marry Dollie Ann McVey, a stunning blond Texan and former Dr Pepper calendar girl. Divorce had always been considered a career killer in Detroit auto circles, and some thought Cole's would sidetrack him. It did not. He and Dollie moved into a tri-level house on Island Lake in Bloomfield Hills and his advance at G.M. continued. He found time to hunt

ducks and pheasants, raise orchids in a greenhouse, tend a minia-
ture Japanese garden in his living room, wire the hi-fi system in his
house, repair his own appliances, train himself as a photographer,
and acquire a pilot's license, all while standing out at G.M. for the
length of his workdays.[6]

What was probably Cole's biggest break at G.M. came as a result
of trouble at Chevrolet, General Motors' largest division, which had
seen its sales slip from 1.5 million cars in 1950 to 871,000 in 1952.
One G.M. executive, president Charles E. Wilson, told another
G.M. executive, Chevrolet general manager Thomas Keating, that
he could have whatever he needed to revitalize the brand. "I want Ed
Cole," said Keating. A third G.M. executive, Harlow "Red" Curtice,
soon to replace Wilson in the top job, called Cole, who at the time
was living out of Cleveland's Lake Shore Hotel in a room outfitted
with sketching tools and a drafting board, to tell him he was the new
chief engineer at Chevrolet.

"How soon do you want me to wrap things up in Cleveland?"
asked Cole.

"Just leave your keys on the desk as you go out," said Curtice.[7]

One of the perks of the Chevrolet job was that Cole at any time
could step out of his office and drive Corvettes at 115 miles per hour
around a test track. More of his time, however, was spent in meetings, including one a few weeks after he started, a corporate planning session where Alfred Sloan Jr., then chairman of the General
Motors board, raised the issue of Chevrolet's fading sales. "I just
happen to have some plans for expanding Chevrolet engineering,"
Cole piped up, "and I'm ready to show them any time you wish."
His plans called for more than tripling Chevrolet's complement of
851 engineers to 2,900. Charlie Wilson pulled him aside after the
meeting and said, "I'll bet that's the first time you ever had your
plans approved without submitting them."

Within weeks, Cole had designed a new Chevrolet V8 engine
with less weight and a 30 percent increase in horsepower. It was a
tough, efficient, reliable, near-perfect engine that would become the
standard at General Motors for the rest of the century, selling over
100 million units and making *Ward's* list of ten best engines of the
twentieth century. Cole had put it into production without building
a test model. "That's how crazy and confident we were," he said.[8]

. . .

By 1956, two years before he fingered the auto industry as a cause
of his worst recession, President Eisenhower had presided over the
opening of General Motors' state-of-the-art, "spectacularly modern" technical center in Warren, Michigan. The new facility was
not one building but a constellation of seventeen major structures
grouped around a man-made lake on a 320-acre campus designed
by the Finnish American architect Eero Saarinen. Celebrated as
the world's largest industrial research complex, it was intended, said
new G.M. president Red Curtice, as a place where four thousand
designers, scientists, and engineers, the core research staffs for the
major General Motors brands, could "think freely of problems yet
unsolved and goals yet uncharted." The press called it a $100 mil-
lion "welcome mat for eggheads," while acknowledging that corporations such as G.M., Bell, and General Electric were scooping
up talent from universities and the defense establishment and by
doing so placing themselves in the front lines of the search for useful knowledge. Eisenhower congratulated General Motors for its
leadership in "furthering new attacks on the technological frontier,"
adding that beyond the frontier "lie better and fuller employment,
opportunities for people to demonstrate yet again the value of a system based on the dignity of human beings, and on their free opportunities in life."[9]

The Saarinen facilities were hailed in *Life* magazine as a "Ver-
sailles of Industry," but not everyone was unstinting with praise. Ed
Cole, for one, had a complaint. It was nothing to do with the campus's eighty acres of manicured lawns, or the reflecting pools and
fountains, or the clean, almost austere lines of the uniformly three-
story buildings of steel and tinted glass. Nor did Cole mind the interiors of the buildings, a fascinating blend of functionalism—brightly
lit spaces with movable wall partitions—with futuristic touches such
as a floating spiral staircase and a round white reception desk that
seemed to hover like a spaceship in a cavernous entranceway. In
fact, the grace and precision of Saarinen's brightly colored glazed
brick, his wood surfaces with inlaid travertine, would seem to have
appealed to Cole's tastes more than a lot of the cars General Motors

was producing at the time. His problem was with the escalators. They were too slow. He ordered them accelerated by 30 percent.[10]

As chief engineer in a semi-sovereign division like Chevrolet, which on its own routinely outsold all of Ford, Cole was encouraged to give his imagination loose rein and to plan for future vehicles. He devoted a skunk works at Chevy to a small-car project. Just after the war, the division had designed a compact model called the Cadet but it was scrapped shortly before Cole's arrival on the assumption that the market was trending toward larger, chromier cars and small would not sell. Cole disagreed and developed a range of small test cars over a period of four years. Some were conventional front-engine, rear-wheel drive cars. Others were daring front-engine, front-wheel drive designs. Eventually a rear-engine, rear-wheel drive prototype was built, disguised under the shell of a Porsche. Cole took it for a spin at the Chevrolet Engineering Center. As a colleague told *Time* magazine, "Ed jumped in the car as if his pants were on fire. The speed limit at the test center is twenty-five miles per hour but Ed sped around at eighty. We kept closing our eyes and praying. Then he pulled up and he could barely talk. He said three words: 'This is it.'"[11]

In July 1956, two months after the Saarinen complex was officially opened, forty-six-year-old Ed Cole was named general manager of Chevrolet and a vice president of General Motors. He spent another year working on his small-car prototype, designing thousands of parts and quietly collecting cost estimates from prospective suppliers. In the early autumn of 1957, just as the Eisenhower recession was showing its fangs and well before the imports were seen as a serious threat to Detroit, Cole, with all of his plans and arguments ready, casually invited his president, Red Curtice, out to Warren to have a look at something.

When Curtice arrived, Cole pulled a canvas sheet from a clay model of a small car unlike anything in the General Motors lineup. It was unlike anything produced anywhere. It had no bulging fenders, no massive bumpers, no toothy grille, no bug-eyed headlights, no long overhanging trunk or sky-raking tail fins. It was low to the ground with straight, elegant lines, an understated but forward-looking design not unlike Saarinen's buildings. It was so uniquely and evenly proportioned, its front end the same length as its back end, that it was not clear at a glance whether it was coming or going. Cole wanted to produce it with a rear-mounted, air-cooled, light-weight aluminum engine instead of the usual water-cooled, front-mounted, cast-iron job. It was a radical proposition from nose to tail.[12]

Cole looked at Curtice, who was looking at the model. He had invited the G.M. president to the Warren complex expressly to reveal this secret project, boldly bypassing the normal channels of new product approval at the company. He knew his odds of a green light would be much improved if he could first get the president onside. Curtice leaned back warily, blue eyes squinting. After a good look, he grilled Cole. Would people buy a small car? What would it require in new plant and equipment? Where would they get aluminum for the engine? Wouldn't a small car simply cannibalize the market for standard Chevrolets?

Cole was ready. He pointed to the fast-rising volume of foreign car sales and produced surveys indicating that Chevrolet buyers were defecting to the import market in search of something different, more economical, and easier to handle and park than the typical Chevy Strassenkreuzer. He revealed plans to convert existing Chevrolet facilities to produce the new car, which would save money (it would still cost hundreds of millions of dollars). He had suppliers of aluminum and price estimates at hand. He displaced Curtice's concerns about cannibalization with urgent appeals to his competitive spirit: "If we don't hurry up and build this car, someone else will."[13]

After two hours of back-and-forth, Cole took Curtice for a test drive. "I think you've got something there, Ed."[14]

The General Motors board approved production of Cole's small car in December 1957, three months before Khrushchev's promise to bury capitalism, and four months before Eisenhower lamented Detroit's fixation on oversized cars. Tempting as it might have been at that moment to let the president and the public know what G.M. was planning, it was going to take time to steer a new car from approval to launch and it was important that the company, if it were to steal a march on Ford and Chrysler in the compact market, keep its project secret even as orders were sent to the toolmakers who would supply the one-off machinery of production.

With corporate espionage among the Big Three incessant and sophisticated, G.M. needed a cover story for what it was doing. It claimed to be updating the Holden, a car produced by its Australian subsidiary. Test models of Cole's new vehicle were hidden under Porsche or Vauxhall body shells and driven through two million miles of trials. Cole himself took one out for a tour of the Colorado Rockies. A launch date was set for the fall of 1959, when the 1960 models would make their debut. In the meantime, despite the company's best efforts, word leaked that G.M. was going small. The *Detroit Free Press* and *Newsweek* reported in March 1958 that both General Motors and Ford were investigating scaled-down designs. Both companies were noncommittal in response to press inquiries. "It is our belief that most American new car buyers will continue to prefer the comfort, convenience, safety aspects, and styling of our standard size American cars," said a G.M. spokesman.[15]

In April, *Automotive News* broke the story that Chevrolet was considering an air-cooled rear-engine vehicle with swing axles instead of the usual straight axles, permitting independent suspension on all four wheels. The new car might also feature unit body (unibody) construction, which meant that the entire frame and body structure of the car would be of a single piece rather than bolted together, allowing for less weight and more rigidity. It seemed an incredible amount of innovation for one Detroit vehicle. Word soon came that Chrysler was fast-tracking a compact of its own.[16]

Meanwhile, evidence of trouble and devastation continued to mount in jittery Motor City. Inventories of unsold vehicles were depleted through the end of 1958, but mostly because the Big Three had drastically cut production. Jobs had continued to disappear and imports had continued to post impressive numbers with expectations of another year-over-year doubling of sales in 1959. *The New York Times* reported the dispiriting news that for the first time in history, the United States no longer produced a majority of the world's automobiles. Europe, Japan, Australia, and South America all set production records in 1958, leading to the building of six million non-American vehicles against Detroit's 5.1 million cars and trucks. As recently as 1954, the United States had claimed 70 percent of the global market. Also for the first time, the States imported more automobiles than it exported, by an almost two-to-one margin. J. Bruce McWilliams, who imported Saabs, predicted that foreign car sales were only several years from reaching 2.5 million per annum, or just under half of the U.S. market.[17]

If sixty-seven import brands were not enough competition, two small U.S. producers were adding to the problems of the Big Three. American Motors Corporation, a distant fourth in the U.S. market, had been pushing small cars for years, in large part because of its inability to compete in the standard-sized market. For 1958, it dropped its practice of bloating its compact Rambler to make it look as big as a standard car and instead slimmed it down to look more like an import. The Rambler, said its marketing department, was the compact of the future, a patriotic alternative to foreign vehicles and the "gas hogs" produced by G.M., Ford, and Chrysler: "Get the only car that gives you the best of both—American big car room and comfort, plus European small car economy and handling ease." The Rambler's sales increased a remarkable 80 percent in 1958 despite an industry-wide drop of 30 percent. AMC turned profitable for the year after a loss of $12 million in 1957.[18]

In a similar move, Studebaker-Packard bet its future on the compact Lark. It was a hit in 1959, leading the company to its first quarterly profit since 1953. The Rambler and the Lark would sell 500,000 units in 1959, which together with the imports brought the small-car market to over one million vehicles, or 15 percent of the U.S. total. Almost all of these cars sold in the $1,400 to $2,000 price range, while the major American manufacturers priced their vehicles from $2,000 all the way up to $13,500 for a top-of-the-line Cadillac. It seemed to many observers as though the Big Three's misreading of the market was bringing both AMC and Studebaker-Packard back from the dead. George Romney, president of AMC, echoed Saab's McWilliams by predicting to the *Detroit Free Press* that small cars would account for half of the domestic market by the mid-1960s.[19]

Encouraging as the results were for champions of the little guy and enemies of the Big Three's supposed oligopoly, it was well understood in Detroit that economic recovery and growth in employment demanded signs of life from the major manufacturers and, in particular, General Motors. It might have been true that the auto industry was large enough to single-handedly pull America out of an economic ditch but not without G.M. and its $3 billion payroll, its procurement operations that supported 26,000 suppliers with $5 billion a year in orders, its dividends of almost $600 million annually to 718,000 stockholders, and its $182 million annual advertising budget (sustaining thirteen separate agencies). In terms of economic output, G.M. was the size of Ireland, Hong Kong, South Korea, and Norway combined. Until G.M. turned around, the future of Detroit, and the prospects for American industry, looked bleak.[20]

As it happened, General Motors' fiftieth anniversary fell in 1958. Having racked up $129 billion in lifetime sales and $11.3 billion in after-tax profits, the company believed a celebration was warranted but the effort seemed forced. The mood in the executive offices of corporate headquarters on West Grand Boulevard was black. Red Curtice, who had realized every Detroit honcho's dream by making the cover of *Time* with his record-setting performance in 1955, was now sixty-five, G.M.'s mandatory retirement age. He exited quietly at the end of the anniversary year with sales off 22 percent and profits down 25 percent.* He was replaced by Frederic G. Donner, a financial man, indicating a deep concern on the board with the company's profitability, which, despite all of the production cuts and a slightly improving market in the last six months of the decade, would shrink by half between 1956 and 1959.[21]

In the middle of the 1959 model year, G.M. finally revealed that Cole's wonder car, the Corvair, a portmanteau of Corvette and Bel Air, would be released with its 1960 models. Ford announced a new compact, the Falcon, and Chrysler its Valiant, both conventional front-engine cars, similar in style to the rest of their parent company lineups.

This news triggered fierce debates in the automotive press

---

* In 1959, Curtice would shoot and kill another retired General Motors executive while duck hunting in Canada, and die himself of an apparent heart attack in 1962. G.M. executives of his era earned a reputation for not living long in retirement. *New York Times*, November 4, 1962.

about who, if anyone, would buy the smaller vehicles. A session on the advisability of small cars at a Society of Automotive Engineers meeting in June was standing room only and there was no consensus on whether the compacts were the future of the industry, whether they would make money, and whether they were safer than standard cars because of their maneuverability or more dangerous based on their lighter weight. The latter was a serious question. "Driving a small car on the highway is like putting a bantam boxer against a heavyweight in the ring," said one expert. Researchers at Cornell raised more doubts by announcing that small cars had a greater tendency than large cars to roll over in collisions. Another unexpected worry was that the small car trend would be detrimental to public accounts in states such as Michigan where taxes were based on vehicle weight. The auto industry was leading everyone into uncharted territory.[22]

Of specific concern to General Motors in the lead-up to the Corvair's launch was criticism of Cole's rear-engine design. The naysaying had begun before anyone outside the company had even seen the car. Lester L. "Tex" Colbert, president of Chrysler Corporation, made a point of stating that his Valiant would have "the engine up front, where it belongs," and Ford released a television advertisement showing what happens to an arrow in flight when its weight is transferred from its tip to its tail. Two British engineers crossed the Atlantic to advise Americans that "it is our very definite opinion that in head-on collisions, it is better to have the mass of the power and transmission unit in front of the vehicle, where its momentum may absorb some of the force of the impact." General Motors had its own experts who attested to the crashworthiness and superior performance of rear-engine cars, noting that Volkswagen, Porsche, and Renault had long relied upon similar setups. They failed to settle the debate.[23]

On the eve of the Corvair's official on-sale date, Ed Cole professed to be confident. "If I felt any better about our Chevy Corvair, I think I'd blow up," he said. His marketing was similarly effusive, advising Americans that on October 2 they would be able to walk into a showroom and "for the first time in Chevrolet's history see two totally different kinds of cars"—the front-engine models they knew and loved, and the "revolutionary Corvair," which was "unlike any car we or anybody else ever built."[24]

The press was agog at the fact that the Big Three had invested almost a billion dollars during a recession in the production and marketing of the three compacts. It anticipated the keenest foreign and domestic competition in the American market since the earliest days of the automotive industry. "Not since Henry Ford put the nation on wheels with his Model T has such a great and sweeping change hit the auto industry," wrote *Time*. Agreed Volkswagen's Heinz Nordhoff from the comfort of his perch in Germany: "Nineteen sixty will be the most interesting year in the history of the U.S. automobile industry."[25]

The first Corvairs began to roll off assembly lines at Chevrolet's Willow Run plant on July 6, 1959, and three weeks later newspaper photographs showed them wrapped in white sheets on the back of transport haulers, headed for dealers across the country. The recession was over and automobile sales had regained a strong pace for both domestic and foreign product. Imports were claiming 10 percent of sales in the Midwest where a decade earlier their share had been less than 1 percent, and an astonishing 17 percent of sales in California. Saab's prediction that imports and domestics would soon split the U.S. market was becoming more difficult to dismiss and, notwithstanding the nation's economic recovery, concerns about America's global competitiveness remained high. How Detroit's new compacts perform, wrote *The New York Times*, "will go a long way in determining the economic health" of the business that employs a large portion of the nation's wage earners.[26]

Three weeks before the Corvair's official launch, Russia dealt another blow to America's presumptions of technological superiority and leadership of the world's future. It followed up Sputnik by firing into space an 850-pound rocket that traveled 236,875 miles in thirty-five hours and crashed into the surface of the moon at a speed of 7,500 miles per hour. It was the first object sent by man from one cosmic body to another and it bore the hammer-and-sickle emblem of the Soviet Union.[27]

The autumn of 1959 was packed with unsettling news of this sort, from reports that Russia had increased yet again its investments in science and technology to announcements that it had accelerated production of household appliances and other consumer goods in response to public demand. A trio of U.S. senators returned home from a fact-finding trip to the Soviet Union to relate that Moscow had assumed world leadership in the development of hydroelectric power. On September 11, the *Detroit Free Press* ran on the top right-hand corner of its front page an excerpt from Nikita Khrushchev's book *For Victory in Peaceful Competition with Capitalism*, outlining the Soviet leader's vision for coexistence with the West and the economic triumph of his brand of communism.[28]

In the middle of that same front page was a photograph of G.M.'s Ed Cole. It was attached to an article on his preview of the Corvair for a crowd of newsmen in the only Detroit building more grandiose than his company's headquarters, the Cass Corridor's sixteen-story neo-Gothic Masonic Temple, largest in the world. Cole confirmed to reporters that his new car was indeed a rear-engine compact. It weighed 2,375 pounds, or 1,385 less than a standard Chevrolet Bel Air. It was two and a half feet shorter than the Bel Air, and a foot narrower. Its eighty-horsepower, horizontally opposed engine was not entirely built of aluminum as originally planned—the six cylinders were cast iron—but Cole could still claim it as the first modern lightweight, air-cooled automobile engine, with anticipated gas mileage 25 percent to 40 percent better than the other six-cylinders in the Chevrolet family. The Corvair was priced from $1,955, at least 10 percent lower than other Chevrolets. Cole went out on a limb and said he hoped to sell 300,000 units of the car in its first year.[29]

Much was made in Cole's presentation and in subsequent Chevrolet advertising of claims that the Corvair, with its unique rear-engine power train and four-wheel independent suspension, contained more genuine engineering advancements than ever introduced on one car before, and that Chevrolet was the first North American manufacturer to conceive, design, and produce a compact car from scratch as opposed to simply shrinking an existing car. It was this clean-slate approach, Cole liked to say, that led him to put the Corvair's engine in the rear, "where it belongs in a compact car."[30]

In preparation for the Corvair launch, Chevrolet dealers were shipped training materials on how to position the vehicle with prospective buyers. Previously it had not been necessary for Chevy salesmen to steep themselves in the emerging arts of audience segmentation. Their cars were mass sellers, designed for everyone. The Corvair, however, was a distinctive vehicle, made for a certain type of driver, and Chevrolet was leery of cannibalizing sales of its existing lines. "In selling cars," advised a seventeen-minute instructional film, "you've got to hit the right sales target with the right sales product if you want to score." The "one particular group of prospects" for which the Corvair was designed was the foreign car owner, a market previously "overlooked" by General Motors. There were 1.4 million imports on American roads at the end of 1959, the film said, most of them noisy, rickety, underpowered, and cramped. They appealed to their owners as functional transportation, easy to handle, inexpensive to buy, and cheap to run. The Corvair delivered all of the import's virtues in a roomier, more comfortable package better suited to American roads and American drivers, and with better service and easier access to parts. Salesmen were informed that the company had sent Corvair brochures to 800,000 foreign car owners. They were encouraged to treat any import shopper who happened by the dealership with more personal attention than a regular car shopper as this is "a person who likes to be different."[31]

When communicating with the outside world, Chevrolet's marketing department seemed to struggle with the new car's positioning. In one commercial, show-business personality Dinah Shore, Chevy's primary spokesperson, sang an adaptation of the nursery rhyme "Frère Jacques": "Safety with a savings, *tout le monde* are craving, le Corvair, le Corvair." While that might have highlighted the new brand's European vibe, another ad had country star Jimmy Dean singing a ditty about the Corvair winning a blue ribbon at the state fair, something that might have applied to any car or truck in the Chevrolet lineup.[32]

The Corvair's launch campaign, comprised of television, newspaper, and magazine advertisements, consumed much of G.M.'s annual $100 million marketing budget. Some ads nodded to the car's styling and its "fashion-crafted interiors." Others boasted of its "safety-girder frame," which provided more resistance to road shocks, and its "safety-master brakes," which permitted shorter and straighter stops, and its "safety plate glass" and "rotary safety door latches," which offered still more protection for drivers and passengers. The advantages of the innovative rear-engine power train were frequently enumerated. It was said to insulate occupants from noise and heat, to allow for a flat floor and improved legroom, and to ensure a "glued-to-the-road traction" in snow, ice, or mud.[33]

Whether or not it was consistent with its import buyer strategy, Chevrolet went out of its way to emphasize Corvair's tanklike traction and stability. It produced a six-minute film of the "Corvair in Action," running figure eights and slalom courses, braking on foam-covered pavement, charging up steep sandy grades and through axle-deep mud, and splashing for miles in a shallow streambed. The automaker insisted that its car had been thoroughly tested and that its power, ruggedness, maneuverability, handling, traction and braking "had all been proved, again and again." These messages were intended less for buyers than for critics of the new car's unconventional rear engine, especially those at Ford and Chrysler.[34]

Chevrolet need not have bothered. Ford was quick with its critiques of the Corvair but not for its engine configuration, a secondary factor in the minds of compact car buyers, who, like most buyers in Detroit's experience, were primarily impressed by styling. The instructional film Ford sent to its dealers emphasized the quality and classic look and feel of its competitor, the Falcon. The Corvair's supposedly modern profile was comparatively "box-like" and "unsightly." Chevrolet engineers had taken "shortcuts in design" and left the car with an "unfinished appearance" that fell "grossly short" of the Falcon's high standard. Chevy used a thin front bumper whereas Falcon had "a husky deep-section bumper" for greater protection. The Corvair's front end was all sheet metal, requiring its owners to scrape bugs off the nose of the vehicle, while the Falcon featured the customary aluminum grille. The Corvair had no rear-seat coat hooks, the air came out of its windshield defroster at a suboptimal angle, its steering wheel was small, its seat material was of inferior quality, its windows were not edged in chrome, and it was narrower than the Falcon and therefore less comfortable for six passengers. Its front-end gas tank was ominously positioned beneath the front passenger's feet and, worst of all, a Christmas tree sticking out of the Corvair's front trunk would block the driver's line of sight and render the car useless.[35]

A twelve-minute Chrysler sales training film introducing the compact Valiant to its dealer network claimed that in a sudden turn the Corvair's heavy rear end would tend to "break loose" and "skid without warning." The bulk of the instruction, however, played up the Valiant's larger size, its 20 percent horsepower advantage, and, most of all, its styling. The Corvair "looks cheap" next to the Valiant, a car that "faces the world jauntily" with its "sport-type aluminum grill," chrome window framing, and faux trunk-mounted spare tire, all familiar elements of big-car design adapted by Chrysler to the compact form. The Corvair, by contrast, took "neatness to the point of austerity" and the sacrifices its designers had made in service of economy were "plainly evident." The Valiant boasted larger door openings, decorative door panels, thicker ceiling insulation, deeper seat cushioning, and a modern push-button radio. Chrysler, too, used an illustration of a Christmas tree sticking out from under the hood of the Corvair to underscore the disadvantages of a rear-engine car.[36]

The press had its own ideas of what was important in the new compacts and its reviews were searching and numerous. *The New York Times* assigned Paul J. C. Friedlander to the Corvair, the only one of the three new vehicles examined by the paper. The use of Friedlander was significant in itself. He was not an auto critic (the *Times* did not often review new cars). He was the correspondent to whom the paper turned to describe and appraise the latest wonders in the field of transportation. Friedlander had taken the first ride on Pullman's new Twentieth Century Limited luxury trains (complete with radio-telephone and barber). He was one of the first aboard the glorious new American Export Lines ocean liner with air-conditioning in every room and two swimming pools. He had flown on Boeing's first jet passenger airplane, the 707, from Seattle to Baltimore at 86 percent of the speed of sound, landing in under four quiet, comfortable hours.[37]

While not an auto critic, Friedlander was nevertheless an experienced motorist, having toured most of the United States, Europe, and South America in a variety of domestic and foreign cars, and having taken racing instruction in England. He picked up the Corvair in Manhattan's Radio City garage and put it through "a fairly comprehensive" weekend workout. He had been following the debates on the car's engine placement. They had been "waged sharply," he said, with all the arguments against a rear-engine car listed and elaborated. That it would steer strangely. That the car would not corner as tightly and smoothly as a front-engine car. That it would float out, weave, or wobble at high speeds because its front end was light, and that the back end would swing wide on turns. After 350 miles in rain and shine over the Long Island Expressway and muddy country lanes, the Corvair "satisfied this motorist that the rear-engine automobile is here to stay." The car cornered neatly at high and low speeds, it steered lightly at all speeds, and it was fully responsive to steering at seventy-five miles per hour, beyond which it began to float a touch.

Friedlander was not uncritical. He ripped the Corvair's lack of storage space, finding it impossible to get two suitcases in its trunk, and he confessed that its compact size made for the "strange sensation" of having to look up at a toll collector, something that could trigger "an inferiority complex." That said, "it was a revelation the way heads turned, traffic slowed and twisted, and pedestrians went out of their way to look at, inspect, and actually welcome the new car."

> I was stopped for a light at Lexington Avenue and Fifty-Eighth Street when a tall young man in his late twenties, did a double take in the middle of the crosswalk, and came back to read the name plate, measure the car from bumper to bumper. He stood there, finally patted the right front bumper gently and approvingly and said, "Good!" before going quietly on his way.[38]

Nick Thimmesch, a future political correspondent and Robert F. Kennedy biographer, also had the reputed demerits of rear-engine cars in mind when he reviewed the Corvair for *Sports Illustrated*. At eighty-five miles per hour on a test track, he found its handling "beautiful" with "no wander or shift." At medium-high speeds, it turned smoothly and on rough gravel at sixty miles per hour it held the road firmly. Thimmesch, too, complained of the shortage of luggage space, and was unenthusiastic about the styling, which to him screamed "economy." On the whole, he judged it "a rear engine honey which represents real pioneering."[39]

The general tenor of the Corvair's reviews was strongly positive. *Car Life* magazine said "the Corvair handles as beautifully and is as safe as—if not safer than—any family car on the road today." The MIT-educated automotive engineer Karl Ludvigsen said in *Sports Car Illustrated* that he found its steering "among the finest I have ever had the pleasure to handle." About the harshest criticism of the Corvair's ride came from *Popular Science* magazine, which found that the traction is outstanding but that it does have a "slight tendency" to oversteer. "This is a car you will have to learn to drive—that heavy rear end may tend to break loose faster in turns on ice."[40]

The last word on the new Chevrolet compact went to *Motor Trend* magazine, then as now the bible of the automotive industry. In its April 1960 issue it proclaimed the Corvair its Car of the Year, the most coveted honor in the motor world. Wrote the magazine's editors, "The choice of the 1960 Chevrolet Corvair was unanimous. Why? For engineering advancement: its air-cooled engine, trans-axle and four-wheel independent suspension. All these combined spell progress and compel us to select the Corvair as the most significant car of 1960." The Corvair also took the 1960 *Car Life* magazine award for excellence in automotive engineering, and it became only the third automobile to win the Industrial Designers' Institute bronze medal, its highest award in industrial design.[41]

If one thing united everyone who worked in Detroit, from executives to engineers to accountants and assembly workers, it was an appreciation for the importance of new car sales. The nature of the appreciation might differ from person to person, with some seeing a high volume of sales as vindication of Detroit's product offerings, others seeing a contribution to shareholder value and stock prices, and still others an opportunity for better pay and extra shifts, but sales always mattered. So as the new Corvairs, Falcons, and Valiants took their places on the nation's showroom floors, representing what *Fortune* magazine called the Big Three's collective and hugely expensive roll of the dice on their own future, there was more than the usual interest around town in the new car data.[42]

Before turning to 1960 models, *Ward's* closed out its reports on 1959 sales, and the news was chilling. It projected that import performance had been stronger than anticipated, on pace for 600,000 units, up from 377,000 in 1958. That capped an astonishing five-year run in which the foreign brands had increased sales in the United States by more than 80 percent per annum, twenty times the rate for domestic automakers. Almost 20 percent of new car buyers in California chose a foreign badge. Import dealers, still struggling to meet demand for their product, now represented 10 percent of U.S. sales, and the compact sector, including Studebaker and Rambler, had expanded to 18 percent of total sales. Analysts noted that if these trends continued just one more year the Big Three stood to be shut out of a third of the U.S. market.[43]

And then everything changed.

Two days before Christmas, *Ward's* released figures indicating that the Big Three's new entries had vastly expanded the market for small cars in October, their first month of sales, and that U.S. compacts outsold imports 70,468 to 51,923. This was a reversal of previous trends that had foreign brands claiming a 60 percent market share. By the new year, more than 100,000 American compacts were being bought every month, most of them from the Big Three. Ford was jubilant. The Falcon accounted for 35 percent of those sales followed by the AMC Rambler at 26.6 percent, the Corvair at 17.4 percent, the Chrysler Valiant at 12 percent, and the Studebaker Lark at 9 percent.[44]

Just like that, after four blighted years of disappointing performance, two years of recession, and endless second-guessing of its executives and its business practices, Detroit was rolling again. Three months of public exposure to the new compacts was all it took for the Motor City to reassert itself as the leader of the automotive world—the brains, backbone, and beating heart of American industry. These first reports of roaring sales squelched all discussion of how automakers had lost touch with consumers and how Detroit was a weak link in America's economic race with the Soviets. The U.S. standard of living suddenly seemed on firmer ground and there were no more complaints from Washington about the quality of American vehicles. The skeptics and the foreign shitboxes had been put in their place. The theme of Detroit's annual auto show would be "Wheels of Freedom."[45]

It took a full year for a clear picture of the winners and losers in this new automotive era to emerge. Import brands were bruised and bewildered, their sales falling sharply from 614,000 to 500,000. Every European model except the Beetle reported declining sales. Italian cars were off 50 percent. There was new talk in the automotive press about excessive supply in the import market.[46]

Among the domestics, it seemed at first glance that Ford had most to celebrate. The Falcon moved an impressive 450,000 units in its first year of production, knocking the Rambler (422,000) out of top spot in the compact field. Its achievement, however, came at the expense of the more profitable standard Fords, which it closely resembled in everything but size and price. The company's total sales dropped, and its share price fell 5 percent on the news. Ford's financials at year's end were disappointing: its market share had fallen by a point and a half to 27 percent; revenue was down from $5.4 billion to $5.2 billion, and profits from $451 million to $428 million. The pre-launch fears that compact cars would cannibalize their makers' higher-margin business were realized at Ford.[47]

General Motors stumbled at the start of the Corvair's first year due to a strike in the steel industry that caught the company shorthanded and forced it to temporarily close most of its assemblies and send 200,000 workers home. (Ford, which received half of its steel supplies from subsidiaries, was less affected, as were the smaller manufacturers, which had adequate supply to weather the shutdown.) Notwithstanding that setback, the Corvair racked up a respectable 230,000 sales in its inaugural year, short of Cole's goal of 300,000 yet good enough for third place in the domestic compact race. The true measure of its success came in G.M.'s year-end report. Standard Chevrolets had managed a strong year even with fresh competition in the showroom. G.M.'s strategy of targeting a new kind of buyer with something unconventional in both styling and technology had proved sound. The corporation increased its market share by a point and a half to 44 percent and registered sales of $12.7 billion with earnings of $959 million, well up from its marks of $11.2 billion and $873 million in 1959. "Falcon is running far ahead . . . in compact car sales," wrote *The New York Times*, "but G.M. is running away with the cash."[48]

In aggregate, it was a great year for the auto sector. A total of 6.6 million cars were purchased, up 10 percent from 1959, second only to the record year of 1955. Most of the growth was driven by the compacts. Detroit now decided to ride the small car for all it was worth. As 1961 got under way, a third of the industry's production was compact. Ford announced that it was planning the introduction of a still smaller subcompact to take on the Beetle. Corvair had supplemented its two-door and four-door models with a convertible, a wagon, and the popular Monza, a luxury model with vinyl bucket seats. The Monza gained a reputation as the poor man's Porsche. G.M. expanded Corvair's Willow Run assembly by 50 percent and announced that Chevrolet, Pontiac, and Oldsmobile would each produce front-engine compacts.[49]

The success of the Corvair and the compacts also seemed to renew Detroit's enthusiasm for automotive innovation. Ford was investigating a four-cylinder engine and front-wheel drive for its subcompact. Pontiac was working on a tilted four-cylinder engine. Chrysler was testing a gas turbine engine that some of its engineers saw as the future of the industry. American Motors revealed a long-range project to build a "revolutionary electric automobile" powered by rechargeable nickel-cadmium batteries. An independent firm, Nu-Way Industries of Lansing, Michigan, was developing its own two-passenger electric car with an expected range of seventy-five miles and a price tag under $1,500. Executives responsible for the Big Three's standard cars were considering aluminum wheels, plastic bodies, and new lightweight, heat-resistant engine alloys that would reduce weight, improve fuel economy, and further blunt the appeal of the imports. Still other ventures receiving attention in the automotive press were automatic guidance systems and "levacars" that would ride on cushions of air. Whether or not there was a market or business case for all this creativity remained to be seen. Nevertheless, the activity further allayed fears that Detroit had lost its spirit of enterprise and capacity for invention.[50]

Another outcome of the compact revolution was a new approach to styling, influenced primarily by the Corvair. Small, slim, neat, with its odd coming-and-going stance and just one straight crease along its side panels from headlight to taillight, it led the industry out of its obsession with bumps, bulges, chrome, and soaring tailfins. Critics at the forty-third Detroit Auto Show found that the fins had all but disappeared among the three hundred 1961 model cars on display and that chrome was "conspicuous by its rarity." The age of excess was over.[51]

The profile of the small-car buyer was rewritten, too, in the wake of the compact triumph. Foreign car owners were no longer cheapskates, bohemians, or anarchists in the eyes of the industry. They were sensible, regular people looking for convenience and economy, often in a second car. California, formerly an outlying colony of nonconformist freaks, was now a car-crazed paradise with six-lane parkways and four-level interchanges where one could divine the secrets of automotive existence. It was to automotive trend watchers "what the Olduvai Gorge is to paleontologists." This embrace of California was helped enormously by the fact that compacts made up almost 45 percent of new car purchases in the state, and that its import business had fallen by half by the end of 1961.[52]

There was no agreement in Detroit on whether all this change would last or recede or lead to something else entirely. Some observers declared people would no longer buy all the car they could afford to impress their friends and neighbors. They would buy as much car as they needed and be satisfied. Others said that the standard car was disappearing and that in future the market would be split between economy cars and luxury cars. Romney of American Motors continued to proclaim the big car a dinosaur and predicted that compacts would comprise more than half the market as early as 1963. This line of thinking led to discussions about whether the popularity of small cars would lead to recessions in the steel and oil industries. Ed Cole, promoted to head of the G.M. car and truck group in 1961 on the strength of his performance at Chevrolet, was among the dissenters: "I cannot accept the view of one of my respected colleagues in the industry that the mouse will eat the dinosaur." He predicted that compacts would continue to sell well but that standard-sized cars would remain the most popular option. Of course, everyone was speculating and opinions varied markedly as tends to happen in times of transformation.[53]

It was not long, however, before some basic questions about the direction of the industry were answered. The imports, after peaking at over 10 percent of domestic sales in 1959, bottomed out at 4.9 percent in 1962. They remained in the range of 5 percent to 6 percent through 1965 and were saved from absolute devastation by the indestructible Volkswagen Beetle, which improved its numbers every year in this period regardless of what was happening in the broader market.[54]

American-built compacts evolved through the early 1960s. Ford redressed Falcon platforms for 1964 and introduced the aggressive-looking Mustang, two weeks after Chrysler had rejigged the Valiant to produce the flashy Plymouth Barracuda. These were personal sports cars as opposed to family vehicles and the Mustang was a runaway success. The tricked-out luxury Monza became the star of the Corvair lineup, often selling as a convertible with a 150-horsepower engine. Automakers were finding that compacts sold best and most profitably in stylish packages with muscle under the hood, even if this made the cars heavier, less efficient, and more expensive than was originally intended in the shift to smaller vehicles. It came to be known as the American way of going compact, and it suggested that the automobile's role as status totem was undisturbed. The majority of buyers continued to lean toward full-sized family cars.

Devotees of true innovation waited in vain for automakers to deliver on their promises of subcompacts, electric vehicles, fuel cells, and floating cars. These, like most radical propositions in the auto world, failed for want of viable technology, cost effectiveness, or a discernible market. In a sense, Detroit was sobering up. Automakers remembered that there are limits to how much change car buyers are willing to accept in vehicles valued primary for dependability, comfort, and good looks. What's more, a manufacturer's finances benefit from consistency and uniformity in the configuration of the product, and suffer when engineers outrun public expectations or build needless complexity into production streams. Inhibitions on the part of both auto buyer and automaker help to explain why the unconventional Corvair, although a respectable performer with about 300,000 sales a year, never became a best-seller like the smart-looking but otherwise ordinary Mustang, and why G.M. did not repurpose its rear-engine power train for other models.

. . .

That is not to say that Detroit became complacent with the import threat in abeyance and its sales climbing to a new record of 9.3 million cars by 1965. Its confidence was high, having executed its hairpin turn on compacts, and its ambition only grew, albeit in a new direction. From the moment the foreign brands began reconsidering their commitment to the American scene, the Big Three began organizing for world domination.

U.S. executives were seized by the fact that the global auto market, which had been relatively slow to develop, was now larger than the U.S. market and growing at a much faster rate. It had doubled in size to seventeen million vehicles in the decade ending in 1963. Detroit wanted a larger piece of the action.

Thus began a new dimension in automotive competition. The global opportunity, said Tex Colbert of Chrysler, was "the most important factor determining the nature of our products, the level of our prices, and the size of our total market. . . . Future success would be measured on the world stage, and the performance of U.S. automakers there would determine the fate of their industry and "have a very important bearing on the strength of the American dollar and the strength of the United States as a world power." Agreed E. P. McKenna, head of Ford's international division, "foreign operations are being placed on a level of equality with domestic operations. . . . American corporations are beginning to act as truly international corporations."[55]

Detroit began pumping its retained earnings into global production in volumes that rapidly exceeded the level of investment it had made in compacts a few years earlier. After booking profits of $1.5 billion in 1963, a record for any U.S. corporation, General Motors announced that half of a massive two-year capital expenditure of $2.5 billion would fund further international expansion. Henry Ford II committed $270 million of his $400 million capital budget overseas. Not to be outdone, Chrysler declared that "by far the largest share of our total investment will be directed toward acquiring and developing facilities abroad."[56]

Global expansion was more complicated than putting American-built cars on boats. Apart from the fact that Strassenkreuzers were too big and costly for global markets, and expensive to ship because of their weight, U.S. exports faced discriminatory quotas and import taxes in foreign markets. A Buick purchased in Europe would cost 50 percent to 150 percent more than at home, and several times more than locally made vehicles, making it prohibitively expensive for all but the wealthiest buyers. Only 104,384 American cars were sold overseas in 1960. The Big Three preferred to play the global game by founding and buying foreign subsidiaries, which allowed them to take advantage of lower labor and production costs abroad while also skirting trade barriers.[57]

Toward the end of 1963, Chrysler took a 35 percent position in Madrid auto company Barreiros, becoming the first American manufacturer to enter the Spanish market. Ford reported that its foreign output, growing at an annualized rate of 17 percent, amounted to a third of its total business that same year. It was embarking on a four-year plan to build an additional 7.4 million square feet of plant overseas. Almost simultaneously, G.M. announced a 27 percent increase in foreign sales of cars and trucks, bringing its total over the one-million mark for the first time in its history. It pushed that number to 1.3 million in 1964. A year after that, it announced a major expansion of its Opel operations in Germany and a new Opel plant in Belgium, upping the brand's production capacity by 35 percent.[58]

In the early 1960s, Detroit's manufacturing facilities outside the United States expanded to thirty-eight countries and 128 million square feet of space, more than a third of the total stateside. What *The New York Times* called "the race for the world automotive market" was going full tilt and Detroit had its major competitors—Volkswagen, British Motors, Fiat, Mercedes-Benz, Standard, Triumph, Volvo, and a scattering of nascent Japanese companies—on their heels.[59]

CHAPTER 6

"THIS MEANS TAKING ON DETROIT"

As an early supporter of his fellow Irish American John F. Kennedy for the Democratic leadership in 1960, Daniel Patrick Moynihan had attended the party's convention in Los Angeles. He wrote speeches for the candidate and was rewarded postelection with the position of special assistant to Secretary of Labor Arthur J. Goldberg. He quickly became Goldberg's protégé and proved himself a skilled bureaucratic operator with his hands in policy initiatives covering poverty, urban affairs, race, health, organized crime, and local architecture. His workload compelled him to write Knopf canceling his contract for a book on traffic safety.[1]

Moynihan did not abandon the issue, however. He believed that he and Haddon had "solved" the road crash epidemic while in Albany, in the sense that physicists solve a problem by arriving at a theoretical conclusion. "It's a very different order of intellectual achievement," he said, "but when the problem is finally faced and solved it will be rather like the first nuclear chain reaction under the stadium in Chicago. I know it will work."* He became Secre-

---

* Scientists attached to the Manhattan Project demonstrated the first man-made, self-sustaining nuclear chain reaction on December 2, 1942, at Stagg Field, a disused football facility at the University of Chicago.

tary Goldberg's surrogate on the President's Committee for Traffic Safety. Later, on his promotion to assistant secretary of labor for policy planning, Moynihan devised a plan to promote his views under the banner of occupational health and safety. Wanting help, he wrote Nader on May 16, 1964: "A serious question. Would you be interested in coming to Washington to work on this subject?"[2]

Five years out of Harvard, thirty years old, unmarried, and having little else on the go, Nader jumped at the offer, abandoning Connecticut for Washington and a sparsely furnished rooming house on 19th Street NW. He was not much changed since law school, only more himself. He had perfected an ascetic lifestyle that required minimal income and still less in the way of creature comforts and companionship. He owned few possessions beyond the mounds of papers and clippings that swelled his files and he seemed always to be wearing the same long trench coat over the same rumpled gray suit over the same gaunt frame. He often ate alone at a Middle Eastern restaurant in his new Washington neighborhood, avoiding pizza, burgers, Cokes, and other popular fare. It was not unusual for him to put twenty-four hours between meals. In the context of a postwar American ethos of material indulgence, he was as extreme in his rejection of prevailing mores as those second-century Christian monks who chained themselves to rocks and ate only grass. Nor was Nader interested in the emerging 1960s counterculture with its blaring music and fashions, its sexual exploration and recreational drug use. Neither hedonist nor dropout, he had a quasi-religious commitment to his ideas and beliefs, to a higher calling, which seemed from his journalism to involve purging his countrymen of their reckless commercialism in favor of less wasteful, less exploitive, more public-spirited lifestyles. He was a secular, twentieth-century Puritan. His self-abnegation and ceaseless devotion to his cause were to him and, later, others, proof of his grace.[3]

Time had not disturbed Nader's unusual work habits, as Moynihan soon learned. Hired for six months at $60 a day, Nader was assigned to room 2314 in the Department of Labor building. He was rarely there during business hours. He tended to arrive in the evening when the building was empty and leave before anyone had arrived in the morning, although he did call on government officials and at congressional offices between nine and five. "He kept odd hours," admitted an amused Moynihan, adding that "his working environment was a sea of papers and books" arranged by organizational principles known only to Nader. He had notes on everything he had read and every phone call he made. He used felt-tip pens when surreptitiously transcribing a phone call because they made less noise than pencils. When speaking with executives outside of government—in the insurance industry, for instance—he did not always make it clear to them that they were on the record with the Department of Labor.[4]

Nader's job, known only to Moynihan, was to write a report identifying the automobile as the primary cause of death and injury on the road, a document that could serve as the basis of legislation that would bring automotive design under federal regulation. He was consumed with the task. "When Ralph talked, it was all auto safety," said David Swankin, who shared room 2314 and found it impossible to move Nader's dial. "Passion and zeal. He had a fantastic desk—piles of stuff, tons of stuff. It was work, work, all work."[5]

Moynihan was pleased with Nader's efforts, if occasionally alarmed by his gusto. "Right away, there developed that tremendous quality of ferreting around that he has. In a matter of days, he was over at Justice, trying to find out if the auto industry might be guilty of antitrust violations."[6]

Moynihan's wife, Elizabeth, would occasionally invite Nader to dinner parties and pair him with eligible young women, in vain. He was uninterested in them, engrossed in his work, certain of its importance and the impact it would have. He was convinced that his approach to traffic safety was so revolutionary that powerful forces were bent on obstructing his progress. "Ralph was a very suspicious man," said Moynihan. "He used to warn me that the phones at the Labor Department might be tapped. I'd say, 'Fine, they'll learn that the unemployment rate for March is 5.3 percent, that's what they'll learn.' But he kept on warning me."[7]

Nader did not finish his assignment in six months. On one occasion, he lost all of his notes in a taxi and had to reconstruct them from scratch. On another, he lost an entire draft. His report was finally completed in the spring of 1965, about nine months after his start, a 234-page text with ninety-nine pages of notes under the title "A Report on the Context, Condition, and Recommended Direction of Federal Activity in Highway Safety." Only a few copies were printed and Moynihan's secretary doubted that even he read the whole document. It was not widely circulated inside government. It may be that no one read it. Moynihan would later tell a reporter he commissioned it primarily so that when advocating for federal regulation of automakers he could say that he had a 234-page report with ninety-nine pages of notes to back his assertions.[8]

In September 1964, a few weeks into Nader's assignment at the Labor Department, Richard Grossman, a book publisher, tracked him down at his rooming house on 19th Street. It was no small feat given that the secretive Nader rarely gave out his address, and that the number of the telephone he shared with three other boarders was unlisted.

Grossman was a university dropout who had dabbled in the advertising business until a family connection helped him land a job at Simon & Schuster in New York. He rose to vice president of the company and quit in 1962 to start his own firm out of a basement apartment near Union Square. An independent spirit attracted to new liberal ideas and thinkers, he came to the vehicle safety issue by way of a *New Republic* article on a spate of lawsuits against General Motors over the design of the Corvair. He approached the author of the piece, James Ridgeway, to suggest he write a book on the subject. Ridgeway turned him down but said "one of the key sources for my *New Republic* article, somebody with trunk loads of information about auto safety, is this guy Ralph Nader."[9]

Grossman took Nader to lunch and learned some of what was in those trunks: technical publications by G.M. engineers, depositions of auto executives involved in lawsuits, patent filings for new and unexploited safety equipment, a confidential California government circular that asked policemen to identify makes of cars with high propensities for crashes. Nader was promptly commissioned to write the book on traffic safety that Moynihan had never found time to produce. He was given a modest advance and a deadline commensurate with a spring 1965 publication date.

·   ·   ·

Abraham Ribicoff, the popular governor of Connecticut, served as a Kennedy floor manager at the 1960 Democratic convention, after which the president-elect offered to name him attorney general. Ribicoff declined, suggesting that the position would be better occupied by Bobby Kennedy. His advice was eventually taken, although probably more because Kennedy's father, Joseph, was pushing the same line. Meanwhile, Ribicoff was appointed secretary of the Department of Health, Education and Welfare. He was the first cabinet member announced by Kennedy, and the first to leave.

Ribicoff's initial months as secretary were unpleasant, in large part because the American Medical Association vociferously opposed and ultimately defeated a bill he had personally drafted to introduce medical care for the aged. Bruised and branded a socialist by opponents of his initiative, unhappy taking hits for the Kennedy team after having run his own show in Connecticut, Ribicoff was looking for an exit before his first year was up. He turned down an opportunity to fill a Supreme Court vacancy, preferring instead to run for an open U.S. Senate seat in his home state. He was elected by a narrow margin of 26,000 votes in 1962.[10]

Enjoying more seniority than other rookie senators due to his cabinet experience, Ribicoff immediately felt at home in what has often been called "the world's greatest deliberative body." He looked like he belonged, a handsome, athletic man, nearly a scratch golfer, with a touch of senatorial gray at his temples. He worked hard, as always. The son of poor Polish immigrants, he had punched a clock in a zipper factory to pay his way through college. After graduating from the University of Chicago Law School near the top of his class, he joined the Connecticut state legislature while still in his twenties, and became a Hartford police court judge at the age of thirty-one. Despite being fifty-two on his election to the Senate, Ribicoff brought to his office the idealism and energy of a much younger man and quickly fell in with a rising generation of liberal Democrats who would begin to wrestle control of vital congressional committees from their conservative, more senior, mostly southern brethren. With that came the ability to set the party's legislative priorities.[11]

In the main, the new liberals shared Galbraith's view that an affluent society blessed with perpetual economic growth could afford to shift its attention from the creation of private opulence to the elimination of public squalor. With production, corporate profits, and private incomes improving rapidly in the early 1960s, the need for such a shift seemed more obvious and necessary than ever. How could a country of enormous wealth tolerate urban blight, poverty, and crime, crowded classrooms, underfunded hospitals, and racial injustice—especially with a man in the White House who appeared to share the reformers' aims?

After Kennedy was assassinated in November 1963, his most ardent followers bathed his memory in the activist liberal light that had been discernible to them, if not to everyone else, while he was alive. They pledged themselves to honor his memory and his sacrifice by realizing the policy objectives they attributed to him. Their mission was enthusiastically supported by Kennedy's successor, Lyndon Baines Johnson, and reinforced by still more liberal Democrats sent to Washington in the elections of 1964.

Galbraith's worldview, meanwhile, was fast finding the mainstream, most conspicuously in a much quoted Kennedy-era commentary in *The New York Times* by economics correspondent Edwin L. Dale:

> The most important continuing issue of American policy and politics over the next decade will be the issue of public spending—what share of America's total resources should be devoted to public as distinct from private purposes. . . . Education is underfinanced. Streams are polluted. There remains a shortage of hospital beds. Slums proliferate, and there is a gap in middle-income housing. We could use more and better parks, streets, detention facilities, water supply. The very quality of American life is suffering from these lacks—much more than from any lack of purely private goods and services.[12]

Although unmentioned by the *Times*, consumer affairs were integral to the new liberal agenda and of great interest to Ribicoff. Kennedy had raised the issue on the campaign trail in 1960 and he returned to it on March 15, 1962, with a message to Congress declaring a consumer bill of rights. He was not the first president to rush to the defense of purchasers. The nation's inaugural piece of consumer legislation had been enacted in 1862 to protect citizens from frauds perpetrated through the U.S. mails. A handful of bills followed, most notably the Pure Food and Drug Act of 1906, a direct consequence of Upton Sinclair's famous meatpacking exposé. Franklin Roosevelt had taken up consumer issues in the New Deal, forming a Consumer Advisory Board in 1933 intended to prevent capitalists from exploiting and misleading the people. The board was ineffective but it did demonstrate to future generations of politicians how consumers could be identified and mobilized as a voting bloc. Roosevelt's exhortations to "think less about the producer and more about the consumer" echoed for decades after his death and inspired Kennedy's bill of rights, which was announced in the White House's Fish Room, a West Wing office in which FDR had mounted angling trophies and conducted his staff meetings.[13]

Kennedy's bill of rights asserted that the federal government, "by nature the highest spokesman for all the people," played an important role in protecting and promoting the interests of consumers, whom it described as the largest and least represented group in the economy: "If consumers are offered inferior products, if prices are exorbitant, if drugs are unsafe or worthless, if the consumer is unable to choose on an informed basis, then his dollar is wasted, his health and safety may be threatened, and the national interest suffers." The bill declared that commercial activity had become far too complex for the average person to cope. "The housewife is called upon to be an amateur electrician, mechanic, chemist, toxicologist, dietitian, and mathematician—but she is rarely furnished the information she needs to perform these tasks proficiently." The particular rights enumerated in the bill were the right of choice in a competitive marketplace for goods and services, the right to be properly informed through appropriate labeling and packaging, the right to be heard if aggrieved, and the right to safety in the use of consumer products. The president also recommended legislation to strengthen regulatory authority over food and drugs, to require truth in consumer lending and in the packaging of goods, and to promote competition and prohibit monopoly.[14]

Consumer activists and Kennedy aides understood the bill of rights as a government response to a groundswell of public concern over unfair business practices. In fact, this iteration of the consumer movement was largely a top-down initiative orchestrated by a small elite of authors, activists, and congressional entrepreneurs. The likes of Galbraith, Lewis Mumford, and C. Wright Mills (who died of his fourth heart attack in 1962) had laid the groundwork with their broad critiques of America's commercial culture and devotion to economic growth. Vance Packard had followed his exposé of the advertising industry, *The Hidden Persuaders*, with an attack on planned obsolescence in American manufacturing, *The Waste Makers*, thus establishing himself as the dean of consumer affairs. Jessica Mitford chimed in with *The American Way of Death* (1963), an exasperated investigation of hard-sell tactics in the funeral home industry. Rachel Carson's *Silent Spring* (1962) arraigned the chemical industry for promoting indiscriminate use of insecticides and herbicides. The latter book became a bible of the fledgling environmental movement, and Carson, through her elegant prose and vast influence, became the true heir to Upton Sinclair, a title many sought but she deserved.[15]

Consumerism and its critics captured the imaginations of liberal-minded congressmen, especially those in tricky political situations. Michael Pertschuk, legislative director for Warren Magnuson, a Democratic senator from Washington, was among the first to exploit the electoral potential in consumer issues, which he described as "homey, usually simple in conception, and of broad general interest." He pointed Magnuson in their direction after he had almost lost his bid for re-election in 1962. Magnuson obeyed, led an initiative to correct abuses in consumer warranties, and enjoyed a long Senate career. Similarly, Estes Kefauver, a Democrat whose progressivism was a liability in his home state of Tennessee, broadened his base of support by using his position as chair of the U.S. Senate Antitrust and Monopoly Subcommittee to campaign for more competition in the auto sector and to regulate the pharmaceutical industry after the Thalidomide scandal.* And Kenneth "Seat Belts" Roberts, out of step with southern Democrats on civil rights, latched on to refrigerator door handles and traffic safety to maintain his political relevance and electability.[16]

During his first year in Congress, Abraham Ribicoff, himself a narrowly elected senator, exploited his position as chair of a Senate subcommittee on reorganization of the executive branch to launch hearings on a federal role in regulating herbicides and the protection of consumers from environmental hazards. He became Congress's leading promoter of Rachel Carson, announcing his intention to hold his hearings the morning after CBS had aired a documentary based on *Silent Spring*. The proceedings commenced the day after the President's Science Advisory Committee had released a report substantiating Carson's arguments on the deleterious effects of pesticides and recommending a reduction of their use.

Carson's book was a gift for a congressional entrepreneur like Ribicoff, containing all of the necessary elements of a high-profile campaign: a disturbing premise, vigorous and solid research, and a call to public action. The book opens with a deliberately alarmist scenario, an "imagined tragedy" in which "a white granular powder" has "fallen like snow upon the roofs and the lawns, the fields and the streams" of the nation. As a result, apple trees produce no fruits, chicks do not hatch, birds and fish disappear. Humans are made sick and they begin to mysteriously perish. Everywhere, writes Carson, is "a shadow of death."[17]

While admitting that her scenario is fanciful, the author insists that "every one of these disasters has actually happened somewhere, and many real communities have already suffered a substantial number of them." The imagined tragedy "may easily become a stark reality we all shall know." The book goes on to describe the speed and alacrity with which new pesticides and insecticides are brought

---

* Thalidomide was a drug developed in West Germany and marketed as a remedy for morning sickness in pregnant women. It resulted in approximately ten thousand cases of infants being born with phocomelia, a condition that involves malformations of the limbs. In half the cases, the infants died.

to market regardless of known or potential dangers to the biosphere. The public, Carson insists, has a right to be protected from these chemicals:

> It is not my contention that chemical insecticides must never be used. I do contend that we have put poisonous and biologically potent chemicals indiscriminately into the hands of persons largely or wholly ignorant of their potentials for harm. We have subjected enormous numbers of people to contact with these poisons, without their consent and often without their knowledge. If the Bill of Rights contains no guarantee that a citizen shall be secure against lethal poisons distributed either by private individuals or by public officials, it is surely only because our forefathers, despite their considerable wisdom and foresight, could conceive of no such problem.[18]

Carson cited Galbraith as a critical influence in her intellectual development. She accepted his assessment of the costs of American affluence, among which she included environmental degradation and the "destruction of beauty and the suppression of human individuality in hundreds of suburban real estate developments where the first act is to cut down all the trees and the next is to build an infinitude of little houses, each like its neighbor." Like Galbraith, she opposed the sanctity of corporate autonomy and complained of "an era dominated by industry, in which the right to make a dollar at whatever cost is seldom challenged." She shared his aversion to automobile culture and hated interstate highways for moving people at speeds sufficient to obliterate nature. Like both Mills and Galbraith, Carson believed government officials, scientists, and engineers were in league with corporate America and its pro-growth agenda. She called upon them to live up to their professional obligations and put the health and safety of the public first.[19]

A best-selling author and a household name by the time she appeared before Ribicoff's committee in 1963, Carson's presence caused a sensation. The hearing room was packed and none of Ribicoff's fellow senators or their staff left during her forty-minute presentation, a rare display of respect. News coverage was plentiful and admiring of Carson, in whose reflected glory the chairman basked. When some months later the author died of cancer, Ribicoff turned his proceedings into a memorial to her. He introduced a resolution in the Senate that the Public Health Service name a proposed environmental health facility after her.[20]

Buoyed by this foray into consumer terrain, Ribicoff was soon asking his policy advisor, Jerome Sonosky, for a list of similar issues on which he might make a difference and hold his momentum. He then picked up the December 20, 1964, *New York Times* and found his next issue without any help.

William Haddon Jr., the man who had stimulated Moynihan's interest in the epidemiology of traffic fatalities, had the previous month published a turgid book called *Accident Research: Methods and Approaches*, coauthored with Edward Suchman and David Klein. Most of the information in the book had been previously, if obscurely, published. The *Times* seized the opportunity of its release to repeat some of the researchers' most striking findings: that the crash rate of women increases dramatically before menses; that overtired drivers are subject to hallucinations and can swerve to avoid imagined obstacles; that pedestrians sometimes stumble at crosswalks because the painted lines appear slippery; that people from broken homes are more susceptible to collisions, as are extroverts, drinkers, and the poor. As a cross-disciplinary roundup of theories and data on all kinds of crashes, whether in the home, on the highway, or at the playground, the book does not push a single remedy, although it is generally favorable to the epidemiological approach of studying interactions among the host, agents, and environment. In the last lines of the *Times* article, an anonymous researcher was quoted as blaming auto manufacturers for traffic fatalities. Detroit refused to allow its engineers to design a crash-proof car, and its executives avoided public discussions of road safety while advertising the power and excitement of their vehicles. It was these last lines that lit up Ribicoff. "It was the first time I'd heard of the car as a factor in accidents," he said. "I was intrigued by the theory of the second collision. This was a new concept to me."[21]

The concept may have been new to Ribicoff but an interest in

traffic safety was not. As governor of Connecticut, he had introduced what might have been the most stringent regime of traffic
enforcement in the land. In January 1956, his state police cracked
down on speeding offenses, issuing penalties of thirty-day license
suspension for a first offense and sixty days on a second. In its first
month of operations, license suspensions were up by 600 percent.
At the end of the month, the governor announced that fatalities had
dropped by a third. After six months, however, the improvements
were evaporating despite continued suspensions. By November,
Ribicoff's troopers had suspended nine thousand licenses and the
fatality count stood at 240, down only slightly from 1955's total of
250 on a year-to-date basis. The variance in fatalities was deemed
statistically insignificant, and the enforcement push a failure, one
that sorely tested the patience of Connecticut voters. Ribicoff joined
the ranks of former Triple-E advocates impatient for a better idea
on automotive safety. A second-collision theory that put the onus on
automakers rather than the driving public he had so recently alienated had obvious appeal. At 8 a.m. on the morning after he read the
Times article, Ribicoff telephoned Jerome Sonosky and asked him to
schedule hearings on the role of the vehicle in automobile crashes.[22]

"This means taking on Detroit," said Sonosky.

"Can you do it?" asked Ribicoff.[23]

Sonosky could.

Around this same time, Daniel Patrick Moynihan found his way
into Ribicoff's orbit and gave further encouragement to his interest in traffic safety and second-collision theories. The senator and
Sonosky both read Moynihan's 1959 article "Epidemic on the Highways." Moynihan's further contribution was to point Sonosky in the
direction of Ralph Nader.

Sonosky and Nader met for the first time in room 168 of the
Old Senate Office Building. "Nader walked in looking then as he
looks now," said Sonosky several years later. "Sallow faced. Wearing
his long overcoat. Carrying a thousand pieces of paper under his
arm. His message was that the auto industry has no right to produce
unsafe cars. We talked for three hours about various aspects of the
issue, and where we should go with it."[24]

The staffer does not appear to have known that there was already a slight connection between Nader and Ribicoff. As a citizen of Connecticut and one of the senator's constituents, Nader had written his office several times requesting government reports and publications on pesticide use, pharmaceutical regulation, and highway safety. Each time he got polite, perfunctory responses from Ribicoff or a staffer. Congressmen are routinely bombarded with correspondence from constituents, many of them narrowly focused on particular issues, just as they are pursued through the corridors of Washington by innumerable single-issue cranks. "This town is full of guys who wander around with stacks of paper under their arms trying to see Senators or bust into magazine offices," said a journalist who knew Nader. "Ralph is one who got through the guards."[25]

Sonosky left his meeting with Nader and immediately called Ribicoff.

"We just struck gold," he said.

"What do you mean?"

"I just met somebody who knows more about auto safety than anybody I've ever come across. I don't have to run around town gathering up various experts. I just found him."[26]

Nader, already on the Department of Labor payroll, was hired as an unpaid advisor to Ribicoff's subcommittee on federal responsibility for traffic safety, which was set to begin hearings early in 1965.

CHAPTER 7

HEAD OF THE CLAN, AT SEA

Frederic G. Donner, serving his seventh year as chairman and CEO of General Motors, looked a lot like every other product to roll off the corporation's executive production line: a bespectacled, fleshy, midwestern male with receding gray hair, cropped close, brushed straight back, and oiled in place. He dressed in G.M. style, dark suits with white shirts and dark ties yanked tight, as though the smallest knot won. He was distinguished only by his accessories. It was not uncommon to see G.M. executives with pocket squares, or tie clips. Donner wore both, and a set of horn-rimmed eyeglasses with an owlish tilt at the hinges. These were flourishes of rank, bold in the moment. Not as bold as his predecessor, Red Curtice, who had allowed himself to be photographed in a sports jacket, but Curtice had been *Time*'s Man of the Year. Donner had made the cover of *Time* in a regular issue.[1]

Donner was known in corporate America as a "businessman's businessman" and "a true financial genius." Among automobile enthusiasts, less appreciative of his executive skills, he was the "ice-blue businessman," the "bean counter." Raised in Three Oaks, Michigan, Donner had studied economics at the University of Michigan and joined General Motors as an accountant, rising on the strength of his orderly, meticulous mind to become the youngest vice president in company history at age thirty-eight. A tour of bombed-out German cities after the Second World War convinced him that the company should reclaim its German subsidiary, Opel, which had been conscripted by the Third Reich during the conflict. As chief architect of General Motors' massive postwar overseas expansion, Donner was catapulted over a block of other candidates into the chairmanship in 1958. A man of regular habits, he split his time between a Fifth Avenue apartment and a twenty-two-room home on Long Island, taking the 7:34 train into the city in the morning and the 6:05 home in the evenings.* He was respected more than loved. He went about his days, said one disgruntled former colleague, displaying "all the emotions of a pancake."[2]

Donner may not have displayed emotions but he did possess them, and in the early months of 1965 he was worried. Not by business. Business could not have been better. General Motors was ringing up record sales, record growth, and record earnings. For an unprecedented fourth consecutive year, G.M.'s net income was right around 10 percent of sales, compared to an average of 7.9 percent in the 1950s. All of this had been accomplished without the assistance of price increases. Indeed, since Donner had taken the top job, prices for his products had been flat or falling despite a 40 percent increase in labor costs and a 10 percent increase in the cost of living. The results were due to efficiencies and high volumes of sales. After moving an average of three to four million vehicles in his early years, Donner had topped 6.1 million in 1964 and 7.3 million in 1965.[3]

The firm continued to control about half the domestic car market and now employed 735,000 men and women, more than the population of Boston or San Francisco. Its payroll was $5.5 billion, which even before retirement and medical benefits was double the net income of all citizens of Ireland. With 127 plants in forty-six countries, its net operating revenues exceeded the 1964 GNP of all but nine nations in the free world. Its sales were greater than those of any other corporate entity in the world and its $2.1 billion in

---

* The physical separation of G.M.'s financial headquarters in New York from its operational headquarters in Detroit was consistent with the independence the company allowed its operating divisions such as Chevrolet and Buick.

earnings for 1965 were 10.6 percent of the total net earnings of the rest of the Fortune 500, and 7.6 percent of the profits of all industry in the United States. The cost of mailing its $1.5 billion in dividend checks to 1.3 million shareholders was $65,000 a year. Postage stamps were a nickel.[4]

It might have seemed to outsiders that Donner would be worried about future growth. A publicly owned company needs a clear path to growing markets and General Motors was tapped out in the United States. Any further expansion at home would have brought charges in Congress that it was trying to swallow the whole of Detroit, if not the whole of the U.S. economy. The company was tacitly prohibited from joining the conglomerate mania that erupted in American business during the Kennedy boom. An outfit such as the Michigan Bumper Company, a one-product auto parts manufacturer founded in Depression-era Grand Rapids, could rename itself Gulf + Western and acquire new companies at the rate of one a quarter, branching out into real estate, sugar, swimwear, professional hockey, book publishing, motion pictures, and many other sectors exotic to the auto industry. Any move in those directions by G.M. would have spurred a congressional inquiry into gigantism and the company's competitive dominance in U.S. industry. Donner, however, was not counting on domestic growth. His overseas experience had been key to his elevation at General Motors and the glittering prize of fast-growing foreign markets was where he and his board of directors saw their future. More than any man in Detroit, Donner was driving American automakers to invest enormous amounts of capital into plants and equipment abroad.[5]

The level of global competition was now formidable. Foreign cars might have suffered a setback in the States but they were performing brilliantly everywhere else. In 1965, international auto sales were two thirds higher than they had been five years before and there were twenty significant foreign automakers producing anywhere from 50,000 to 1.2 million units annually. The postwar German and Japanese economies were both building strong automotive industries with what Donner, whose own international efforts were just getting under way, called "the latest and best in plant layout, tools, equipment and methods." Not only did they have new expertise and cheap labor but they were building small, inexpensive, one-liter compacts well suited to the smaller incomes and tighter spaces of overseas markets. West Germany was managing twice the automotive export growth of the United States. Japan was doubling West Germany.[6]

Donner's strategy was to double down on investments in the production capacity of his major overseas brands. He built new automobile manufacturing capacity in Germany, England, and Australia, and new engine manufacturing plants in Mexico and South Africa. G.M. was also assembling vehicles in Peru, Venezuela, Argentina, Uruguay, Switzerland, Belgium, Portugal, and Denmark. The corporation was buying its way into foreign markets and learning to produce different cars for different buyers accustomed to different driving environments.[7]

Despite the vast sums of money involved, Donner's moves in global markets went almost entirely unnoticed in the American press. Since taking office, he had tripled his industry-leading foreign investment, spending just under $1 billion annually on new plant, equipment, and special tools, with a quarter of that flowing overseas even though foreign markets brought only 13 percent of his revenue. The direction of a company's investment capital is always the best clue as to where it sees its future, and Donner was all-in on foreign markets.[8]

With the numbers failing to speak for themselves, Donner emphasized his overseas strategy in annual reports and other communications. He rarely spoke off corporate premises on any subject beyond his operating results but in 1962 and 1964 he made major addresses to the International Congress of Accountants and the U.S. Foreign Trade Convention. His subject on both occasions was the changing nature of global commerce and how the United States needed to lift its head from the domestic scene if it was to hold its position of leadership in the markets of tomorrow. Patterns of trade and investment were combining to create "a new kind of capitalism," "a truly worldwide market" for goods and services that would be served by "worldwide businesses." The "modern industrial corporation," said Donner, would be an institution "transcending national boundaries," one with the capacity to adapt its products and manufacturing processes and marketing methods to new countries and new consumers. By making cars on four continents and reshaping its product line to suit non-American buyers, G.M. was already in transition to this new way of operating.[9]

Donner's objective in drawing attention to G.M.'s global future was to convince his own government, world governments, and international trade bodies to foster a business environment that encouraged private investment and the free movement of capital. He also aired specific complaints about trade barriers, taxation and currency issues, access to information and talent, and the inability of foreign populations to buy shares in General Motors or their local G.M. subsidiary. That he was speaking out on issues of public policy, a rare move for a Detroit executive, was further testament to Donner's commitment to global expansion. He might not have been able to gap a spark plug but he had a clear and far-reaching vision of the future of his company and American enterprise, and he was doing his best to educate and rally his countrymen to an appreciation of their international opportunity. After his speeches were delivered, he published them in book form with McGraw-Hill, yet another highly unusual move for a G.M. executive.

It bothered Donner that the size of his overseas bets and his work as an apostle of globalism were overlooked by a financial press that continued to caricature G.M. executives as shortsighted midwestern bumpkins. It seemed to him symptomatic of a larger problem. He could not put a precise finger on it—it was just an impression—but he sensed that General Motors and the American people, or some segments of American public opinion, were not on the same page. Impressions and feelings were not Donner's strong suit. His first impulse when faced with a problem was to quantify it. Impressions do not readily lend themselves to quantification, although Donner tried.

In 1964, General Motors commissioned a study of public attitudes toward big business in America and General Motors in particular. Ira O. Glick of Social Research Inc. conducted in-depth interviews of a representative sample of four hundred Americans in three major cities. He found that public sentiment was favorable to big business. General Motors, overwhelmingly, was the first company that came to mind when people thought of big business, followed at a considerable distance by Ford and U.S. Steel. Four in five Americans named G.M. as the most powerful company in America, and placed it among the most successful. Amid a field of leading industrial concerns including Ford, General Electric, U.S. Steel, Standard Oil, and AT&T, G.M. stood out as the most forward-thinking of the bunch. It was elevating the reputation of big business generally. Its dominance in the automotive field, far from worrying Americans, appeared to rouse their admiration. "General Motors cars," wrote Glick, "still retain the public's vote of preference and loyalty for being the best cars in style, performance, dependability and value—and especially in capturing the unique mood of the current market—and there is no hint in these interviews that this pattern of choice will alter to any noteworthy extent during the coming model year." There were "extremely few criticisms" of any Detroit automobiles on the basis of safety, and G.M. was considered the safety leader. It was also the automaker most would prefer to work at or invest in by margins of four to one.[10]

Glick attributed General Motors' high standing in part to a booming economy, a strong sense of national well-being, a high level of interest in the automotive industry, and widespread experience of the company's products and awareness of its reputation. Respondents had a clear and appreciative view of the General Motors brand. They personified the company as "an energetic, dynamic man who comes from an old-line, influential background." He is familiar with wealth and power, polished, well-groomed, well-educated. Outside of work, he is socially responsible, gregarious, elegant in his lifestyle choices, and a paternal "head-of-the-clan" figure in his large family. He is socially responsible and conducts himself with "a general tone of reserve." Most interviewees could not name a single General Motors executive.[11]

The picture was not uniformly bright. A rump of 20 percent of Americans were hostile or very hostile to big business. They blamed management for strikes in the auto industry, traffic congestion, and air pollution. A still smaller minority of people were aware of antitrust issues. A few people complained that their own G.M. cars were lemons. Others were concerned about speed and racing. There was modest awareness and acceptance of the idea of big government acting as a countervailing force to big business, although more people were frightened of big government than big business. Most believed that automakers were "serving the public welfare in responsible and appropriate ways." On the whole, Glick found "extremely few complaints or criticisms directed against auto manufacturers or their products." General Motors, by all appearances, was at a reputational zenith.[12]

That Glick failed to quantify Donner's unease did not dissipate it. There were too many portents. Congress, alert in its own way to public opinion, was seized with the automobile industry. While manufacturers were growing accustomed to more attention from legislators, it seemed now that Detroit was replacing its major supplier, the steel industry, as Washington's enemy-in-chief. "I can't remember a time when a Congress has come up with so many legislative proposals," a Detroit lobbyist told The Wall Street Journal. Automakers were being investigated for mistreating their dealers, price-gouging, using high-pressure financing tactics, squeezing out competition, polluting, and taking a lax attitude toward safety. The familiar cry that mammoth General Motors needed to be broken up seemed louder than ever on Capitol Hill, and the notion could not be taken lightly so soon after the company's largest shareholder, the du Pont family, had been forced to divest its G.M. stock.

As a preventive measure, Donner led a radical corporate transformation. He created a single body-making plant for all of his divisions, a degree of centralization that took from Chevrolet, Buick, Cadillac, Plymouth, and Oldsmobile their ability to build their own cars. This made it exceedingly difficult for, say, Chevrolet to be carved out of the G.M. family by trust-busting congressmen and set up as a self-sufficient entity. In Alfred Sloan's universe, Donner's moves against the autonomy of G.M. divisions were heresy, but Sloan had never faced so dire an antitrust threat.[13]

The hazard posed by the safety issue was less distinct. It had nowhere near the congressional momentum of antitrust, and the public and car buyers couldn't have been less interested. But safety worried Donner. His attitude toward safety was similar to that of all automakers. He understood that his company, his peers, and their predecessors had worked hard to design cars that evaded crashes and held together on impact. Outsiders, he believed, underestimated the industry's concern for traffic safety and its tangible contributions to preventing injuries and fatalities. In this, he was correct.

Since the days of the Model T, the industry had adopted lower stances and wider wheelbases in its vehicles for improved stability. It had learned to build cars with stiff steel frames that did not crumple on light impact. General Motors had introduced the one-piece, all-steel "Turret Top" roof in 1934, which, while not impregnable, was far superior to anything before it (and especially the open cars that had predominated in the early years of automotive mass production). Electronic ignition systems had replaced dangerous crank starters. Brake lights and taillights had become standard equipment in the 1930s. Headlamps, mirrors, lighted dashboards, electronic wipers had been introduced and improved. Larger windshields allowed for enhanced sightlines and shatterproof glass reduced one of the primary dangers of the auto crash. Hoods were equipped with safety locks so they could not be blown open by winds on the road. Padded dashboards were first made available in 1947. The screeching two-wheel brakes of early vehicles had been supplanted by four-wheel mechanical brakes followed by hydraulic brakes followed by power brakes. The location of primary vehicle controls, including pedals and knobs and shifts, was standardized to answer the problem of unfamiliarity.[14]

All of the major automakers had followed General Motors' 1924 lead in establishing massive proving grounds where the handling and performance of vehicles were tested in a range of conditions from tight curves to slippery surfaces. When G.M., on its own initiative, began subjecting its cars to frontal crash tests by driving them into stationary concrete barriers (1934), and started using dummies in these tests to measure the impacts on humans (1955), its methods were again adopted by its competitors. The Big Three hired safety specialists within their engineering departments, and their automobiles were believed even by their critics to be the safest in the world. Measured by deaths per registered vehicle or fatalities per millions of driven miles, they were.[15]

While safety was seldom at the fore of Detroit's marketing messages, it was a regular topic at industry gatherings. For instance, at the 1950 annual meeting of the Society of Automotive Engineers, a symposium provided detail on how vehicles were designed to maintain the safest possible proportions in "the relation of the seat to the steering wheel, steering column, foot pedals and the height of the hood; the distance from the seat to the floor, and the amount of headroom that is provided." These and other factors, it was reported, took "precedence over an attractive appearance."[16]

It was true that Detroit's marketers were not keen to lead with safety, but their reluctance was based in experience. As far back as 1936, Chevrolet promoted the advantages of its steel body and hydraulic braking with an illustration of a wife and mother saying, "I want them to have the safest car that money can buy!" A year later, G.M. deliberately built safer cars and marketed them on the strength of safety. The 1937 Plymouth offered "safety interiors," with every detail inside the car "recessed or padded or redesigned for the protection of passengers . . . to eliminate minor mishaps inside the car, bruises in case of sudden stops, torn clothing . . . barked knuckles."[17]

Unfortunately, the 1937 Plymouth was slow off the car lot, and other efforts at selling safety were no more successful. The rear-engine Tucker of 1948 boasted of its "safety and solidity," the "soft crash pads that line car and dash," and a windshield designed to pop out if hit from the inside. A year later, Chrysler advertised its crash padding, "a safety feature of major importance! Front passengers, especially children, are given new protection against possible injury in the event of sudden stops or collisions by the new sponge-rubber Safety-Cushion [which] extends across the top part of the dash, and is upholstered in leather to match the interior." The Nash Airflyte in 1950 became the first North American car to offer seat belts as an option. Buyers were not enticed in significant numbers by any of these offers or improvements.[18]

A larger safety effort was made in 1951 by Kaiser Motors, an aggressive postwar automaker based in Michigan and owned by California industrialist Henry J. Kaiser. A pioneer in fiberglass car bodies and a retail partner of the gigantic Sears Roebuck chain, the Kaiser firm was determined to crack the dominance of Detroit's Big Three through innovation. In 1953, it drew on the Cornell research of Hugh DeHaven and others to build and market the "world's first safety-first car." In addition to padded dashboards and recessed instrument controls to protect the head and face from injury, it featured more glass and less metal in the driver's sightlines to eliminate blind spots. Kaiser offered these improvements without sacrificing anything in the way of looks, winning more than its share of design awards. This bold effort to carve a distinct positioning for the company as the safe car builder produced disappointing sales and the company was soon out of the passenger car business.[19]

The greatest safety push by a Detroit manufacturer came from Ford. It made the "Lifeguard Safety Package" on its Fairlane and Crown Victoria models the centerpiece of its 1956 marketing campaign. Employing the latest Cornell research (after making a $200,000 grant to the university's crash research program) as well as learnings from its own crash test facilities, Ford installed as a standard feature a deep-center steering wheel of the sort recommended by the medical community, as well as improved door latches, padded dashboards, recessed instrument panels, and seat belts. It boasted that its innovations could lead to at least a 35 percent decline in automobile injuries. The company hosted a two-day national safety forum with physicians, lawyers, insurance executives, and crash experts to sanction its new approach to the market. The seat belts were a relatively successful option where available but a mere 2 percent of the company's buyers paid extra for safety features. Chrysler and General Motors, both of which offered similar safety options on certain models while continuing to focus their marketing on the proven messages of styling, performance, and status, sold well at Ford's expense. It would be a long time before another North American automaker centered its pitch, as *The New York Times* said, "on new ways to avoid getting killed inside a car." Ford returned to conventional marketing techniques for 1957 and its sales recovered.[20]

Detroit undertook all of these safety efforts well before the nation's physicians, Congressman "Seat Belt" Roberts, and the tort innovator Harold Katz weighed in on highway crashes. Ford's Lifeguard package was in production months before the first appearance of Dr. Shelden's influential article in *The Journal of the American Medical Association*. Virtually all of the physicians' recommendations already had been tried by the industry. Door latches, steering wheels, and dashboards had been improved. Padded dashboards and headrests had been made available as options, and as standard features on some models. It was for good reason that the traffic safety community believed the manufacturers were doing their part. Indeed, most existing state safety regulations were post facto formalizations of voluntary industry innovations such as headlights, windshield wipers, and rearview mirrors.[21]

Donner, like his peers, believed the cause of safety was best served when the industry was permitted to develop its own safety standards. He opposed government-mandated safety standards on the grounds that automakers knew better than bureaucrats the viability of safety technologies. When in 1964 the General Services Administration (GSA) was authorized by Congress to require all automobiles purchased by the government to include padded dashboards, stronger windshields, and other safety equipment, and fourteen states were requiring lap belts installed in the front seats of automobiles, Donner grumbled that unwanted cost increases were being foisted on consumers, but complied. Notwithstanding that Glick's research had found even the most sophisticated Americans uninterested in road safety, G.M. made seat belts standard equipment in all vehicles, adjusted to the GSA requirements before they were official, and generally ramped up its attention to safety issues.[22]

In the spring of 1965, Donner spoke on the occasion of the fortieth anniversary of G.M.'s proving ground, its key facility for improving the performance and safety of automobiles. The profitability of the business, he said, depended on its ability to adjust to the public's ever-changing priorities, including issues of safety, which needed to be balanced against other qualities such as reliability, comfort, economy, and appearance. A G.M. policy handbook, approved by top management, went further, stating that safety was a higher priority than profitability: "Management will, from time to time, identify areas of public concern in which General Motors must involve itself seriously, in the public interests, for its own security. Highway safety is one such area." It must be considered "apart from commercial considerations," and its requirements "may at times run counter to strictly commercial considerations." Decisions of this nature would be left to the CEO, advised by internal committees struck to investigate issues of public interest.[23]

Donner had done all this yet still wondered if he was correctly reading the prevailing winds and responding adequately to outside pressure. He worried that there was more to safety than met the eye. Not only were Washington and the medical community alert to the issue but it was metastasizing in unpredictable ways.

Seemingly out of nowhere, ambulance chasers were descending on G.M., in force. The company's legal department was being bombarded with personal injury suits alleging that its vehicles, particularly the Corvair, were crashing and killing or injuring people because they were negligently designed. These were the suits *The New Republic* had noted. California law firms no one had heard of before were generating cases by the dozen. They all followed the same template and made the same arguments, suggesting a degree of collaboration among plaintiffs' attorneys who seemed to think they were on to something big.

The term "ambulance chaser" was coined by the *New York Sun* in 1896 and made its first appearance in *The New York Times* three months after that fateful evening in 1899 when Henry Hale Bliss stepped off a trolley to become America's first automobile fatality. It referred to unscrupulous lawyers who specialized in personal injury lawsuits, particularly of the man-versus-machine variety, which is to say that the automobile and the ambulance chaser grew up together. As cars became more ubiquitous on America's streets and collisions became more common, so, too, did personal injury lawyers. They seemed to intuit that mass motorization and the havoc it inspired spelled boundless opportunity for enterprising members of the bar.[24]

In fairness to personal injury attorneys, some were proper and competent practitioners who did laudable work on behalf of legitimately injured parties. These were often overshadowed, however, by those who literally chased ambulances to crash scenes in hopes of signing up clients, or trolled hospital wards for crash victims whom they could coach on what to say and how to act in order to shake a settlement out of a driver or a driver's insurer. In 1928, a cabal of New York attorneys was found to be paying druggists, doctors, and police officers to bring in injury cases and assist in their prosecution. Policemen would receive $10 for referring victims with bruises and $25 for those with fractures.[25]

Still other personal injury lawyers were determined to find injury and damages where none, in fact, existed. Early in their existence, personal injury specialists came under suspicion from governments and responsible legal practitioners for their high incidence of false and fraudulent collision claims. In 1927, the New York City district attorney arrested nine men and women for staging sham car crashes to swindle insurance companies. In one celebrated instance, an attractive young woman had brought suit against an insurer and a wealthy young man in whose car she had allegedly been hurt. She claimed partial paralysis and was on the verge of collecting a tidy sum before the defense procured photographs of her playing leapfrog with another man on a beach.[26]

In 1929, a special prosecutor brought more than a hundred actions against members of the New York bar for unethical and illegal conduct in personal injury practice. That prompted a resolution of the Association of the Bar of the City of New York to curb or eradicate the "evil practices" of lawyers in pursuit of crash cases. It accused them of preying on the poor and the ignorant, of encouraging perjury, and undermining public confidence in the administration of justice. The crackdown was largely ineffectual.[27]

There was more at issue with ambulance chasers than their unseemly haste and sometimes fraudulent claims. Even the relatively respectable ones tended to play by their own rules. For instance, they worked on contingency fees, taking a percentage (usually a third) of any settlement rather than charging an hourly rate of compensation, a practice viewed by some of their legal colleagues as discreditable to their gentlemanly profession. The chasers were also aggressive about drumming up business despite a canon of the American Bar Association's Code of Professional Ethics against solicitation of "those with claims for personal injuries or those having other grounds of action in order to secure them as clients."[28]

That personal injury lawyers were able to withstand this pressure and stay in business was due in part to their contention that they represented a democratization of justice in America. Rules against solicitation, they argued, were anticompetitive measures adopted by bar associations to protect established firms from ambitious upstarts. Contingency fees, they continued, were necessary to bring the cost of legal action within reach of indigent crash victims, and to align the interests of counsel and client. Personal injury lawyers, moreover, were useful counters to claims agents at insurance companies who were also known to rush to the bedsides of crash victims urging them to sign releases of claims before they understood the extent of their injuries and/or their ability to collect. Ambulance chasing could be a two-way street.[29]

Through the first half of the twentieth century, bar associations made no headway against the personal injury practitioners apart from curbing their ability to aggressively advertise their services. The fundamentals of their trade were thus unchanged by the 1950s. Even the rates paid to tipsters were similar: $10 for patients with fractures below the knee; $25 for fractures above the knee; $50 for internal injuries. Every once in a while, a district attorney would make a show of rounding up corrupt lawyers and their accomplices, as when seventeen attorneys and seven runners were arrested in July 1954 for their part in an ambulance-chasing ring that covered nineteen hospitals and operated with "the smooth efficiency of a supermarket." The American Bar Association voted to make ambulance chasing grounds for expulsion of its members, and cracked down further on the ability of attorneys to advertise, again to minimal effect.[30]

What had changed most by the 1950s was the size of the personal injury industry. A half century of auto collisions had fueled high volumes of business. New firms were popping up in every city to meet demand and their cases clogged the courts: the backlog reached thirty months in the Bronx and forty-three in Manhattan. This growth was driven in part by shifts in social norms. Earlier in the century, crash victims had been reluctant to sue, even in cases of negligence. There was a stigma around being a plaintiff, trying to collect from others for one's own misfortunes instead of suffering fate in a stalwart fashion. This ethic of individual responsibility waned as the decades passed. Increasing numbers of people felt comfortable resorting to the courts to settle disputes and receive compensation for injuries. By the 1950s, many felt they were leaving money on the table if they failed to collect over a wrong.[31]

Adding more fuel to the personal injury boom were the plaintiff-friendly changes in torts noted by Harold Katz, a new willingness of courts to pay out on the basis of pain and suffering as well as a victim's direct costs, and the increasing generosity of juries with crash victims.

Against the personal injury onslaught, businesses and property owners, not to mention homeowners and drivers, loaded up on liability insurance, which, perversely, made them even juicier targets for crash victims and their lawyers. Insurance companies could not raise rates fast enough to keep up with awards. Payouts skyrocketed from $700 million to $1.8 billion in bodily injury and property damage cases in the course of the 1950s despite the death rate per insured vehicle dropping and the rate of injuries increasing only slightly. Between 1956 and 1959, casualty stock companies lost $700 million on collision insurance. The whiplash claim, along with diagnoses of recurring headaches and post-crash personality changes, brought some of the larger awards and settlements.[32]

All of this business meant that ambulance chasers were in the money. They now practiced in large offices with solid walnut doors and heavy brass fittings and expanses of clear glass to better display all the zeroes on the framed settlement checks lining their boardroom walls. They were also organized. The umbrella of the National Association of Claimants' Compensation Attorneys (later the American Trial Lawyers Association) defended the practices and integrity of its members and opposed legal reforms that threatened their business.

The association held conventions and seminars on how to engineer rich verdicts and otherwise serve the crash-prone public. It described personal injury practitioners as "the most articulate, the best-trained, the most experienced and effective advocates of fundamental rights that the world has ever known." This might have been an exaggeration but the lures of financial gain and public attention were undoubtedly attracting a higher level of legal talent to the field, and encouraging more specialization, whether in auto collisions, plane crashes, or medical malpractice.[33]

Top-flight personal injury practices now employed multiple attorneys, friends of the poor and downtrodden, strong in human sympathies, high in public profile due to regular newspaper and television appearances. They continued to be shunned by established firms and country club sets but they were increasingly at home in the Democratic Party. Their high profiles helped with business development, as did ensuring that all members and employees of the firm were widely acquainted with physicians, nurses, hospital residents and interns, policemen, and clergy. Some firms had prop departments with artificial limbs and skeletons for anatomical display in the courtroom, along with scale models of automobiles, traffic intersections, trains, oil derricks, and other instruments of harm. Some had photo departments to produce under appropriate lighting glossy, gory shots of crash scenes and their injured clients with bandages, casts, and pained expressions. Still others employed theater-trained casting directors to assist experts and other witnesses with their jury presentation skills.[34]

All of these personal injury lawyers, said one of their number, dreamed of cases that could be explained to juries in bright colors and sharp contrasts: beauties versus beasts, Davids versus Goliaths. While most cases involved shades of gray, practitioners labored to make their plaintiffs appear as pure as a jury would find plausible. Believing that jurors were never as alert and discriminating as law texts suggested, they dialed up the action and emotion in their presentations. "To play on the heartstrings of the jurors for a deserving claimant is good advocacy and a noble act," said one plaintiff's attorney. "Being an advocate is an old and honorable profession. The Israelites had Moses as their advocate with Pharaoh. The sinners have their advocate with the Father. We are the advocates for the poor, the sick, and the helpless—millions of deserving claimants. Drive hard for your verdict."[35]

A standard auto industry response to the rise in torts was that the law was being abused by shamelessly self-seeking personal injury lawyers to shake down deep-pocketed manufacturers. Detroit, for the most part, still read torts as saying that a manufacturer could only be held responsible for injuries in a crash if the product was dangerous when used as intended. Cars were not built with the intention that they be used in collisions, therefore manufacturers were not liable for injuries that incurred because someone drank too much, drove into a ditch, and dented his head on a dashboard. Used correctly, an automobile was harmless.

Frederic Donner's own view was more sophisticated and went

beyond his industry's reading of the letter of the law. He accepted that automakers had a civic responsibility to make cars as safe as reasonably possible. He was undoubtedly aware of the sharp rise in personal injury suits against his company, and that the Corvair was being singled out for its unusual rear-engine design, but whether he was briefed on the nuances of torts and the new avenues of legal attack being employed against G.M. is difficult to say. He appears to have left the details to his legal department and concerned himself with the big picture: his sense that his company was somehow out of step with the times, and under attack from new and nebulous forces. There was something in the air, and the lawsuits and safety concerns were simply manifestations of it. In search of a better understanding of his changing environment, Donner departed once more from his corporation's traditions and turned to outsiders for help.

A preacher's son and navy pilot turned public relations specialist, Earl Newsom was the most trusted and respected man in his field. He ran a small shop, Earl Newsom & Co., and tended a short list of prestigious clients ranging from Price Waterhouse to the Rockefeller Foundation. It was Newsom to whom Standard Oil turned when confronted at the height of the Second World War with embarrassing evidence of its associations with Nazi Germany. It was Newsom whom CBS retained to rebuild a reputation destroyed when *The $64,000 Question*, its popular quiz show, was found to be rigged. Keeping a low profile, charging high fees, and working only with senior management, Newsom was not a conventional PR agent. He did not issue press releases or deal with reporters. He was a strategist and counselor, analyzing problems, explaining them to the executives responsible, and recommending solutions to be carried out by others. His primary deliverable was a memo. Tall, fit, and authoritative in manner, he spent most of his days reading and thinking behind a large semicircular desk in his New York office, pulling an endless supply of Kent cigarettes from a brass box by his telephone. He had a reputation for integrity, insisting to corporate leaders that public opinion was sovereign, and that candor and transparency were essential to the satisfactory resolution of any public relations problem.[36]

Newsom had called Donner in January 1964 to wish him a happy New Year and to chat him up. Donner unloaded his worries, telling Newsom that he knew how to handle every part of his business operations but struggled with G.M.'s place in the public domain. "I must confess that it is a subject at which I am wholly at sea," he said. "It is to me entirely amorphous." He described his concerns about Washington, the Corvair litigation, and union negotiations, and his fear of what would happen "when we inevitably slip." The conversation led to meetings, which led to Newsom's engagement. His brief was to "appraise continuously the public opinion climate in which the company is operating, to offer creative suggestions on actions the company might take to improve its position within this climate, and to help where advisable in carrying out the suggestions."[37]

In March 1965, Newsom sent Donner a two-page memo (the chairman insisted on brevity) referencing the "revolutionary changes" afoot in America and around the world. People were "demanding reform and the immediate correction of assumed injustices," he said, and using aggressive tactics, including direct action, lawsuits, protests, riots, threats of violence, and, occasionally, violence to enforce their demands. Given the constraints of space, Newsom did not cite the Freedom Riders confronting racial prejudice in the Deep South or any other aspects of the civil rights movement, nor the Berkeley student protests over free speech, race, and the Vietnam War, nor Betty Friedan's challenge to gender roles in *The Feminine Mystique*, nor any other particular uprising. It was sufficient to note the waves of social unrest and acknowledge that new standards of morality and behavior were evolving, and new notions of rights, especially among the young. The ability of General Motors to continue to prosper and grow, said Newsom, "depends upon its responses to the constant change in social, economic, and political values of its environment. It is subject to the force of public opinion."[38]

Newsom believed it imperative for Donner to "get off the defensive and into a public posture of serious concern about the problems that are bothering people today in areas where G.M.'s operations are influential." There was no hiding from or withdrawing from the outside world. The corporation must seize the initiative, engage with its critics and the world of ideas, and contribute to thought leadership. If it did not learn to hold its own in public debate, it would be "at the mercy of men in government, labor, and elsewhere, who seek to pre-empt leadership and are more practiced in shaping the public attitudes that make up a corporation's environment." In short, it would lose what was essentially a power struggle with its critics and, in doing so, lose control over its destiny. Unlike the pollster Glick, Newsom saw a mistrust of corporations among the public at large, and a growing sense that they were not living up to their social responsibilities and that government intervention or regulation was advisable to prevent abuses of power by business. He believed people were more susceptible to G.M.'s critics than the corporation might think.[39]

On the basis of his discussion with Donner and other members of G.M.'s inner circle, Newsom & Co. concluded that the laws and beliefs that ruled life in the corporate hierarchy were out of touch with "economic, social, and political" developments in contemporary America. It recommended that General Motors broaden the interests of its executives, augment *Road & Track* subscriptions with *The New Republic*, bring intellectuals to Detroit for discussions with management and the board, hire and promote executives comfortable in the world of ideas. These men should be capable of answering challenges to the power of large corporations, not in a defensive or dogmatic way, but rationally and in the spirit of open discussion. They should be able to explain the role and benefits of large corporations, how their large reserves of capital were essential to the efficient production of heavy goods, how they develop new and better products that enhance consumer choice, create well-paid jobs, and support communities.[40]

The measures Newsom suggested for external engagement were pedestrian. Magazine articles, speeches, and white papers on the benefits of large corporations in contemporary society. Tours of college campuses. Newsom was especially concerned about students. Research showed that undergraduates did not "place business and industrial corporations high on their lists of significant modern institutions." They did not identify with commercial values or corporate leadership. They were anti-materialistic and showed a preference for such service projects as the Peace Corps and the civil rights movement. By engaging in "free-wheeling discussions" with students, G.M. could dispel preconceptions and introduce them to the "many ways in which our modern corporation is dealing with fundamental social needs of mankind."[41]

On the particular issue of safety, Newsom had examined public opinion research by Gallup and other organizations dating back to 1949 and found that the public consistently displayed a Triple-E mindset, blaming crashes on negligent and reckless drivers, and believing more driver training, better roads, regular automobile inspections, and more enforcement were appropriate safety remedies. Interest in seat belts and other car safety equipment or improvements was tepid, at best, as was support for limiting the speed of cars to sixty-five miles per hour. Roughly half of male drivers and a third of all drivers had experienced a crash of some sort, suggesting that people knew the dangers of automobiles and had adapted to them. The safety issue, Newsom believed, was not being driven by public concern but by "a relatively small segment of the public" with an outsized influence in the political climate. Given the chance that the broader public might latch on to safety as a concern, he recommended G.M. engage in thoughtful, evidence-based discussions with its opponents.[42]

The efforts of Newsom & Co. were appreciated by Chairman Donner but there were signs that progress would be elusive. One was that Donner, for all his goodwill, wanted quick fixes to problems that could not be solved by pulling levers or adding lines to budgets. True engagement with the issues raised by Newsom required patient, long-term attention and effort, and no one at G.M. seemed ready for that commitment. Newsom was assigned to work with the company's internal public relations department, which naturally resented the intrusion of outsiders less familiar with the nuances of the automobile marketplace and dismissive of G.M.'s previous and ongoing communications efforts. General Motors was also reluctant to move alone on what it said were industry issues: it was accustomed to fighting public battles through its trade group, the Automobile Manufacturers Association (AMA), which acted as a shield to protect corporate brands. (The existence of the AMA also forestalled the automakers from competing on the appeasement of their critics in and out of government, a form of rivalry that would be expensive to all.) G.M.'s unwillingness to stand on its own practically ruled out original, dramatic, or otherwise impressive responses to public pressure.

More important than any of this, time for action had run out. Weeks after Newsom delivered his memo to Donner, who was vacationing in Ojai, California, the Detroit automakers were invited to appear before Senator Abraham Ribicoff's hearings on traffic safety. No amount of public relations was going to substantially alter the climate of opinion before that date.

CHAPTER 8

"I INTEND TO BE A CRUSADER"

Like every Congress to meet since the inaugural and much smaller United States Congress gathered for the first time at Federal Hall in New York City in 1789, the 89th Congress was, by its own estimation, an auspicious group, energetic, high-minded, and intent on exerting a positive and powerful influence on affairs of state. What distinguished the 89th from so many of its predecessors was that important voices outside of its ranks agreed that it might be auspicious.

Democrats had made sweeping gains in both houses in the 1964 elections. The aged coalition of conservative Democrats and Republicans that had frustrated progressive legislation in the 88th was now impotent. *The New York Times*, surveying the incoming forces and noting that the majority of the Democratic gains found liberals or moderates supplanting conservatives, declared that the nation could expect "a satisfying future for the legislative components" of Lyndon Johnson's Great Society.[1]

Determined to meet expectations, the 89th, from its opening session on January 4, 1965, until its close nine months later, operated at breakneck pace. It tackled health insurance for the elderly, mental health care, hospital improvements, education funding, science policy, arts funding, low-income housing, urban renewal, voting rights,

immigration, the minimum wage, the length of the workweek, cigarette warnings, insecticides, fungicides, rodenticides, farmworkers,
railroads, illicit drug trade, bail practices, the gun problem, the high
costs of lawmaking, the march of communism, and the conflict in
Vietnam. Favored by Democratic supermajorities in both houses
and a legislatively ambitious president in the White House, the 89th
was enormously productive. It generated 27,618 pages of the *Congressional Record* (not counting 6,693 pages of appendix), introduced
14,587 bills, 910 joint resolutions, 595 concurrent resolutions, 790
simple resolutions, and made 563 laws. These numbers left all of the
89th's postwar predecessors in the dust. Among its many pieces of
landmark legislation were the Social Security Act, the Voting Rights
Act, the Housing and Urban Development Act, the Federal Cigarette Labeling and Advertising Act, the Immigration and Nationality Act, and the Elementary and Secondary Education Act. All in
one spectacular session.[2]

Notwithstanding that productivity, the 89th, like every Congress, did a great deal of work that went for naught, or that was
so trivial it might as well have gone for naught. In addition to the
1,759 hours dedicated to proceedings on the floor of their respective
chambers, hours during which the 89th's legislative landmarks were
forged, members of the Senate and the House of Representatives
spent countless additional hours in the wood-paneled and marbled
rooms of the Russell and New Senate Office buildings participating
in hearings. Committee hearings, subcommittee hearings, legislative hearings, oversight hearings, investigative hearings, confirmation hearings, and ratification hearings—endless days and nights of
hearings, sometimes dealing with important legislation and other
times arguing for the designation of a historic site or a national bird
or questioning the necessity of hiring an additional fourteen men
with scrubbing machines to make the marble corridors of the Ray-
burn House Office Building sparkle, the latter a rare concern for
economy in the 89th.[3]

Most of these hearings made no dent on the course of events in
Washington, let alone the nation. Little of what was said in session
was actually heard by anyone beyond the battalions of stenographers
paid to transcribe testimony, and almost all of what was recorded

was too insignificant to make its way into the commodious volumes of the *Record*. The perorations of congressmen and their witnesses in these proceedings were of no more consequence than the murmurs and coughs and scraping chairs that accompanied them day after interminable day.

All of which is to say that when Abraham Ribicoff, chairman of the Senate Subcommittee on Executive Reorganization, began three days of hearings into the "Federal Role in Traffic Safety" in room 1318 of the New Senate Office Building at 9:45 on the morning of March 22, 1965, odds were that his initiative and every word spoken in its record would go for naught. Only two of his eight colleagues on the senatorial panel that Ribicoff had convened for the proceedings bothered to attend that day. The senator addressed himself to a near-empty room:

> Today we begin a long-range series of hearings into the role of the Federal Government in the field of traffic safety. We will examine and review from top to bottom those agencies—both public and private—federal, state, and local, which direct and support the nation's traffic safety efforts.[4]

Ribicoff had two points to make off the top. The first was that there existed what he called a "traffic safety establishment," extending from local police forces to state traffic safety commissions to the President's Committee for Traffic Safety. This establishment was a far-reaching and powerful fraternity of mostly public officials who were responsible for the state of traffic safety. He included in it sixteen separate federal agencies, all of which had a hand in the issue, and Ribicoff would hear from the more important of these in his opening sessions. "We will endeavor to establish exactly what the present federal role in traffic safety is, how much is expended to support it, how it might duplicate and overlap, and how it might be improved."[5]

His second point was that the traffic safety establishment was failing, that the "awful carnage on our roads and streets" was continuing and worsening. "In the past minute, twenty accidents have taken place," he said.

One-half hour from now, three Americans will be dead who right now are alive. And for every half hour of this day and the days to follow, three more human beings will lose their lives on our nation's roads and streets. . . . As a result of traffic accidents which occurred in 1964, 47,800 people have already died, and before the records are closed the total is expected to exceed 48,000 which is 10 percent more than the 1963 fatalities which numbered 43,400.[6]

That rise in traffic deaths above the usual thirty-odd thousand range was new and unexplained, adding urgency to the subcommittee hearings. Even more significant, as the senator noted, was that the deaths per 100 million miles driven had inexplicably risen from 5.3 in 1962 to 5.5 in 1963 to 5.7 in 1964, a rare reversal of the steady decline in the fatality rate that had held since the Great War. "If the current increase in the traffic fatalities rate continues," warned Ribicoff, "deaths will rise to 100,000 a year by 1975."[7]

Ribicoff went on to question the priorities of a nation that was spending more than $1 billion to ensure the safety of three astronauts traveling to the moon but spending less than one hundredth of that amount to protect 190 million citizens from death or injury on its roads. He then invited his first witness, the carefully selected, like-minded Gaylord Nelson, U.S. senator from Wisconsin.

Nelson repeated and expanded upon Ribicoff's litany of alarming statistics, noting that auto collisions were the number one cause of death for Americans aged five to twenty-nine. Nelson put the second-collision theory on the record and blamed "the unsafe nature of the car itself" for the high rate of traffic fatalities, claiming that a "simple reconstruction of the vehicle" would reduce the annual death toll by more than half. The holdup, he said, was in Detroit, where profits were more important than saving lives. "The slightest mention of safety standards," he said, "seems to cause panic in the automobile industry."[8]

Before closing, Nelson enumerated the safety features required in vehicles purchased by the federal government thanks to the legislative efforts of crusading congressman Kenneth Roberts— anchorages for seat-belt assemblies, padded dashes, recessed instrument panels and controls, impact-absorbing steering wheels, safety door latches, anchored seats, four-way flashers, safety glass, dual braking systems, standard bumper heights, standard P-R-N-D-L gear shifts for automatic transmissions, sweep-design windshield wipers, glare reduction surfaces, exhaust emission controls, safety wheel rims, backup lights, and an outside rearview mirror—and told the hearing that he had just introduced a bill to expand these standards to include collapsible steering columns, anchors for shoulder safety belts, and specific types of safety glass, among other features. He also wanted the standards applied not only to government-purchased cars but to all cars sold in interstate commerce. Ribicoff supported these initiatives wholeheartedly.

The next witness, Postmaster General John A. Gronouski, supervisor of a fleet of 88,000 vehicles, took Ribicoff off course. Gronouski revealed that he had contracted with General Motors to improve the safety record of Post Office trucks, which, among other problems, were running over children at the rate of fourteen per year. By installing backup beepers, mirrors at the bumper line so that drivers could see kids playing beside their trucks, and by implementing driver tests and remedial training and rules requiring collision reviews and proper vehicle maintenance, Gronouski and G.M. had in a decade reduced the Post Office crash rate from 130 per million miles to 30 per million miles. He was also very keen on seat belts and had worked with G.M. to improve the quality of those installed in Post Office vehicles.[9]

Ribicoff did not congratulate the postmaster on this progress. He was taken aback that Gronouski had contracted for a $115,000 safety study with the very same automakers that had "shirked their responsibility in the safety research field." It seemed to him absurd, like paying a criminal to fight crime. When the senator suggested that the automaker had a conflict of interest in studying safety problems in which its vehicles were implicated, and added that G.M. at least should have done the study for free given its volume of business with the Post Office, Gronouski countered that G.M. had the finest facility in the world for safety research and that almost the whole of his fleet, which included many right-hand-drive trucks and three-wheeled mini vehicles, was purchased from specialty suppliers. He saw no conflict of interest.[10]

Another annoyance for Ribicoff in the postmaster's testimony was the intervention of one of the two panelists in attendance, the Republican senator from Wyoming, Milward Simpson. A veteran of the Great War, a graduate of Harvard Law, and former cowpuncher and professional baseball player, Simpson was sixty-eight years old with a perfectly round bald head and a voting record rivaled in its conservatism by that of Barry Goldwater (both senators were among the six Republicans to oppose the Civil Rights Act in 1964). Simpson saw no need to point fingers at Detroit. He thought that "major companies like Ford and General Motors" were far ahead of the state governments when it came to fighting for road safety. He also believed that progress was slow on the issue because it required the "buying public" to wake up and understand the value of such equipment as seat belts. Ribicoff allowed the senator from Wyoming to put his thoughts on record without interruption but neither encouraged him or engaged with him.[11]

The rest of the day brought only more aggravation for Ribicoff. General Alfred M. Gruenther (retired) arrived to represent the President's Committee for Traffic Safety and give a stalwart defense of the Triple-E approach to traffic safety. He also undermined the senator's opening contention that traffic fatalities per million vehicle miles were increasing based on the results of the two most recent years of data. He introduced to the record a chart showing that the death rate had been 35 per million miles driven in 1925 when Herbert Hoover and his experts began pushing improvements in education, enforcement, and engineering. By 1946, that figure had fallen to 9.8, and by the early 1960s it was below 5.5. The general considered the slight increase in the death rate per million miles driven in the two most recent years an anomaly. On the whole, he insisted, the postwar road safety record was remarkable given that 46 million more drivers had been licensed, 52 million more vehicles were on the road, and 580 billion more miles had been traveled in that period of time. More vehicles driving more miles on the same roadway systems increase the risks of collisions significantly. If the 1946 fatality rate had held, said Gruenther, 1.095 million Americans would have died in traffic in the interval. Instead, the fatality toll was 713,000 thousand, a difference of 382,000 lives. "That's more people than there are in the State of Wyoming," he said. "And those 382,000 lives weren't saved by luck."[12]

What Ribicoff dismissed as the traffic safety establishment, General Gruenther considered authorities in their fields, and he credited them with the gains he had cited. Their continued embrace of the Triple-E program was "the only realistic hope" of continued or accelerated improvement.

Gruenther was not lacking in authority. A graduate of West Point and the youngest four-star general in U.S. history, he had been Supreme Allied Commander in Europe before his retirement, decorated by the United States and thirteen other governments. He also owned stellar credentials as a humanitarian, having served as president of the American Red Cross between 1957 and 1964. Before leaving the stand, he told Ribicoff that in his experience as a member of the President's Committee for Traffic Safety, automakers had been generous with facts, figures, and safety information, and "very cooperative" in the fight to save lives.*[13]

The last witness of Ribicoff's first day was Lawson B. Knott Jr., acting administrator of the General Services Administration, responsible for procurement of the federal fleet. He testified that the GSA did all it could within the bounds of its statutory authority to promote traffic safety. Its two primary means of doing so were to set a national example by encouraging extensive use of safety devices in vehicles, and to insist on specific safety features for cars procured by the government each year, now numbering sixty thousand. Knott described how the seventeen specific safety features had been determined in consultation with government agencies, technical experts, safety organizations, and the automobile industry. They covered the major concerns that had been raised by Congressman Roberts and the medical community over the previous decade, and were scheduled to go into effect with government purchases in the 1967 model year. Knott expected that further requirements would be introduced

---

* General Gruenther's analytic powers were so keen he was known as "the brain" by admiring army colleagues. President Eisenhower once called him "one of the ablest all-around officers, civilian or military, I have encountered." He held the Distinguished Service Medal with two oak leaf clusters, and was the recipient of honorary degrees from thirty-eight American colleges and universities, including Harvard, Yale, and Columbia. His spare time was dedicated to refereeing bridge tournaments and writing a book about the game, *Duplicate Contract Complete. New York Times*, May 31, 1983.

in the years to come. He had hopes for antiskid devices, headrests designed to prevent neck injuries, and improvements in fuel tank placement to prevent post-collision fires.[14]

Ribicoff congratulated Knott on the introduction of his vehicle safety standards and asked who gave the best advice on their development. Detroit, came the answer. Ribicoff asked what use automakers made of this knowledge. The witness credited them with significant progress in safety but allowed that they had not done enough on their own to prevent the imposition of GSA standards, which was the answer sought by the chair. Knott nevertheless added that the industry's response to the government's purchasing requirements had been "generally favorable," and his co-witness, H. A. Abersfeller, commissioner of the Federal Supply Service, further subverted the chair's line of questioning by pointing out that some automakers had already installed headrests on seats to prevent whiplash, notwithstanding a lack of research to support their efficacy. "At this point in time," said Abersfeller, "we have had the utmost and finest cooperation from the industry."[15]

The next exchange between Ribicoff and Knott was curious. The senator compared the thorough investigations of plane crashes by federal authorities to the relatively cursory investigations of traffic crashes by police forces and asked Knott if there was not, as a result of casual police methodologies, a lack of reliable data on the true causes of road deaths: "To a great extent we are guessing on all this, are we not?"

Knott agreed with Ribicoff. He went further and admitted that his team's work rested on a shaky empirical foundation: "We had hoped in the development of the standards that we could look to someone who could tell us how many lives we might save by any one of the seventeen standards we are proposing. We found the statistics . . . not to be that precise." He added that the acquisition of reliable data should be "the most significant part of the safety program." Neither man appeared uneasy about imposing standards despite an acknowledged lack of information. What they had, ventured Knott, was good enough.[16]

The subcommittee adjourned for the day with Ribicoff having endured a rough ride from the traffic safety establishment.

. . .

The next morning at 9:30, hearings resumed in a different room in the New Senate Office Building. They would move to a third room the day after that, but on each occasion the results were much the same. Only one of Ribicoff's eight colleagues deigned to attend, and the testimony presented frequent challenges to the chair's views on traffic safety.

One particularly unhelpful witness was the man who had replaced Ribicoff as secretary of health, education, and welfare, Anthony J. Celebrezze, who shared the chair's sense of urgency over traffic death tolls and believed himself uniquely positioned to effect change. "Virtually the entire department" that Ribicoff had abandoned, said Celebrezze, was seized with concern for traffic safety and it was expending millions of dollars to learn more about the issue. As the secretary ran through the long list of research grants he had made, sixty-four in total, it became clear that he was indeed serious about traffic safety, and a firm devotee of the Triple-E approach to its management. Under questioning from Ribicoff, he described how during his earlier career as mayor of Cleveland (1954–61) he had decreased annual traffic fatalities from 118 to 64 by education programs, improvements in visibility at intersections, a squad of motorcycle officers specially trained in road safety, and other measures.[17]

Celebrezze was not averse to improving the crashworthiness of cars. But more padding in cars, he said, was not going to prevent drunk drivers from crashing into light posts, bashing their skulls against dashboards, or pitching themselves through windshields. He saw more utility in his broader approach to the problem. "We agree with most authorities that the causes of traffic accidents are very complex and that the prevention of traffic accidents will be equally complex." He was particularly interested in the human dimensions of safety. It concerned him that more than half the fatalities in Cleveland during his time as mayor involved alcohol, and that drivers refused to wear seat belts. He had been deeply impressed by research that he said "conclusively proved that the universal use of seat belts would greatly decrease the number of deaths and the severity of injuries inflicted in traffic accidents."[18]

As Celebrezze continued to assert that the traffic safety establishment was succeeding, that automakers were "very cooperative," that their product was reasonably safe, and that there was no need to consolidate into one department all federal traffic safety initiatives as the chair wished, Ribicoff's frustration began to show. He accused Celebrezze of doing too little to publicize the safety research undertaken by his own department, and of treating the automotive industry as a "sacred cow." Detroit, he insisted, "is dragging its feet" on safety. Manufacturers complained that unwanted safety features merely added to the price of automobiles yet they had no qualms about equipping cars with "a clock that does not work for which they charge," among other "useless and expensive" extras.[19]

Having worked himself up, the chairman laid his cards on the table: "I intend to be a crusader for traffic safety on a national basis. May I say this—I expect somebody in the federal government to start being a crusader for traffic safety in the executive branch." Celebrezze declined Ribicoff's invitation to join in a crusade against the industry, repeating his beliefs that more could be accomplished by dealing with negligent, careless, and drunk drivers and by convincing people to wear seat belts, which were by now standard on vehicles.[20]

Ribicoff was similarly exasperated by the testimony of another cabinet member, John T. Connor, secretary of commerce as well as head of the Interdepartmental Highway Safety Board. A Harvard Law graduate and former Marine who had co-chaired Johnson's 1964 campaign, Connor, too, believed that the safety establishment was making real progress. He noted that almost all of the safety features wanted by the chair had "already been incorporated in these automobiles by the manufacturers." Ribicoff protested that some were as yet optional rather than standard equipment. Connor said they were in the process of being installed as standard equipment, as per GSA guidelines, and meanwhile were available to anyone who wanted them. He refused to denounce the auto industry.[21]

Another witness from the Commerce Department was Rex Whitton, the federal highway administrator, who spoke of how his strategy for highway safety took into account the car, the driver, highway engineering, and driving conditions, among other factors. What he called a "systems" approach was simply another term for the Triple-E. He was especially proud of the highway engineering innovations pioneered by his administration, including center-line striping, no-passing zones, shoulder widening, safe-speed marking, guardrails, the minimization of railroad crossings, and longer sight-lines on bends in roads. These and other measures had "contributed substantially to reducing the collision death rate from 16.7 persons per 100 million vehicle miles in 1934 to 5.7 in 1964." On its own, the introduction of dedicated turning lanes had brought the fatality rate per million vehicle miles from 9.7 to 2.8 on newly completed sections of interstate highways. The simple introduction of a merge lane at a busy intersection in Virginia had reduced crashes by 70 percent, injuries by 56 percent, and eliminated deaths completely over a two-year period. Whitton spoke with great enthusiasm and specificity of the research being done on the causes of collisions on particular highways, on rural roads in general, and in urban settings, and how the learning from these efforts promised further reductions of fatality rates. Ribicoff admitted to being impressed by Whitton's work but his questions were limited to matters of state cooperation, budgets, and road signage between Washington and the Dulles Air-port.[22]

The inability of Celebrezze, Connor, Whitton, and other wit-nesses to frame the problem as he framed the problem served only to convince Ribicoff that they did not care about traffic safety as much as he cared about traffic safety. Their unwillingness to advo-cate for second-collision solutions, their insistence in rattling off proofs of the success of Triple-E methods, meant to him that they were doing nothing at all to improve the situation. "I am looking for someone in the federal government who says to himself, 'This is a horrible thing. No civilized society should close their eyes to the continuous slaughter on the highways. This is something that I am willing to get involved in and do something about.' "[23]

The only witness apart from Senator Nelson of Wisconsin to wholeheartedly agree with Ribicoff that the problem was horrible and that almost nothing was being done about it was the most junior witness to appear, a lanky young man with a large Irish face, rosy cheeks on pale skin, unruly eyebrows, incipient jowls, and lepre-chaun ears. Daniel Patrick Moynihan, assistant secretary of labor, arrived to declare in testimony and through the articles he placed on the record that the Triple-E approach was so much "ignorant superstition." It focused overwhelmingly on automobile users who were too numerous and too incorrigible to be managed. Education was wasted on them. The reckless characteristics of drivers were so manifold that it was "hopeless to think of doing anything about them for the limited purposes of traffic safety." Enforcement, which Moynihan defined as the "massive fines, imprisonment, punishment, and extortion which have been imposed on [the people] in the name of traffic safety," was an outrage. "We have been making a nation of felons of ourselves." He allowed that engineering developments affecting signage and the design of roads had reduced crashes but, all in all, the Triple-E was discredited, deficient in its theory, "uniformly practical," and the practice could not be said to have advanced very far when forty thousand people were dying in traffic each year.[24]

The rational theory of road safety, said Moynihan, was the second-collision theory. It required the traffic establishment and automakers to stop looking at crashes as unusual and avoidable and face up to the fact that they are inevitable. "One of every four automobiles manufactured ends up with blood on it," he said. "That is a high failure rate." Best to address the problem in epidemiological terms by controlling the agent, by which he meant automobile design. He asked why no one had demanded that Detroit simply place a control on a car that makes it impossible to run a red light.[25]

Moynihan's certainty on the importance of second-collision theory and his denigration of practical experience allowed him to dismiss out of hand the hundreds of agencies and thousands of professionals engaged with the Triple-E, as well as the successes they claimed. There were only "ten scientists" in the country who, in accordance with the second-collision theory, were attempting to make cars crash-proof. That they were so few was evidence that America had "done almost nothing about the problem of traffic safety." It was obvious to Moynihan that the time for federal regulation of automobile design had come. Detroit had made no real technological advances in fifty years. Its executives had displayed "considerable obtuseness" in making bloated, overpowered, overpriced cars with benign tailfins. He expected that a concern for safety would have to be forced upon the indifferent industry, and he noted that there were precedents for transportation regulation in the rail and aviation sectors.[26]

Coming in quick bursts of emphatic speech, sprinkled with scientific terms, "quantum" and "etiology," Moynihan's testimony was enchanting to Ribicoff. He thanked the witness for his "very, very pertinent comments" and his wisdom, and groused to him about Secretary Celebrezze's inability to grasp the issues. "You make a lot of sense in almost everything you do, Mr. Moynihan. I appreciate your coming here."

Ribicoff asked his staff to have Moynihan's testimony transcribed that very day and dispatched to Secretary Connor in Commerce: "I am just curious about what reaction they may have."[27]

Pleased as he was that Moynihan had laid down the correct theory and implicated the real offenders, Ribicoff seemed less cognizant of another aspect of his witness's contribution to the record: his devastating critique of the state of knowledge in the field of traffic safety. As part of his dismissal of the Triple-E strategy, Moynihan had emphasized that after decades of effort "we know almost nothing." The information available on traffic collisions was scant and unreliable. Little data was gathered at crash scenes beyond time of day, speed estimates, driver characteristics, and type of vehicle. What data was collected was subject to standards that varied significantly state to state, and police force to police force. There existed no central collection of data that permitted research on crash rates, or injury and death rates, by make and model of car. "It is my impression and it is the firm opinion of research workers for whom I have the greatest regard," said Moynihan, "that with perhaps one or two exceptions all the vast accumulation of data about automobile accidents over the past half century has contributed almost nothing to our understanding of the cause and prevention of accidents." Several government officials had voiced similar concerns about problematic data, which, of course, posed challenges for the second-collision school of traffic safety as well as for the Triple-E, but they failed to raise eyebrows at the hearings.[28]

Nor did Ribicoff display an interest in the expert criticisms of Moynihan's views on the need for federal regulation of automobile design that were appended to an article he submitted to the hearings. The automotive engineer R. N. Janeway said that while it was true that Washington had instituted safety regulations in the railroad field, it had "never dictated the design of rolling-stock equipment. The railroads have regulated that themselves through their own system." (Another expert noted that the federal government had simply required a minimum level of safe performance of aircraft manufacturers: "the design has not been done by the bureaucrats.") Janeway found Moynihan's contention that there has been no real technological development in the automobile in the last fifty years to be "hardly defensible." Rather, there had been "tremendous progress. And I think most people who buy cars are aware of this, even though perfection has not yet been attained." He had no problem with government regulating highways and traffic, and he expressed the hope that Detroit would do more to regulate itself to forestall any initiative by Washington because "it would be a very, very great calamity if the federal government were to be in a position to dictate the design of automobiles."[29]

Thus ended the first session of Senator Abraham Ribicoff's hearings on the federal government's role in traffic safety.

Ribicoff's panel reassembled less than four months later on July 13, by which time Martin Luther King had returned home from his march on Selma, Alabama, Students for a Democratic Society had rallied 25,000 Vietnam War protesters in Washington, and astronaut Ed White had stepped out of the Gemini 4 space capsule to complete the first space walk by an American. Change was afoot in room 1114 of the New State office building, as well. Ribicoff now found himself joined on the rostrum by three colleagues, a record attendance for his nine-member panel.

The hearing room was abuzz with spectators, photographers, and reporters. The excitement was due to the scheduled appearances of two witnesses from Detroit, Frederic G. Donner, chairman of the board of General Motors, and James M. Roche, president of the company. These barely distinguishable eminences sat side by side at the witness table as though they were prepared to audit the Senate rather than testify before it. When they put their gray heads together to whisper, news photographs made them appear conjoined.

Donner and Roche had prepared intensively for the hearings. They worked for a company obsessive about appearances, a company known to replace signatures in its annual report if they appeared fussy or weak. Donner and Roche had rehearsed questions and honed their answers and subjected their prepared statements to several drafts and outside advice from Newsom & Co. Some close to the corporation nevertheless believed it was a mistake for the top executives to attend. Why legitimize Ribicoff's quest? Send a crew of lawyers and engineers and not a single headline would issue from the proceedings. But Donner and Roche were eager to demonstrate their concern for traffic safety and their willingness to collaborate with government and account for their actions and products.[30]

Representing the largest automaker, G.M.'s executives were invited to appear before their competitors. They had sent prepared statements to Ribicoff's panel in advance. In an intended gesture of goodwill that would strike some as cynical, they had made a $1 million donation to traffic safety research at the Massachusetts Institute of Technology weeks before appearing. They further announced that they would be introducing six of the seventeen safety requirements of the GSA as standard features in 1966 models, a year ahead of schedule.[31]

Ribicoff's team was also prepared. Ralph Nader had been a regular in the Senate subcommittee's offices in the basement of the Old Senate Office Building. He was not paid by the subcommittee (still being on the payroll at Labor), and he did not appear on lists of Senate employees. No one else in the basement knew what he was doing there, sitting at his desk late into the evening with his charts and papers spread out in front of him, but his role was critical. "Nader was my prime resource, period," said Ribicoff's aide, Sonosky, who doubled as staff director and general counsel to the subcommittee. "I didn't need anyone else. He had everything." Sonosky and Nader would meet and talk for hours about the issues, what questions to ask witnesses, and how to handle technical material. "Sometimes I had to shut him up," said Sonosky. "He was fixated." Information and tactics they developed circulated among the offices of Ribicoff, Moynihan, and freshman senator Robert F. Kennedy, who was expected to participate in the hearings.[32]

A study of the panel's first session, and particularly its witness schedule, might have urged more caution on the part of the G.M. men. It telegraphed Ribicoff's strategy. He was not intent on an open inquiry into the best approach to reducing deaths and injuries on the road. If he were, a logical starting place would have been to invite (as he initially promised he would do) state and local officials responsible for traffic safety and vehicle regulation, as well as law enforcement experts, academics, highway engineers, and safety councils, all of whom had experience and expertise to share. That is how Congressman Kenneth Roberts had proceeded a decade earlier. Instead, Ribicoff largely dismissed these parties as tainted by their adherence to an outdated Triple-E credo. They were ignorant of second-collision theory and the role of the automobile in deaths and injuries. He did not want to engage them; he wanted to usurp them. Using second-collision theory as a club to beat his way to a new federal mandate for traffic safety, Ribicoff instead spent his first three hearing days demonstrating to his satisfaction that various federal departments and agencies responsible for traffic safety were ignorant of the automobile's role in crashes and fatalities. He next invited Detroit's honchos, intending to demonstrate their inattention to second-collision theory as a further proof that federal intervention was warranted.[33]

A second reason for inviting Detroit's leaders was that they would attract media attention. The hearings, admitted Sonosky, "were almost totally press-oriented." Still, General Motors' top executives appeared as requested and heard the senator, with his opening words, express irritation that he needed even to build a case for federal regulation of automobiles: "The federal government can control the contents of my wife's tube of lipstick but it lacks even a policy regarding the 3,500-pound super-powered piece of machinery she and I and millions and millions of others use daily."[34]

Donner read a prepared opening statement declaring that General Motors took a broad view of traffic safety issues, which he said made sense given the great many variables involved in collisions of complex machines moving at great speeds on all kinds of roads, in all kinds of conditions, with drivers of varying levels of skill and conscientiousness behind the wheel. He did address the role of the vehicle, signaling that G.M., to some extent, had been paying attention. He pointed to the great improvements his company had recently made in safety glass, door latches, steel roofs, windshield wipers and defrosters, headlamps, and other equipment. He spoke of G.M.'s participation in crash injury research projects conducted with the Automotive Safety Committee of the American Medical Association and the University of Michigan Medical School, and similar studies at Cornell and Wayne State universities aimed at improving passenger protection and minimizing injury in the event of collisions. He mentioned G.M.'s new $1 million grant to MIT. He elaborated on the thorough testing G.M. did on its cars at its proving grounds and listed off collaborations on road safety with the Automotive Safety Foundation, the Automobile Manufacturers Association, the National Highway Users Conference, the Auto Industries Highway Safety Committee, the President's Committee for Traffic Safety, the National Safety Council, the Highway Research Board, the Society of Automotive Engineers, state motor vehicle administrations, and other members of the so-called traffic safety establishment.

To preempt the inevitable questions about why General Motors did not install new safety technology in its automobiles the moment it became available, Donner explained that the company operated in a "climate of public acceptance." It recognized "the basic freedom of the customer to pay the cost of tailoring a car to his own specifications or rejecting whatever he may not want." If it were to force on people "things they are not prepared to buy, we would face a customer revolt, and we want to stay in business." New safety features were thus subject to an evolutionary process. Customers had to be sold on advances, convinced of their usefulness and their contribution to safety. The turn signal, he said, is now universally recognized as an enormous advance in communications among drivers and its contribution to safety might be considered self-evident, yet when it was first introduced as an option, only a small minority of buyers were willing to pay for it. Eventually the turn signal caught on and became standard equipment. Similarly, seat belts, introduced as options in 1956 G.M. models, were ordered by a mere 10 percent of owners as late as 1962. They were made standard equipment in 1964 under legislative pressure, yet research showed that only a small minority of drivers wanted or used them.[35]

President Roche followed Donner and addressed the safety improvements in G.M. cars with more specificity. He described how researchers at the proving grounds used computers, high-speed photography, crash sleds, and crash dummies to measure and better understand the dynamics of collisions. Highly technical studies of steering, braking, cornering, and acceleration were undertaken to enhance the driver's ability to avoid collisions. He noted that G.M. would be meeting thirteen of the seventeen new GSA safety requirements a year early, in its 1966 models, and added that while the company believed a couple of the standards were unrealistic, all would be met by 1967. Just the same, he said, safer vehicles "cannot be viewed as a panacea" for highway safety.[36]

Ribicoff's initial questions were unremarkable. He asked Donner if G.M. would absorb the expense of meeting the new GSA standards, estimated at about 3 percent of the cost of an automobile. That the costs of regulation are typically passed along to consumers through higher prices is a constant frustration for regulators, especially when inflation is a concern, as it was for Johnson Democrats. Donner recited the many factors that go into the pricing of a vehicle, including market demand and competitive pressures, before admitting the obvious: the additional expense would be added to prices because G.M.'s first responsibility was to return value to its shareholders.

Ribicoff asked why automakers seemed to believe that safety does not sell cars. Donner answered that safety did not make a great marketing slogan but that some safety features added to a vehicle's marketability, and any car had to be considered fundamentally safe or people would not buy it. Asked how much G.M. spent on actual safety research, by which Ribicoff meant, it came out after some back-and-forth, second-collision research, Donner replied that the company did not segment spending by type of safety or theories of safety, adding that myriad elements of an automobile contribute to safety, even seemingly tangential features such as strength of steel and the quality of suspension.

Roche expanded: "Our expenditures for research and development and experimental work in this area are so interwoven with our regular engineering and development programs that it would be almost an impossibility to segregate them."[37]

Ribicoff sprang his first trap: "You talked about safety door latches and hinges. You say you already meet GSA's requirements.

Could you explain, then, why the doors on General Motors cars seem to tear off to a far greater extent than other cars?"[38]

The senator was reading from a 1964 study by crash experts at Cornell that found doors on G.M. vehicles were more than five times likelier than Chrysler or Ford doors to be torn off in crashes. This random piece of data threw the G.M. witnesses into disarray. Neither Donner or Roche was immediately familiar with the report. Nor was Harry Barr, their vice president of engineering, who was also in attendance. Barr seemed to recall having seen raw data from Cornell on the doors of G.M. cars but claimed not to have seen any evidence that they performed better or worse than any other doors.[39]

"I think this is something that certainly needs looking into," said Ribicoff, now giving way to a fourth member of his panel who had joined the proceedings late, Senator Robert Kennedy of New York.[40]

"Do I understand you that you haven't studied these records at all?" said Kennedy, glowering from under his forelock. "Was this information made available to you prior to the time [Ribicoff] gave you the report of Cornell?"

"Senator Kennedy, I have not observed this personally," answered Barr. "I am sure if the data is available we do have it in General Motors."

"Isn't it well known in your company that Cornell makes these studies?"

"Yes, sir."

"As everybody considers this an important matter, I would think that you would have a close working relationship with Cornell."

"We do have."

"And with their studies."

"We do have."

"How can you appear before this committee and not even know about it?"

"I believe the data requires more study on our part, sir," said Barr. "We do have information on the General Motors door locks, and we are very good in this area."[41]

It had been the better part of a decade since Kennedy as a young Senate aide had badgered Jimmy Hoffa and suspected communists in hearing rooms but he had not lost a step. "I'm not an expert and

I have just been sitting here for a few minutes but I don't gather . . . that there is a very high priority given to the question of safety by General Motors at the moment. . . . What surprises and somewhat shocks me is the fact that [Cornell] makes this study, it has been continuously making this study, makes this material and information available to you. Yet here are the three top executives of the company and not anybody, not one of them knows anything about it. It doesn't seem to me that that is giving it the highest priority."[42]

Alarmed by the senator's aggression, Donner stepped in to defend his engineer and G.M., relaying the important improvements the company had made to its door locks in recent years to prevent passengers from being thrown from cars in the event of crashes. He proposed to show the panel a film he had brought demonstrating these improvements. Kennedy, reluctant to let go of the study, interrupted.

"The fact is that the study, an objective study not made by your company, has been made, and none of the executives of the company appearing before this committee know anything about it or have studied it or analyzed it or can give an explanation of it."[43]

"Let me just explain for a minute," said Donner, who tried another explanation only to be cut off by Kennedy again.

"But does the Cornell study indicate that you have done well?"

"I don't know if you were in the room . . ."

"Could you just—does the Cornell study indicate that you have done well?"

Donner restated Barr's contention that G.M. only received data from Cornell on its own cars, not those of its competitors.

"Let me just ask the question again," insisted Kennedy. "Does the Cornell study indicate that you have done well."

"Well, that depends on the period. We consider that we have gotten our door locks . . ."

"I think you can answer that question. Isn't the Cornell study critical of General Motors?"

"Oh, possibly," surrendered Donner.[44]

Barr, flipping through a copy of the report, was able to object toward the end of this exchange that the study ignored further improvements to post-1963 G.M. models. He might have gone further but Ribicoff changed the subject, having established to his satisfaction the dangers of Donner's door locks. He used the opportunity to lecture the executives:

> Should the automobile industry always be lagging behind waiting for somebody to tell them something has to be done? It would seem to me that you would be in a position to know what has to be done beforehand as well as anybody else in our society. . . . It would be better if a Congressional hearing did not have to say you ought to put seventeen [safety] devices into an automobile. I would hope the time will come when the automobile industry will do whatever they have to do for safety without waiting for the federal government.[45]

At this point, Senator Carl Thomas Curtis, a short, round-faced Nebraska Republican, grew impatient with his congressional colleagues and began to question their emphasis on the car as the primary problem in road fatalities: "What I would like to have brought before me by somebody is an authoritative determination as to . . . what it is that causes these accidents that these people are getting killed in, whether it is driving errors, winding roads, or mechanical failures of the product they are driving." He asked the witnesses how often mechanical failure of a car caused automobile crashes. Donner cited National Safety Council data that said 90 percent of collisions involved driver error and another 7.5 percent involved drinking and driving, and that 2 percent were attributable to mechanical failure.[46]

Ribicoff, displaying impatience of his own, interrupted Curtis to say the causes of first collisions were well known. "I am referring to the so-called second collision which so few people are aware of." Curtis protested that he had been shown no evidence that the design and manufacture of automobiles was to blame: "I just don't see how we can apply a solution until we have the problem defined." But Ribicoff had effectively shut him down, allowing Kennedy to resume his offensive.[47]

When had General Motors made its donation to MIT, asked Kennedy. On hearing that it was recent, he characterized the donation as a publicity stunt. G.M. pleaded that it had been motivated by recent promising findings on human tolerance to injury out of the University of Michigan. The senator was unimpressed: "Tell me how much money General Motors spent on these matters?"

"MIT is $1 million," said Donner.

"That is for the future," said Kennedy.

"That is prospectively."

"What have you spent so far?"

"Sir, I don't believe it is a matter of what we have spent."

"Well, I am interested in it. You might not be, but I am, and I am just asking you."

"We don't know, Senator, how to add all these things up."

"You don't?"

"Because they are scattered all over . . ."

"General Motors doesn't know how to add them up?"[48]

Donner tried to explain that some money was spent in research, more through the Automobile Manufacturers Association, and in other directions. He asked if Kennedy wanted to know about pure research, or development and testing, or reliability, or other matters.

"I will ask you some specifics about it," said Kennedy, confident he had the witnesses on the run. "How much money have you spent to find out how many children . . . fell out of the back of an automobile because of a faulty latch or lock?"

The executives had no answer.

"How many children have fallen out of General Motors cars?" asked Kennedy. "Last year?"

"I don't quite know how you would find that out," said Donner.[49]

Kennedy toyed with the executives, asking more questions he knew they would be unable to answer about their safety spending, and taunting them for their failure. When Roche finally coughed up a hard number, estimating that the company spent $1.25 million in the previous year on external safety research, Kennedy went for blood.

"What was the profit of General Motors last year?"

Roche answered, "I don't think that has anything to do . . ."

"I would like to have that answer if I may. I think I am entitled to know that figure. . . . You spent $1.25 million, as I understand it, on this aspect of safety. I would like to know what your profit is."

Donner tried to brush Kennedy back, saying that he was in attendance to discuss safety not finances.

"What was the profit of General Motors last year?" repeated the senator.

"I will have to ask one of my associates," said Donner.

"Could you, please?"

"$1,700 million," replied Roche.

"What?" asked Kennedy.

"About $1.5 billion, I think."

"One billion?" asked Kennedy.

"$1.7 billion," said Donner.

"About $1.5 billon?"

"Yes."

"You made $1.7 billion last year?"

"That is correct."

"And you spent $1 million on this?"[50]

At the end of its appearance, General Motors was finally permitted to show its film on the history of its vehicle safety improvements. For all intents and purposes, however, the show had ended when Kennedy drew from Roche a safety spending number he could compare to G.M.'s massive profits. The juxtaposition was fatal. Kennedy berated the executives for making so much and spending so little on safety when there were more than forty thousand Americans dying on the road every year. Donner and Roche tried to explain that the $1.25 million figure was for external safety spending, not the sum total of the company's safety expenditures, but the fact that they could not specify the sum total negated their point and brought more abuse from Kennedy: "I cannot believe General Motors does not have this information."[51]

Ribicoff and Kennedy brought the proceedings to a close by congratulating one another on their commitment to improving traffic safety when so many of the individuals and organizations nominally responsible for safety were sitting on their hands. Newspapers and television reporters reveled in the drama of the day, almost universally at the expense of the automakers. "Bobby Baits GM Officials in Auto Safety Hearing," read the front page of the *Detroit Free Press*, before going on to elaborate how Kennedy had "turned a polite discussion about auto safety into a biting cross-examination" of Donner and Roche.

It was a stellar moment for the young senator and he had thoroughly enjoyed it. Nick Thimmesch, the former Corvair reviewer, now a *Time* magazine staffer, accompanied Kennedy on the drive to his estate in McLean, Virginia, in the evening after the hearings. They ripped along the Beltway at seventy-five miles per hour. The top was down on Kennedy's massive Lincoln Continental. Along the way, the senator inveighed against the villainous Detroit moguls, his safety belts lying unused beside him on the leather seats.[52]

During the hearings, Ralph Nader, the Ribicoff panel's expert-in-chief, had sat behind a door in the chamber and passed slips of paper to Jerome Sonosky inside, supplying information and ideas for lines of attack. The more they worked together, the more Sonosky was impressed with Nader. He developed a conviction that his source had a future as a public figure regardless of his quirks and obsessive nature. Sonosky raised this prospect with Nader and received in response an enigmatic "Hmmm." When Sonosky suggested that Nader write a book on traffic safety, Nader gave him an uneasy smile and did not acknowledge that he had one in the works.[53]

Nader's book, in fact, was late. His publisher, Richard Grossman, had planned its publication for the spring of 1965. He wanted it in the market for the opening rounds of Ribicoff's hearings and, ideally, for Memorial Day weekend, which was reliably prolific of fatal car crashes and media stories on driver safety. By the appointed date, however, Nader, finishing up his report for Moynihan while also advising the Ribicoff panel, was far behind on the book. A small publisher with a lot riding on Nader, Grossman could not afford further delay. He traveled midsummer from New York to D.C. and took a room at the Gramercy Inn on Rhode Island Avenue. He set up two typewriters. Nader joined him with suitcases full of legal briefs, patent filings, newspaper clippings, government papers, and academic reports. They worked together day and night on their manuscript.[54]

By this time, publisher and author had no shortage of models for their book. The Kennedy era produced a shelf of passionate social critiques designed to jolt readers out of an assumed intellectual complacency. Joining Carson's *Silent Spring*, Mitford's *The American Way of Death*, and Betty Friedan's *The Feminine Mystique* were Michael Harrington's *The Other America*, which argued that 30 percent of the nation lived in poverty, and Jane Jacobs's *The Death and Life of Great American Cities*, a self-described "attack" on prevailing theories of urban life and city planning. All of these books were published in a burst between 1961 and 1963, and while each is rooted in a particular subject, the authors share a commitment to upending conventional ideas about American politics and society. Activists as much as journalists, antiestablishment by temperament, they wrote with their anger and urgency at the surface of their prose.[55]

As a group, the authors were determined to shift America's concern from the perpetuation of economic growth to unease about the consequences of growth. They related the different social evils they addressed to the nation's commercial economy and unprecedented affluence. They dismissed established authorities as robotic purveyors of conventional wisdom, and wealth creators as self-seeking vulgarians. Counterarguments that social ills are complex and difficult of solution were answered with a version of the man-on-the-moon argument Ribicoff had used in the early days of his proceedings: if America, the wealthiest society in the history of mankind, is capable of landing a human on the lunar surface, surely it has the resources and know-how to deal with poverty, inequality, urban blight, and crooked funeral directors. All that is missing is commitment, which the writers had in spades, and which their provocative books were intended to foster in others.[56]

The authors identified the roots of the social problems they addressed in the leadership of smug, homogeneous, unaccountable, self-perpetuating elites who had rigged the system for selfish ends. The leaders might be politicians, bureaucrats, corporate chiefs, or patriarchs, or some cross-disciplinary cabal of these types. The system might be a social order, a policy process, or an industry. The victims, largely oblivious to the manner in which they were being manipulated and abused, might be housewives, consumers, or the indigent. Details varied case to case but each author saw ordinary people suffering from the stupidity, greed, or indifference of those in positions of authority. By way of remedies, they called for the expansion and protection of individual rights, and the application of scientific expertise, and intelligent public policy.

None of the books was generated in isolation: each reflected a growing appetite for social change in America and around the world. Authority was under attack from every direction in the early 1960s, as might have been expected after a half century of devastating global war. New voices and new ideas were claiming the public stage and setting in motion such diverse phenomena as the civil rights movement and the Second Vatican Council. A new group consciousness flourished among minorities—feminists, homosexuals, Blacks, Hispanics, Indigenous peoples—all insisting on their rights and joining the rebellion against the status quo. Liberalized divorce laws and birth control were shaking the foundations of the nuclear family, and a new bohemianism featuring recreational drug use, sexual liberty, casual dress and grooming, left-wing politics, various mystic fascinations, and rock 'n' roll music gained popularity among the young (and not so young). The cultural revolution of these years was so broad, diverse, and complex as to frustrate encapsulation but the new literature of protest was as much a part of the times as Bob Dylan's antiwar anthems and Odetta's rendition of "Oh, Freedom" at the March on Washington.[57]

Nader was selective in his attachment to this broad movement. He demonstrated far more interest in Native American issues than African American issues. He had little to say on alternative lifestyles, or on poverty. He wore a tie, clipped his hair, avoided alcohol and drugs, and was clueless about popular culture. Yet he, too, was antiauthoritarian, outraged by perceived social evils, and committed to fight for change. It was the conflict between people and capital, consumers and corporations, that most animated him. He admired Carson and Mitford, and Moynihan's office had ordered him a copy of Friedan's book during his time on the Department of Labor payroll.[58]

The narrative strategy for Nader's book draws heavily on *Silent Spring*, particularly in its opening chapter. Nader and Grossman sought to dramatize the problem of traffic safety as vividly as Carson had her environmental concerns. They tell the story of Rose Pierini, a Santa Barbara woman who was driving at a speed of approximately thirty-five miles per hour on Hollister Street when she suddenly lost control of her automobile, a 1961 Chevrolet Corvair. The vehicle swayed right toward the curb, made a sharp cut to the left, and rolled, according to a police officer on the scene. He found her severed arm with wedding band and wristwatch attached as he approached the car. When the officer reached Mrs. Pierini, blood was gushing from the stub of her arm. A lawsuit brought against General Motors and its dealer, Washburn Chevrolet, alleged that they had built and sold an inherently unsafe automobile, and after three days of court testimony in which it was learned that a student employee at the dealership had improperly filled the tires of the Pierini Corvair, G.M. settled with the plaintiff for $70,000. The company was glad to issue a check, writes Nader, rather than continue a trial that "threatened to expose on the public record one of the greatest acts of industrial irresponsibility in the present century."[59]

G.M.'s rear-engine wonder car, in the author's view, is "a one-car accident" and proof that Detroit routinely prioritizes fancy styling and profits over safety. In a cost-cutting measure, the corporation failed to install stabilizing equipment necessary for the car's suspension. As a result, the Corvair, with most of its weight over the back wheels, suffers from too much positive camber, meaning that its back wheels tend to tuck under in tight turns at higher speeds. It is "one of the nastiest-handling cars ever built," says one test driver quoted in the manuscript. "The tail gave little warning that it was about to let go, and when it did, it let go with a vengeance few drivers could cope with." In an instant, says Nader, the car could reach a critical point at which "there is a sudden rear-wheel tuck under . . . a horrifying shift causing violent skidding, rear-end breakaway or vehicle roll-over." He holds that G.M. knew of these deficiencies and had the means to correct them but, loyal to "that bitch-goddess, cost reduction," did not begin to do so until its 1964 models, by which time a million Corvairs had been sold.[60]

Nader blames Chevrolet's president, Ed Cole, and his G.M. colleagues for prioritizing increased profits over the safety of their customers. These executives chose to depend on differential air pressure in the Corvair's front and rear wheels (fifteen pounds per square inch and twenty-six pounds per square inch, respectively) to counteract the car's handling issues. Nader called around to Chevrolet dealerships and found salesmen who were themselves confused about the correct air pressure required front and back of the Corvair. How, then, was the average driver to know? Is it reasonable, asks Nader, to expect him or her to read the owners' manual? With the wrong pressures, he continues, the Corvair can flip in a sharp turn at speeds as low as twenty-two miles per hour. It is no wonder to him that more than one hundred lawsuits have been filed alleging inherent instability in the design of the Corvair.[61]

Nader goes on to reveal the many other ways he holds Detroit primarily responsible for 45,000 road deaths and $8.3 billion in property damage every year. Automakers alone know the weaknesses and dangers of their vehicles yet they do not share their test data with the public. They possess the technology and expertise to prevent people from dying in crashes yet do not use it, preferring to keep costs down. Nader points to manufacturer patents for collapsible steering columns that have never left the drawing board.

The automakers, amoral and sociopathic in Nader's telling, dazzle car buyers with expensive new paint colors and body shapes and gadgets while installing weak brakes, fragile glass, inadequate sightlines, failing headlights, leaking gas lines, defective hood latches, sticky accelerators, and inferior tires. They build cars with crazy amounts of speed and power, cars that in crashes impale drivers on steering columns, split passenger heads on finely beveled metal dashboards, crush the eyeballs of children on protruding knobs, eject occupants into oncoming traffic, spear pedestrians with tailfins and hood ornaments, and pollute the air. When challenged on their negligent design and shoddy workmanship, Detroit executives, says Nader, take refuge in the defeatist argument that a crash-proof vehicle is impossible to build and that better drivers, better roads, and more enforcement are the sure routes to traffic safety.

Not content with nailing Detroit, Nader presents the industry's attitude toward safety as symptomatic of "a much deeper malaise that radiates beyond corporate borders into society." He posits the "closely knit traffic safety establishment" comprised of state and municipal safety officials, bureaucrats, law enforcers, and nonprofit safety organizations, and accuses it of abetting Detroit in avoiding culpability for mayhem on the highways by preaching the Triple-E gospel. Underlying their perverted conception of the public good, he says, is "the view that highways and vehicles were built about as well as could be expected under existing technology, and that traffic crashes were therefore traceable to willful, careless, irresponsible, or incompetent drivers." He exempts from this sweeping generalization the few governmental officials and medical professionals who have spoken out against the design flaws of American cars.[62]

Among the chief culprits Nader identifies in the traffic safety establishment is the influential, nonprofit National Safety Council. A public service organization committed to the Triple-E, the council receives some of its financial support from the auto industry and is therefore compromised, he writes. The American Automobile Association, the American Legion, the International Association of Chiefs of Police, the National Congress of Parents and Teachers, and the American Bar Association, all of which promote education and law enforcement as solutions to traffic problems, are to Nader similarly tainted, as is every organization that works with them. They have all contributed to the consensus that drivers rather than automakers are chiefly to blame for injuries and fatalities on the road. Legislators and administrators at the state level, and the legal system, too, have bought the auto industry's line that responsibility for collisions lies with drivers. As a result, traffic laws, crash investigations, insurance claims investigations, and statistical reporting are primarily concerned with identifying driver fault. Nader quotes Moynihan's opinion that Detroit and its allies are eager to keep responsibility for traffic safety at the state rather than the federal level because officials at the lower level are incompetent and/or uninterested in solving the safety problem.

The evidence in favor of blaming carmakers for highway deaths is to Nader so compelling that there can be no honest disagreement over the correct approach to saving lives. The motives of his opponents are therefore suspect and almost universally impugned. He sees an alarming conspiracy among medical professionals, police chiefs, insurance agents, auto repair shops, funeral homes, and others whose financial interest is dependent on a steady supply of highway injuries and fatalities. Thousands of jobs depend on the death toll, says Nader: "[This] is where the remuneration lies and this is where the talent and energies go." Everyone in this crash injury system, masterminded from Detroit, has incentives to sell and crash more cars and block efforts to save lives through better vehicle design. Prevention does not pay.[63]

The manuscript is nothing if not dogged, brandishing fact after fact, argument after argument, in chain-mace style. It is preachy, prosecutorial, sarcastic, and uncompromising. Where data can't be found to support his arguments, Nader blames the secrecy of automakers. If a driver crashes after reaching for his cigarette lighter and mistakenly turning off his headlights, or after putting his car into reverse when he intended to slot it into drive, or after stepping on the accelerator when he intended the brakes, Nader faults automotive design. Some of his questions about Detroit's methods and products are entirely valid. How, for instance, could an automaker build a car that required the length of a football field to brake from cruising speed?[*]

The influence of Rachel Carson is evident not only in narrative strategy but in Nader's revolt against the perceived right of industry to make a dollar at any cost. Also, in damning the ethical failings of the engineering and medical professions, both of which, he maintains, have failed to rise up against corporate malfeasors. Whereas Carson expands on JFK's bill of consumer rights to assert the right of people to be protected from environmental degradation, Nader proclaims a doctrine of "body rights." People must be protected from insults to their flesh, for if anything is sacred, says Nader, quoting Walt Whitman, "the human body is sacred."[64]

Other influences on the manuscript that emerged from the twin typewriters in the Gramercy Inn include Moynihan and Haddon, who are felt in its discussion of second-collision theory and the epidemiology of car crashes. Nader outdoes Moynihan's contention that one in four U.S. cars will wind up with blood on it, predicting

---

* Braking was nevertheless an area where the industry was voluntarily seeking to improve its performance. Each of the Big Three participated in the January 1965 Pure Oil Performance Trials in Daytona Beach (an annual event), where the average V8 stopped in twenty to twenty-five fewer feet from sixty mph than the year previous (most stopped in 175 to 200 feet). G.M.'s Buick Wildcat placed first in its class with 165 feet, an improvement of fifty-seven feet year-over-year for that car. G.M. took five firsts in seven classes in all three events: fuel economy, acceleration, and braking. *Detroit Free Press*, January 28, 1965.

that one in every two will kill or seriously injure an occupant. Large swatches of testimony from the early Ribicoff hearings are included, including Kennedy's demolition of G.M. over its unfamiliarity with Cornell safety findings and the small amounts it spent on accident research. Nader also cites data and passages from filings and speeches by personal injury lawyers, including those he had assisted in their lawsuits against G.M. over the Corvair.[65]

All of this notwithstanding, by far the most direct influence on Nader's manuscript is the report he wrote for Moynihan at the Labor Department. Written while the author was employed by the federal government, the report is a first draft of his book manuscript. It covers the supposed Corvair travesty, Detroit's recalcitrance toward safety issues, its overemphasis of styling and its failure to use known lifesaving technology, the perceived shortcomings of the Triple-E strategy, the development of second-collision theory, the epidemiological approach to car crashes, the capture of the traffic safety establishment by auto manufacturers, the Detroit-led conspiracy to keep responsibility for road safety at the state level, the wanting ethics of engineers and doctors, the sanctity of human flesh and the need for body rights. Both texts end with uncompromising calls for the creation of a federal regulator to impose strict safety standards on American-made cars.[66]

Some sections of the book manuscript, including its treatment of the crash injury industry and the manner in which private and public services profit from highway collisions, are lifted almost intact from the Moynihan report. Some of the report's subtleties, including a few kind words for the Triple-E, are lost in transition, as are many of the worst excesses of the author's idiosyncratic prose style. Nader's obscure references, convoluted attempts at humor, and descriptions of the Triple-E approach to safety as a "neatly conceived teleological explanation staffed by propositions invulnerable to disproof because of their tautological armor" were presumably eliminated in Grossman's editing.[67]

The Moynihan report is not credited in the new text. It would have been inconsistent with Nader's presentation of himself as an independent researcher, a lone wolf, an image universally accepted by his admirers and critics. The romantic fantasy of a single voice fighting a complex and powerful establishment is crucial to the era's protest literature. The impartiality and credibility of the author's call for federal regulation of the automobile industry would be undermined if he was known to have worked on his manuscript while being paid by a federal office determined to force that regulation. Also, the Ribicoff panel planned to call Nader as a witness. There is a hard line in legal ethics between witnesses and advocates: the first brings impartial evidence and the latter interprets that evidence to build a case; working both sides, confusing these roles, is regarded as prejudicial to everyone concerned. This perhaps solves the mystery of why Nader's report for Moynihan was never placed on a public record, and why he refused to be a full-time employee of the Labor Department, insisting on "the ad hoc nature" of his appointment and asking that Labor bureaucrats "delete my name" from project reports.[68]

The lack of credit to the government report does not change the fact that Nader, while at Labor, was an insider sharing in the immense power of the federal state. Through Moynihan, he enjoyed direct access to the President's Committee for Traffic Safety, the Interagency Committee on Safety, the Interdepartmental Highway Safety Board, and the Division of Accident Prevention at the Department of Health, Education, and Welfare. He worked with members of the Department of Defense, the Department of Commerce, and the Federal Aviation Administration on elements of automotive transportation policy. He assisted in the drafting of the General Services Administration's new safety standards for automobiles, the first stage of federal regulation of Detroit. He used Moynihan's office as cover to draw research from such diverse organizations as Cornell University, the Society of Automotive Engineers, the American Medical Association, the American Standard Association, NASA, and the New Zealand Transport Department. Throughout his almost two years in the department he enjoyed a degree of privilege and access that General Motors would have envied. His book was an inside job.[69]

Moynihan's secretary, through whom Nader often funneled his requests for information, was also in touch with tort lawyers pursuing claims against General Motors. In particular, the secretary approached Harney, Ford & Schlottman, the obscure California firm that had filed at least a dozen Corvair suits. Moynihan's office asked for details from its trials including names and addresses of certain organizations and expert witnesses, depositions and inter-rogatories of expert witnesses and manufacturers' experts, and so on. Harney, Ford & Schlottman had represented Rose Pierini, the subject of Nader's shocking first chapter.

After twenty-two days at the mercifully air-conditioned Gram-ercy Inn, Grossman was satisfied that he had a publishable text. He returned to New York to prepare it for printing, aiming for a November release. The book needed a title. Grossman liked *Unsafe at Any Speed*, a line lifted from *Insolent Chariots*, the journalist John Keats's 1958 screed against the motorization of American life. Nader was not fond of it but it stuck.[70]

CHAPTER 9

SOMETHING STUPID

In the days after chairman Donner and president Roche appeared before the Senate subcommittee, unfavorable reviews of their performance rolled off the nation's presses. *The Wall Street Journal* declared it "dismal" and quoted a congressman as saying, "I really wouldn't have believed they could be so bad." The *Journal* guessed that the hostility of Ribicoff and Kennedy "came as a shocking surprise to the auto magnates," who were "astonishingly ill-prepared" for the onslaught. The failure of the executives to convincingly manifest concern for safety made infinitely more probable "the thing the auto men wish most to avoid: federal instructions on how to build cars."[1]

The G.M. camp reviewed the clippings and came to the conclusion that Donner and Roche were "clobbered." Kennedy was fingered as the culprit. Donner was doing well, speaking in a slow, deliberate manner, without interruption, until 11:15 a.m. when the junior senator from New York arrived late from a Senate roll call. Without having heard the executives' opening statements, he began a belligerent line of questions and derailed Donner. "His sarcastic thrusts had the press section giggling," noted one internal document. It was thought that neither Donner nor Roche photographed well. They did not look "like warm-hearted, generous men. The photo showing them with their heads together conferring on some point made them look like a couple of defendants."[2]

The Chrysler Corporation, appearing the day after G.M., fared no better. Its executives boasted of their safety innovations and put on the record a list of fifty safety features introduced on Chrysler vehicles over the years, underlining that most were invented by the industry and available long before prompted by lawmakers. Seat belts had been offered at no cost since 1961 and as standard equipment since 1964 and in backseats since 1965, and Chrysler was now experimenting with shoulder belts despite a Gallup poll showing only one in seven drivers could be relied upon to wear any kind of belt. This was part of the company's larger argument that there was already more safety built into vehicles than motorists were willing to purchase and use.[3]

Harry Chesebrough, Chrysler's group vice president of product planning and development, suggested the federal government could make a great contribution to traffic safety by establishing a center to study the contributory causes of crashes. In the meantime, he urged caution in imposing specific approaches to safety or automobile design given the preliminary and dynamic state of research. It takes time to study and test new theories and technologies, he said, noting that successful innovations such as hydraulic brakes and all-steel construction were regarded skeptically by safety experts when they were introduced. Similarly, in the early 1950s it was still believed that the crash victim was safest if thrown clear of the vehicle. Cornell crash injury research, funded by the automobile companies, disproved that theory and Detroit quickly and voluntarily improved latches and locks on its doors. Chesebrough had just finished saying that the idea of a completely safe automobile, while an admirable goal, "is not in the realm of the attainable," and that a narrow focus on vehicles was "short-sighted," when Ribicoff, pleading time pressures, cut short the company's presentation and moved directly to questions.[4]

Chesebrough's first mistake under examination was to insist to the subcommittee chairman that a car buyer was entitled to all the safety he wanted. "This to me is a shocking thing," said Ribicoff. "What is your responsibility to produce a safe car . . . ? You are talking about an item that last year killed 48,000 people." The senator would refer to automobiles as "the most lethal weapons of all time" in the course of the day. Companies should acknowledge that people are stupid and reckless, he said, and give them the protection they need rather than the protection they want. Kennedy then stepped in to badger Chrysler about its safety spending. Despite the earlier embarrassment of Donner and Roche on this point, Chesebrough and his colleagues had no precise number for Kennedy. Kennedy mocked them for bringing six assistants to the hearing room and still failing to answer a simple question. Ultimately, he answered for them: Chrysler was spending $250 million a year on advertising and "a small percentage of that" on safety. This was as embarrassing as the contrast between G.M.'s profits and safety spending but was of no real interest to the media. Chrysler was not General Motors.[5]

American Motors, the third automaker to appear before the panel, recommended the Triple-E approach to traffic safety and complained about consumer apathy—"so much apathy, and actual resistance" to seat belts and vehicle maintenance. President Roy Abernethy, downgrading the importance of second-collision theory, said his first priority was to prevent crashes and, secondly, to package occupants. Better steering and braking, better headlights and comfort features for driver alertness, would do most to keep motorists secure. He, too, failed to answer the question of how much his company spent on safety, and he doubted the need for a collapsible steering column. Yet AMC was treated gently compared to its predecessors at the witness table. Ahead of its appearance, the subcommittee's staff had spread the word to cooperating senators, including Kennedy, that AMC deserved a break because of its support for dual operating brakes.[6]

One of the GSA's seventeen mandatory safety features, dual brakes were frowned upon as unnecessary by other manufacturers. The theory of dual brakes, as Chesebrough had explained to the panel, was that a car should have a hydraulic brake circuit for its two front wheels and another for its two back wheels. That way, if one circuit were to fail, the other would conceivably remain in operation. "We have not found any evidence that [circuit failure] is a contributing factor to accidents," said Chesebrough. "Our experience indicates that failure of the hydraulic circuit of brake systems is not a sudden thing. It is one that comes because of improper maintenance, and gives plenty of warning." Nevertheless, the dual brake system remained a high priority among Detroit's critics. AMC viewed them favorably, and also held the view that highway deaths had reached a point where manufacturers should consider "force-feeding" safety technology on customers. Its executives escaped unscathed.[7]

Ford, conspicuously retrograde in its vigorous support for automobile racing, took full advantage of being the last manufacturer to appear. Company president Arjay Miller had used the extra time to come up with an answer to the inevitable question of how much Ford spent on safety: a whopping $138 million annually. While agreeing with G.M. and Chrysler that it was impossible to precisely segregate safety costs, his company had considered the expenses of internal and external safety research, proving-ground activities, driver-training programs, and portions of the costs of prototype developments, basic design work, vehicle development, and quality control in arriving at its number. Miller also brought a ten-point plan to advance road safety that included second-collision research, an increased emphasis on safety in advertising, and specific recommendations for an enhanced federal role.[8]

Ribicoff was charmed: "If you follow through with these ten points, the other automobile manufacturers will do the same. Everything we have done in this committee will have been justified, and I think that the committee will have made a contribution toward automobile safety, and so will the automobile industry. This is the first time where there is an indication of a willingness to go beyond routine, to cooperate with government." Miller was thus forgiven his skeptical comments on collapsible steering columns, dual braking systems, the anti-whiplash headrest, and his view that elements of Cornell's crash research were not as technologically advanced as that of automakers. He was also permitted a defense of increased power and acceleration as useful in avoiding collisions, based on a Bureau of Public Roads study that low-horsepower cars are more likely to crash than high-horsepower cars.[9]

Although its moment had passed, General Motors, learning from Ford's example, quickly forwarded to the subcommittee its own comprehensive estimate of safety spending, including research, testing, engineering, and driver training, of $193 million a year. It also dug into the Cornell report on door failures with which the senators had ambushed Donner and Roche and developed a better response than the executives had been able to summon on the fly.

The Cornell researchers had examined close to 25,000 injury reports to determine whether cars in the early 1960s had better door latches than cars dating from the early 1950s. They found overwhelming evidence of improvement. Doors on the earlier cars, which had no safety latches, opened in 42 percent of crashes while the later models opened 23 percent of the time. Leadership in door latches had been shared since their installation by G.M. and Chrysler, although in the most recent model year (1963) there was "no statistically significant difference" among the Big Three.[10]

The Cornell experts, however, were not interested in latches per se. They were concerned with doors opening for any reason in the course of crashes. Sometimes latches were to blame, other times hinges. Still other times, improvements in latches and hinges resulted in damage to the areas surrounding them, resulting again in unwanted door openings and passenger ejections. Because companies used different technologies on hinges and latches, their doors failed in different ways. What mattered to Cornell was the frequency of any kind of door opening because open doors were what made occupants vulnerable. General Motors' doors opened in 21.1 percent of crashes, not as good as Chrysler but better than Ford. The three Detroit automakers had shown marked improvement over the previous decade, and each was significantly below the average of all automakers (including the smaller domestic and foreign brands).

Ribicoff's data on doors being torn off completely, as opposed to simply opening, was a single, obscure data point buried deep in a study with literally thousands of data points. It was not viewed as vital by the researchers, and there was no good reason to expect G.M.'s top executives to have been familiar with it. Donner had been correct in asserting that his company had made real progress in the security of its doors. The company made some of these points in a post-appearance letter from Roche to Ribicoff, and stressed that its progress in this area had been made without legislative prompts or threats. Ribicoff entered the letter into the hearing record along with G.M.'s estimate of its total safety expenditures, but the headlines had already been written and hardly anyone would read the formal record of the proceedings.[11]

. . .

Other arguments and defenses undoubtedly occurred to the men at General Motors after their appearance. What struck them hardest, however, was how much their world had changed. There was that old 1953 remark by former G.M. president Charles E. Wilson: "For years I thought what was good for our country was good for General Motors, and vice versa." It was frequently misquoted as "What's good for General Motors is good for the country," and misinterpreted as evidence that a G.M. executive could not distinguish between corporate interests and the public interest or, alternatively, that he believed the country should be run to improve G.M.'s profitability. What Wilson had meant was that he thought the country and General Motors were on the same team, and that they should look out for one another's interests. It was a simple nod to the Cold War Consensus: America's future depended upon its ability to keep its capitalist economy firing on all cylinders. Yes, there were disagreements about union settlements and monopolistic behavior, among other issues, but the two sides understood one another. That was no longer the case.[12]

G.M.'s head of public relations, Anthony DeLorenzo, told Ed Cole in the aftermath of the Donner-Roche appearance that their company and their industry were now "targets of a disturbing, rapidly growing, and often fact-distorting campaign to indict motor vehicle design as the major contributor to traffic deaths and injuries." The integrity of the company and its executives was in doubt, along with their goodwill, intelligence, and competence. The leaders of the Big Three, some of the highest-achieving businessmen on the planet, accustomed to reverential or, at least, friendly reception on Capitol Hill, were being hounded with the hostility and cheap tactics usually reserved for suspected communists. Their products, formerly viewed as technological marvels, showpieces of American ingenuity, proofs of the superiority of the American way, were now "lethal weapons," and the automotive sector, once the glory of the world's most powerful economy, was a conscienceless killer of tens of thousands of innocent American people. The world, or some significant part of it, had profoundly changed.[13]

Indeed, G.M. and its critics scarcely spoke the same language

anymore. Time and again during the hearings, the likes of Ribicoff and Kennedy would ask questions about Detroit's concern for
safety, by which they meant the importance of second-collision
theory. Time and again, Donner and his peers would answer with
an emphasis on crash prevention measures such as better steering
and braking, better roads and driver training, not realizing that
these responses, in the eyes of their inquisitors, made them look
ridiculous, obtuse, and quite possibly corrupt. Members of the press
giggled.

If Donner had been wholly at sea on public relations before the
hearings, his entire company was now dismasted in a public relations storm. There were internal disagreements on how to react.
The Newsom group, feeling that it had been correct in its assessment of the revolutionary shift in public values and the consequences for automakers, believed the company's critics had a point.
General Motors was overly preoccupied with commercial matters.
It had more safety knowledge and technology than it was using, the
interior designs of its cars did not put the welfare of occupants first.
Large sums of money had been spent testing the strength and reliability of vehicles but only one engineer in a lonely outpost was
carrying out design research from a second-collision perspective.
During the Ribicoff hearings, the company had displayed the "organizational arrogance one expects in an authoritarian state."[14]

It was an open question, so far as Newsom's experts were concerned, whether General Motors had a conscience, some place
"where moral, ethical, and public-responsibility questions are continually and carefully examined." They could not help but think that
if the company had "put public safety very high on its list of worries, it would have done more." It seemed to them to have grown
too large and sclerotic to adapt to social change and live up to its
responsibilities as a corporate citizen. It was evasive and defensive,
leaving the impression at the hearings that there was something to
the charge that it was a big, rich corporation heedlessly endangering
the lives of women and children, a narrative too juicy for ambitious
congressmen and critics of corporate America to pass on.[15]

The consultants doubled down on their recommendation that
General Motors move with the times, accept the legitimacy of its
critics, and engage in sincere public debate. The company should

talk safety continually, reveal the facts of G.M.'s leadership in the field, and reverse its antiquated policy of avoiding public discussion of specific design changes in future products, at least where safety was concerned.[16]

These recommendations rankled some at General Motors, particularly DeLorenzo in public relations. The company already talked safety continuously, he told Newsom. It produced and distributed millions of safety brochures, and developed and launched annual safety marketing campaigns. It placed safe-driving advertisements in magazines and newspapers every year before Memorial Day, ran a safety speakers' program, made traffic safety documentaries for public schools, and established a green pennant program to reward schools with good safety records. DeLorenzo's department was in the process of rewriting every G.M. owner's manual to place a greater emphasis on safety. He responded point by point to Newsom's proposed actions, noting that G.M. was currently doing or had previously tried virtually everything on the list.[17]

As far as DeLorenzo was concerned, General Motors was doing everything that might reasonably be done for safety without seriously damaging its finances or repelling consumers. Newsom, he believed, had a vested interest in convincing the company that it was out of touch and in need of the consultancy's services. The bigger the problem, the more hours the consultancy could bill. Its suggestions, moreover, were in DeLorenzo's estimation surrenders to the radicals and their overhyped second-collision theory. A former wire service journalist and a sixteen-year veteran of the corporation, DeLorenzo preferred to fight on G.M.'s terms: agree that the death rate must be reduced; remind people that American cars and highways were the safest in the world; insist on the company's longstanding and continuing support for crash prevention and passenger safety; refuse to be the fall guy for Ralph Nader and a grandstanding pack of mendacious politicians.[18]

DeLorenzo's outlook appears to have been popular among G.M. executives. James Roche would soon tell a convention of General Motors dealers: "A scapegoat is not a solution. It may serve as an emotional substitute but workable solutions to problems like this demand factual information and objective, cooperative effort." He had earlier called on the auto industry as a whole to disprove the "unjustified" criticisms of Detroit's product. "We want to build safer cars," he said, but "we can't afford to indulge in what might seem like lofty ideals, at the cost of immobility, a lower standard of living, and the risk of falling behind in the world-wide competition."[19]

Nevertheless, there was some recognition at G.M. that the corporation and the industry needed to show flexibility to protect the business. All outstanding items on the General Services Administration's list of required safety equipment were fast-tracked. In a post-hearings flurry of brochures and presentations, G.M. built second-collision notions into its otherwise broad-based safety program. It tried to seed positive stories in *The Saturday Evening Post* and *Look* magazine, and it talked to Disney about a traffic safety film. The Automobile Manufacturers Association appointed a committee "to undertake at once the preparation of plans for a cooperative program to expand the industry's efforts in the field of automotive safety, particularly in the area of crash prevention, safety research, and the problems of the 'second collision.'" The University of Michigan received a $10 million grant ($8 million of it from G.M. and Ford) to establish a highway safety institute that would develop a comprehensive approach to highway safety which included the crashworthiness of the automobile. It was to that time the largest corporate gift ever received by a university for any purpose.[20]

The second-collision concessions and largesse were prompted by fear of federal regulation. G.M. hoped its contrition and compliance would convince Washington to back off. In case Washington wasn't getting the message, it also warned of the likely negative consequences of regulation. "Such regimentation of our industry would be most unfortunate," said Roche.

> Our industry has an outstanding record of progress which can be attributed, in large measure, to the pressure of free competition—pressure to innovate, develop and improve—pressure to produce better value for our customers whose approval determines our success. Government regulation would discourage competition as we have known it. The regulatory standards would tend to become the maximum as well as the minimum. Regulation would have a severe and adverse effect upon our business. It would substitute rigidity

for flexibility—bureaucratic approval for public approval. It would make the industry less, rather than more, responsive to our customers' changing needs and tastes.[21]

Roche's assessment of the effects of government regulation of an industry was conventional and largely defensible. Although only about 20 percent of the nonagricultural economy was regulated at the time, it was well established that government intervention in a market, however necessary, tended to stifle innovation, competition, responsiveness to customers, and that regulatory standards tended to become the maximum as well as the minimum of an industry's efforts (it was also known that the effects of regulation ranged from mild to severe depending on the regulatory approach and the industry in question). It was further understood that an industry threatened with regulation would respond angrily and lobby to preserve its independence, as Roche and General Motors were doing, emphasizing the "private" in private enterprise, insisting on the rights of property owners, and proposing to pass along to consumers the costs of regulation.

It is difficult to overstate how destabilizing the prospect of regulation was to General Motors. It amounted to a nightmarish manifestation of Chairman Donner's impression that the corporation was out of step with some important segment of society. It seemed to confirm DeLorenzo's suspicion that G.M. was in the bull's-eye, also Roche's sense of being a scapegoat. Their reaction was entirely predictable.

As the executives were doing their best to ward off an incursion by Washington, Yale political psychologist Robert E. Lane was updating his groundbreaking work on a seldom discussed aspect of regulation. Lane saw government supervision of business not in simple economic terms but as a conflict in the mores and belief systems of competing elements in a community. It worked like this. Some business activity that businessmen saw as a normal and defensible part of their industry would be fingered by critics as detrimental to society, and government would take it upon itself to correct the problem. While the targeted businessmen would complain long and hard about the financial implications of regulation, the real cost, Lane found, was to self-image. The captains of industry, perceiving themselves as high-status contributors to the community, competent and honorable providers of important goods and services, creators of wealth and jobs, were suddenly accused of serious transgressions and pilloried as incompetent, thoughtless, heartless, greedy, degenerate, shameless, or otherwise villainous people. The charges were leveled by actors whose values and motives the businesspeople did not understand, who in their eyes lacked expertise and experience of their field and were not qualified to judge. They had never made a sale, turned a profit, built a business. They did not even compete in the real world. This collision of values challenged the belief systems and self-respect of the business leaders to an extent that Lane assessed as traumatic. Their status within the community was diminished, an outcome that exacted "a toll of anxiety, frustration and dejection beyond all relation to the economic cost."[22]

The psychic costs of regulation or regulatory threats were largely unspoken, according to Lane, because confident and imperious men of affairs did not admit to personal injury, and because doing so would not advance their cause. They instead clothed their hurt and bewilderment in economic arguments, resisted their impending depreciation, and bargained with government. They hoped that the causes of friction could be smoothed over, that their businesses would retain their freedom of movement, and they themselves would return to the nation's good graces.

None of this amounted to a reason not to regulate business in the public interest, or an excuse for cranky behavior by businessmen. It did suggest, however, that in proposing regulation of the most critical sector of the American economy, legislators would have been wise to adopt a low-key and collaborative approach in order to enhance safety without disrupting the confidence and operations of the automakers. It was in America's interest to have both safer cars and a revved-up General Motors: 58 percent of General Motors' gross profit went to state and federal taxes, making the American people, in effect, its largest shareholder.[23]

In the wake of Ribicoff's hearings, G.M.'s brass, as Lane would have predicted, was rattled, injured, and hoping that things could be smoothed over. The senators had had their fun, embarrassing executives of the world's largest corporation, winning headlines, sitting for television interviews, and reminding their constituents of their existence. It was now time for sanity to prevail, for the nation's attention to shift back from highway death tolls to the millions of gleaming new automobiles rolling off Detroit's assemblies. The company believed this was an achievable outcome, even if a best-case scenario.

It is not known if the company discussed worst-case scenarios. What might happen, for instance, if the senators turned up the heat, and the media piled on, and G.M.'s executives did something stupid?

General Motors' hopes for a season of peace and reconciliation in the second half of 1965 were almost immediately dashed. Its critics had been emboldened rather than satiated by the subcommittee confrontation. Senators Kennedy and Ribicoff took victory laps that fall, making speeches and writing articles on traffic safety and how to improve it. At year's end, they released a joint statement announcing that 720 Americans had been killed in a seventy-eight-hour period over the Christmas holiday. Once again, they professed to be amazed that Detroit had not used its scientific and technological prowess to build a crash-proof car. The answer, they said, was federal regulation of Detroit.[24]

Another group of G.M. tormentors, the plaintiff's attorneys, were similarly animated, notwithstanding the fact that since settling the Pierini case the corporation had twice convinced juries in Corvair suits that there was nothing defective or negligent in the car's design. The attorneys continued to bring new cases and escalate their rhetoric. Less than two weeks after the Ribicoff hearings, Harry M. Philo, a former Ford assembly worker with a degree from the Detroit College of Law and a personal injury practice, made a sensational speech about the Corvair before a Miami convention of the American Trial Lawyers Association. It was a step-by-step guide to launching an action against General Motors for negligence in the design of 1960–63 Corvairs.[25]

Philo maintained that the car's rear suspension was inadequate and that a gust of wind, a tight curve, or a bump in the road could cause a driver to go out of control at speeds as low as twenty-two miles per hour, resulting in severe injury or death. He guessed that more than ten thousand crashes of this nature had already occurred and claimed that General Motors had been aware of the car's deficiencies yet produced it anyway. Philo held that the Corvair was more than a one-off failure: it was symptomatic of corruption in the heart of Detroit. The auto industry had been negligent in failing to provide the American public with crashworthy vehicles. It was sacrificing safety to pad its profits. Philo did not mention in his speech that he and his firm were representing a plaintiff in a Corvair design case in Clearwater, Florida.[26]

In the midst of the trial lawyers' new offensive landed Nader's book. The first comments on *Unsafe at Any Speed: The Designed-In Dangers of the American Automobile* appeared on October 8, 1965, in the *San Francisco Chronicle*, which called it "a searing document that may become the *Silent Spring* of the automotive industry." The newspaper also compared it to Jessica Mitford's *The American Way of Death*. On November 30, *The New York Times* reported Nader's claim that a traffic safety establishment was shielding the auto industry from scrutiny and criticism (it followed the next day with complaints from the American Automobile Association, among others, that his comments were untrue and misleading). *Unsafe at Any Speed* was briefly but favorably reviewed along with nine other automobile books in the *Times* a week later, and *Science* magazine welcomed it with yet another version of the man-on-the-moon argument: "When a society that can put a man in orbit cannot guarantee his survival in a collision at twenty miles per hour, then the cause is more likely to be an underdeveloped public policy than an underdeveloped technology."[27]

General Motors became aware of *Unsafe at Any Speed* around the time of its mention in the *Chronicle*. The corporation noticed that Nader was using many of the same arguments and citing many of the same corporate speeches, documents, and patent filings that the personal injury lawyers used in their pleadings. Like them, Nader claimed that G.M. had always been aware of the Corvair's shortcomings and that its failure to correct them was indicative of Detroit's venality, although the author outstripped the plaintiff's attorneys by suggesting on a television broadcast that lethal car designs were premeditated: "When you continue to design cars at a level of safety that is not commensurate with the needs of the public, one wonders whether indifference doesn't blend into something more conscious and more willful." The existence of some link between Nader and personal injury lawyers was obvious and alarming to legal staff at General Motors. The nature of the link, however, was unclear.[28]

What G.M. did know about the Corvair suits was that almost all of them were emerging from two hubs. The first was the Los Angeles firm of Harney, Ford & Schlottman, which had made itself liberally available to the media after its settlement of the Pierini suit, expanding its Corvair business. It was now involved in the vast majority of active Corvair cases, which by G.M.'s count numbered 106, for a total of $40 million in claims. The corporation suspected Harney of using unscrupulous means to win new Corvair clients. A lurid account of the Pierini case had appeared on the front page of a cheap tabloid called *Midnight* in March 1965 with the headline "150 Lawsuits Charge: G.M. Cars Are Death Traps—Hushed-up Evidence Revealed in Court." A break from such usual *Midnight* cover fare as "Virgins Make Lousy Wives" and "Adultery Can Save Your Marriage," the article mentioned thirteen Corvair cases in addition to Pierini. Three of these had yet to be served, one had yet to be filed. All of them were brought by Harney, whose firm thus appeared to have cooperated with the story. This seemed to G.M. a possible violation of the American Bar Association's prohibitions against soliciting work through advertisements or press commentary. The corporation also suspected that Harney might have paid or otherwise encouraged Nader to write the unsigned *Midnight* piece, as well as *Unsafe at Any Speed*.[29]

The other locus of Corvair activity was the Detroit law firm of Goodman, Crockett, Eden, Robb, & Philo. It was pursuing cases in Florida and Michigan. G.M.'s counsel had been disturbed by the "unsupported and sensational charges" in Philo's well-publicized speech in Miami and believed it to have been timed to influence juries against the manufacturer. General Motors considered bringing bar association grievances against Philo for violating professional ethics restraining lawyers from discussing pending cases in public. The company also knew that Nader and Philo were connected. The author had attended a gathering of plaintiff's attorneys, including some from Philo's firm, at the Harlan House Motel in Detroit where a film of tests allegedly proving the instability of the Corvair had been shown.[30]

From a certain angle, Harney and Philo were familiar opponents to General Motors' legal department, typical hustlers in the
morally liminal world of personal injury law: noisy, aggressive, devious, working on contingency fees, playing to the emotions and cre-
dulity of juries. They might get their hands dirty, but they generally
worked within the confines of the legal system and were mercenary
enough to accept settlements. Ralph Nader was something else. Try
as they might, G.M. lawyers could not get the measure of him.

It was tempting to see Nader as a journalist-activist in the fashion of Rachel Carson, who had also testified before a Ribicoff panel.
Carson, however, was a trained scientist, a noted expert in her field,
with a long history of publications in *The Atlantic Monthly* and *The
New Yorker* and best-selling books to her credit. Nader was not an
engineer or an automotive specialist. His publication history was
relatively thin and obscure, and he made no pretense of scientific
objectivity.

Perhaps, then, Nader was more lawyer than writer? He had
graduated from Harvard Law and practiced for a time in New
Haven. His unedited prose was more legalistic than journalistic, as
evinced by his recent 153-page article, "Automobile Design Hazards," in *American Jurisprudence Proof of Facts*. He was loudly cheering the Corvair suits, calling them "the most signal development in
the history of applying tort law to motor vehicle design." Yet Nader
did not appear in court. He had no known cases. He had stated
publicly that he had abandoned legal practice. What's more, lawyers
collect fees, and no one was known to be paying Nader.[31]

And then there was the fact that Nader's only known employment was his stint at the Labor Department and his association
with the Ribicoff committee. Both roles had been mentioned on
the cover of his book. He seemed to be putting himself forward as a
government consultant or a political actor but, again, the roles did
not fit. Consultants have listed telephone numbers, and they tend
to get paid, whereas Nader had worked for Ribicoff as an unpaid
volunteer. Political actors have offices, portfolios, constituencies,
parties, and Nader, apparently, had none.

Nader was a mystery to General Motors. Not a real author. Not
a real lawyer. Not a real consultant or political agent. Yet somehow

all of these things, and he was popping up everywhere. "Who the hell is this guy?" one G.M. attorney asked his colleagues.[32]

No one individual in General Motors' legal department of fifty to sixty attorneys would ever claim credit for the idea but by November 1965 it was understood internally that Ralph Nader had to be investigated. The emerging image of him as a lone crusader for the public good, a central theme of his book publicity, cut no ice at G.M. Maybe he was setting himself up for a run for office, or as an expert witness. Maybe he and his book were part of an "organized nationwide publicity campaign to pretry the Corvair cases by television, newspaper, and magazine, and to precondition prospective jurors in the cases still to be tried throughout the United States." He had to have an angle, whether political, legal, or pecuniary, and General Motors had to know what it was.[33]

On November 18, 1965, Aloysius Power, head of G.M.'s legal department, ordered an attorney on his staff to call Royal Globe Insurance Co., G.M.'s product liability insurer, to ask whether it had an investigator in Connecticut. Royal assigned a man named William F. O'Neill of East Hartford to poke around Winsted to see what he could learn about Nader, his background, character, and qualifications.

O'Neill devoted about a week to the assignment. He learned that Nader's father owned a local restaurant in Winsted and that its food was good and the place seemed well run. The Nader family appeared to be unremarkable, although Ralph's brother, Shafeek, seemed to have attended "half the colleges in the country and is now back working in back of his father's lunch counter." There were rumors that Shafeek and his father were anti-Semitic. The acting police chief in Winsted had known Ralph from boyhood and described him as a brilliant student who broke scholastic records at the high school before attending college. Another local remembered him as "a swell kid with a brilliant mind." O'Neill learned that Nader had received an A in Chinese at Princeton despite rarely attending class. He had practiced law for a short time in Hartford, taught history at night school for a time in the same city, and appeared as a concerned citizen before the Connecticut state transportation committee to share his views on automobile design. Nader had never registered a car in Connecticut and he had not been in town much, if at all, for the previous two or three years. He was said to have moved to Washington, D.C.[34]

Finding nothing of value in O'Neill's report, and seeing no diminution in the volume of lawsuits against the Corvair, Aloysius Power decided that an upgrade was in order. One of his staffers, Eileen Murphy, volunteered to use her contacts in D.C., where she had worked with the civil division of the Department of Justice, to find a better investigator.

A poised, tough-talking brunette with fashionable dark-framed glasses, Murphy was a rarity at G.M., a female executive. As the company's law librarian, she had oversight of all research activities in the legal department. She had compiled a thick dossier on Nader. "We had every tape, every piece of film, everything he'd written, from the time he'd been at Harvard. . . . I can remember three tape-recording machines going at the same time, just transcribing tapes of interviews or talks that Nader had given. We had volumes of Nader transcripts that would be, altogether, about sixteen inches thick, and then we had a four-inch-thick binder on him. We had a *lot*." But the lot they had raised more questions than it answered, hence the need for investigative support.[35]

With Power's permission, Murphy contacted Richard Danner of the Washington-based law firm of Alvord & Alvord three days before Christmas. We have "a problem in the legal department having to do with a Mr. Ralph Nader," she said. Could Danner "recommend a competent investigative organization to handle this matter?" A former FBI special agent who had been called to the bar in middle age, Danner said yes.[36]

Because of holiday travel and personal illness, Murphy and Danner did not meet in person until January 11. In the interim, Nader was busy promoting his book. On January 5, he and Grossman pulled a publicity stunt in Detroit, inviting the heads of the major automakers to discuss safety at a press conference in the Sheraton-Cadillac Hotel in Detroit. As expected, the executives did not materialize but Nader used the opportunity to enlighten reporters on Detroit's failings and to predict that General Motors would be forced to recall and modify the suspensions on 1960–63 Corvairs. It would be cheaper, he declared, than defending the corporation against the blizzard of lawsuits brought by victims of the car's faulty design.[37]

From Detroit, Nader traveled to Des Moines, Iowa, to testify in traffic safety hearings organized by the state attorney general, Lawrence Scalise. The Big Three were invited, too, but declined to attend. Nader described Detroit's absence as "a shocking display of contempt" for the people of Iowa, and proof that the automakers had "much to hide" from the public and more "to be ashamed of for their past, present, and expected performance." He repeated his complaints about Detroit's failure to build a crashworthy vehicle, and added that the operational controls of the company's cars were booby traps that overloaded the capacities of drivers and caused crashes. He thought criminal sanctions would be useful in forcing automakers to mend their ways, and made it clear that toppling Detroit was as much a part of his agenda as improving safety: "Power is the only language this industry understands, as befits any Goliath ranking so high on the corporate brutality index for so long with so little challenge."[38]

It was not lost on G.M.'s legal department that a favorite Nader source, Dr. Paul Gikas, research director of Physicians for Automotive Safety, also testified in Iowa, as did Dr. Thomas Manos, an associate professor of engineering at the University of Detroit and a star witness for attorneys bringing suit against the Corvair. The hearings received national attention, as did a simultaneous appearance by the tort attorney Harry Philo before a Michigan Senate study committee on traffic safety. Philo repeated parts of his Miami speech, including his views on the "horrible" instability of G.M.'s only rear-engine vehicle. He described the 1960–63 Corvairs as "the worst crime that's happening in Michigan today" and urged the state to ban them from its highways. "If the Corvairs are allowed to continue to operate, I think the legislature is derelict in its duty."[39]

Aloysius Power was outraged that Philo had been permitted to present himself before the State Senate as national chairman of the safety committee of the American Trial Lawyers Association (ATLA) rather than as a plaintiff's attorney with a pecuniary interest in Corvair suits. He wrote an angry letter to the chair of the Michigan highway committee complaining of Philo's disregard for ethical prohibitions on discussing litigation in public forums, underlining the disadvantage at which G.M. was placed by maintaining its silence on the Corvair in accord with its ethical responsibilities.[40]

When Eileen Murphy finally met Richard Danner in his K Street offices, she handed him O'Neill's report, a brief biography of Nader she had prepared, and some press clippings. According to Danner's later testimony, Murphy said that G.M. wondered about Nader's "absence of objectivity" and suspected that he was connected with attorneys bringing Corvair suits. She wanted to know more about his legal practice, his government employment record, his sources of income, associates, movements—a complete background check. Did he drink, and what accounted for the "nervous habit of sniffing" he had displayed at a recent press conference? Was it pneumonia or "a dope addiction"? Murphy and Danner agreed that some sort of pretext would have to be invented for the investigation but Murphy was happy to leave that to Danner and his investigator.[41]

Danner's investigator was Vincent Gillen of New York, another lawyer and former FBI agent whom he had previously retained to interview potential witnesses in court cases. He considered Gillen to be "competent, businesslike, and ethical." The two met January 13 in Danner's office. They discussed the investigation, which Danner considered perfectly legal, a routine matter of the sort "conducted every day in connection with business, industry, or the practice of law." He passed to Gillen the short Nader biography, the O'Neill report, and the news clippings. They agreed that the best pretext for the investigation would be a pre-employment check. Gillen and his associates would pretend to be acting on behalf of an employer about to offer Nader an important position and ask questions about his education and employment histories, his personality and character, "his prejudices, political leanings, sources of income and any other area which might embarrass any employer." The prospective employer would not be revealed. Gillen was to report to Danner once or twice a week on his progress.[42]

A barrel-chested man with a deep voice and kinky steel-gray hair brushed straight back, Vincent Gillen was a graduate of Fordham University and Brooklyn Law School, and the proprietor of Vincent Gillen Associates, the New York franchise of Fidelifacts Inc., a national chain of private investigators run mostly by former FBI men. "I am a professional fact-finder," Gillen liked to say. "I work for those who will pay me." He was proud of his client list, which ran to reputable organizations as opposed to suspicious spouses. He had worked for Metropolitan Life and in 1960 had reconnoitered the Kennedy campaign on behalf of the Republican National Committee. Danner did not appear to have been aware that Gillen had previously undertaken assignments directly for General Motors.[43]

Explaining the investigation to his associates, Gillen used an agreed-upon pretext: the subject, Ralph Nader, was a freelance writer and attorney, and author of a book highly critical of the automobile industry. An unnamed "client of our client" was impressed by Nader's intelligence and talent and was thinking about offering him a job. Before committing, however, it needed to know more about Nader. "Our job is to check his life and current activities to determine 'what makes him tick,' such as his real interest in safety, his supporters, if any, his politics, his marital status, his friends, his women, boys, etc., drinking, dope, jobs—in fact, all facets of his life." The probe might require surveillance, he added, but only on the express order of Vincent Gillen.[44]

Everyone involved in the investigation understood its sensitivities. Rather than hire its own detective, General Motors had worked through a legal intermediary, shielding itself with attorney-client privilege. Danner and Gillen would also claim to be operating attorney to attorney, although an initial invoice was forwarded under the letterhead of Gillen's detective agency rather than on legal stationery. Gillen instructed his operatives to show caution: "We must be careful not to arouse the ire of Nader. Keep in mind that he is a brilliant fellow and a good writer and he could, no matter how unjustly, write something about us which would be rather damaging. Hence it is important that interviews be handled with great discretion and under a suitable pretext."[45]

As General Motors was setting up its investigation, its predicament with its critics was intensifying. Harry Philo had made contact with Robert F. Kennedy and his Democratic colleague Gaylord Nelson of Wisconsin. The senators were interested in Philo's Miami speech.

Kennedy circulated it to the Ribicoff subcommittee as information for future hearings, and pressed the Department of Commerce to look into the design of the Corvair and whether "remedial action for the remaining Corvairs still on the highway is desirable." Kennedy also began encouraging Corvair owners who had been in crashes to pursue litigation against General Motors and to seek publicity in doing so. When Philo, in his capacity as national chairman of the ATLA's safety committee, asked Kennedy to throw his weight behind the organization's new highway safety campaign, the senator gladly complied.[46]

The ATLA's campaign was a new pitch of safety activism. While ostensibly concerned with reducing the highway death toll, it served to institutionalize the Nader-Ribicoff claim that Detroit's "lethal" product designs were premeditated and responsible for killing fifty thousand Americans a year. Its slogan was "Stop Murder by Motor." Daniel Patrick Moynihan, who was then preparing an article for *The Public Interest* denouncing the "brute greed and moral imbecility" of the auto industry, was invited to deliver the keynote at the campaign's launch on February 2, 1966. Ralph Nader made an appearance, and Senator Kennedy commended the ATLA's focus on traffic safety, "perhaps the greatest of the nation's public health problems," and its particular emphasis on the "sacred cow" of vehicle design.[47]

Here was the new General Motors nightmare. Its disparate enemies, legal, political, and journalistic, had found each other and were collaborating against the corporation. They were developing and amplifying one another's arguments and compounding one another's legitimacy. They were vilifying the Corvair, disgracing the corporation, and threatening it with still more legal pressure and federal regulation. It boggled G.M.'s collective mind that a rabid author/attorney and people it regarded as ambulance chasers had more pull in certain legislatures than the world's largest corporation, yet it could not be denied. DeLorenzo had been on the money with his assessment that G.M. and its executives were targets of an organized and vicious campaign: they were now being publicly accused of murder. And right in the middle of it all was the relentless, inexplicable figure of Ralph Nader. "He was all around us," lamented a G.M. lawyer.[48]

CHAPTER 10

ANARCHY ON WHEELS

Lyndon Johnson had demonstrated enormous personal restraint in the aftermath of the assassination of his predecessor, John F. Kennedy. His public manner was solemn, his voice soft and controlled. It was an unaccustomed and uncomfortable pose for perhaps the most excitable of White House occupants yet he held it for four months, until Easter weekend 1964 when he invited members of the press to his sprawling Hill Country ranch on the north banks of the Pedernales River, just down the road from his boyhood home in Johnson City, Texas. There, he finally cut loose.[1]

Eager to show off his 2,700-acre spread and its pigs, Angora goats, and Hereford cattle, he jumped behind the wheel of a late-model Lincoln Continental convertible, cream-colored with suicide doors. A cup of Pearl beer in hand, he waited impatiently as four reporters, three female and one male, piled into his passenger seats. "Whoooee!" he yelled. "Whoooee!" Stepping on the gas, he jounced the car over open fields, dodging livestock and dung heaps. "The cows are fat," he shouted. "The grass is green. The river's full, and the fish are flopping!"[2]

Johnson pushed a button beneath his dashboard to blow a horn that sounded like a bellowing cow, stampeding his heifers. He treated the ladies in the backseat to a graphic account of the mating life of a prize bull. "Mr. President, you're fun!" gushed Marianne Means, a Hearst newspaper correspondent who had recently finished the first of her five marriages and who was reputed a mistress of John Kennedy (in fact, she had been sleeping with one of JFK's press secretaries). Mr. President met her smitten gaze and, having finished his beer, filled his cup from hers.[3]

Trailing in the Lincoln's dust were five other vehicles, including one driven by the president's wife, Lady Bird, who, like her husband, clutched a Pearl in her non-steering hand, but neither she nor the Secret Service detail could hold the presidential pace. As Johnson hit the two-lane highway and cruised along at eighty-five or ninety miles per hour (the local limit was seventy) a reporter in the car commented on his speed. Rather than slowing, the leader of the free world took off his broad-brimmed hat and used it to cover his speedometer. Coming up behind two vehicles traveling near the legal limit on a long rise, he veered into the left lane to pass and remained there as he approached the crest of the hill. A surprised driver coming in the other direction swerved off the pavement to avoid a presidential collision. Said a reporter alert to the line of succession in an administration with no vice president: "That's the closest [House Speaker] John McCormack has come to the White House." Johnson, amused, ventured that McCormack would make a fine commander-in-chief.[4]

LBJ's neighbors were accustomed to his reckless ways. "Lyndon enjoys fast boats and fast cars," said an Austin businessman. "He took me on a motor boat ride when he was vice-president. He was real happy when he gunned her and we lost the Secret Service men trying to follow us in another power boat." But apart from Ms. Means, who became a regular private visitor to the Johnson White House, the press corps was affronted. "I have been assigned to covering presidents since the Truman Era," said a White House photographer. "I have never gone through a more frightening and impossible effort. I was keeping up with him at one point. I looked at my speedometer and it read 90." Added a reporter: "I have no doubt that Mr. Johnson is a good driver but accident statistics are high on the roads. Anything can happen. . . . The president should be using a chauffeur."[5]

Johnson was hurt that some of the invited reporters wrote about his driving escapades in the days following their visit. Newspapers from coast to coast clucked their tongues and reviewed a litany of previous episodes of scandalous presidential driving, starting with Ulysses S. Grant piloting his rig through the streets of Washington and challenging others to race, and ending with Eisenhower's limousine outrunning police cars on the way to his Gettysburg farm. When on April 4, 1964, Johnson was asked point-blank at a news conference about putting himself and his passengers in danger in his automobile, he waved off the question: "I am unaware that I have ever driven past seventy."[6]

As he began the second full year of his mandate in 1966, Johnson already had a litany of legislative accomplishments to his credit. Indeed, if volume of bills passed is the mark of a great reformer, he had better claim to the title than either Woodrow Wilson or his idol, Franklin Roosevelt. Yet just twelve months into his first full term, the ground was shifting fast under his administration and it was increasingly apparent that his Great Society was teetering. Despite preaching quality over quantity with respect to priorities in American life, Johnson had opted for quantity over quality in legislation, churning out more than a hundred bills of wildly uneven merit. For every triumph such as the Voting Rights Act of 1965 or the Immigration and Nationality Act of 1965, there were several others, including many measures in his celebrated War on Poverty, that were ill-conceived, poorly executed, underfunded, or otherwise destined to disappoint. A more prudent executive might have paused at the beginning of 1966 to consolidate gains and ensure his legacy, especially with the escalating war in Vietnam commanding greater shares of his attention and his budget. Not Johnson.

Even with interest rates rising and inflation threatening and tax hikes begging, he refused to accept that America could not simultaneously support a large-scale war and his ambitious social agenda. He took comfort in telling Americans they were "in the midst of the greatest upsurge of economic well-being in the history of any nation." The Gross National Product had increased by a third from 1960 to 1965 and personal incomes by slightly more. Corporate profits were high, farm incomes were high, wages were high, and unemployment was low. "Can we move ahead with the Great Society programs and at the same time meet our needs for defense?" he asked. "My confident answer . . . is yes." He insisted that Americans had fathomed the mysteries of economic growth and proved that "recessions are not inevitable." They had learned how to achieve prosperity and to sustain it and they now had to make the most of the opportunities it presented.[7]

In his State of the Union Address on January 12, 1966, days before the launch of the ATLA's Stop Murder by Motor campaign, Lyndon Johnson proposed 113 new measures ranging from efforts to clean up American cities to laws preventing discrimination in the housing market to the creation of a federal department of transportation. The latter had been telegraphed in 1964 and, indeed, kicked around Washington as far back as Eisenhower's 1961 budget address, but it was not until Detroit executives had been embarrassed before Ribicoff's panel that anyone had drafted a bill. That thirty-five different federal agencies were employing 100,000 people and spending $5 billion annually on transportation-related concerns "made it almost impossible to serve either the growing demands of this great Nation or the needs of the [transportation] industry," said Johnson. The speech also called for highway safety legislation to more specifically address "the destruction of life and property on our highways."[8]

There were so many new initiatives in the State of the Union that the transportation news was scarcely noticed by the media. A day later, Johnson was asked dozens of questions in a long press conference. None touched on transportation, never mind that the president had proposed to establish only the thirteenth executive department in the history of the Republic (and the second in two years after Housing and Urban Development in 1965).

Senators Ribicoff and Magnuson and other champions of an enhanced federal role in transport and road safety were exhilarated by Johnson's initiative and eager for more detail, which the president soon provided. The new department would bring together the Bureau of Public Roads, the Federal Aviation Agency, the Civil Aeronautics Board, the Great Lakes Pilotage Administration, and various other offices. It would rationalize and coordinate their activities, engage in new research and development, take advantage of new technology, clear institutional and political barriers to change, encourage industry to give the consumer more for his transportation dollar, and contribute to America's ongoing efforts to build a nation on vast and diverse lands. "In a nation that spans a continent," he said, "transportation is the web of union," the powerful $120 billion network on which prosperity and convenience depend. He further justified the department by pointing to expected growth in traffic on roads and in the skies in the decades ahead and the resulting threat of a "transportation paralysis."[9]

For the most part, the administration relied on the surface plausibility of the argument that centralized and rationalized federal agencies were better than scattered and loosely coordinated federal agencies. It asserted that a larger federal presence would alleviate the highway death toll and congestion in major urban centers but made little effort to explain precisely how these improvements would materialize, or how they would be measured. Nor did it explain what exactly was wrong with the existing system, which had met America's urgent postwar need for mobility during the greatest growth spurt in its history. Like Ribicoff and the advocates of a federal department who had appeared at his committee, the administration ignored the various interagency committees and interstate bodies that already existed to rationalize and coordinate policy across the country.

With so many bills in the hopper, speed was essential for Johnson on the transportation file, so there would be no task forces or commissions of inquiry or periods of study to demonstrate the need for the new department. Nor would the administration consider alternatives such as the Hoover commission's 1948 recommendation that the various federal transportation agencies be centralized within the Department of Commerce. In the rush for legislative trophies, much would have to be taken on faith.

The safety component of Johnson's transportation initiatives was embodied in two bills: the National Traffic and Motor Vehicle Safety Act, which allowed for the imposition of federal vehicle design standards, and the Highway Safety Act, which set standards for highway safety programs at the state level. These additional acts lent to Johnson's transportation package an emotional momentum that a bill creating a transportation department could never muster on its own. "There is no single statistic of American life more shocking than the toll of dead and injured on our highways," Johnson told Congress. "Each day we kill 135 of our fellow citizens—each year we injure three million more." The United States spends billions of dollars in medical research to conquer disease and prolong life "yet we still put up with the senseless slaughter of thousands of Americans on our highways." The president spoke of "families stung by grief" and projected that if trends held, "one out of every two Americans will one day be killed or seriously injured on our highways." He noted that more Americans had died on the roads than in all of the nation's wars, and averred that there was "cause for sacrifice in Vietnam" but "no cause for suicide at home." America must "replace suicide with sanity and anarchy with safety."[10]

Like some of Ribicoff's witnesses, the president asserted that the safety problem and the death toll were revelations and that safety officials were either ignorant of highway butchery or standing idly by in hopes that the situation would improve on its own. He said that the auto industry had not made safety a priority. His employment of the phrase "we kill" suggested something deliberate about the traffic toll, and while he did not speak of a traffic safety establishment, his promise to reorganize the President's Committee for Traffic Safety and support it entirely by federal funds echoed Nader's assertion that existing safety agencies had been co-opted by the automobile industry.[11]

Johnson promised that his safety act would give particular attention to research into the causes of highway crashes because the present state of knowledge was "grossly inadequate." He nevertheless felt comfortable calling for comprehensive legislation with $700 million in new money attached to it. As though acknowledging the inadequacy of the government's grasp on the problem, he threw that money in every conceivable direction, asking for more collision data collection, better emergency medical services, more support for state and local safety programs. There would be new funds for the three discredited E's—driver education, engineering, and enforcement—as well as for second-collision priorities.[12]

Despite the scattershot approach, Johnson made clear that the core objective of his legislation was regulation of the automobile itself. "Proper design and engineering can make our cars safer," he promised. "Vehicles sold in interstate commerce must be designed and equipped for maximum safety." He asked the General Services Administration to begin "a detailed study of the additional vehicle safety features" that should be required for the federal fleet. He recommended that the Commerce Department be given authority to determine the safety performance criteria for all vehicles sold. If, after two years, the secretary of commerce felt that voluntary standards had failed to move Detroit to significant improvements, he would prescribe nationwide mandatory safety standards and prohibit the sale of new vehicles failing to meet his standards. Not even the threat of federal regulation of the nation's most important industry lifted the proposed legislation to the status of a major story.[13]

Days later, the president continued to use strong language on traffic safety in his letter to the American Trial Lawyers Association at the launch of its Stop Murder by Motor campaign. "You and I know that the gravest problem before this nation—next to war in Vietnam—is the death and destruction, the shocking and senseless carnage that strikes daily on our highways. . . . There can be no excuse for a nation that tolerates such anarchy on wheels."[14]

While those convinced of the centrality of second-collision theory and keen to see Detroit regulated were happy with Johnson's attention to safety, his suggestion that the industry be allowed time to voluntarily raise its game was unwelcome. A two-year delay in implementing high standards for crashworthiness, they argued, was tantamount to sentencing another 100,000 Americans to die. They were determined that the final drafts of the administration's safety package be as tough and immediate as possible. With Johnson aiming to sign legislation before the November midterm elections, which could erode his command over both chambers of Congress, the crusaders' challenge was to make the emotional momentum behind the proposed bills so powerful that none could stand in its way.

While appearing at state safety hearings in Iowa early in 1966, Ralph Nader began to think he was being followed. "I had a feeling," he said, "that I was under surveillance in Des Moines between the dates of January 7 and January 13. It took the form of a kind of uneasy feeling [regarding] a gentleman who was in my vicinity twice on the first floor of the Hotel Kirkwood and once outside my room on one of the upstairs floors." Despite a lack of evidence, Nader could not shake his suspicions of a tail. He took them to his host, Attorney General Scalise, who, having no experience of Nader's paranoiac tendencies, was alarmed that someone might be attempting to harass his witness. The Iowa Bureau of Criminal Investigation was alerted. It found nothing worth investigating and dropped the matter.[15]

Nader was not being followed in Des Moines, at least not by G.M.'s investigator, Vince Gillen, who had only been hired on the last day of the author's Iowa testimony. The detective's investigation was slow to take shape. On January 25, his men conducted interviews in the Winsted-Hartford area but not a single person they contacted knew where Nader could be found. It was thought he might be in Washington. Gillen sent a work request to another former FBI agent, David Shatraw, at Arundel Investigative Agency in the D.C. satellite of Severna Park. Shatraw took the job but as late as February 3 had yet to locate Nader.[16]

Over the next several weeks, Gillen and his investigators spoke to fifty or sixty people in Winsted, Boston, and Washington. They interviewed Nader's neighbors, classmates, teachers, editors, and public service colleagues, and learned, as O'Neill had before them, that their subject was widely regarded as intelligent, hardworking, and uncontroversial in his personal affairs. Typical of the interviewees was the publisher of the Winsted newspaper, who said Ralph was a "fine man," not at all like his brother, Shafeek, or his father, Nathra, who were "the type of people that if you throw them in the river will float upstream." Vale and others attributed anti-Semitic attitudes to Shafeek and Nathra but virtually everyone in town cautioned against visiting those sins upon Ralph. Interviews of Princeton and Cambridge associates were similarly complimentary to Nader.[17]

Gillen drove to Concord, New Hampshire, to speak with Nader's Harvard classmate Frederick Hughes Condon, to whom *Unsafe at Any Speed* is dedicated. Not long after his graduation, Condon had fallen asleep at the wheel of a Plymouth station wagon and overturned in a ditch, leaving him paraplegic. Now working as an insurance executive, he told Gillen that Nader was "intelligent, capable, modest, and hard-working," that he had a fine character and no known political affiliations. Asked why his friend was not married, Condon picked up the inference of homosexuality (sodomy was still illegal in the vast majority of states), denied it, and said that Nader had not yet met the right girl.[18]

Condon saw that Gillen kept a tan briefcase on his lap throughout their conversation. He thought it might conceal a tape recorder. It did not, but the investigator suspected Condon had one. As he was leaving the office, Gillen tried to pry from Condon anything he knew about Nader's driving record, including whether he had a license. The detective left empty-handed.[19]

More productive were interviews with Nader's former Washington associates. Frank McElroy was chief of the Office of Industrial Hazards at the Department of Labor while Nader was employed by Moynihan. Responsible for compiling statistics on occupational injuries, McElroy's unit was diverted by Moynihan to gather and analyze traffic safety statistics. Moynihan was "furious," McElroy recalled, when the gathered numbers did not conform with the outcomes he had expected. "Moynihan was very critical of me and . . . claimed that none of the statistics were worth the paper they were written on." Nader also reviewed the unit's results and agreed with Moynihan. McElroy remembered both men going out of their way to gather all possible information related to traffic injuries from private organizations and other government agencies and being "not only critical of the committees or units that gathered these records, whether private or governmental, but of the people who did the work." He felt they were out to get the auto industry. "Nader really has an ax to grind when it comes to the automotive industry," he said.[20]

Another Labor official, Robert Gidel, director of the Occupational Safety office in the Bureau of Labor Standards, resented that Nader had been billed to his office when he worked exclusively for Moynihan. It also rankled that Nader was appointed as a consultant rather than having to compete for a staff position which would have exposed his lack of qualifications and experience, and that Nader was paid at a Grade 15 level, which amounted to a handsome $15,000-plus annual income (the average U.S. household income in 1964 was $6,590). Gidel said that Nader was on the Labor payroll for a year and a half, right through to the fall of 1965, covering the period during which he was volunteering as a consultant to Ribicoff, and the period during which he did much of the research and writing of his book. Gidel was correct: Nader was paid $60 a day for two concurrent appointments that stretched from April 30, 1964, to October 24, 1965, days before the publication of *Unsafe at Any Speed*.[21]

One of the best leads uncovered by the investigation, so far as Gillen was concerned, was that Nader had helped Connecticut representative George Eddy prepare bills on traffic safety, and testified in favor of those bills as an independent witness without disclosing his handiwork. This suggested that Nader, long before the Ribicoff hearings, had prejudicially blurred the line between witness and advocate. "That would make him look pretty silly," wrote Gillen, "if he . . . was promoting his own bills and suppressing that from the legislature."

Another interesting finding came from the branch manager of Hirsch & Co., a brokerage with offices on 17th Street NW in Washington, who said that Nader had become a client in July 1965, around the time the Big Three were testifying before Ribicoff's subcommittee. One of the four stocks held by Nader, said the manager, was Ford Motor Company. The detectives suspected that the author might have been trying to profit from the damage done to G.M. at the hearings by holding shares in its main competitor.[22]

Largely because of his investigation's slow start, Gillen, with little to show his impatient client, resorted earlier than he had anticipated to placing Nader under surveillance. The Arundel agency had finally located Nader at his Washington rooming house but by February 6 quit the job, pleading a heavy workload. Gillen sent two men of his own to pick up where Arundel left off. It was tedious work, and unproductive. At 1 p.m. on February 7, for instance, the detectives followed their subject from his rooming house to his bank to the National Press Building. They noted that Nader wore a gray coat, a green-and-white plaid scarf, gray suede gloves, and no hat despite the cold. He carried in his hand a manila envelope. Once inside the National Press Building, "he walked to a retaining wall containing floral decorations, set down the manila envelope (8x12) . . . and for perhaps thirty seconds engaged himself in tying his shoelaces, both left and right." He picked up the envelope, the contents of which were never discovered, and through a side door entered Costin's Sirloin Room. He ate an uneventful lunch.[23]

On February 9, Gillen decided that the double-shift surveillance was an expensive waste of time and canceled it. He did, however, continue with spot surveillance, which was supposed to commence on February 10 when Nader was scheduled to step out of the shadows and appear as a witness before Ribicoff's subcommittee. It was his preparations for this appearance that had kept Nader indoors for much of the week, frustrating the surveillors. By the time Gillen's men contacted the Senate office and learned the time of Nader's appearance, they were too late. The witness was almost finished.[24]

The next day, a detective saw Nader emerge from his rooming house at 1:20 p.m. and followed him to the New Senate Office Building but lost his trail indoors. The detective gave a description of Nader to a guard inside the entrance but the guard, mistaking a news reporter who looked like Nader for the genuine article, pointed him in the wrong direction. Worried that he could not cover so large a building alone, Gillen's man called an associate to join him. The two men lurked in the corridors for about forty-five minutes until a Capitol police officer asked them what they were up to. Working, they said. The officer asked them to leave, and they did. It was yet another unproductive day.[25]

Gillen sent reports once or twice a week to his intermediary, Richard Danner, who forwarded them to Detroit, where they were read with great interest and, as the weeks passed, disappointment. While Nader's connection to the Corvair suits was one focus of the investigation, it was not all that interested General Motors. Eileen Murphy, in her communications with Danner, had wanted to know about Nader's associates, his personal habits and relationships, whether he drank or used drugs. She had not come out and asked for dirt but it was clear from her instructions that dirt was wanted by G.M., and as February drew to a close Danner and Gillen had delivered precious little in the way of dirt or even new information. She expressed her displeasure to Danner:

I am still disappointed with the odds and ends we are receiving. It strikes me that the reporting is being duplicated by two or three people doing the same thing but not knowing of each other. It also strikes me that everyone is going overboard to impress us with what a great, charming intellectual this human being is—Eagle Scout type. There are too many variances for this to be accurate. One does not place 396 out of 462 in [his Harvard] class and be a hot shot at everything he is supposed to have undertaken.[26]

Murphy asked that Nader's military record be scrutinized. "What did he do for six months in the Army? What type of discharge did he receive?" She wanted more on Nader's driving record and any collisions in which he had been involved, and more on how he had come to be employed at the Labor Department. She had read in the Ribicoff subcommittee transcripts Nader's unsupported anecdote of a child decapitated by a glove compartment door during an auto crash. "See if this gem can be uncovered as to where, when or how he was involved." Murphy also suggested a look at certain aspects of Nader's freelance writing career. "Well friend," she signed off, "have fun. I will be talking to you. Call if anything great appears."[27]

For Murphy, the pursuit of Nader was not personal. She admired his stamina and devotion to his cause. "I really, in a way, enjoyed what he was doing. I'd say, 'Keep it up, baby!' or 'Keep it up, Ralphie baby!'" For Murphy, Nader was a professional challenge. She knew that he was sharing information and arguments with Corvair plaintiff's attorneys and that he was supporting the ATLA's Stop Murder by Motor campaign. She knew of his recent long article in *American Jurisprudence Proof of Facts*, and a 1965 piece in the ATLA's *Trial* magazine where he described auto crashes as an "epidemic of blitzkrieg proportions" and "an assault on the biosphere," and lectured his readers on how to bring evidence in design liability cases, using the Corvair as his chief example. This was firm evidence that Nader was goading, directing, and applauding the plaintiff's attorneys but it did not mean that he had a stake in the litigation against the corporation, which is what the legal department most wanted to prove.[28]

What looked like G.M.'s best lead was that the American Trial Lawyers Association had been promoting Nader as an expert in Corvair litigation to its 25,000 members. When an Oklahoma lawyer wrote the ATLA in June 1965 looking for help, Thomas Lambert, an ATLA editor, said that Nader was working for lawyers representing litigants in Corvair design cases (which turned out to be untrue) and offered up his services: "We also suggest that you write to Ralph Nader, 53 Hillside Avenue, Winsted, Connecticut. Ralph is a lawyer who has developed expertise in the area of automobile manufacturer liability. Ralph has a substantial amount of information on the Corvair." An attorney in Amarillo, Texas, received similar assistance from Lambert, and Nader's name and expertise were also noted in an ATLA newsletter. While the ATLA maintained lists of experts on such items as defective lawnmowers, exploding bottles, and poisonous hair dyes, Nader appeared to be the only Corvair design expert promoted by the organization.[29]

Better still, from the automaker's perspective, Nader was named as counsel on a brief on appeal in another auto liability suit: *Barbara June Muncy and Charles Muncy v. General Motors Corp.* before the U.S. Court of Appeals Fifth Circuit. In that case, decided on April 10, 1964, the plaintiff was a pedestrian who had been hit by a runaway Chevrolet (not a Corvair) in which the ignition had not shut off after the driver had removed the key. The suit claimed G.M. had improperly designed the ignition switch. The jury had brought a verdict against General Motors, which was appealing the decision. G.M.'s counsel saw this as evidence that Nader had a stake in design lawsuits against their company.[30]

All of this work, like Gillen's investigation, was performed delicately. G.M. shared the investigator's view that it was best not to arouse the ire of Nader or anyone with whom he was associated, whether plaintiff's attorneys or U.S. senators.

Nevertheless, Gillen's investigators themselves came under scrutiny in the month of February. Word spread quickly among interested parties that two detectives had been evicted from the New Senate Office Building while tailing Nader. A Capitol policeman who owed his position to Ribicoff's patronage informed Jerome Sonosky of the incident. A second Capitol policeman, Marshall Speakes, pulled Nader aside as he was leaving the building to tell him what had happened. On learning of the operation, Nader decided to go to the press, as Gillen had feared he might.[31]

Washington Post journalist Morton Mintz was at his desk on Saturday morning, February 12, when his phone rang and a receptionist told him a Mr. Nader was waiting downstairs to see him. An investigative reporter known for his work on Thalidomide, the hazardous morning sickness drug, Mintz covered the consumer affairs beat at the paper and was celebrated by his peers for his "capacity for indignation." Nader had read him and liked his style. He introduced himself to the reporter and said that a Capitol policeman had just confirmed his suspicions that he had been under surveillance in recent weeks. Mintz heard him out but did not feel Nader's claims warranted a story. He said he would look into it, and he did. He found the policeman, Marshall Speakes, who confirmed to the reporter what he had told Nader but added nothing more.[32]

Mintz still doubted he had a story when, late in the day, he relayed what he had heard to Laurence Stern, his news editor. Stern was startled. He had just spoken to another *Post* reporter, Bryce Nelson, who had been told by a Capitol policeman at the Senate Office Building that *he* was being followed. Tall, dark, and lanky, Nelson was the newsman who had been mistaken for Nader. Putting these pieces together, Mintz wrote a story for the next day's paper: "Car Safety Critic Nader Reports Being Tailed." He recounted the policeman's mistaking Nelson for Ribicoff's witness and added that Nader suspected the detectives were employed by an automaker because his book dealt harshly with the industry.[33]

The implications of an automaker spying on Ribicoff's witness were immediately clear to G.M.'s opponents. Sonosky would later claim that on hearing of the tail, he picked up the phone and told Ribicoff that they were guaranteed to get strong safety legislation as a result. Nader, too, felt it was a big story—bigger than the *Post* had reported. A number of his acquaintances had been in touch to congratulate him on being in line for a significant employment opportunity. They had been interviewed by individuals posing as representatives of a prospective employer, one Nader was sure did not exist. His friend Fred Condon, who had not fallen for the employment pretext, called to warn him that Gillen was poking around. Furthermore, Richard Grossman had heard from Dexter Masters, who reviewed *Unsafe at Any Speed* in *Consumer Reports* magazine, that a "smooth-talking fellow" from something called the "Gillian agency" was fishing for personal information about the book's author. Nader took this information, and more, to *The New Republic*.[34]

Nader had a knack for finding and earning the trust of journalists sympathetic to his causes. "When I get a story from Ralph," said one, "I don't have to double-check his facts." *The New Republic* was a small-circulation liberal magazine of ancient and respectable lineage. Influential in the first half of the twentieth century, it had found itself marginalized during the Eisenhower years. Much like its occasional contributor Arthur Schlesinger Jr., it had enjoyed a rebirth with the election of Kennedy, whom the editors had supported and who was seen carrying a copy of the magazine aboard Air Force One. By the mid-1960s, *The New Republic* was flirting with the New Left, a loose coalition of radical and Marxist activists and intellectuals dubbed "new" by C. Wright Mills to distinguish them from the traditional left and its obsessions with labor issues. The magazine's opinions were becoming more provocative and its investigations harder hitting. The reporter James Ridgeway was a rising star at *The New Republic*, thanks in part to his friendship with Ralph Nader.[35]

Like Mintz of *The Washington Post*, Ridgeway found Nader to be idealistic, earnest, comprehensive in his research, colorful in his quotes, and politically compatible. He appeared to have no institutional attachments and professed no political ambition. That he treated all of his information as closely guarded secrets and was reluctant to share his telephone number made him seem authentic. Nader had spoon-fed Ridgeway the information for his August 24, 1964, article in *The New Republic* entitled "The Corvair Tragedy," the same piece that had convinced Grossman to sign Nader to a book deal. Now Nader walked through Ridgeway's door again with something that promised to be far more explosive.

CHAPTER 11

EXPOSED

The event at the New Senate Office Building missed by Gillen's tardy detectives was Ralph Nader's star turn as witness before Senator Ribicoff's ongoing hearings into the federal role in traffic safety. It was February 10, 1966, and the hearing room was packed. Nader was just three minutes into his presentation, speaking quickly, punctuating his points by chopping the air with his hand. "The 1966 Ford advertisements boast of 'engineering magic,'" he said. "The expectant reader . . . learns that this 'magic' is composed of an optional stereosonic tape system and a station wagon tailgate that swings open for people and pulls down for cargo. With such 'magic' our space endeavors would have gotten us no further to the moon than Mount Everest."[1]

From empty promises, Nader moved to the viciousness of automobile advertisements he claimed were intended to "stir the animal" in the car buyer. "It is aimed not at the reason of men but at their ids and hypogastria. Can there by anything less than a fundamental contempt for the consumer in the following advertisements . . ."[2]

"I don't like to interrupt," said Senator Carl Curtis of Nebraska, interrupting for the second time already.

"Yes, sir," said Nader

"But I don't understand your language. 'It is aimed not at the reason of men but at their ids and hypogastria'? If I ever bought a car for those reasons, nobody explained it to me."[3]

Nader elucidated Freud's concept of the id and located the hypogastria in the lower region of the abdomen.

Curtis shook his bald head: "The id refers to the subconscious aggressive pattern?"

"Yes, sir."

"I want a car that I can really hit somebody with and smash him dead, is that what you mean?"[4]

Nader brushed aside the question and began reciting lines from automotive advertisements: the Buick Skylark was a "Son of a Gun"; the Buick Riviera was a "red-blooded car that makes hearts beat faster and the adrenalin flow"; another vehicle was "cheaper than psychiatry"; another ad encouraged buyers to "drive it like you hate it."[5]

Nader next lit into the "aggressive and ferocious" brand names with which Detroit christened automobiles: Thunderbird, Cobra, Mustang, Wildcat, Cougar, Barracuda, the Plymouth Fury, and the Marauder, "which means literally 'one who pillages and lays waste the countryside.'"[6]

"Now, let me ask you," Curtis interjected again, "what does the name of an automobile have to do with the solid construction there or lack thereof?"

Nader said he was making the point that advertisements and names reflect the automobile manufacturers' view of their products. Detroit was living in and encouraging a "dreamboat fairyland" appealing to man's basest instincts and distracting attention from the fact that cars are "a form of transportation that kills."

"You've kind of lost me. I listen to radio and it tells me to put a tiger in my tank," said Curtis, referring to a long-running Esso gasoline campaign. "Does that make me a dangerous driver?"

"Senator," replied Nader, "the reception of the audience to the advertisements is not a uniform one. I would be the first to agree that you would not be within the most impressional class of receivers of this information."[7]

They quarreled briefly about how "impressional" and "unsophisticated" the driving public might be, after which Nader was allowed to read two more pages from his statement unmolested.

He was beginning to address the liability of automakers for faulty design when Curtis struck again.

"Are you a lawyer?"

"Yes, sir."

"Have you sent out any advertising to lawyers or others or any announcements making yourself available as a consultant with reference to litigation in this area?"

"Are you asking that question directly of me?"

"Yes."

"Or of another group?"

"You," said Curtis.

"Have I sent out circulars saying that I would be a consultant in litigation dealing with these problems? No sir."

"Has anyone sent out any for you?"

"Not to my knowledge."

"I want to know whether or not lawyers or a single lawyer has been informed through some type of advertising direct or otherwise of your talents and availability as a consultant in litigations involving accidents where cars are involved."

"I know of no such advertisements, Senator. It would be highly unethical."[8]

With that last sequence of questions, Senator Curtis, the pudgy, folksy former country lawyer and conservative Republican from Nebraska who had been skeptical of Abraham Ribicoff's hearings from their start, revealed himself to be not merely a partisan of plain English, a defender of the common sense of common people, a skeptic of contemporary psychological theory as applied to auto advertising, and a stickler for ethics, but a voice of American automakers and, in all probability, General Motors, whose legal department had earlier spotted the promotion of Nader's services in an American Trial Lawyers Association publication. Curtis is unlikely to have fallen upon this specific line of questioning on his own.

Although unable to get Nader to confess to any crossing of lines, Curtis had put on record his suspicion that the witness was compromised by association with personal injury lawyers. And he kept at it. When Nader indicted Detroit's designs, Curtis quoted experts claiming that fewer than 20 percent of car crashes could be attributed to the vehicle and its mechanics, and that most of those

were due to improper maintenance. He objected to Nader's claim in
the first line of *Unsafe at Any Speed* that "the automobile has brought
death, injury, and the most inestimable sorrow and deprivation to
millions of people." If car design, rather than reckless driving, was
the major cause of death and injury, said Curtis, people would refuse
to get behind the wheel.

The public, answered Nader, might indeed be more reluctant to
drive if it understood that automobiles were ill-equipped to protect
occupants in the inevitability of a crash.[9]

Point by point, Curtis kept up his challenges, undermining the
witness's composure and ruining the momentum of his address. It
was not what had been intended by Jerome Sonosky, Nader's sponsor at the subcommittee. Keen to make a leading man of Nader, or
at least to canonize *Unsafe at Any Speed*, Sonosky wanted something
like Rachel Carson's visit to Capitol Hill in 1963, a reverential affair
that none had dared interrupt. Instead, Nader's appearance was
combative and disjointed.

Sonosky kept an eye on Senators Ribicoff and Kennedy, wondering if they would intervene, but they seemed content to hold fire
and leave the fight to Nader. At least, they did until Curtis wandered
into dangerous terrain.

"Have you ever been an employee of this committee?" asked the
Nebraskan.

"No, Senator," said Nader.

"Have you ever been a consultant?"

"I have not been a paid consultant to the committee. Let me
explain."

"Have you been a consultant to them or any member or any part
thereof . . ."

"Why don't you let the witness answer?" asked Kennedy.[10]

Nader replied to Curtis that Senate committees have limited
staff resources, making it incumbent on any citizen possessing
knowledge of a particular problem and proposals for its solution to
make this information known, "candidly and forthrightly." So he
had offered his assistance to the subcommittee and its staff.[11]

"Did you give time to the staff?" asked Curtis.

"In what way, Senator?

"In assisting this committee with the subject."

"My efforts were only in the sense of putting forth what I thought were relevant facts to the subject of inquiry."[12]

Curtis demanded to know when Nader had joined the subcommittee. The witness said he had joined in the early summer of 1965 and worked off and on until late summer.

"Have you ever been an employee or a consultant of any branch of the federal government?" asked Curtis.[13]

Nader, who like other witnesses had not been placed under oath, admitted to having been employed as a paid consultant to the Department of Labor on and off between the middle of 1964 and the spring of 1965, working on traffic safety. His approximate answer hid approximately half of his tenure.

"When did you do the work on this book?" asked Curtis.

"That book, Senator, had its gestation almost a decade ago when I saw a little girl decapitated when a glove compartment door opened in a car that collided at fifteen miles per hour."[14]

It was an answer designed to forestall follow-up questions but Curtis pressed on, unperturbed, possibly aware that G.M.'s investigators were beginning to doubt that the decapitated girl (or almost-decapitated girl, in other Nader tellings, sometimes at fifteen miles per hour, other times at twenty-five miles per hour) had never existed: "When did you do the work on this book?"[15]

"The writing of the book was done early in the sixties and in the early part of 1965."

The senator said he was curious as to how Nader could have written a book while working for the Labor Department and volunteering for the subcommittee, and he was obviously intrigued by the possibility of connections or overlap between these endeavors, and between Moynihan's office and Ribicoff's staff. He did not appear to have the whole story but he was nearing uncomfortable truths: that Nader had done substantial research for *Unsafe at Any Speed* while at Labor and that an early draft of the book was written there; that Nader was employed for longer than he was admitting; that he was being paid by Moynihan in Labor as he volunteered with Sonosky. Curtis may not have known that Nader was Sonosky's prime resource at the subcommittee but he seemed to appreciate that Nader was not as advertised, and in cahoots with Moynihan and Ribicoff.

Had Nader known that he would have a book to promote when he volunteered for the subcommittee? asked Curtis. Well aware that Richard Grossman had initially scheduled the book's release to coincide with the opening of the hearings, Nader, after some dodging, coughed up a "Yes."[16]

"Will the Senator yield?" asked Ribicoff.

"Yes," said Curtis.

"The first time I ever saw Mr. Nader," said Ribicoff, "is when he walked into this room today."[17]

It was an odd statement, an answer to a question that no one had asked. It revealed Ribicoff's sensitivity to the ethics of the situation, as did a lengthy follow-up in which he tried to present Nader as a random expert who had stumbled in and out of the subcommittee's offices leaving hardly a trace:

> My understanding is that Mr. Nader came around and talked to the staff of this subcommittee about this problem. Representatives of the manufacturers of automobiles, I would say, are in the committee staff's office much more than Mr. Nader. . . . The subcommittee's staff is courteous, listens to all points of view for or against any proposal. I would hope that anyone that had anything to offer of a constructive nature would come to the subcommittee staff and that the subcommittee staff would be courteous to anyone that came in. Mr. Nader never received any compensation for coming and talking with the staff. The staff is available to all the members of the subcommittee, and anyone else interested in the problems of traffic safety no matter who they may be.*

Kennedy, also alarmed at the direction of Curtis's questions, tried a filibuster on the author's merits. He commended Nader for working in the Department of Labor, and for assisting the subcommittee, and for writing his book. He protested Curtis's implication

---

* Some of his interview subjects had left Vincent Gillen with a clear impression that Ralph Nader and Senator Ribicoff had indeed met before this appearance. No evidence to that effect has been produced. Gillen Memo, December 26, 1966, Gillen Papers, Baker Library, Harvard.

of wrongdoing, which he exaggerated to put the Nebraskan on the defensive. "As I hear the questioning of Mr. Nader, it sounds like he is a criminal of some sort, or is guilty of some crime," said Kennedy. "I am surprised, if I may say so, there seems to be a concerted effort to prevent Mr. Nader from giving his testimony before this committee."[18]

Curtis calmly countered that he had not accused Nader of any crimes but was curious about his self-interest.

"How many books have you sold?" he asked the author

"I don't see that that has the slightest bit to do with this," said Kennedy.

"Well, I do. I think that he . . . is using this forum here to sell books."[19]

The witness was saved by a bell ringing to call senators to a vote.

When the panel reconvened after a long recess, Nader was permitted to read the rest of his statement, with its warning that America was committing "extinction by automobile," into the record without obstruction. He held nothing back, stating his belief in an organized scheme to prevent investigation of the automobile's role in road carnage and calling for criminal penalties for manufacture of "a defective automobile dangerous to life." He piled on technical language and obscure vocabulary, and toward the end placed on the record a series of patent applications that to his mind proved that automakers had more and better safety technology than they were using. When the author was finished, Ribicoff led him through a series of questions in answer to which Nader suggested that automakers, led by General Motors, had a secret gentleman's agreement to retard progress on safety research and development.[20]

Strangely, Ribicoff also waltzed Nader through a staged admission that *Unsafe at Any Speed* contained a significant error. Nader had quoted a G.M. engineering journal as saying that door latches were "dictated by styling requirements." This was evidence in support of Nader's core thesis that styling took precedence over safety in Detroit. The senator asked why the author had left out another sentence that read, "Since no compromise can be made to safety, it is established policy to design from the strength standpoint so as to make the lock as rugged and durable as possible." Ribicoff might also have asked why Nader had put two sentences together from different pages in the engineering journal to construct his evidence, eliminating important words and another sentence that stated that safety, reliability, operating ease, and reasonable cost, in that order, were "the most important considerations" in deciding the means of latching. Clearly prepared for the question, Nader answered good-naturedly:[21]

> I must say, Senator, you certainly have looked the book over carefully. I don't have the article in front of me, but I will certainly accept your statement that there were missing after the first sentence several dots indicating intermittent material. I will also say that while I have to take responsibility for this, it must have been a typographical error. I am very careful in taking statements of that kind and putting them as they appear. When books are published, you get typographical errors. In the index, there is Stupebaker instead of Studebaker. I am sorry. That will be corrected in the next printing, if there is one.[22]

Having enabled Nader to dismiss as an innocent typesetting error what might otherwise have appeared as a willful act of misrepresentation, and having dealt with the matter affably before his enemies could confront him, Ribicoff and Kennedy continued to throw softballs at the witness until the senator from Nebraska, as though waking from a midday nap, put himself back on the case.

Curtis picked up Nader's comment about a lack of reliable data on automobile collisions and got him to agree that policymakers needed more objective and accurate information before they could hope to understand "the whole picture." He asked Nader if he had possessed the whole picture of what caused crashes when he wrote his book. The author acknowledged that he did not have the whole picture but believed he had enough information to support his conclusions. Unimpressed, the senator read with undisguised scorn from a section of *Unsafe at Any Speed* suggesting that medical, law enforcement, insurance, auto repair, and funeral services all have a vested interest in maintaining a high level of road carnage.

Nader said his meaning was simply that the energies and resources expended by those services in "wiping up the blood" of collisions should be devoted instead to prevention. Curtis insisted that a plain reading of the text meant the aforementioned professionals were thwarting safety measures to ensure the continuation of what Nader had called "economic demand for these services running into the billions of dollars."[23]

"What other bodies have you testified before?" asked Curtis.

"I have testified in Iowa," said Nader.[24]

Curtis quoted Attorney General Lawrence Scalise as saying in *The National Observer* that the immediate effect of his hearings "would be to give Iowa lawyers an important source of testimony that might be used in damage suits against manufacturers." Curtis read another quote from *The Des Moines Register* describing Scalise's initiative as an attempt to open up "a wide, new area of litigation" by demonstrating that auto design "plays a significant role in the deaths and injuries resulting through auto accidents."[25]

Without giving Nader an opportunity to respond to the implication that he and Scalise were tools of the plaintiff's attorneys, Curtis asked the author if he had ever referred to the *Automotive News* as "the only factual publication in the automotive field." Knowing where the senator was headed, Nader answered that "the article you are about to refer to was an extra departure from that tradition of responsible journalism." Curtis then read into the record comments from the *Automotive News* on *Unsafe at Any Speed:* "Yet, in quoting five times from the *Automotive News* in his book, almost always he selected the negative facts reported on any subject while ignoring completely the accompanying positive facts in the story." Nader insisted he had selected the relevant facts.[26]

"Now," continued Curtis, "the *Automotive News* on January 17 said this: 'But when Nader was repeatedly asked the key question: what percent of 1965 highway deaths and injuries were caused by car design, he was unable to answer.'"

"It is not correct. That is one of many distortions," said Nader.

"All right, how many of the injuries and deaths that occurred in 1965 were caused by car designs?"[27]

Nader admitted "we don't have this information" but added that studies showed that three quarters of deaths and serious injuries occurred in collisions at under fifty miles per hour. The knowledge and technology exists, he said, to "easily build cars that will protect occupants up to that level of collision." Therefore, "seventy-five percent of motorist [deaths and] injuries were caused by car design." Curtis returned to his preferred data showing that 80 percent of crashes were caused by reckless driving, sparking a dispute over whether it was more important to prevent collisions or injuries.[28]

Making one last stab at connecting Nader to personal injury suits, Curtis said: "Now, I asked you before the recess if there had been any advertisements . . . directly or indirectly by you or by anybody else holding you up as a consultant for lawyers and litigants in reference to traffic accidents."

Nader stuck to his denial but this time used the opportunity to speak in defense of product liability law.

"The area of what I call the judicial protection of bodily rights is in its infancy," he said. It was only now being articulated, much as civil rights emerged in the 1950s, and just as civil rights required time to be accepted, he continued, body rights would be increasingly recognized as legitimate even if some people looked upon them with contempt and ridicule. There was "nothing dirty," said Nader, about holding manufacturers to account for negligent or defective product design. "I see nothing more proper than an attempt to articulate these rights, to bring the facts out into the public domain outside of the chrome curtain."[29]

"What is the chrome curtain?" asked Curtis.

"The chrome curtain is that which hovers around the automobile industry and makes it extremely difficult, for example, to ask the industry or the tire industry to give this legislative body and other Senate committees the test data that show whether their tires are safe or not safe."[30]

The Nebraskan seemed amused that Nader would adapt to the economic engine of America the Iron Curtain metaphor used to describe the nation's mortal enemies in the Soviet sphere. He asked if the National Safety Council, the Automotive Safety Foundation, and other organizations were behind the chrome curtain and encouraged Nader to speak at length on how some organizations were entirely behind the curtain, others had one leg behind it and the other in front, and still others stood in front of the curtain yet "accommodated to the principles that operate in the automobile industry and the traffic safety establishment."[31]

When Senator Kennedy announced that time was running out, Curtis asked to pose one more question. He wanted to know if Nader had bothered to interview automobile manufacturers and confront them with his complaints and charges before publishing them in a book. Nader said he did. When Curtis asked who he had met and when, Nader said he had attended two industry conferences, one in 1964 and another in 1965, but he could not name anyone to whom he had spoken before Kennedy announced, "The hearing is recessed."[32]

"Hello, Mr. Gillen. This is David Sanford at *The New Republic* magazine. I understand from Mr. Fred Condon and also from Mr. Dexter Masters that you have been making inquiries concerning a person by the name of Ralph Nader. I wonder what the reason for that investigation is—why are you doing it?"

"I have no hesitancy in telling you but I am puzzled as to why you are asking me," said Gillen. "I might ask you the same question."

"I know Mr. Nader."

"Oh, you do. What is your name, sir?"

"The name is David Sanford."

"You are with *The New Republic*—you one of their staff or what?"

"Yes, exactly."

"Are you the owner, or what?"

"Reporter—what is your agency's interest in regard to Mr. Nader?"

"That is the damnedest thing I've ever had asked me. I don't get your point. What is it in relation . . ."

"Why is it you are investigating Mr. Nader?"

"I return the compliment. Why are you asking me?"

"Well, I have already answered a couple of your questions. I want . . ."

"You told me your name and the fact you are with *The New Republic*."

"Right, and you have spoken with Dexter Masters and Fred Condon concerning Ralph Nader, right?"

"No."

"It's not?"

"No."

"I thought you just said it was."

"I have said we have made some inquiries regarding Nader. We make lots of inquiries."

"So what was the purpose of the inquiry?"

"I spoke with Hughes, I mean what's his name, Condon, myself. Another man in our organization spoke with Masters—are you—listen, Sanford, I have been in business a long while and I have never had a third person call me up and ask me why I am investigating a second person."

"Who employed you to make the inquiries about Ralph Nader?"

"Well, who employed you to ask me?"

"*The New Republic* employed me to ask you," Sanford laughed.

"Look, we don't divulge the clients. That's axiomatic, elementary in our business—you should know that."

"Were you employed by General Motors?"

"General Motors would be the last one to employ me for anything like that, I should imagine."[33]

Vincent Gillen surreptitiously recorded this conversation with *The New Republic*'s David Sanford on Monday, February 28, 1966. Despite his denials, Gillen knew that his cover story for the Nader investigation was thin and that he was near to being exposed. He appears to have immediately notified his client, Richard Danner, of the magazine's call. Danner appears to have alerted his client, General Motors. By day's end, Danner got back to Gillen to say that the operation was on hold.

In the next morning's mail, Gillen received a letter from Danner that had been written a few days earlier, advising him of Eileen Murphy's unhappiness with his results to date:

> I am attaching hereto a copy of a letter dated February 25, 1966 from our client. As you can gather from the letter and I certainly note from my telephonic conversations,

these people are not too happy with the investigation, nor am I. It just does not seem to me that good investigative techniques are being used and too much time has been spent in detailing long-winded dissertations on the same subject, namely, that Nader is a brilliant fellow who went to Princeton and to Harvard and who wrote a book. . . .

You know and I know from what we have learned to date about Nader that this fellow hasn't hit a lick of work in years, apparently living by his wits and he just couldn't be that perfect. Frankly, I think we are going to have trouble justifying your bills unless information is unearthed that hits a little closer to home wherein Nader's background is concerned. . . .

I think it would be well to stop interviewing Nader's friends, get to digging into his bank accounts, stock transactions, sources of income, etc., or if you think this is impossible, let me know and we will see what the client wants done.[34]

Notwithstanding the suspension of his investigation, Gillen wrote Danner a three-page single-spaced letter on March 3 to thank him for his candor and to say that it was "only through such a frank expression of views that we can best serve your client's interests." He stated his hope that some of the investigative reports his office had produced since the date of Eileen Murphy's complaint had addressed her concerns, and he shifted some of the blame for "long-winded dissertations" to G.M. with the suggestion that Miss Murphy might not be accustomed to reading investigative reports, which, of necessity, contain raw feeds of intelligence that overlap, reinforce, and sometimes contradict each other. He then warned that his investigation was coming under pressure from friends of Nader, and from the author himself: "We are dealing with a fellow who will seize upon anything to further his ends. The *Washington Post* item is an example. Everything that might be construed by Nader as having been done by us, he apparently attributes to us."[35]

It is inevitable, Gillen told Danner, that Nader will discover he is under watch. Unless a client is willing to bankroll an expensive

long-term investigation, or a detective is willing to breach the various state laws governing his trade, a subject is bound to learn that
inquiries are being made. It is then up to the investigators and the
client to stick to their cover story and "not get sucked into making
any admissions." Gillen enclosed with his letter a verbatim transcript of *The New Republic* phone call, a full report of his investigation, and a list of thirty-six additional leads that might be followed.
He said that Nader had been an "interesting and stimulating assignment" and that he hoped to be able to finish the job.[36]

He would not have the opportunity. At the very moment Gillen's
letter was making its way from New York to Washington, a new edition of *The New Republic* was landing on newsstands. On page eleven
was an article by James Ridgeway entitled "The Dick." Its opening
paragraph declared that Nader, who had been hoping that his book
would lead to a "knockdown public fight" with the auto industry,
instead found himself "locked in a subterranean struggle against an
uncertain enemy." From there, Ridgeway and his uncredited colleague, David Sanford, unleashed a series of claims that Nader had
been spied upon and harassed by shady figures thought to be linked
to the auto industry.[37]

The reporters retold the story of the investigators following
Nader into the New Senate Office Building and revealed that agents
from the Gillen-affiliated firms of Allied Investigating Service of
Washington and Management Consultants of Boston had visited
the author's friends and associates, asking personal and professional
questions under the guise of a pre-employment interview. It was
mentioned that Nader's landlady and his broker had been contacted.
Fred Condon's account of his face-to-face meeting with Gillen was
treated at length.

In addition to Nader's suspicions that he had been followed in
Iowa, the story described a similar incident on his return from an
appearance on *The Mike Douglas Show* in Philadelphia. Arriving at
the airport minutes before his flight's departure time of 3:30 p.m.,
Nader rushed to the gate and noticed that two men seated on a
bench nearby rose and followed him up the gangway. They took
seats near him and seemed to be interested in him. When the plane
landed at Washington's National Airport, Nader hurried into the

terminal, wove in and out of a number of doors, and jumped into a taxi. Watching the road behind him as he approached the city, he was satisfied that he had shaken the two men.[38]

Ridgeway reported that Nader had received odd phone calls at his rooming house in early February, including six on the evening of February 9, as he was writing his opening statement for his appearance before Ribicoff's subcommittee.

"Mr. Nader, this is Pan American," said one caller before hanging up.

"Why don't you go back to Connecticut, buddy-boy," said another.

On the evening of Sunday, February 20, the story continued, Nader walked up the street from his rooming house to a drugstore and was standing at the magazine rack when a young, attractive brunette approached him and said, "Pardon me. I know this sounds a little forward. I hope you don't mind, but can I talk to you?" She said a few of her friends often gathered to discuss foreign affairs and asked if Nader would join them. He politely refused with the excuse that he was from out of town. She persisted, saying there was a meeting that very night. Nader said he was not interested and turned his back. The girl left.

The following Wednesday afternoon, Nader stopped at a Safeway store near his home to buy a package of cookies. There were perhaps thirty people in the store, he told Ridgeway, including women, children, and a few single men. As he was standing in the cookie aisle, a young woman, blond and wearing slacks, approached him to say, "Excuse me, but I need some help. I've got to move something heavy into my apartment. There's no one to help me. I wonder if I can get you to give me a hand. It won't take much time. Will you help?" Nader said he was sorry but he was late for a meeting. This woman, too, persisted. "Please," she said. "It won't take long." Nader again refused. The woman turned straight around and left the store, although there were a number of other people in the aisles who might have helped her.

Nader told the magazine he believed the women were honey traps, and that "the auto companies would like to get anything they could to discredit him as a future witness before congressional committees considering traffic safety legislation."[39]

The New Republic had contacted Allied Investigating Service in Washington and Management Consultants in Boston. Neither firm had anything to say. Ridgeway disclosed Sanford's interview with Gillen, albeit in an uncharitable manner. The order of the detective's quotes was shuffled to give the impression that he had accidentally revealed in the course of the call that his client was a party mentioned adversely in Nader's book. While his answers to Sanford were hardly polished, Gillen did manage to stick to his cover story and only spoke of people being adversely mentioned in Nader's book in response to a direct question. He did admit to reading Nader's book and to thinking as he read it, "he'd better know what he's talking about or somebody might yell."

"Is somebody yelling?" asked Sanford.

"All I can say is, it is good for Nader," said Gillen.[40]

On March 6, two days after Ridgeway's article was released, *The New York Times* picked up the story, repeating all of the allegations from *The New Republic*, including the harassing phone calls and the attractive women. The newspaper asked around Detroit if anyone had launched an investigation into Nader, described as a "leading independent critic" of the auto industry. It was known in Detroit, said the *Times*, that some automakers kept investigators on staff, including former FBI agents, to conduct counterespionage work on car designs, and to do background checks on potential executives. All of the major automakers dismissed the idea of spying on Nader as ridiculous. Unnamed executives were quoted as saying, "think what a blunder it would be if a company was caught at it." And, "you can bet that if one of us was doing it, it would be a lot smoother. If we were checking up on Nader, he'd never know about it."[41]

The *Times* had noticed that the same day Gillen was in Maine asking Condon whether Nader had a car or a driver's license, Frank Winchell, chief engineer at Chevrolet, was responding to Nader's claims before Michigan's Senate Highway Committee. He, too, wondered about Nader's driving record: "I don't even know if he has a license."[42]

The New Republic and *The New York Times* stories were ammunition enough for Abraham Ribicoff to rise on the floor of the Senate on March 8 to condemn the surveillance and harassment of Ralph Nader, and to draw a connection between these activities and the

author's appearance before his subcommittee. He demanded a federal investigation into apparent attempts to intimidate a federal witness. "Someone," said the senator, "wants either to discredit Mr.
Nader or induce him not to testify further." Ribicoff proclaimed
himself certain that his "fellow senators would agree that the operations of the Congress will suffer acutely should any citizen feel
himself restrained from coming forward to offer his opinions and
counsel on matters of public policy. But more than that, no citizen of this country should be forced to endure the kind of clumsy
harassment to which Mr. Nader has apparently been subjected since
the publication of his book." The senator cited a section of the
criminal code providing for fines and imprisonment for threatening
or intimidating a witness in any proceeding before a federal agency
or in connection with a congressional inquiry.[43]

All of the major Detroit manufacturers refused comment on
the spying and harassment allegations. It was only after the stories
had landed and Ribicoff had called for a federal investigation that
G.M.'s top brass were informed that their company was culpable.
With chairman Frederic Donner on the other side of the planet,
touring his operations in Australia and New Zealand, it fell to president James Roche to deal with the mess. There were fierce arguments on the fourteenth floor of corporate headquarters as to what
the company should do. Be quiet about its role? Admit that its legal
department had hired detectives and argue that the investigation
of Nader was lawful and proper (the legal department's position)?
Roche insisted on an admission and personally wrote the first draft
of the company's statement which, on release, read as follows:

> General Motors said today that following the publica-
> tion of Mr. Ralph Nader's criticisms of the Corvair in writ-
> ings and public appearances in support of his book Unsafe
> at Any Speed, the office of its general counsel initiated a
> routine investigation through a reputable law firm to deter-
> mine whether Ralph Nader was acting on behalf of litigants
> or their attorneys in Corvair design cases pending against
> General Motors. The investigation was prompted by Mr.
> Nader's extreme criticism of the Corvair in his writings,
> press conferences, TV and other public appearances. Mr.

Nader's statements coincided with similar publicity by some attorneys handling such litigation.

It is a well-known and accepted practice in the legal profession to investigate claims and persons making claims in the product liability field, such as in the pending Corvair design cases.

The investigation was limited only to Mr. Nader's qualifications, background, expertise and association with such attorneys. It did not include any of the alleged harassment or intimidation recently reported in the press. If Mr. Nader has been subjected to any of the incidents and harassment mentioned by him in newspaper stories, such incidents were in no way associated with General Motors' legitimate investigation of his interest in pending litigation.[44]

The admission was front-page news across the country. On March 10, Ribicoff was back on his feet on the Senate floor to announce that he was inviting the president of General Motors, its detective agencies, and Ralph Nader to appear before his subcommittee on March 22. In addition to witness harassment and possible violation of the U.S. criminal code, he said, the Senate must consider the additional issue of a witness's right to testify before a committee of the U.S. Congress without fear of character assassination: "I resent character assassination in any form and I expect General Motors to back up its charges concerning Mr. Nader's connection with pending Corvair litigation."[45]

Senator Kennedy, too, was aghast: "It seems anybody in the United States who is critical of the Corvair is subject to investigation by General Motors." His colleague, Senator Gaylord Nelson of Wisconsin, argued with G.M.'s claim that it had only been interested in routine legal matters, noting that Nader's friends and colleagues were approached by detectives "making lurid inquiries" into his personal life, his drinking and dating habits, and that attractive women had tried to lure him into compromising situations. "The information is compelling that General Motors was responsible for much of this sordid thing."[46]

Nader agreed. Was it "routine," he asked, "for General Motors to hire people to ask about one's sex life, religious practices, politi-

cal affiliations and credit ratings? Is it routine for General Motors
agents to ask for information of professors of law at Harvard and
other associates of mine on the wholly false pretext that I was being
considered for a 'lucrative research job'? Against such a faceless and
privileged prober, who knows what other 'routine' invasions of privacy have occurred which cannot be detected by an individual who
becomes the target of such abusive assaults."[47]

On March 11, Fred M. Vinson Jr., assistant attorney general in
charge of the Justice Department's Criminal Division, telephoned
Senator Ribicoff to tell him that the Federal Bureau of Investigation
would immediately investigate the alleged intimidation of his witness, Ralph Nader.

CHAPTER 12

PLAYING A LOSING HAND

Ralph Nader's appearance before Abraham Ribicoff's traffic safety subcommittee had drawn a record crowd, including six members of its senatorial panel, two more than had shown when General Motors testified, and a full complement of reporters, lobbyists, aides, and onlookers. "You bring out very good attendance," Ribicoff had told the witness. Howard Pyle, president of the National Safety Council and a charter member of what Nader and Ribicoff called the traffic safety establishment, was not so favored. He also appeared before the subcommittee in its third session. The only senator in the hearing room to hear him testify was Ribicoff and the press seats were vacant. This no doubt irked Pyle, whose presentation was a full-on rebuttal of Nader, Moynihan, and others who believed second-collision theory was the solution to traffic safety.[1]

A former war correspondent, Republican governor of Arizona, and deputy assistant to President Dwight Eisenhower, Pyle was thoroughly briefed, as might be expected of the head of an organization claiming possession of the largest safety library in the world. He introduced the National Safety Council to the empty chamber as a not-for-profit public service organization, founded in 1913 and chartered by Congress. Its mandate was to promote safety in every walk of life, with special attention on the causes of accidents and the most effective measures of their control. Governed by a large board of directors composed of men and women from industry, the academy, labor organizations, civic organizations, and the national government, it operated on funds raised from public and private sources. It maintained a staff of statistical, educational, and engineering technicians to assist with its work. It also acted as a clearinghouse for safety information of all kinds, publishing eight magazines, including one on traffic safety, with a combined circulation of 2.5 million.[2]

In his opening remarks, Pyle took polite umbrage at his critics' suggestion that the council and the rest of the safety community did not care about the nation's highway death toll and had failed to make progress against it. The council, he said, had devoted tremendous time and energy to what was an enormously complex problem. There were no magic formulas or silver bullets in traffic safety: the only real answer was sustained attention to laws and ordinances, education and public information, engineering of both highways and vehicles, motor vehicle inspection, and research. He freely acknowledged that no one had done enough: not automotive design engineers, not safety researchers or academics, not educators or law enforcers, not governments at either the national or local level. Nevertheless, great strides had been made, and the work was ongoing.

Off the top, he tackled the recent rise in road fatalities per year, both in absolute terms and per million miles driven, statistics that Nader and others had identified as proof of the NSC's incompetence and the need for federal intervention. The numbers begged the question: if there was any merit at all to the council's approach, which at its core stressed education, enforcement, and engineering, why were more people dying?

Pyle noted that the most recent data showed 49,000 deaths in 1965, an increase of 3 percent over the previous year, down from increases in the range of 7 to 9 percent in the previous four years, despite a 37 percent increase in road mileage over that time. The rate of deaths per hundred million vehicle miles, which had increased from 5.2 to 5.7 between 1961 and 1964, allowing critics to project horrendous increases in morbidity out into the distant future, had declined to 5.6, the same level as it had been in 1958 when there were 25 percent fewer cars in the road, traveling far fewer miles.[3]

The bump in absolute deaths in the early 1960s, said Pyle, could be accounted for by the sharp increase in travel alone. The opportunity for two-vehicle collisions, the deadliest kind of crash, increases exponentially rather than proportionately with an increase in mileage, and two-vehicle collisions had increased by a third between 1961 and 1965. A major factor behind the increase in mileage was an explosion of new motorists. The bulk of them were baby boomers who, being as reliably dangerous as any generation of young drivers, were making their own contribution to the mortality rate. As were small cars, which now represented 17 percent of the entire American fleet (compared to 2 percent in 1958); they were twice as likely as large cars to see their occupants killed in a crash. And motorcycles were gaining in popularity, especially among the young and reckless, killing 1,500 a year compared to 725 only four years before. Still more damage had been done, said Pyle, by steadily increasing highway speed limits. Drivers were twice as likely to be killed in collisions at sixty-five miles per hour as at fifty-five. Finally, statisticians had determined that traffic morbidity was affected by money: as the business cycle peaked so, too, did the number of people expiring on roadways, and the United States was well into the longest and most vigorous upturn in its history.[4]

Given record numbers of motorists driving record numbers of miles at younger ages, at higher speeds, and in smaller vehicles, it was a wonder that the crash rates, on the whole, were stable, said Pyle. He had some ideas about what was keeping fatalities in check. A small but significant portion of the driving public had adopted seat belts, saving an estimated five thousand lives a year. Better door locks and interior vehicle design had made a difference, as had improved driver training and the proliferation of limited-access divided highways. The death rate per million miles on the U.S. interstates was now 2.6, almost a third of the rate on the nation's unimproved highways and rural roads, a striking demonstration of the importance of engineering to traffic safety. Similarly, 1,063 cities had maps identifying collision hot spots and traffic engineers had put 300,000 man-days into eliminating the hazards at those locations.[5]

Pyle had data on single-car crashes, two-car crashes, urban crashes, rural crashes, pedestrian crashes, drunk-driving crashes, and many other kinds of crashes. He informed Ribicoff of a modernized traffic signal system on a four-mile stretch of road in a midwestern city that had resulted in a 13 percent increase in capacity and a 21 percent decrease in collisions. Switching to issues of enforcement, he mentioned a study in thirteen states that found 46 percent of vehicles failed periodic motor vehicle inspections. His abundance of information did not merely answer accusations that the traffic safety establishment had no interest in research; he left a strong impression that the subcommittee would have been better served by inviting him at the start of its deliberations.[6]

All this was prelude. Pyle next walked Ribicoff through the council's eighteen-point strategy for traffic safety, which included highway upgrades, funding to fix high-collision locations, improved crash investigations, intensified driver training, better crash research and record keeping, drunk driving measures, emergency response systems, as well as vehicle design and other items. He entered into the record forty pages of supporting evidence (with ten appendices) explaining the rationale and expected return for each of the eighteen points, which the council estimated would save 25,000 lives a year if enacted. This comprised the bulk of Pyle's presentation, and his answer to characterizations of the National Safety Council as heedless and ineffectual.[7]

About halfway through his statement, Pyle noted that half of fatal crashes involved alcohol and that legislators were sleeping on this aspect of the safety problem. That seemed to sting Ribicoff, who was interested in the faults of automakers, not lawmakers. He opened his examination of Pyle with a defensive speech about the many licenses he had suspended while governor of Connecticut. He failed to address Pyle's recommendation, supported by the American Medical Association and the U.S. Public Health Service, that blood alcohol tests be used to establish a clear baseline for determining driver impairment (as opposed to the rough and often indulgent judgment of law enforcers and juries). While declaring himself an enemy of the habitual drunk driver, Ribicoff betrayed a lenience toward the casual impaired driver before he steered the conversation back to his own priorities.[8]

The first of these was a federal mandate for traffic safety. Like other advocates of new federal legislation, Ribicoff insisted on one national nexus of responsibility on traffic safety as opposed to the "anarchy" of fifty states following individual policies. He was appalled at several premises underlying Pyle's plan: that states were capable of managing the road safety problem, that the federal government already had enough of a role and possessed all the tools it needed to have a greater impact, if only it would choose to use them. From Ribicoff's point of view, this was a second heresy on top of Pyle's earlier argument that the problem was not as alarming as advertised.[9]

Pyle agreed that the states could do more to save lives but he reminded Ribicoff that nothing had worked to make seat belts standard equipment in automobiles until several states independently passed laws requiring them. Wisconsin moved first in 1961, followed by twenty more states in the following two years, and the automakers bowed to the inevitable, making seat belts standard. Congress had wanted nothing to do with the issue. Allowing states to pursue their own priorities might do more to advance the cause of safety, suggested Pyle, than having the federal government in charge.[10]

The notion that fifty states would create anarchy, he continued, was bunk. Congress had already legislated the creation of interstate compacts to encourage standards in vehicle safety equipment and licensing of drivers, and the vast majority of states had signed on. A Vehicle Equipment Safety Commission had been established to further coordinate the activities of state motor vehicle administrators. Washington had also used its highway funding powers to direct the states to create highway safety commissions, and it could use the same stick to beat more uniform reforms out of governors if it pleased.

The best and most effective federal tool for improving safety features of automobiles, said Pyle, was the General Services Administration, which had already insisted that automakers competing for its massive annual vehicle purchases install virtually every safety item on the American Medical Association's wish list. This set an example for the interstate compact's vehicle safety standards, not to mention every other purchaser of automobiles. Detroit, bowing to the inevitable, had agreed to make this equipment standard. The

Safety Council's position was that the secretary of commerce should demand that automakers report regularly on their progress in safe vehicle design and that the GSA use these reports as the basis for still higher standards for federally purchased vehicles.

"We insist that you already have the role" of federal oversight, said Pyle. His implication was that all Washington lacked was the political will to fill the role, which was another sacrilege so far as Ribicoff was concerned. He claimed that it had been the threat of his hearings, and not the GSA, that moved the automakers. The timing of Detroit's decisions supports Pyle's version of events, but he was happy to give Ribicoff credit and he encouraged him to continue with his oversight. All the same, "no new legislation is necessary."[11]

As Pyle went on to speak of the vast amount of collaborative work among the U.S. Public Health Service, the U.S. Bureau of Public Roads, the Interdepartmental Highway Safety Board, the President's Committee for Highway Safety, the Governors' Conference, the National League of Cities, the National Association of Counties, law enforcement agencies, the medical community, and the National Safety Council, Ribicoff shifted tactics from insisting that no one cared and nothing was being done about traffic safety to questioning the independence and integrity of those doing the work. He asked Pyle a series of questions, the burden of which was to locate the origins of the Safety Council's eighteen-point plan in proposals launched in the 1940s by the Automotive Safety Foundation, a Detroit trade association. Pyle demonstrated that his plan had in fact emerged from a 1946 White House conference on traffic safety.[12]

Ribicoff tried another angle. He established that the 1946 White House conference had eventually evolved into the President's Committee for Traffic Safety, and that Pyle had been chairman of that organization's policy advisory council, and that his predecessor as chairman had been a representative of the industry's Automotive Safety Foundation. His implication was that "the keynote to the whole safety program of the United States, the attitude of the action program which says this should be a local and state program," had been guided by lobbyists funded by the auto industry. Without denying that automakers had been at the table, Pyle insisted that his action program was composed by many hands representing diverse interests.[13]

Ribicoff further pursued the notion that the National Safety Council and the rest of the traffic safety establishment were shills for automakers by asking Pyle, "Can you cite any articles on the subject of vehicle design critical of automakers in your publication during the last ten years?" This question went to the heart of Nader's theory that the manufacturers were using their money to manipulate the safety establishment into blaming educators, enforcers, and road engineers for fatality rates while shielding Detroit from criticism.[14]

In response, Pyle produced twenty-five NSC research reports calling for better seat belts, windshields, door locks, interior cushioning, and other safety improvements to automobiles. A number were written by second-collision pioneer Hugh DeHaven, and several more were either by or about Congressman Kenneth Roberts, who had brought second-collision theory to Capitol Hill in the 1950s and fathered the GSA's standards.[15]

Pyle next pulled out an additional twenty-four articles on motor vehicle design from a National Safety Council publication which featured on its editorial board William Haddon, who had been Daniel Patrick Moynihan's second-collision guru at the New York State Health Department, and Ross McFarland of the Harvard School of Public Health, originator of the epidemiological approach to traffic safety. Another twenty-two speakers had addressed these same subjects at the council's National Safety Congress. Finally, Pyle told the hearings that the National Safety Council's 1964 Metropolitan Life Award for Research on Accident Prevention had been given to second-collision researchers, as had its 1965 award.[16]

Although he evidently failed to move Ribicoff with this testimony, Pyle had laid down important challenges to the chairman's thinking. It was facile to lay the slight 1961–64 bump in the fatality rate at Detroit's door, and unreasonable to project that small selection of data into a future catastrophe that was going to kill or seriously injure every second or third American. That the traffic safety issue had not been finally solved did not negate decades of important, effective, and reasonably well-coordinated work by public and private parties across the country. There was no shameful neglect, no anarchy, nor, evidently, any great wastage of money on useless programs. Automobile design had not been ignored by the establishment and there was compelling evidence that emphases on education, enforcement, and engineering solutions were working and should continue to be central to safety programs. Indeed, the drunk driving problem, the failure of almost half of car owners to maintain their vehicles, and the underutilization of seat belts, which had been proven to save lives, were reasons for more, not less, attention to driver behavior. Pyle had also made the uncomfortable suggestion that the unwillingness of politicians of any stripe to impose on drivers (i.e., voters) was a more significant obstacle to progress than anything happening in Detroit. To his mind, the case that federal intervention would improve traffic safety had yet to be made.

Two of Pyle's most interesting contributions to the subcommittee were never heard by his meager audience. They were slipped into the written record for the benefit of the handful of people who bothered to read it. The first was a potent attack by National Safety Council experts on the testimony of Daniel Patrick Moynihan, who had projected a coming forty million crashes because "almost nothing" had been done about traffic safety. Moynihan, in their estimation, tended to be "freewheeling in his rhetoric," internally inconsistent in his arguments, unaware of his own department's literature, highly selective in his facts, and often wrong in those facts. Among the omissions and errors made by Moynihan, who liked to say that the first step to solving any social problem is to measure it, was a mathematical mistake that doubled his collision projection number beyond what the data supported.[17]

The second contribution landed on the record several weeks after Nader had appeared before the subcommittee and repeated his accusations from *Unsafe at Any Speed* that the National Safety Council was an unprofessional organization of "public relations" men who were "suffocating" rather the helping the fight against traffic safety. Nader's view was that the council was tainted by its acceptance of funds from Detroit, that it conducted "no research," had "not devised any accident prevention measures" nor any engineering requirements for safe design, and that it had deemed American cars crashworthy on the questionable authority of the Automobile Manufacturers Association. He maintained that a council executive had once proposed a policy on vehicle design only to have the idea quashed at a weekend meeting between the council's board of directors and auto executives aboard a yacht on Lake Michigan. On the whole, said Nader, the council's performance was "bankrupt."[18]

Nader, answered the National Safety Council, had never interviewed anyone at the organization, nor given it an opportunity to respond to his allegations. The council's eighteen-point action plan, which Nader claimed had not been updated since 1949, had been updated three times in the 1960s alone, with special emphasis on vehicle design. The council had criticized Detroit for emphasizing speed and power, for its involvement in racing, for its dangerous hood ornaments, for doors that opened in crashes, and for its reluctance to promote seat belts. It noted that Congressman Roberts's initiative to use GSA purchasing power to improve safety equipment in cars, which Nader called "a stroke of legislative genius," had, in fact, been facilitated and promoted by the council. (Nader would subsequently protest in an angry letter to Ribicoff that he "did discuss Council problems with Council personnel," but provided no details.)[19]

As for Nader's charge that the National Safety Council had been bought off by industry and reduced itself to "endemic servility," Pyle advised that only 6 percent of its funding came from automakers, and that thirteen of its 201 board members were employed in the industry (and half of those were employee safety officials at their companies). The 1958 yacht trip that had inspired Nader's innuendo had not been arranged for auto executives to pressure the council into soft-pedaling vehicle design. Rather, an automobile executive who served on the council's executive committee had arranged for the Automobile Manufacturers Association to meet with council because "he felt strongly that the industry should give particular attention" to its views on seat belts and safe vehicle design. Failing to convince the automakers to adopt its views, the council proceeded with a seat-belt campaign in partnership with the U.S. Public Health Service and American Medical Association.[20]

The National Safety Council's was the most comprehensive rebuttal to the case put forward by the second-collision evangelists but it was hardly alone. The Ribicoff panel had also heard from the Post Office of its happy collaboration with General Motors on safety improvements; from Senator Milward Simpson of Wyoming

on how the state legislatures had outperformed the federal government on traffic safety; from General Gruenther of the President's
Committee for Traffic Safety on the cooperative attitude of Detroit
and the successes of the safety establishment; from Paul Fannin,
former head of the National Governors' Conference Committee on Roads and Highway Safety, who said that coordinated state
programs had achieved more for traffic safety in the previous five
years than had been accomplished in the preceding sixty-five years
of automotive history, and warned that rigid federal standards in
a competitive, complex industrial field would inhibit rather than
encourage technical improvement; from the head of the General
Services Administration, who lauded Detroit's command of vehicle
safety technology and its favorable response to new safety standards; from the commissioner of the Federal Supply Service, who
had received the "utmost and finest cooperation from the industry,"
which he said was at times installing new safety technology well in
advance of the application of federal standards; from the secretary of
health, education, and welfare and the secretary of commerce, who
each endorsed the National Safety Council's approach to safety and
found the automakers cooperative and progressive.[21]

The crash safety experts at Cornell University, whose work was
generally regarded as definitive by the second-collision school, also
had bones to pick with Nader. They advised Jerome Sonosky in the
summer of 1965 that their laboratory supported a well-rounded
approach to traffic safety, one including education, engineering,
enforcement, and traffic control as well as vehicle design. They were
cautious about promising any improvements in survival rates by
modifying car interiors. In their estimation, not enough research had
been done to justify even the GSA's new safety standards. Indeed, no
theoretical framework existed for evaluating the effectiveness of any
particular equipment standard imposed on Detroit, especially given
the wide range of crash circumstances, with cars and passengers of
all shapes and sizes moving at variable speeds, in variable road and
weather conditions. As far as performance of existing cars was concerned, the drivability and control features of North American cars
were "excellent." Their crashworthiness might be improved with
"better understanding of the vehicle collision and structural collapse
process, as produced by valid mathematical models of the phenom-

enon." The development of such a rational basis for design criteria would require four to five years of planning and research.[22]

Notwithstanding his reliance on its data, Nader had smeared Cornell's Automotive Crash Injury Research Project in *Unsafe at Any Speed*. He described it as a pawn of Detroit for accepting industry grants. He claimed that it was "suppressing" research results on steering columns and other items at the behest of the Automobile Manufacturers Association. The researchers told Sonosky that their work "would not exist" without the support of the automobile industry. They were grateful for its funding and also for their direct pipeline to Detroit's proprietary research and information. Industry money had no effect on their scientific integrity, and the data on steering columns had not been fully released because researchers had yet to find "scientific evidence of its relationship to injury." Some state laws precluded the kind of public disclosure Nader was demanding of all of Cornell's research. Finally, the Cornell project was a research organization, not an advocacy group. All of this information went into the voluminous hearing record, but was not otherwise heard.[23]

Scientists at UCLA's Institute of Transportation and Traffic Engineering felt burned by Nader, as well. He had lumped them in with other organizations he believed to have been bought by Detroit. "Industry didn't give us five cents," said UCLA's Robert Brenner, a PhD in safety engineering. He believed Nader's activist zeal made him impatient with and dismissive of scientists taking a careful approach to facts.[24]

Still more testimony and evidence against the need for aggressive federal legislation and regulation of Detroit came from Harvard's McFarland, who independently and in the midst of the Ribicoff hearings made an optimistic presentation to a White House Conference on Health saying that "a great deal of progress" was being achieved to eliminate "built in" or "design" errors in automobiles. The climate for crash research and safety programs was more favorable than ever before, he continued, and new concepts and knowledge were being imported from the fields of biostatistics, medicine, engineering, and psychology, all of them "providing fresh impetus for experimental studies."[25]

Thus, by the time General Motors' detectives had been busted by *The New Republic* and James Roche had signed off on the corporation's apology, strong counterpoints had been made to every important argument in the arsenal of Nader, Moynihan, Ribicoff, and company. Indeed, it was quite possible to look at the full record and see the second-collision gang as injudicious, if not reckless in its handling of evidence, incurious about the true causes of road carnage, overzealous in its pursuit of legislative trophies, and shabby in its treatment of honest researchers and public servants, to say nothing of the auto industry.

No one was looking at the full record, however, and G.M.'s executives prepared for their return visit to the subcommittee under a cloud of headlines about private dicks and honey traps.

The son of an Illinois funeral director, James Roche was soft-spoken, self-effacing, folksy, tactful, loyal, reliable, and hardworking, qualities that would have served him well should he have entered the family business. Instead, he studied accounting through a correspondence school and joined General Motors as a bottom-rung statistician at the age of twenty-one. Over time he displayed a flair for marketing and sales rare in an abacist. He was launched onto the corporate fast track and in 1965 became the first Roman Catholic to reach the presidency of a corporation so WASPish, according to *Time* magazine, that "the hierarchs belong to the same Masonic lodge." He often attended mass before work on weekday mornings and was thought by some to be "gallantry personified," and by others to be "too much a gentleman" for his position.[26]

It had been Roche whose head was conjoined with Frederic Donner's in photographs from their earlier appearance at Ribicoff's subcommittee (duplicative as they seemed, the president was a couple of inches taller than the chairman, longer of face, thinner of lip, and weaker of chin). It had been Roche's mortification, after almost forty years of dedication and relentless toil at General Motors, to confess to Bobby Kennedy under heated questioning the exact amount of the company's massive profits, and it had been Roche's misfortune to be alone in headquarters when the detective scandal hit, and to have the company's admission released under his signature. With his senior colleague still traveling, it would also be Roche's burden to appear again before Ribicoff on March 22, 1966, in an attempt to explain the corporation's inexplicable probe of Ralph Nader.

It was a searing experience for Roche. Five years later he would observe its anniversary to the precise minute and remember in detail all that occurred. Every chair under the great chandeliers in the Caucus Room of the Old Senate Office Building was filled, leaving rows of onlookers to stand at the back. Roche sat near the front in a leather-seated armchair at a wooden table with three television cameras trained on him. Crouching before the TV tripods was a row of newspaper photographers. Roche faced an imposing dais that accommodated Senator Ribicoff, Bobby Kennedy, and the slouching, bemused figures of Senator Fred Harris, Democrat of Oklahoma, and Senator Henry "Scoop" Jackson, Democrat of Washington. Republican Milward Simpson was the fifth member of the panel. Senator Carl Curtis, Detroit's ally earlier in the hearings, was nowhere to be seen.[27]

Roche was not supposed to lead the day's proceedings but the first scheduled witness, Ralph Nader, failed to answer the bell. His name had been called, and called again. The hearings took a fifteen-minute recess and still he did not show. Ribicoff reluctantly invited Roche to come forward and asked him "as a matter of formality, in keeping with the rules of the committee," to take an oath. Roche was the first witness in the subcommittee's record to be so honored, and the oath was anything but a formality. Ribicoff had opened the morning's session with these words: "There is no law which bars a corporation from hiring detectives to investigate a private citizen, however distasteful the idea may seem to some of us. There is a law, however, which makes it a crime to harass or intimidate a witness before a congressional committee."[28]

Accompanying G.M.'s leader to the witness stand was Theodore Sorensen, a practicing lawyer and former John F. Kennedy aide who had been hired to advise the company and, by his presence, instill caution in the late president's brother, a personal friend. Sorensen sat demurely by his client's side with his briefcase on his knees as Roche, his hands shaking, a sober expression on his long face, his fleshy neck spilling over his snug white collar, began his contrition:

I deplore the kind of harassment to which Mr. Nader has apparently been subjected. I am just as shocked and outraged by some of the incidents which Mr. Nader has reported as the members of this subcommittee.[29]

Roche said he did not know of or approve of the investigation when it was initiated but he took full responsibility "for any action authorized or initiated by any officer" of his corporation related to Mr. Nader.

While there can be no disagreement over General Motors' legal right to ascertain necessary facts preparatory to litigation . . . I am not here to excuse, condone, or justify in any way our investigating Mr. Nader. To the extent that General Motors bears responsibility, I want to apologize here and now to the members of this subcommittee and Mr. Nader. I sincerely hope that these apologies will be accepted. Certainly, I bear Mr. Nader no ill will.[30]

As Roche understood the investigation, it had begun the previous November when Nader's book had been released criticizing G.M. and its Corvair, and it was "wholly unrelated" to his role as a witness before the subcommittee, which was not announced until several months later. Its purpose was to determine Nader's relation to the more than one hundred lawsuits pending, all of which alleged that 1960–63 Corvairs were unsafely designed. G.M. had a legal duty to shareholders to defend these suits, and to investigate the collisions and parties in question, and the merit of their arguments. The company saw a concerted effort on the part of a few trial lawyers handling Corvair cases to stimulate additional suits. It wanted to know if these counselors were libeling G.M. or its products, or transgressing any bar association canons. It sought to determine if any witness or author of any document that might wind up in court as evidence was entitled to the legal definition of expert. These, said Roche, were the narrow purposes for which Nader had come under investigation.

There has been no attempt by, and it has at no time been the intention of, General Motors Corp, or any of its officers or employees to annoy, harass, embarrass, threaten, injure or intimidate Mr. Nader, to invade his privacy, to defame his character, or to hinder, impugn, coerce, or prevent his testimony before this or any other legislative body. Nor was any attempt made along those lines with respect to any other critic of General Motors.

I personally have no interest whatsoever in knowing Mr. Nader's political beliefs, his religious beliefs and attitudes, his credit rating or his personal habits regarding sex, alcohol, or any other subject. Nor for the record was any derogatory information of any kind along any of these lines turned up in this investigation.[31]

Sweating under the brilliant chandeliers and television lighting, Roche cautiously added a plea that the senators not interpret the investigatory episode as a reflection on G.M.'s concern for traffic safety. The death toll remains too high, he said, and the car, like the driver and the road environment, bore some responsibility for that. "I am urging our engineers and experts on to greater heights, to be pioneers in automotive safety." He pledged G.M. to cooperate with the subcommittee and with all constructive state and federal legislative initiatives on traffic safety, and then gave himself up for interrogation.[32]

The senators offered Roche congratulations on his forthright and sincere apology, and their questions were not especially taxing until Kennedy took his turn. He pulled out G.M.'s statement from March 9 admitting the existence of the investigation and, in his inimitable style, posed a series of questions that led Roche first to agree that his company had on that date disavowed any harassment of Nader while claiming that its investigation was strictly routine and legal in intent. Kennedy then obliged Roche to admit that the investigation, having poked into Nader's personal life and subjected him to surveillance, was not at all routine and could reasonably be considered harassment. This was followed by a touchy exchange in which Roche first tried to explain how the misrepresentations in the March 9 statement could have occurred, and next claimed that he and his senior staff knew nothing about Gillen's decision to use in his investigation a pre-employment pretext that involved delving into Nader's family background, sex life, and political beliefs. Kennedy eventually gave way to Ribicoff, who, waving a sheaf of investigative reports that had been delivered to G.M.'s legal department, compounded the witness's embarrassment by pointing out that the reports often had more to say about what Nader ate for lunch than the Corvair lawsuits: "There was very little inquiry concerning Mr. Nader's legal activities."[33]

Roche had no answers to these charges. He absorbed blows meekly until Ribicoff and Kennedy eventually punched themselves out, and was fortunate that he wasn't abused more for attempting to rationalize the corporation's dirt-digging. "May I thank you, Mr. Chairman, and gentlemen, for your courtesy," said the president of the world's largest industrial enterprise as he retired from the witness stand.[34]

Next to be sworn in was Aloysius Power, who as the corporation's general counsel tried to justify the investigation from a legal perspective. He came armed with reams of material raising questions about the author's involvement with attorneys suing G.M. over the Corvair. He said that he had been concerned on initiating the investigation that lawsuits involving the design and safety of complex products often turn on expert testimony, which made it necessary to determine whether Nader was a potential witness, and if he was qualified to fill such a role. Power was further troubled by apparent breaches of the Canons of Professional Ethics of the American Bar Association, which prohibit lawyers from public discussion of pending litigation, as well as from solicitation of professional employment by advertisements or personal communications, or by such indirect advertisements as "furnishing or inspiring newspaper comments." These lines appeared to have been crossed by attorneys handling Corvair suits.[35]

As soon as the first Corvair actions were filed in 1962, said Power, anonymous advertisements began to appear in newspapers across the country inviting "other attorneys representing plaintiffs in similar suits" to contact a post office box number. The number of suits subsequently multiplied, most of them brought by the Harney firm in California, which had handled the Rose Pierini case. Denied the opportunity to present all of his evidence against the Corvair when the Pierini case was settled out of court, Harney had nevertheless shared it with the media, resulting in another burst of Corvair suits. Power told the subcommittee of the inflammatory 1965 report in the supermarket tabloid *Midnight*—"150 Lawsuits Charge: GM Cars Are Death Traps: Hushed-up Evidence Revealed in Court"—which had contained excerpts from Harney cases that had yet to be served or even filed. Stories of this nature led to still more suits and more pressure on General Motors to answer to its public and its shareholders.[36]

The American Trial Lawyers Association, Power continued, appeared to have taken a special interest in promoting the services of Ralph Nader as a Corvair expert. Long before the publication of his book, the ATLA had described Nader as an "author, attorney, and one of America's foremost research authorities on legal and public questions," and made his availability known to several dozen lawyers. It was perfectly appropriate, said Power, for G.M. to inquire into the identity of Nader and his technical qualifications as an expert when the ATLA was beating a drum for him. The company wondered whether Nader, whose criticisms of the Corvair mirrored those of the Harney firm, had a financial interest in some of the cases and if his writings were "part of an organized nationwide publicity campaign to pre-try the Corvair cases by television, newspaper, and magazine, and to precondition prospective jurors in the cases still to be tried throughout the United States." Furthermore, the investigation had interviewed a senior official at the ATLA who said Nader had, in fact, done paid consulting work for lawyers representing Corvair litigants, including David Harney (this claim was false).[37]

It particularly annoyed Power that even after G.M. had triumphed in two complete jury trials of Corvair design cases in the summer of 1965, plaintiff's attorneys had continued to make highly publicized speeches—he cited Harry Philo's appearances before the ATLA convention in Miami and the Michigan Senate's hearings on traffic safety—repeating arguments about the Corvair that had been unanimously rejected by juries. Nader had done the same in public testimony and in his book. There was a single sentence in *Unsafe at Any Speed* on the adverse jury decisions. There was no mention of them at all in the Corvair chapter as excerpted in *The Nation*.[38]

Like Roche, Power claimed that detective Vincent Gillen, and not G.M., had decided to pry into Nader's personal life and that nothing untoward had been found there and that no efforts to disparage Nader had been made, however often he accused the automaker of sacrificing the public's safety on the altar of profitability.

Power's attempt to unload the unsavory aspects of the investigation on Gillen rightly left the senators cold. Not all of the investigation had concentrated on legal matters, said Ribicoff. Senator Harris asked how the company's lawyers did not know something was amiss when reading reports from the detectives in which Nader's acquaintances were asked over and over again why he was not married and if he had any vices. The subcommittee also had in its possession handwritten notes by G.M. librarian Eileen Murphy asking Richard Danner to find out about Nader's drinking habits and the cause of his sniffing problem. Power admitted that these questions, and the decision to put Nader under surveillance, had nothing to do with Corvair litigation, and his presentation about Nader and the tort industry went for nothing.

The morning closed with Ribicoff addressing Nader, now in the audience, directly: "And may I say to you, Mr. Nader, that I have read these reports very carefully, and you and your family can be proud, because they put you through the mill, and they haven't found a damn thing out against you."[39]

The afternoon session opened with Nader on the witness stand, apologizing for his lateness that morning. He could not find a taxi, he said, an experience so frustrating he "almost felt like going out and buying a Chevrolet."

Nader said he had been hurt by G.M.'s investigation: "It is not easy for me to convey in words what I had to endure and what my family has had to endure, as anyone subjected to such an exposure can appreciate. However, I certainly stand ready to reply to questions which the subcommittee may wish to ask."[40]

Speaking into three microphones with a pencil in his hand and an untouched glass of water by his side, Nader repeated his views on traffic safety, the "creative lethality" of automotive stylists in Detroit, and the uncommon dangers of the Corvair. He said he had worked at no charge for Corvair litigants, although he admitted to being a paid party to another suit alleging negligent design of a different G.M. vehicle. He defended the advertising of his services in legal publications on the grounds that he was working for free. These were the housekeeping components of his presentation. His larger ambition was to frame "the attempt to obtain lurid details and grist for the invidious use and metastasis of slurs and slanders" as something more than an assault on his "self." It was "generalizable," he said, as an encroachment by large companies upon the public interest.[41]

Nader railed at length on the unaccountability of corporate America, and how it represented an "authoritarian pocket" in the democratic framework, operating outside the law and taking advantage of "systematic immunities" from oversight and prosecution. The vast majority of Americans had chosen to "surrender to the system" rather than fight corporations for truth and justice: "How much has this nation lost because there are men walking around today with invisible chains?" He congratulated himself on dissenting from the "suffocating orthodoxy of the times" and fighting for the public interest and against "corporate transgressions." He was not challenged by the panel on these points.

It was not entirely a cakewalk for Nader. Senator Kennedy asked if the author had any training as an engineer (he did not), and if he had any hard data indicating that the Corvair was less safe than other cars. Nader danced around the question. Kennedy repeated it several times, insisting on a straight answer until, finally, the witness admitted that none existed. He fell back on an insistence that none was necessary because expert opinion had found the car to be dangerous.[42]

Nader was also forced by Kennedy to defend the small notice he had given in his book to jury trials that had favored G.M. He claimed that his publication schedule had not allowed for the addition of late-breaking information, and added that jury verdicts, vulnerable to "the frailty of the judicial process," were not final in any event. Tests needed to be done "on an objective proving ground with adequate instrumentations." This line of questioning from the New York senator suggests that General Motors had made the right move by hiring Ted Sorensen, although this part of Nader's testimony did not much interest the press.[43]

. . .

While Roche and Nader would dominate the headlines on the day, the star of the show in terms of entertainment value and fresh perspective was the gruff, wavy-haired figure of Vincent Gillen, president of Vincent Gillen Associates, who was pleased to inform the subcommittee that in addition to earning both his postsecondary degrees at night school and working for the FBI and such illustrious American companies as Metropolitan Life and Otis Elevators, he had served with Air Force Intelligence in the Second World War, taught management and industrial relations at Hofstra University, served as president of the Long Island Industrial Job Development Corporation, was a member of the Long Island Association of Commerce & Industry, and president of the parent-teachers association at his daughters' Brooklyn high school.

"I appreciate this opportunity to inform you frankly and fully about the investigation of Ralph Nader," Gillen said. "It involved no harassment; no intimidation; no attempt to defame; no following him around the country; no telephone harassment, no recordings, and no women." He offered to open all of his corporate records to anyone who might want to challenge him on these points.[44]

Yes, admitted Gillen, he had recommended a pre-employment pretext for the investigation of Nader. It would encourage interview subjects to speak to detectives, and prevent those same subjects from jumping to the conclusion that Nader had done anything embarrassing or wrong. It was designed to protect rather than subject Nader to character assassination. Gillen insisted that none of the questions asked by his investigators were different from those asked in typical government background investigations: "Let me put this ridiculous subject to rest by categorically saying that no investigator asked any embarrassing questions or intimated anything lurid." He did apologize for the fact that his detectives had followed Nader into a government building, saying that it had been a decision made on the fly by an operative fearing that he might lose his mark.[45]

Gillen was the only person on the day's record who found nothing discomfiting or disreputable about his trade or his investigation. He captivated the hearing's audience. James Roche sat in the spectator's gallery listening attentively and scribbling in a notebook.

Kennedy went hard after the detective for conducting an investigation under a pretext. "What you mean was you were conducting an investigation under a lie," he said.[46]

Gillen calmly reminded Kennedy that as U.S. attorney general he had overseen the Federal Bureau of Investigation where similar techniques were used: "You get very little investigative material if you conduct it openly on all occasions, sir. You know that."

"I understand that, but what disturbs me . . ."

"If you understand it, why don't you leave us do it then?"[47]

Kennedy answered that it was harassment, to which Gillen responded that every conversation was civil and polite and typical of other pre-employment investigations. No one was harassed.

The senator asked why the detective agency had not simply contacted Nader with its questions instead of using a pretext: "Why didn't you give him a ring if you didn't have anything to hide?"

"What?"

"Why didn't you give him a ring and tell him what you were doing if you didn't have anything to hide?"

"What would you suggest I tell him?"

"I suppose maybe you could start with the truth. 'I am conducting an investigation that is under a pretext.' I don't know. How would you express it?"[48]

Gillen had no idea how to express it and instead spoke of the success he had enjoyed during his FBI career interviewing people under pretexts, drawing them out, learning their life stories.

"But, you see," said Kennedy, "that your objective was to obtain a good deal of information, and you were proceeding under a false pretext."

"Oh, Senator, come on. Come on. For goodness sake, where did I learn to do this? In the FBI."[49]

All inquiries about Nader's personal life, insisted Gillen, were simply intended to keep up the pretext of a pre-employment interview in which personal questions were typical. They were made over and over again because "when you conduct an investigation under a pretext, you have to carry it out completely. If you do anything less, or inject extraneous matters, you run the risk of losing the pretext." Hence the lack of overt questions about Corvair litigation. The detectives had waited for the matter to be raised organically by interview subjects, and it was, once by an executive at the ATLA, and again by a friend of Nader's mother who had been told that Ralph was consulting with attorneys as an expert on automobile crash cases.[50]

Gillen had not had time to follow up on those leads (the ATLA had given him the names of three personal injury lawyers whom Nader was supposed to have worked with) before the plug was pulled on the investigation. "I stand on the quality of our reports," said Gillen. "I submit my integrity to the scrutiny of all."[51]

Before leaving the stand, Gillen was comfortable enough to tease the New York senator, saying that he was a constituent, that Kennedy was always writing him for his vote, and that in the past, at least, he had given it.

Ribicoff got no further than Kennedy with the detective, although he tried: "Your entire investigation, Mr. Gillen, had to do with trying to smear a man, the question of his sex life, whether he belonged to left-wing organizations, whether he was anti-Semitic, whether he was an odd ball, whether he liked boys instead of girls. The whole investigation was to smear an individual, and I can't find anything of any substance in your entire investigation over these weeks that had anything to do basically with whether or not he was tied up with plaintiff's attorneys that had to do with Corvair cars."[52]

Gillen answered that he had already explained his methods, that Ribicoff had no sworn testimony that he had ever used a term like "odd ball" or otherwise smeared or slandered Nader. "And," he finished, "I don't think that it is appropriate for me to come here as a witness and be smeared myself."[53]

The detective did General Motors a huge favor in his testimony. He kept to himself the fact that he had years before undertaken at least two dozen investigations not through the lawyer Richard Danner but directly for the company's legal department. Most appear to have been routine but one looked into a Harlem civil rights group that had been protesting the absence of African Americans in G.M.'s New York offices. Another investigated a former G.M. employee who had gone to work for the United Auto Workers. These additional assignments, which suggest that G.M. resorted to private investigations more frequently and broadly than its executives admitted, would not come to light for several years.

All in all, it was a terrible day for General Motors, notwithstanding Gillen's brio. There was general sympathy for Roche in the media and in Detroit. The Newsom company's assessment of his testimony—"It was extremely awkward and he did extremely well"—was echoed in the press. Nevertheless, the larger story, carried prominently on all three television networks and as the lead item on the front page of *The New York Times*, was best summed up by Judd Arnett of the *Detroit Free Press:* "How could General Motors, supposedly the world's best-managed big business, have been so stupid as to have authorized an investigation of Ralph Nader?"[54]

CHAPTER 13

KILL SHOT

Previous to the revelation that General Motors had been investigating Ralph Nader, the Johnson administration had been split on how far to push Detroit on safety. One faction, led by Commerce Secretary John Connor, supported a safety bill giving the industry a two-year window to voluntarily improve. Another faction, including Ribicoff and presidential aide Joseph Califano, wanted stringent and immediate federal safety standards. The president, in his 1966 State of the Union Address, leaned to Connor's view. After news broke of the automaker's spying, Ribicoff said that the two-year delay in the president's proposal was intolerable and more Democrats were inclined to agree. Unfortunately for Ribicoff, one of those inclined to agree was his colleague from Washington, Warren Magnuson, who had two decades of seniority over him and was head of the powerful Commerce Committee, a more appropriate venue than Executive Reorganization for deliberations on traffic safety regulation.[1]

Elected to the Senate in 1944, Magnuson was one of the chamber's more popular figures, charming, gregarious, sodden. *Time* magazine called him a "Cadillackadaisical Democrat" who lived for "the tinkle of ice water coming down a hotel hallway." Notwithstanding his tendency to forget or butcher people's names, the cigar ash on his suits, the frequent razor cuts on his face, and what one newspaper called his "spindly legs" supporting "a turnip torso in defiance of all laws of gravity," he had gained renown as the "playboy Senator." He had once made himself late for the opening of a session by chasing to Hawaii the Hollywood starlet Toni Seven, whose own legs had won prizes from the Society of Photographic Illustrators. Early in the administration of his close friend LBJ, Magnuson had attended a black-tie state dinner, stayed over at the White House, and emerged from the sleeping quarters the next morning in rumpled tuxedo at the side of an attractive woman in wilted gown.[2]

After the overnight debacle, the senator had taken himself off the market and married a Seattle widow with the president, who was rumored to have insisted on the arrangement, as his best man. The housebroken Magnuson proceeded to make major contributions to the 89th Congress's orgy of legislation by championing the consumer issues that had resurrected his endangered political career in the early 1960s. He pushed hazardous toys out of the market, slapped cancer warnings on cigarette packages, and insisted on truth in advertising. Magnuson had been uncharacteristically slow to the automobile file, however, letting Ribicoff steal a star turn before a large media audience. By early 1966, with the nation watching and the likelihood of legislation much improved, Magnuson awoke to the opportunity and pulled rank, hosting seven days of testimony in March and April on S.3005, a companion to the new Department of Transportation bill, drafted by the White House "to provide for a coordinated national safety program and establishment of safety standards for motor vehicles in interstate commerce to reduce traffic accidents and the deaths, injuries, and property damage which occur in such accidents."[3]

After declaring his hope that the second session of the 89th be known as the "automobile safety Congress," and his intention to saddle Detroit with immediate safety standards, Magnuson invited the eclipsed Ribicoff as his first witness. It was a charitable sop to the junior senator. Ribicoff was followed by a familiar cast of characters including the commerce secretary, Howard Pyle from the National Safety Council, Ralph Nader, and Ford vice president John S. Bugas, who represented Detroit in his capacity as chairman of the Automobile Manufacturers Association safety committee.[4]

Little of importance was added to what Ribicoff had already put on the record. The deliberations pivoted on questions of whether to move fast or slow, how much discretion over standards to leave in the hands of the secretary of transportation, and how much to worry about the cost of safety regulation to the consumer. The industry had few allies in its view that voluntary standards were sufficient and that the costs of new safety equipment were problematic. Nader and Detroit were in fierce agreement that the secretary of transportation could not be allowed too much discretion over standards, the former fearing that he would not ask enough of the industry, the latter fearing he would ask too much. There were nods at the hearings toward the long-standing issues of incomplete and often contradictory research on the true causes of crashes and the best measures for saving lives, but no serious grappling with them. There was no time. The White House wanted its legislation delivered before the midterm elections in November.

Overshadowed though he was by Magnuson, Ribicoff refused to leave the picture, or to abandon to chance or congressional deal-making the stringency of safety regulations. On April 5, as the Commerce Committee hearings were winding down, he sent telegrams to the presidents of the four largest automakers demanding that they send him "a complete listing of all bulletins, notices and other correspondence relating to product or equipment defects or failures since 1960." Nader had informed him of the industry's quiet practice of recalling vehicles, either from dealers or owners, to fix problems discovered after their release. He and Ribicoff saw the practice as proof that manufacturers were unloading shoddily made and perhaps dangerous goods on vulnerable customers. They bet that the public would be startled by the volume of recalls, and they were right. The gambit put Ribicoff back on the front page and returned him there a month later when he reported the results of his requests. Since 1960, 8.7 million cars had been recalled by America's major manufacturers out of 47 million produced.[5]

Detroit protested that the recalls were effective measures to ensure the quality of their vehicles and evidence of its strong sense of responsibility for its manufactures. Many recalls, it noted, were related not to safety but to the comfort and convenience of drivers, or such relative trivia as paint blisters. Ninety percent of suspected defects, moreover, had either been addressed or found not to exist.

James Roche of General Motors said that even with extensive pre-market testing, it was inevitable that problems would materialize on vehicles with fourteen thousand parts, many of them moving. He congratulated his firm on its diligence in fixing every known error, almost entirely at the company's expense.

Ribicoff was unconvinced. One in five Detroit cars was faulty, he insisted, and he was bothered that the manufacturers had not tracked down the last 10 percent of affected owners. He admitted that given the information provided, he could only guess at the significance of the problems that prompted recalls but with 155 of 426 recall campaigns involving brakes, steering, or suspensions, it seemed to him that roughly a third were safety related, and that these must be a primary cause of highway carnage. "It shatters once and for all," he said, "the myth that accidents are invariably caused by bad driving. From now on we must be concerned—not just with the nut behind the wheel but with the nut in the wheel itself, with all the parts of the car and its design. When the steering assembly on an automobile comes apart because a bolt or nut was improperly assembled or omitted entirely, there is likely to be an accident. It's that simple."[6]

Media reports tended to favor Ribicoff's alarming opinions on the meaning of his data. *The New York Times* printed Roche's response in full but gave more prominence to the senator's insistence that he had discovered the real cause of America's traffic safety problem even as it noticed that he spoke in "guesses and generalities." It was obvious, said the newspaper, that the recall revelations would further batter the reputations of automakers and increase the amount of litigation they faced while increasing the likelihood of stiffer safety legislation, which, of course, was Ribicoff's goal.[7]

With this round of stories, Ribicoff had managed to at least momentarily resume his position as the leading force behind safety legislation, shoving even Magnuson to the sideline. On the release of the recall data, the *Times* described the senator from Connecticut as a public-spirited fighter who "when he gets his teeth into a good, meaty, high-calories political issue . . . does not let go easily." The paper admired his ability to keep a grip on a commanding issue with only three years of Senate seniority when colleagues "with five times his service have never succeeded so well." It allowed that this work was probably necessary given "the rather grudging 27,000 vote" margin of Ribicoff's electoral victory.[8]

A month later, *The New York Times Magazine* ran a long profile of Ribicoff, detailing how he had outmaneuvered his more established colleagues on highway safety. It described how he had sat before television cameras in a neat dark suit to unveil his list of automobile defects, playing with his horn-rimmed eyeglasses in a "professorial way," his moon-shaped eyebrows arranged to give "just the desired effect . . . of deep concern and thoughtful sincerity." The article also revealed a dirty fight for the spoils of credit on the safety file. Some of Ribicoff's colleagues ripped him as an opportunist who chased easy headlines on simpleminded consumer issues. Nader, having led the senator by the nose on safety, was stung to see him celebrated: "When Ribicoff moves, people don't say here is a guy who is far out. They say, if Ribicoff is moving, the tide can't be far behind."

"The fuss over the investigation of Nader certainly has dramatized this thing," the senator returned. "But what's needed is somebody to translate a cause into concrete legislation."[9]

Although no one was entirely sure what to make of them, the recall numbers seemed to give those arguing for firm and immediate regulation of the automobile industry an empirical case to bolster their raw appeals to conscience. Ribicoff, Magnuson, the White House, Nader, and other advocates of regulation continued to recite gruesome statistics, the "50,000 useful and promising lives lost," the "families stung by grief." They repeated stories of decapitated children, all those recalls, and the embarrassment of auto executives. They pounded the table until Congress felt compelled to do something, anything, to dampen the flames they had fanned.[10]

On September 9, 1966, Johnson signed the National Traffic and Motor Vehicle Safety Act, which allowed for immediate safety standards to be imposed on automobiles sold in interstate commerce. The bill stood apart from previous federal regulation of business by boldly imposing new industry-wide standards rather than cautiously reacting, on a case-by-case basis, to the actions of individual companies. It had been shot through committee to rare unanimous approval by both houses of Congress within four months of Magnuson's hearings. The final draft had been completed with Senate aides shuttling back and forth between separate rooms occupied by Lloyd Cutler, chief lobbyist for Detroit, and Ralph Nader, representing the second-collision advocates. Johnson also signed the related Highway Safety Act creating an agency eventually known as the National Highway Traffic Safety Administration (NHTSA), which administered standards and required states to have uniform highway safety programs in order to qualify for full federal highway funding. Four weeks later came the legislation creating the Department of Transportation.

Senator Ribicoff had been invited to the White House for the formal signing of the September 9 bills. Afterward, Sonosky and Ribicoff drove off in the senator's Ford Mustang. On Pennsylvania Avenue they saw Howard Pyle of the National Safety Council on the sidewalk, stopped, and waved. Pyle walked over and stuck his head into the car to say hello, adding, "Senator, your seat belt's unbuckled."[11]

Sixty-seven years after Henry Hale Bliss had stepped off his trolley to become America's first traffic fatality, half a century after it had refused responsibility for the nation's traffic safety, the federal government had claimed oversight of the issue and committed itself to regulating the world's most important manufacturers. The principal reason for this "radical departure from the government's traditional, respectful hands-off approach" to the sacrosanct automobile industry, wrote Elizabeth Drew in *The Atlantic Monthly*, was that politicians had discovered that "beyond the merits of the issue, automobile safety was good politics." People loved their cars but nobody really loved an automobile company and the result had been "a political car-safety derby, with politicians jockeying for the position out in front."[12]

Drew had watched the legislative process from ringside as congressmen and their staffers tripped over one another to leak her stories about which of their colleagues was "mangling the bill now." Asked why they saw fit to vote unanimously for Detroit's regulation, congressmen cited the behavior of automakers rather than any confidence in the substance of the legislation. Substance, wrote Drew, was beside the point. Kennedy's drubbing of the General Motors executives over the amount of their safety spending was seen to have damaged Detroit's credibility, as did the company's later assertion that it spent $193 million on safety in 1964—"I saw the 'tilt' sign light up," said one legislator. Nader's anecdote about a girl being virtually decapitated by a glove compartment door made a strong impression, although there was no collision report or police testimony or news clipping to back it up. G.M. spying on a critic was considered devastating. "It was the Nader thing," said a senator. "Everybody was so outraged that a great corporation was out to clobber a guy because he wrote critically about them. At that point, everybody said to hell with them." Agreed another: "When they started looking in Ralph's bedroom, we all figured they must really be nervous. We began to believe that Nader must be right." Dan Cordtz, who covered the story for *Fortune* magazine, wrote, "Many strong supporters of auto safety legislation agree that G.M.'s conduct . . . was the most important single factor in establishing a congressional climate conducive to the passage of a tough safety bill."[13]

The National Traffic and Motor Vehicle Safety Act deliberately shifted the focus of America's long-running concern for road safety from drivers to vehicles. A day after signing the bill, President Johnson named William Haddon, who had been Daniel Patrick Moynihan's tutor on second-collision theory while working for the state of New York, to helm his new safety agency. Because Congress in its haste had not provided the agency much in the way of resources, and had left undefined the words "reasonable," "practical," and "appropriate" among other modifiers of its standards, Haddon's was a difficult job. His shop became the locus of future conflicts over safety regulation. Most of his proposed standards would become subject to lobbying and heated controversy. Litigation with the industry became routine.[14]

Another challenge for Haddon was his own view, broader than Nader's, of the safety issue. He did not see failure or recklessness in the industry's recall data: "In the production of anything as complex as a motor vehicle, and produced under tight schedules in as large numbers, it is virtually impossible to guarantee that no defective vehicles will ever reach consumers." It was thus reasonable to make provisions for their immediate correction. And notwithstanding his firm grasp of second-collision theory, Haddon looked beyond the vehicle to engineering, education, and enforcement for solutions. He had researched eight years of single-car crashes in Westchester County and found that 70 percent of drivers had been under the influence of alcohol. Fixating on the vehicle, to his mind, would not eliminate road fatalities in these cases, an outlook that put him at odds with anti-Detroit zealots. Nader, who on Haddon's appointment said that he was "superbly equipped, a really dedicated person," soon turned on him for supposedly surrendering to the automakers. Haddon would later say that to Nader, "the possibility of the invidious immediately becomes the fact of it."[15]

Within two years of his appointment, Haddon had managed to propose ninety-five safety standards for American vehicles and enact twenty-nine, although most were already met by automakers due to General Services Administration requirements. The focus of automotive regulation expanded in the late 1960s and early 1970s as growing public awareness of urban air pollution brought a barrage of new legislation aimed at fuel economy standards and automotive emissions. While their broad objectives were laudable, their implementation was aggressive and haphazard, much like the safety regulations.[*16]

Through that time, the National Highway Traffic Safety Administration did not waver from its primary concern for the crashworthiness of automobiles. A section of the Highway Safety Act advising research into whether or not the states should be pushed to move against drunk drivers went nowhere. The administration soon pushed its total of imposed vehicle safety standards above fifty and won along the way the ability to force recalls on automakers. It also became obsessed with one particular element of second-collision theory, viewing passive safety systems as the ultimate goal of regulation. This was especially the case when President Jimmy Carter appointed Nader's colleague Joan Claybrook as head of the

---

* Some of the new regulations were managed by NHTSA, and others by the new Environmental Protection Agency. Costs were high for manufacturers and consumers. Lawsuits between Detroit and Washington were endless. Some of the regulations were at cross-purposes: early emissions controls, for instance, undermined fuel economy, while the push for fuel economy resulted in smaller vehicles, which set back safety.

NHTSA. Air bags, entirely passive, requiring nothing of incorrigible vehicle occupants, became a holy grail for the administration, never mind that the technology was far from ready, and that the public was no keener on air bags than it was on seat belts.[17]

Regardless of the difficulties encountered in implementation, the new traffic safety legislation was a watershed. It took no time for other entrepreneurial congressmen to figure out that standing for the people against private greed and corporate recklessness could work in other sectors of the economy. Between 1967 and 1973, twenty-five substantial consumer and environmental regulatory bills were passed and hundreds more were considered. Existing agencies like the Federal Trade Commission and the Food and Drug Administration became more vigilant about consumer interests. One hundred twenty regulatory programs were implemented between 1969 and 1979. The number of people staffing regulatory agencies tripled and government spending on regulatory enforcement increased by a factor of nine over that same period. The *Federal Register*, a publication that details Washington's regulatory actions, exploded from 15,000 pages when the Corvair was launched to 86,000 pages by 1980. Prior to the Ribicoff hearings, regulated industries in the United States represented 7 percent of Gross National Product, by 1978, 30 percent. The regulatory state expanded into food, cosmetics, credit instruments, packaging and advertising, monopolies and pricing practices, and air and water pollution. Additionally, all fifty states had by 1975 created consumer protection agencies and thirty-nine had passed consumer protection statutes.[18]

The victimized consumer was all the rage. Activists, staffers, and politicians, especially those with weak ties to the business community, faced American capitalism in a frankly adversarial pose, armed with shocking facts and moral outrage. Said the actor Betty Furness, now President Johnson's special assistant for consumer affairs: "You gave us nylon but didn't tell us it melts. You gave us insect spray, but you didn't tell us it would kill the cat. You gave us plastic bags, but didn't warn us that it could, and has, killed babies. You gave us detergents, but didn't tell us they were polluting our rivers and streams. And you gave us the pill, but didn't tell us we were guinea pigs."

President Johnson echoed Furness: "Women are tired of meat with worms in it, blouses that burn, and pipelines that blow up under their houses."[19]

Time recognized the new consumerism as another manifestation of "an age of discontent that has roiled campuses and ghettos," never mind that it had sprung "primarily from the comfortable middle class." The anger and the fury were unmistakable. The magazine saw only good in this, signs that Americans were better educated, harder to fool, willing to subject old certitudes to new doubts and to question authority. It put Nader and the Corvair on its cover under the banner "The Consumer Revolt," suggesting that the author was the head of a righteous grassroots movement.[20]

Not all the regulatory action was in government. New developments in the legal system added a belt to the federal government's suspenders. Tort law continued its expansion from what Yale's George L. Priest has described as "a relatively minor mechanism for dealing with a small subset of accidents" into an institution aspiring to "regulate all industries and social activities, making it the most significant regulatory body in American society." The law increasingly imposed on manufacturers a responsibility to reduce hazards inherent in defective products whether or not they were negligently designed or made. Even if a crash could not have been prevented by a better product, making the manufacturer liable was viewed as providing a form of insurance for consumers. Thus the costs of injury were said to be "internalized" to the injury-causing entity, or corporation, which was presumed rich enough to bear the cost.[21]

Building on the idea of requiring corporations to cover the costs of injury, the courts curtailed legal defenses available to manufacturers while expanding liability standards to cover almost any malfunction. They also allowed greater scope for recovery of noneconomic damages such as pain and suffering. Class action procedures, by which private law claims were aggregated, came of age in the mid-1960s, allowing entrepreneurial attorneys to argue harms on behalf of hundreds of thousands of individuals, effectively industrializing torts and threatening huge economic loss upon defendants. Because of the enormous risk they presented, class action claims were almost never litigated to judgment; both plaintiffs and defendants preferred to manage their costs and risk through negotiated settlements.

For many attorneys, tort actions were simply another line of business. For others, and for activists like Ralph Nader and James Ridgeway who assisted them, there was clear political intent. "In recent years," said Ridgeway, who after *The New Republic* cofounded the radical newsletter *Hard Times*, "the trial lawyers have mounted a devastating attack on American corporations. Their suits begin simply as damage claims, then broaden into attacks on the conduct of the corporation, tracing in the most fundamental radical manner the injury of individuals back through the corporation hierarchy. They show in great detail how corporate officials engage in calculated plunder and injury of the populace." Ridgeway saw the courts replacing legislatures as the venue where "the evils of the business system" were exposed and corrected, and the exploitive system of commercial consumption was challenged and defeated.[22]

All of these developments contributed to a vast and seemingly endless expansion of tort liability. From 1950 to 1990, direct tort costs grew at an astonishing average annual rate of 11.3 percent, from $1.8 billion a year to $130.2 billion, more than three times the rate of growth in the economy.[23] These high costs might be justifiable if social objectives are being served, but they seldom are. Torts can't be said to promote justice because few cases are brought to trial and those that do are likely to end in defeat. Most are settled out of court, without findings of guilt or innocence. Torts are notoriously weak as a deterrent and as punishment for transgressors since most have insurance. Nor do they serve well as a compensation system for the injured: most victims, whether of auto crashes or medical malpractice, never recover their full losses (and nearly as many nonvictims as victims are compensated thanks to the culture of settlements and questionable jury outcomes). Studies have shown that the lion's share of moneys raised through tort actions winds up in the pockets of lawyers rather than those of victims.[24]

Nevertheless, Americans were convinced, in the moment, that the actions of congressional and legal entrepreneurs against corporations were necessary. In addition to the surge in legislative and legal actions, newspapers and other media outlets began hiring consumer advocates and impressing upon the public the myriad ways in which businesses large and small worked against its best interests. As early as 1969, seven in ten Americans believed more legislation was required to protect their health and safety, and their confidence in product and service retailers and advertisers continued to decline through the ensuing decade. Behind all of this activity was an unwavering confidence that public interest advocates and the minds governing America had at their disposal the means and expertise to protect citizens. Nader, again, received credit for "moral leadership of the movement." A majority of Americans believed it was "good to have critics like Ralph Nader to keep business on its toes."[25]

CHAPTER 14

NO DEFECTS, NO NEGLIGENCE

The consequences of the safety crusade were not limited to new legislation, consumer activism, and momentum for tort actions. Corvair sales had been decimated even before G.M.'s private eyes were discovered. The Detroit Auto Dealers Association recorded 503 Corvair sales in the first two months of 1966 compared to 1,128 in 1965. Within days of the corporation's apology to Nader, a Detroit Chevrolet dealer reported that the car was "off real bad in both price and volume," that discounts of 10 percent were required to close a deal for a new model, and still deeper cuts for preowned vehicles. General Motors slashed production of the car to 32,043 units in the first quarter of 1966 from 65,172 in the first quarter of 1965, and reduced the workweek at its Willow Run plant to three days. The sales data crushed what had otherwise been a fine start to 1966 for the Corvair: it had placed first in the annual Pure Oil Performance Trials with a fuel economy of twenty-five miles per gallon, and in another competition demonstrated itself to have the best brakes in its class.[1]

In the months following, Ralph Nader appeared on a CBS special report hosted by Charles Kuralt where he compared the dangers of riding in American-built cars to sitting "in a roomful of knives," and on NBC's *Meet the Press* where he said, once more, that the automobile industry was "outside the law" and that driving Detroit vehicles was akin to shaving with a "jagged razor blade." Chevrolet engineer Frank Winchell was quoted in some of the same programs and press reports but his statements that the "Corvair's capabilities were greater than the capabilities of [its] drivers and the highways on which [it] is driven," and that its range of controllability was "equal to or better than any other car" of its class, were no match for Nader's frightening rhetoric. And employed as he was by the corporation that had made a humiliating public apology for spying on Nader, Winchell's credibility was suspect. Corvair's sales plummeted further. Chevrolet moved 1,899 Corvairs in the first ten days of May compared to 6,213 the year before.[2]

That spring, United Auto Workers officials attending their annual convention in Long Beach, California, speculated that General Motors would drop the Corvair from its 1967 production lineup. They leaked to the press a rumor that Willow Run was scheduled for a shutdown of eight to nine weeks starting in July. A Chevrolet spokesman called that story "a dirty stinking lie" and insisted that G.M. remained committed to the Corvair. The corporation admitted that sales were declining due to "increased competition from intermediate-size cars and adverse publicity."[3]

Eighteen hundred shareholders attended the General Motors annual general meeting in May 1966, including Evelyn Davis, a New York investor waving 212 proxies. She failed in her bid to nominate Ralph Nader to the automaker's board of directors. Three doctors representing Physicians for Automotive Safety were jeered by shareholders for stating from the floor that the corporation's safety plans had been "paltry, frugal, tardy, incomplete, makeshift, and hastily conceived." Said an employee-shareholder in the crowd: "I like all those knobs on the instrument panel and I would never use seat belts."[4]

Nader was credited in the *Detroit Free Press* with stealing the show at the annual meeting without having attended. That observation likely prompted the newspaper to publish its own profile of him, introducing Nader to its readers as a best-selling author, a household name, and the talk of the industry. What was remarkable about the piece was Nader's presentation of himself to the *Free Press*'s reporter as a lone, courageous crusader for truth who pre-

ferred his mission to food, drink, sleep, or sex: "It's far more important for me to have my gratification in the safety movement than
in the traditional ways. When you're in the front lines you can't go
home to mother. You have to fight and sleep in order to fight some
more. . . . Besides, I can't work eighteen hours a day and have time
for anything else."[5]

Nader saw himself as living a great romantic adventure: "It seems
ridiculous but there were meetings on dark streets, in lonely places,
disguised telephone conversations." That he was fighting Detroit
against impossible odds motivated rather than deterred him: "What
sustains me is the knowledge that I can't win. But at least I'll be able
to civilize things a bit more." It was an attitude perfectly matched to
the times: stories of solitary, righteous heroes fighting losing battles
against corrupt systems were box-office gold for Paul Newman (*Cool
Hand Luke*), Richard Burton (*The Spy Who Came in from the Cold*),
and countless other actors in the 1960s.[6]

Contrary to its earlier assertions, Chevrolet did close the Willow Run plant for the entire July–August period in the summer of
1966. Chevrolet tried aggressive rebates and produced 1.5 million
glow-in-the-dark bumper stickers reading "I Love My Corvair" but
by autumn, with sales off 54 percent year-to-date, tens of thousands
of unwanted Corvairs were collecting dust on dealer lots. By the
end of 1966, which Chevrolet labeled "a difficult year," only 73,000
Corvairs had found homes compared to 204,000 in 1965.[7]

Ed Cole's revolutionary small car was now unsalable, firmly
lodged in the public mind as a death trap. Before the safety controversy, Corvair had enjoyed some of the highest ratings in quality surveys of G.M. owners; it was now near the bottom on almost
every count, even on items like body workmanship and upholstery
which had nothing to do with safety. It did not matter that Nader, in
his last appearance before Ribicoff's subcommittee, had been unable
to answer Senator Kennedy's request for empirical proof that the
Corvair was any worse than any other car. All of Detroit was waiting for the announcement that the Corvair would be discontinued.[8]

To G.M.'s great frustration, the car's sales were tanking at the
very moment that courts were nearing unanimity on the soundness
of the Corvair's design. This had been what Kennedy was getting at
when he asked Nader about court decisions involving the Corvair

and *Unsafe at Any Speed*'s neglect of jury verdicts favorable to the automaker in Clearwater, Florida, and San Jose, California. A third trial played out in the months immediately following the close of Ribicoff's hearings.

The third case involved sixteen-year-old Don Wells Lyford, who around 10 p.m. on May 16, 1960, was killed behind the wheel of a new Corvair on the curvy two-lane Carmel–Pacific Grove Cutoff in Monterey County, California. Believed to have been speeding at the time, Lyford lost control of his car on a turn and crashed into an oncoming Plymouth. His divorced parents, Mary Jane Drummond and Don Lyford, sued General Motors and two Chevrolet dealers for wrongful death and asked $250,000 in damages. The plaintiffs were represented by the Harney firm in Los Angeles. Many of Nader's ideas, arguments, and rhetorical strategies were applied in the case, indirectly putting *Unsafe at Any Speed* on trial.[9]

The plaintiffs in *Drummond v. General Motors* appealed to the well-established legal principle that a manufacturer must exercise reasonable care in the manufacture of a product so as to avoid unreasonable risk of causing physical harm to its users when they are using the product for the purposes for which it is intended. Specifically, they argued that the design of the Corvair was defective, that it had too much weight in the rear, that its suspension was inadequate, that it was dangerous in the hands of the average driver, and that G.M. and its retailers were negligent in adopting the design. They further argued the new doctrine of strict liability, which had been embraced by California courts. It held that G.M. need not have been negligent in creating its design in order to be responsible for the vehicle's flaws. If the automaker exercised reasonable care yet still created a defective vehicle and someone was injured or killed while using it in an ordinary fashion, the manufacturer was liable.

Unlike the previous Corvair jury trials, the Drummond case was argued before a judge, the Honorable Bernard S. Jefferson of the Superior Court of Los Angeles County. This was significant because Nader had been dismissive of the abilities of juries to reach the right conclusions in automotive design cases.

Over fifteen weeks, the court filled 9,599 pages with testimony from forty-one witnesses, most of them experts: engineers, police investigators, auto magazine editors, university professors, racing car drivers, and employees of General Motors. Among the 240 exhibits allowed into evidence were eyewitness testimony, photographs, films, a scale model of the road where the crash occurred, minute examinations of the skid marks left by Lyman's car, and a full-size model of the controversial rear-end suspension of the Corvair. The plaintiff introduced technical discussions of lateral acceleration, centrifugal force, road friction, oversteer, understeer, slip angles, and wheel camber, all of which was intended to convince the court that the Corvair was prone to suddenly and without warning produce a vicious oversteer that would cause the driver to lose control and, often, roll the vehicle.

Judge Jefferson gave careful consideration to the patent applications that Nader and the plaintiff's attorneys had relied upon to argue G.M.'s negligence, including one from 1956 by Maurice Olley, former head of research and development at Chevrolet, which was purportedly critical of swing-axle independent suspensions such as the one on the Corvair. The judge looked at film of Corvairs in test runs provided by both the plaintiff and the defense. He pondered the after-market stabilizers produced by independent manufacturers to increase the stability of the vehicle after its 1960 release, and G.M.'s decision to upgrade the suspension in 1964 models of the Corvair, both of which had been seized upon by critics as proof of G.M.'s initial failure to build a safe car. He also considered the argument that G.M. advertisements stating that the Corvair offers "glued-to-the-road traction for cornering and driving on ice, mud or snow"—that it "handles like a quarter horse and rides soft as eider down"—constituted a disingenuous promise or warranty to the buyer.[10]

In his seventy-page decision, Judge Jefferson determined that Olley's patent application was discussing a different type of swing-axle suspension than the one introduced on the Corvair. He found nothing incriminating in the test films. The automaker's decision to upgrade the suspension in its 1964 models was not proof of the inadequacy of earlier Corvairs. Rather, an improvement had been made, one that had been in development at G.M. for a decade and not available for use when the Corvair debuted in 1960. To read any upgrade on late-model cars as a criticism of earlier models, declared

Jefferson, would discourage innovation and shortchange consumers. Nor was the existence of an aftermarket stabilizer for the Corvair (similar accessories were made for Porsches and Volkswagens) indicative of anything more than the fact that every car on the road could be upgraded if an owner so desired. There was no law imposing upon car manufacturers an obligation to design and manufacture the safest possible car irrespective of cost and appeal to the buying public. All vehicles, wrote Jefferson, represent a compromise between the best that could be made and what could be produced economically and marketed successfully.

The judge criticized General Motors for using imprecise language in a section of the Corvair owner's guide that dealt with tire pressure—the corporation's own engineers could not decipher it—but said it had no bearing on the Lyford collision. Finally, the notion that G.M.'s ads could be construed as misrepresentations of material fact was rejected: a reasonable purchaser would see them as expressions of opinion, salesmanship, puffery, rather than taking them literally as had Nader and the Lyford attorneys.

The Corvair might be different from front-engine cars but different is not inherently defective, Jefferson wrote in summation. Regardless of whether a car tends to oversteer or understeer, it is incumbent on the driver to learn the behavioral characteristics of the vehicle, and operate it prudently under prevailing conditions. All automobiles have limits to their controllability, points beyond which they present a serious danger to their drivers, and those limits vary from car to car. An oversteering car reacts differently on a sharp turn at high speed than an understeering car, but both will go out of control beyond their limits. The judge found no compelling evidence that the Corvair was more inclined to spin out on tight corners than a conventional understeering car. The reason that the plaintiffs had film of the Corvair rolling in tight curves while G.M. had film of the Corvair successfully executing tight curves was simply that the plaintiffs had wanted to roll the car while the G.M. engineers had not. Jefferson was impressed that Don Lyford's stepfather, as owner of the fated vehicle, had driven the car under various conditions and at challenging speeds and had found nothing wrong with it. His only warning to his stepson had been that the

Corvair handled somewhat differently than the car he was accustomed to driving. It was only after the crash, upon reading criticisms of the car by Nader and others, that Drummond became convinced of its design flaws.

Jefferson faulted the deceased in the crash. It had been "foolhardy" of him to drive too fast on a dark and tricky road in an unfamiliar vehicle. The judge's findings with regard to the Corvair were unequivocal:

> It is the Court's conclusion that the Corvair automobile of the 1960 through 1963 variety is not defectively designed nor a defective product; that no negligence was involved in the manufacturer's adoption of the Corvair design; that the Corvair matches a standard of safety which does not create any reasonable risk of harm to an average driver; that the cause of the May 16, 1960 accident and the death of Don Wells Lyford was due solely to the actions of said deceased and not to the design or any handling characteristics of the Corvair automobile. Judgment will be for the defendants.[11]

The Jefferson decision prompted an Associated Press wire story, although major newspapers, including the *Chicago Tribune, The Boston Globe,* and *The Arizona Republic,* were as blasé in their treatment of it as *The New York Times,* which placed it on an inside page next to its wedding announcements. It went unnoticed that Ralph Drummond, the stepfather, was a law partner of David Harney, who was handling forty-seven Corvair suits. Nor did much attention attend the consequent collapse of the Corvair personal injury industry. Harney admitted that the Drummond decision had made further actions untenable and settled the rest of his G.M. suits out of court in January 1967. A third of these cases were dropped for no payment, and the rest for the token sum of $350,000, or 1.3 percent of the $25 million asked. G.M. would eventually clear all but two of its Corvair cases at minimal cost.*[12]

---

* G.M. was sued 294 times for damages of over $100 million relating to the Corvair's design. Apart from the Pierini settlement, a Texas jury found the Corvair defectively designed and in 1979 awarded Harold L. Bryant, who suffered brain

Legal vindication had no effect on the Corvair's sales. In the first half of 1967, G.M. produced 11,304 units compared to 58,016 in the first half of 1966. That trend continued for the rest of the year, during which the *Times* called the car a "disaster." Only 15,000 more Corvairs were made in all of 1968. A few auto journalists noted that the Corvair's sales might have declined even without the safety scandal. A new generation of sporty vehicles, led by Ford's Mustang, was capturing the public's fancy. But there is an enormous difference between manageable decline and sales that fall off a cliff. The safety scandal, not the Mustang, killed the Corvair. Despite 1.7 million units sold, Chevrolet's rear-engine vehicle would in future appear on lists of crackpot automotive innovations alongside swivel front seats and Chrysler's backseat record player.[13]

In another bitter victory for General Motors, Cornell's Automotive Crash Injury Research Project released in December 1968 an enormous study of crashes in thirty states dating back to 1956. It found that the major cause of traffic fatalities and serious injuries for all cars was ejections, usually caused by rollovers. It offered a rare brand-by-brand look at collision outcomes, something Nader had long been demanding. In crashes in which rollovers were the principal cause of injury or death, occupants were ejected from Volkswagens at a rate of 31.1 percent, from foreign sports cars at 42.9 percent, and from the Corvair at 13.9 percent. The range for other American-built cars was 17.7 to 40.0 percent. In non-rollover crashes resulting in deaths, Corvairs performed on par with other North American– and European-built cars. This provided perhaps the best answer to Senator Kennedy's question about empirical data on the Corvair's safety relative to other cars. It came too late to help the Corvair.[14]

Rumors were published throughout 1968 that General Motors would finally discontinue the car. On May 13, 1969, it was official. "GM Drops Corvair," wrote *The New York Times*, "A Failure at Age 10." Nader, whose book had by now sold 55,000 hardcovers and another 200,000 paperbacks, danced on its grave: "General Motors

---

stem damage in a 1965 accident with a 1962 Corvair, $2.4 million. This says more about the unpredictability of jury outcomes than it does about the design of the Corvair.

can perform a public service by recalling the old Corvairs . . . and attaching ride-stabilizing parts. Corvair stability gets worse with age, and the poor people and the teenagers end up with those old ones."[15]

Notwithstanding the Corvair's departure from the G.M. lineup and its legal vindication, Nader refused to abandon his prosecution of the car's design. In September 1970 he wrote letters to Nixon's Transportation Secretary John A. Volpe and Senator Ribicoff alerting them to the existence of previously unseen G.M. films that "conclusively prove the Corvair to be uniquely unstable with unprecedented rollover capability unlike any other American car." The vehicle had been captured rolling at speeds as low as twenty-six miles per hour. G.M., said Nader, had suppressed evidence to Ribicoff's subcommittee. It had "manufactured and maintained a massive lie," and engaged in a "massive conspiracy."[16]

Ed Cole, who wore the Corvair's "spectacular failure," and who had succeeded Roche as president of General Motors, told reporters that the films in question were of tests to evaluate the effect of experimental parts on the handling characteristics of the Corvair, and that Nader's representation of them was "irresponsible and false." Ribicoff nevertheless investigated Nader's claims. He concluded that G.M. did not mislead his subcommittee and declared the matter closed. This seems to have ended the senator's relationship with Nader, who claimed the investigation had been bungled. Ribicoff's investigators told the press that Nader had become uncooperative in their dealings.[17]

Under further pressure from Nader, who claimed that "the best place to test the Corvair is on an objective proving ground with adequate instrumentations," the new National Highway Traffic Safety Administration organized a thorough, independent test of the Corvair to determine, once and for all, whether the vehicle was unsafe relative to other cars on the road. It appointed a blue-chip advisory panel including Edwin Resler, a professor of aerospace engineering and an expert on crash research at Cornell; Paul Wright, a professor of civil engineering at Georgia Institute of Technology; and Ray Caldwell, a racing car builder and graduate of Harvard Business School. The panel was told to review all relevant literature on vehicle stability and handling, examine all evidence brought by Nader, his associates, and officials of the Department of Transportation and General Motors, and produce a conclusive evaluation of the Corvair.[18]

The panel spent two years on the project, including four months of road tests at College Station, Texas, during which a 1963 Corvair was put through its paces alongside three other compacts of similar vintage, a 1962 Falcon, a 1962 Volkswagen, and a 1963 Renault, all of them operated by robots and monitored by the latest scientific instruments to avoid the subjectivity of human drivers. The panel's findings were that "the handling and stability performance of the 1960–63 Corvair does not result in an abnormal potential for loss of control or rollover and it is at least as good as the performance of some contemporary vehicles both foreign and domestic."[19]

The researchers noted that when driven around tight curves at excessive speed the car would tend to oversteer rather than understeer, which might not be expected by a driver accustomed to conventional domestic automobiles (the NHTSA, still under pressure from Nader, would later advise Corvair owners of this fact). However, they could find no "critical speed" beyond which the Corvair was unsafe. Its rollover rate was the same as the other light American cars. The much anticipated smoking-gun films were not representative "of the practical driving environment" and proved nothing. The report essentially confirmed the review of *Consumer Reports* magazine, which had tested the Corvair on its release and found that while its tendency to oversteer rather than understeer might be undesirable for some drivers, it presented "no problem" in normal driving conditions and it made possible "some important handling gains."[20]

A relentless Nader called the NHTSA report a "shoddy, internally inconsistent whitewash" of the Corvair's "notoriously unsafe handling." Assisted by future NHTSA head Joan Claybrook, he maintained the Corvair testing had been "rigged." The panel's testing procedures and model selection were biased. He complained that new tires rather than old tires had been installed on the 1963 Corvair, and that the 1963 model was configured slightly differently from earlier models. There was also too much passenger weight added to the Corvair in the tests, which along with the weight of the test equipment had further altered results. He accused the engineers who had performed the tests of a cover-up.[21]

Nader continued to attack the Corvair's handling, to no avail, although he did finally win a modest victory on another matter. He alleged that heaters in 1965 Corvairs leaked fumes into the passenger compartment. Subsequent field tests confirmed that in some cars that had not been properly maintained, carbon monoxide and other fumes could escape the engine compartment to the interior. The NHTSA said the evidence was insufficient to order a recall, and G.M. protested that there was no problem if owners maintained their vehicles. The automaker nevertheless agreed to notify owners of the possibility of problems in their heating systems, and how to correct them at their own cost.[22]

In 1970, Nader managed a larger victory. Almost from the moment Roche had apologized for G.M.'s investigation of Nader, the author and his lawyers began organizing a suit against the automaker for invading his privacy. The goals were to hold G.M. accountable for its surveillance, expand the privacy rights of individuals, and fund more consumer activism. Nader's counsel, Stuart Speiser, took the case on a contingency basis:

> The tort lawyer's dream of the perfect case usually involves a completely pure plaintiff (such as a nun) who has been injured outrageously by a "target defendant," someone who makes a ready target for the jury's righteous indignation and can also pay a large judgment (such as a drunken millionaire playboy driving an expensive sports car at breakneck speed). As I watched James Roche apologize to Ralph Nader on nationwide television, I was convinced that we had the dream case at last. Whatever Ralph Nader had become to idol-hungry admirers—knight in shining armor, champion of the consumer, the last honest man, even a sex symbol—in my narrow sights he was one thing above all else: the perfect plaintiff. And General Motors was a perfect target defendant: hated by millions of disgruntled car owners and

unlikely to get sympathy from a jury when it came to fixing damages.[23]

With his dream case in hand, Speiser filed a claim of $2 million in compensatory damages for mental distress and $5 million for punitive damages, naming G.M. and Vincent Gillen as defendants. Speiser launched a second suit against the detective for defamation. Gillen had told a newspaper reporter that Nader was imagining himself to have been followed in various places where he was not followed and ought to see a psychiatrist. When the legal department at General Motors foolishly declined to help Gillen in his defamation suit, the detective switched teams and dumped in Speiser's lap documentation demonstrating clearly that he had been instructed to pry into Nader's personal affairs, and that he had conducted other wide-ranging investigations for G.M. After failing with various legal maneuvers to have the evidence thrown out, General Motors, tired of the bad publicity and wanting rid of Nader, settled the invasion of privacy claim without any admission of wrongdoing for $425,000, a fraction of the original ask but far more than any previous award for a similar claim.[24]

That Nader squeezed a handsome settlement out of General Motors contributed mightily to his legend. If Roche's apology had been Goliath's fall, G.M.'s $425,000 check was his severed head held aloft to idol-hungry admirers. It made Nader, the pure plaintiff, almost skeptic-proof. He faced remarkably few questions about his work on the government dime, his having served as both prosecutor and witness for Ribicoff, his various outrageous and unsubstantiated claims and ruthless attacks on experts and public servants, his mishandling of important facts and quotations, and the massive conspiracies that failed to materialize.[25]

One of few Nader skeptics was David Sanford, the *New Republic* writer who first interviewed Vince Gillen about his investigation on behalf of General Motors. Having grown wary of the crusader, Sanford in the mid-1970s wrote a small book, *Me & Ralph*, asking hard questions about Nader's reported ownership of Ford Motor Company stock; his apparent purchase (with his brother Shafeek) of an expensive home in Washington while he still claimed to live an austere rooming-house lifestyle; the contradiction between his demands for transparency on the part of corporations and his secrecy about his own personal and business affairs; and how the various public advocacy entities he had created, including the Center for Study of Responsive Law, the Public Interest Research Group, the Tax Reform Research Study Group, Public Citizen, the Corporate Responsibility Research Group, and the Public Citizen Litigation Group among many others, amounted to a public interest combine more complicated and secretive than General Motors (it would eventually expand to twenty-nine organizations with combined revenues of $75 million).* Nader and his associates refused to cooperate with Sanford, dismissing him as a corporate stooge. His book passed with small notice. Nader placed in the top ten of Gallup's list of most admired men several times in the 1970s, and a Harvard Law School publication called him "the most outstanding man ever to receive a degree from this institution," over the likes of Oliver Wendell Holmes and Louis Brandeis.[26]

---

* According to a 1970 Gannett News Service report, Nader's Safety Systems was fined by the Internal Revenue Service for actions "jeopardizing charitable purposes," including, on one occasion, short-selling the stock of a company Nader was attacking. *Forbes*, September 17, 1990.

CHAPTER 15

THE DEATH OF ALFRED P. SLOAN

The fate of one rear-engine wonder car does not matter enormously to a manufacturing empire like General Motors. The Corvair was a single vehicle in a Chevrolet lineup that included Impalas, Bel Airs, Biscaynes, Caprices, and many other models, and Chevrolet was one division (albeit the largest) of several within the General Motors family. Had the damage from the safety siege been limited to one nameplate, had Nader and company simply blown a Corvair-sized hole in G.M.'s hull, the corporation might have sailed into the future little the worse for wear. But the damage was not limited to the Corvair.

To appreciate the impact of the safety controversy on the whole of General Motors, it helps to step back to the very eve of the Ribicoff hearing when the corporation was comfortably atop the Fortune 500 rankings and confident that its 1965 model year had broken all records in sales volume, sales revenue, and profits. Its executives had in their possession a fresh Ira O. Glick study that told them General Motors was considered by Americans the undisputed leader of the auto industry and, by an overwhelming margin, the most powerful and successful corporation in the land. It was widely admired for the styling, reliability, and value of its products, to say nothing of the performance of its share price. A Gallup study of college students rated G.M. ahead of General Electric and every other American company in terms of outstanding products and corporate performance and contributions to society.[1]

Safety was not a serious issue in the public mind. Americans blamed drivers for blood on the road and thought that more driver training, more enforcement, lower speed limits, mandatory vehicle inspection, and seat belts were the answers to the problem. They believed their cars were built with their protection in mind and to the extent that they thought about safety, they considered crash avoidance rather than crashworthiness the salient issue.[2]

Yet another demonstration of G.M.'s dominance of American business at that moment was the presence in bookstores of the recently published memoir of its retired chairman, Alfred P. Sloan. For a memoir, *My Years with General Motors* offered little in the way of personal revelation from the man who had built G.M. into the world's largest manufacturer and raised the bar for organizational excellence throughout American industry. Rather, in the course of telling the story of General Motors from conception to colossus, Sloan delivered an extended essay on his approach to corporate management. It was a serious effort, five years in the making. Published to immediate acclaim at the end of 1963 and released as a mass market paperback in 1965, it was well on its way to becoming one of the best-selling business books of all time, studied by aspiring Sloans around the world for generations to come. No less an authority than Peter Drucker would call it the best book on business management ever written.[*3]

Now ninety years old and widowed, Sloan was enjoying a fulfilling retirement, rare in its longevity for a top General Motors executive. In addition to his book, he was keeping a close eye on the

---

* Microsoft cofounder and voracious reader Bill Gates has said of *My Years with General Motors*: "This is probably the best book to read if you want to read only one book about business." Walter A. Friedman, a professor at Harvard Business School, added in 2014 that despite wholesale changes in the business environment since its publication, Sloan's book reveals more than any other single volume "what it takes to build a company around a compelling strategy." http://favobooks.com /enterpreneurs/46-billgates.html; https://hbr.org/2014/03/my-years-with-general -motors-fifty-years-on.

automaker in the capacity of chairman emeritus. He was overseeing an impressive range of philanthropic activities through the Alfred P. Sloan Foundation. He lived in a commodious apartment overlooking Central Park at Fifth Avenue and 53rd and went daily to his office two blocks away, often carrying in his coat pocket a sandwich neatly wrapped in paper. He gave every indication of being happy and healthy until February 15, 1966.[4]

As a prime indicator of consumer confidence and the health of the broader American economy, new car sales were publicized widely and regularly in the 1960s. Newspapers and wire services issued updates at annual, quarterly, monthly, and ten-day intervals. General Motors' numbers for the first ten days of February were released on February 15, the first set of data fully reflecting national publicity for *Unsafe at Any Speed*, Nader's appearance at the Iowa hearings, the launch of the Stop Murder by Motor campaign, Harry Philo's bid to have the Corvair banned from Michigan roads, and January's leak that the White House was preparing a bill to regulate automakers. G.M.'s sales results were grim: down 22,850 units from the same period in 1965. The damage crossed almost every G.M. nameplate and was deep enough to drag all of Detroit to a net decline of 15,500 units for the period. It was the first significant break in Detroit's remarkable five-year expansion.[5]

Suddenly unwell, Sloan was taken that same day from his apartment to New York's Memorial Sloan-Kettering Center, so named in gratitude for his $4 million gift two decades earlier. He was dead of a heart attack within forty-eight hours.

Sloan's obituary in *The New York Times* filled a page. Henry Ford II hailed him as "one of the small handful of men who actually made automotive history." The *Times* called him "a quiet, selfless executive" with organization and management skills "amounting almost to genius." However magnificent his contributions to the nation's business life, said the paper, they were dwarfed by his philanthropic endeavors, in particular grants and gifts totaling $23 million that had made the Sloan-Kettering Cancer Institute one of the world's foremost cancer research centers. Sloan's estate provided another $90 million to charity, including a $10 million gift to the Sloan School of Management at his alma mater, the Massachusetts Institute of Technology.[6]

. . .

It is impossible to say whether the condition of his beloved corporation had anything to do with the timing of Sloan's demise. He was
ancient. Yet he had been in "excellent health" until February 15.
Regardless of causality, he may be counted fortunate to have missed
all that visited G.M. in the months and years to follow.[7]

In response to its February decline, General Motors did what
it usually did when sales slumped. Organized for scale, firm in its
belief that its half share of the American automotive industry was
the key to its success, the corporation ramped up its advertising and
offered discounts to make up lost sales. These tactics cut into the
company's profits but protected its all-important market share. An
uptick in sales followed in March.

Sales pressure is a short-term tactic, however, and the recovery
proved unsustainable, especially in the wake of Roche's apology. In
April, G.M.'s sales were down almost 5 percent from the previous
year while Ford and Chrysler improved slightly. By the end of the
first half of 1966, General Motors sales were off 7 percent, with
Chevrolet down 10 percent. The Corvair, accounting for 38 percent
of the Chevrolet decline, was a big piece of Chevy's problem but
hardly the whole of it.[8]

A clearer window on the depths of the company's woes was its
share price. It hit a high of $105 in the first weeks of 1966, dropped
to $101 on the release of the early February sales data, and fell to $95
after Gillen's detectives were exposed. When the April sales figures
were released, it sank to $88, and on the further announcement that
the company, struggling with a bloated inventory of unsold vehicles,
was cutting production not only at Corvair plants but in two California facilities that assembled regular-size G.M. cars, it hit $85.

"For five straight years," wrote *Time* magazine in May, "the U.S.
economy has enjoyed unprecedented good times, and no company
has benefited more from the prosperity or contributed more to it
than General Motors. Now that the sales of the nation's biggest and
most influential manufacturer are slowing down from spectacular to
merely excellent, the rattling at G.M. has raised doubts about the
direction of that greater engine, the U.S. economy."[9]

As G.M. goes, they said on Wall Street, so goes the market. The Dow Jones Industrial Average, which had reached a new high of 995 points simultaneous with G.M.'s peak, followed the automaker down, plummeting by 16 on news of the production cuts, the largest drop since the Kennedy assassination. By the end of June, the Dow was at 871 points, off 13 percent from its high. G.M.'s share price was meanwhile at $80, meaning that a quarter of the company's $8.4 billion market capitalization had evaporated in six months. "Uncertainty," said *Time*, "has replaced confidence with disconcerting suddenness." Michigan governor George Romney, the former head of American Motors and a proponent of federal automotive safety legislation, warned that overheated criticism of Detroit and its products was threatening to send the entire auto industry and the national economy "into a tailspin."[10]

The national economy had problems of its own. The Johnson administration's high social spending, combined with the mounting costs of the Vietnam War, were raising prospects of inflation, higher interest rates, and tax increases. The Federal Reserve moved interest rates from 4.5 percent at the start of 1966 to 6 percent in September, dampening consumer spending and compounding Detroit's troubles. Ford and Chrysler, too, announced production cuts, although not as deep as G.M.'s. It is difficult to say how much of the latter's share price decline was due to its own problems and how much to the broader economy, but the Dow's slump, as much as 21 percent in 1966, was nowhere near as sharp as the automaker's.[11]

By the end of 1966, G.M. had sold 8 percent fewer cars than the year before, its revenue had slipped for the first time in five years, and profits had slipped from $2.1 billion to $1.8 billion, or 14 percent. The company's net income as a percentage of sales, which had averaged over 10 percent the previous four years, was reduced to 8.9 percent, indicating that it had indeed been spending more to sell fewer vehicles. Coming off a record year, these numbers were disappointing but not terrible. The same could not be said for the share price. For generations one of the most reliable performers on the New York exchange, it traded at $66 by year's end, representing a 37 percent loss of shareholder value and a $3 billion hit to G.M.'s market capitalization. Six months further down the road, interest rates had returned to 4 percent, the Dow had recovered most of its loss, Ford's share price had almost entirely recovered, yet G.M. was still off more than 20 percent.[12]

Throughout 1967, General Motors surveyed public attitudes on everything from simple matters of customer loyalty to larger questions of corporate social responsibility. The responses help to explain G.M.'s underperformance. The safety controversy, in addition to killing the Corvair, had tainted the company's brand, and that taint had spread like a cancer throughout the entire General Motors world. One survey conducted by Ira O. Glick determined that the Ribicoff hearings and Washington's decision to regulate Detroit had produced "pointed anger and heightened fears" about American cars. Some consumers had been convinced that 1966 automobiles did not carry sufficient safety equipment, leading them to postpone purchase decisions, contributing to that year's sales slump. While the eventual introduction of new safety standards reassured buyers, General Motors "does not fully share in the attitude improvement" that followed the new laws. The feeling was that G.M. had done "less than it could (and should) have done in regard to the safety of its products until forced by the government to introduce changes." Its seeming recalcitrance prompted "considerable amounts of disappointment or even anger." The controversy had left "an emotional residue."[13]

The emotional residue expressed itself in a variety of ways. Most broadly, it affected perceptions of General Motors relative to its peers, resulting in "diminished corporate esteem." Respondents were suddenly less inclined to view G.M. as the nation's leading automaker, and more inclined to doubt its capacity to do anything right. The corporation was accused of living off its past reputation. Its "total image" had been damaged by "Nader's charges and their aftermath," and the study concluded that "in the emergent future G.M. is likely to lose still more power and prestige."[14]

The public's jaundiced views of General Motors leached into perceptions of its product. For many respondents, safety and quality were two sides of the same coin. There emerged a general conviction that late-model American cars were cheap, tinny, poorly finished, and prone to rust and breakdown. All automakers were suspected of failing to manufacture top-quality vehicles but "the brunt of complaint and disappointment" centered on G.M., which was compared unfavorably to its past as well as to Ford and Chrysler. The extent to which G.M. cars had been recalled was widely exaggerated by respondents, who were also "vigorously critical" of the company's styling, which had long been a strength, as well as the durability and value of the cars. "Even those consumers most inclined to praise [G.M. cars] are less convinced of their superior qualities or that only G.M. offers this kind of product."[15]

The researchers found the opinions of respondents to be imprecise, emotional, and poorly articulated, unrooted in "rational standards or objective measures," but "deep-seated" nevertheless. And they were supported by a survey of G.M. brand loyalty that showed it slipping from 82 percent in 1964 to 73 percent by the middle of 1966. Chevrolet, the heart of the corporation, fell to 60 percent.[16]

By the end of 1967, another Glick survey found that while anger at G.M. as a corporate entity had abated somewhat, the taint remained. Criticisms of its styling and quality were persistent. Its cars were seen as deficient in excitement, newness, youthfulness, sportiness, and other desirable automotive qualities. G.M. might continue to think of itself as "bold, imaginative, innovate, an industry leader," Glick told its executives, "but people don't believe it. So it's not true."[17]

In certain respects, General Motors answered this tide of bad news forthrightly. Ed Cole wrote an internal memo committing the company to "aggressively pursue the necessary research and development to assure that G.M.'s products continue to be as safe as possible." He wanted to be able to claim leadership in automotive safety, not simply meeting but wherever possible exceeding the government's new standards. The company distributed 700,000 booklets on safety subjects, launched a new safety program involving 2.5 million schoolchildren, produced nine motion pictures on safety, and fielded its executives and PR professionals to deliver 575 safety talks and speeches. Instructed to display humility, G.M. executives admitted publicly that their competitors were closing the gap on quality: "They have greatly improved their products. Their cars are attractively designed. They have style. And customers find their quality and performance acceptable." The company also broke with its policy, long considered a competitive necessity, of never speaking about its research-and-development projects until they were ready for the consumer market. It revealed its innovative work on gas turbine engines, Stirling external combustion engines, electric drives powered by batteries and fuel cells, and "molten metal power systems."[18]

These were positive moves but nothing that would solve G.M.'s larger predicament. The blighting of a corporate brand creates serious problems across a business. Competitors are emboldened. Investors pull back. Regulators pile on. Customers are angry or, at least, wary, and they have long memories. Everything a company produces looks like damaged goods, raising the costs of marketing and forcing the acceptance of either lower sales or lower margins (if, like G.M., a company is determined to protect its market share). In either event, the share price is likely to decline, and investors will stand back further. The result is a kind of system failure.

Fixing a damaged brand is exceedingly difficult. The precise problem is often difficult to identify. There is always something ineffable about a brand, however diligently marketers might work to define it, and top executives, most of whom have risen from finance or product roles, can find it difficult to get their accustomed grip. No sooner had the Glick research found its way to G.M.'s executive suite than arguments broke out over what it meant.

The Newsom group and its allies saw nothing in the research to dissuade it from its view that the world had changed. American corporations were now expected to demonstrate a high level of social responsibility, and General Motors was failing to adapt. The company was run by detached financiers and engineers who were preoccupied by cars and spreadsheets, men whose every public utterance read as though it had been written by committee, men remote from the human concerns of the average consumer, and unfamiliar with elite opinion. These men also averaged almost sixty years of age, which Newsom thought was part of the problem. Appearing to the world as out of touch, unapproachable, robotic, arrogant, and mean, G.M. was wide open to attacks from the likes of Nader.

General Motors product, from this perspective, was not the problem. The attacks had begun and caught on at a time when G.M. was indisputably the best automaker in the world, spending far more than any other company on research, and leading in inno-vation. To a certain extent, the attacks seemed to have been invited by G.M.'s undeniable success: "the silk hat gets the snowballs," said one insider. Ford had been on a roll with its Mustang, as happens from time to time with individual automakers, but there was no objective evidence of a sudden deterioration in the quality or mar-ketability of G.M. cars. The models that had informed the glowing surveys at the end of 1965 were almost exactly the same as those that were suspect at the end of 1966. Thus the company's behavior, not its product, was at issue.[19]

The corporation's PR chief, Anthony DeLorenzo, agreed that times had changed:

> In years past, if a company made a quality product, paid good wages, earned a dividend and was a good neighbor in the plant community, you couldn't ask for more. Well, today there is an influential segment of the public that is asking for a lot more, and often. Many writers, teachers, professional people, and especially politicians and government officials are fostering a broad new doctrine of industry responsibil-ity. To begin with, these people wish to hold an industry accountable for any social problem vaguely associated with its product. Under this doctrine, for example, a brewery is held responsible for beer cans littering the wayside. In the case of the auto industry, this means such problems as air and water pollution, highway safety, junk cars, auto theft, and urban congestion. In a much broader sense, industry is expected to provide active assistance in improving the qual-ity of American life and helping solve such great social prob-lems as the poverty, ugliness, and blight of our big cities.[20]

DeLorenzo also agreed that G.M. had to accept its social responsibilities. It had to spend less time shouting about cars and more time listening to what was happening outside the boardroom doors. All the same, he believed the automaker had been adjusting and that its problems had been overstated by self-ordained critics, Nader in particular. DeLorenzo found consolation in a minority of editorial comment that had taken Nader apart for his "paternalistic, paranormic, and somewhat myopic vision," and he looked forward to the time when the press corps would realize that Nader had overplayed his hand by emphasizing the automobile over other aspects of road safety.[21]

Harry Barr, G.M.'s vice president of engineering, was also critical of "certain public officials seeking personal publicity" who swarmed the company "like vultures" and held it entirely responsible for problems of safety, air pollution, and traffic snarl that were impossible for automakers to solve on their own. DeLorenzo and Barr disagreed with Newsom not on the need for G.M. to adapt, but on how far it had to go in heeding critics. Social problems, they maintained, were the domain of governments, not automakers.[22]

Newsom and DeLorenzo also disagreed over the role of the product. DeLorenzo read Glick's studies as saying that consumers were focusing on G.M.'s demerits as a corporate citizen because it had lost its aura as the world's leading automaker. Thus it needed to build some hot new cars and market the hell out of them. "We need to proceed from tangible, real things," he said. If the new Chevrolet Camaro could beat back the Mustang, sales would improve, G.M. would regain the benefit of the doubt, and people would realize the company was actually a good corporate citizen. This disagreement led to heated meetings and unfriendly memos being passed back and forth in the executive suite. Newsom partisans, upset that Cole made them report up through DeLorenzo, were wondering if G.M. was capable of changing. DeLorenzo suspected, accurately, that the consultants were trying to get him fired. Earl Newsom had been coaxing Chairman Roche on the need to hire an outsider as head of public relations, perhaps a young hotshot from IBM.[23]

Neither side in the debate had a real answer. DeLorenzo may have been right that an exciting new vehicle would have alleviated the pressure on G.M., but only to a point. Glick's surveys showed people were happy with G.M. cars right up until the safety issue arose. Product was not central to G.M.'s struggles.

The notion that G.M. was out of touch was similarly overstated. There is no doubt that G.M. could have moved faster on safety and managed its public relations better. It might have been quicker to pick up signs of trouble, of which there were many: the rise of the second-collision theory as a cure-all for traffic safety, the intellectually fashionable demonization of the automobile, the rise of the consumer movement, the congressional embrace of Rachel Carson, the flurry of Corvair lawsuits, the behavior of the federal government toward Detroit's largest supplier, the steel industry. But, in fairness, the Newsom people had gained their seat at the table because Frederic Donner was worried about the world outside his plants. And G.M. was by prevailing standards a decent corporate citizen, more concerned about traffic safety than the public at large, equal to the expectations of the safety establishment. It was also doing more outside its walls than had been credited, whether through its jobs program for Detroit's hard-core unemployed or by holding its prices and delaying capital spending, when asked, to help Washington combat inflation.

Had G.M. done everything asked of it by Newsom, hiring young executives with broad outlooks, exerting thought leadership through the universities, moving further and faster on safety, the outcome would have been the same. Driving still would have been inherently dangerous. Drivers still would have been reckless and unwilling to pay for safety. The death toll still would have jumped in the early 1960s. Swifter adoption of safety features would have meant nothing to critics who believed Detroit was stubbornly refusing to build an entirely crash-proof car. Intellectual critiques of corporate influence, commercial culture, and the antiauthoritarian tenor of the times would have been undisturbed, along with the expansion of tort law. The ambitions of Nader and Ribicoff for federal regulation, and the legislative aggression of the Great Society, would not have been affected. And General Motors would have remained the largest, richest target for aspiring giant killers. The confluence of forces against the corporation was not to be appeased. G.M., of course, set fire to its own defenses by spying on Nader, compounding its reputational damage, but the crusaders by that point were already over the walls.

For the next several years, General Motors executives did what was expected of them. The overriding responsibility of any public company is to protect its shareholders. At G.M., protecting shareholders required executives to keep sales volumes and revenues high, safeguarding the all-important market share, even if the company had to spend more to do so. And it did spend more. Annual reports from 1966 to 1968 all tell the same story of higher promotional expenses and steeper sales discounts in order to maintain market share.

This worked insofar as the company continued to sell a respectable average of 6.5 million cars a year through the rest of the 1960s. With journalists and analysts accustomed to evaluating the company on market share, sales volume masked some of G.M.'s weakness. But the higher spending killed the company's margins: from $2.1 billion in 1965 to $0.61 billion in 1970. Net income as a percentage of sales (another measure of profitability) dropped from just over 10 percent to 3.2 percent. As a result, the corporation's share price reached a new low in the first month of 1970: $64.50, or 39 percent off its 1966 peak (the Dow also remained off its peak but by 18 percent).[24]

That 40 percent of G.M.'s shareholder value was still missing four years after the corporation's ordeal did nothing for morale at headquarters. Despite their apology for their treatment of Nader, their acceptance of the regulation of their industry, and the safety improvements they had made to their vehicles, G.M. executives remained villains, enemies of the public good. Their days as national benefactors and exemplars of America's commercial genius were over. Their self-respect and their worldview were shattered. As Robert Lane had predicted in his work on the psychological effects of business regulation, they suffered "a toll of anxiety, frustration and dejection beyond all relation to economic cost."[25]

In a speech to the Executive Club of Chicago on March 26, 1971, the five-year anniversary of his apology to Nader, James Roche expressed the hurt and bewilderment that accompanied the lost stature of his ilk. He condemned "the enemies of business" in America who equated profits with immorality and spread a "cloud of suspicion and distrust over all we have achieved and hope to achieve." These enemies were "threatening the entire free enterprise system, assaulting America's reputation, and creating an unfairly negative image of American business." They wanted to "alienate the American consumer from business" and "tear down long-established relationships which have served both well." Roche gave particular attention to the likes of Nader who "jump from cause to cause, going wherever popularity or expediency lead, using whatever means are at hand, inflaming any issue that promises attention." Naderites were subjecting business to "a form of harassment" and misleading government and the courts into further persecution of business. Corporations were being blamed for all of America's social ills:

> Business didn't create discrimination in America, but business is expected to eliminate it. Business didn't bring about the deterioration of our cities, but business is expected to rebuild them. Business didn't create poverty and hunger in our land, but business is expected to eliminate them.[26]

Time and again, as Lane foresaw, Roche returned to the unbearable loss of stature he and his colleagues had suffered, how "the climate of criticism has dulled the reputation of business. . . . We read and hear little that is good about business." It was an ill-advised pose, wounded and self-pitying. He certainly had enemies but he exaggerated the demands on the business community. He also gave Nader an opportunity to accuse him of "corporate McCarthyism" for describing his critics as un-American.[27]

Nevertheless, Roche's speech captured something important about the course of American capitalism in the 1960s. He had become a vice president at G.M. in the late Eisenhower years when Washington, while unafraid to upbraid, investigate, and impose on the firm, had at least recognized its contribution to American prosperity and understood that the national interest to some extent depended on Detroit's success. Ten years down the line, the company was on the outside; enemies it had never known before were on the inside, working with Washington to embarrass and constrain General Motors, still the largest engine of prosperity in America, without regard to its contributions.

CHAPTER 16

THE END OF DETROIT

There is a standard narrative of the decline of the U.S. automotive industry that takes 1973 as the critical point, "before which the U.S. auto industry enjoyed world-wide pre-eminence and unchallenged dominance of the domestic market." A sudden surge in oil prices toward the end of that year prompts a large number of American car buyers to abandon Detroit's massive and relatively expensive cars for smaller, more fuel-efficient imports from Japan and Germany. Rather than meet this challenge with inexpensive compacts of their own, U.S. auto executives, "people who had made their way up by taking as few risks as possible and never letting their eyes waver from the bottom line," sit on their hands. Fat and sclerotic after decades of immense profits and minimal competition, willfully blind to the inferior quality of their vehicles, they dismiss the foreign brands as cheap knockoffs of American originals and wait for their former customers to return to their senses. This is the same fatal attitude they had taken several years earlier when Ralph Nader had to drag them "kicking and screaming into the age of auto safety." As D. C. Jackson, a onetime *Fortune* magazine publisher and Eisenhower insider, said: "There is a certain special stupidity and narrowness that exists in many of the more successful businessmen in this country, more so in the Midwest than other places, and nowhere else as much as Detroit."[1]

Spurning domestic automakers, the narrative continues, American car buyers learn that small imports are not only inexpensive but dependable and easy to drive. They are "fun." They are innovative. Foreign designers are installing four-wheel independent suspension and putting their engines over their driving wheels, eliminating the drive shaft with its rear-seat hump and extra weight. And foreign cars are made in plants in Germany and, especially, Japan where payrolls are not bloated and executives are wiser, nimbler, more innovative, and harder-working. This moralistic sublot applauds the defeat of America's decadent, dog-eat-dog capitalism at the hands of a "communal, state-guided capitalism . . . tailored to benefit a more complicated assortment of interests," as David Halberstam put it in *The Reckoning*.[2]

By the late 1970s, when U.S. automakers finally admit the magnitude of their problem, imports have seized more than 25 percent of the U.S. market and Detroit is too late, too hidebound, too incompetent to catch up. Washington has to step in to protect the domestics by placing quotas on Japanese imports. Even this is insufficient to halt the long, humiliating slide that will finally see the heads of Ford, General Motors, and Chrysler before Congress in 2009 begging for a bailout. The emphasis in this standard narrative is always on the avoidable failures of the arrogant and ineffectual executives running U.S. automotive companies. The unmistakable conclusion, in Halberstam's best-seller, in an important 1980 Department of Transportation report, and many other accounts of the auto industry, is that Detroit failed America.[3]

There is some truth to this version of events. The crisis of 1973 did happen, rendering Detroit's powerful, gas-guzzling automobiles less salable. American automakers were arrogant and their executives did stupid things. They did not mount a successful competitive response to the second wave of imports, and the 1960s had not been the most innovative decade for American cars. In the end, Detroit required a bailout.

The narrative is nevertheless incomplete and unsatisfactory. Detroit's troubles did not begin in 1973. Industry data and the financials of General Motors and its competitors show that the critical moment in the decline of Motor City, the year everything started to unravel, was 1966. The second import invasion was under way well before the spike in oil prices: foreign models started to regain a significant market share in the United States in 1966, right around the time when Ribicoff and Nader opened their campaign to convince Americans that Detroit was murdering them with unsafe vehicles. After averaging 5.5 percent of the market from 1961 to 1965, foreign models leapt to 9.7 percent in 1966 to 12.5 percent in 1967 to 16 percent in 1968. These years were prime time for the safety crisis and G.M.'s brand blight.

By the end of 1970, imports accounted for two million vehicle sales in the United States, 24 percent of the market, a new record. Despite only marginal gains in quality before the late 1970s, they held that level, vibrating between 21 percent and 27.5 percent, through the 1973 oil crisis and the rest of the decade. Of course, evolving consumer tastes and the lack of American-made subcompacts also contributed to the success of the imports, but G.M.'s finances and internal surveys show that the safety crisis and the company's response to it had already created widespread dissatisfaction with American and, especially, General Motors automobiles. Consumers were encouraged to think twice about Detroit and visit the showrooms of the imports, thus reshaping the market in unhelpful ways. The crisis of 1973 merely solidified the trend toward foreign cars and perhaps brought Detroit's competitive issues to greater public notice.[4]

It is customary for top executives in any leading industry to receive too much credit in good times and too much criticism in bad, and Detroit was no exception. Its leaders may not have been geniuses but even allowing for the decision to spy on Nader they were not possessed of special stupidity. Many of the same men who had produced an entirely new line of import-beaters for 1960 were still at work, and some, like Ed Cole, were in higher positions in their respective companies by the end of the decade. They were not sitting on their hands. They continued to veer away from the Strassenkreuzers of the 1950s, producing a string of beloved sporty midsize coupes, Mustangs, Camaros, and Firebirds, that remain among the more popular automobiles ever sold. There were significant technological innovations in the 1960s. General Motors, for instance, released the front-wheel drive Olds Toronado in 1966 and a year later a Cadillac Eldorado with front-wheel drive and optional front disc brakes, as well as variable-ratio steering and automatic level control, both world firsts.

There is no evidence of decline in the quality of Detroit executives between the 1940s and 1970s, however much abuse they took toward the end of that period. The relevant question is not what happened to executive talent but what changed in the business environment, and what changed in America, that could account for Detroit's failure to answer the bell when the second import invasion occurred.

The renewed competition from foreign cars called for an innovative new import-beater, something bold and marketable, as the Corvair had been a decade earlier, but smaller still and less expensive. As it happened, G.M. was working on such a car. Ed Cole had been aware of the need for a subcompact as far back as the Corvair launch. America, he said at the time, was "entering the era of specific driving needs" and people would buy cars to suit their individual requirements. He had never stopped thinking about subcompacts. By 1967, he was personally overseeing the development of G.M.'s first, the four-cylinder Chevrolet Vega, released at the end of 1970.[5]

While G.M. had the right idea, producing a bold new car was more difficult in the late 1960s than in the late 1950s. The appetite for technological innovation in Detroit was reduced, not for lack of imagination but because of risk. Everyone in Detroit knew the story of the Corvair. The most innovative Detroit vehicle in a generation, with four-wheel independent suspension and an engine over its driving wheels just like certain celebrated imports, it had been attacked pre-release by competitors and auto experts for being different from other cars, and savaged post-release by safety activists and the tort industry for supposed dangers rooted in those differences. There was nothing particularly wrong with the Corvair yet it had been made into a weapon against General Motors. Why court the reputational, legal, and regulatory risk of more technological innovation when surveys showed car buyers were largely content with what was already on offer? Far more sensible to innovate on design, comfort, power, sportiness, and gadgets.

Producing a new car from scratch was also expensive. It had been expensive in the late 1950s, too, but General Motors' net income and share price were relatively steady at that time, notwithstanding a recession. Now the company had cost pressures, squeezed margins, a tanking share price, and a blighted brand. A subcompact would increase the company's exposure to the low and less profitable end of the automobile market, the last thing it needed while trying to rebuild its profitability.

Adding to these financial pressures was the broader economy. The fiscal excesses of the Johnson administration were continuing to make life difficult for all American businesses in the late 1960s. Price inflation, well under 2 percent annually in the five years before 1966, climbed to just under 6 percent in the five years after. The costs of steel and other automotive inputs rose significantly. G.M.'s labor costs grew at 6.5 percent in the inflationary period between 1966 and 1973 with a roughly constant number of employees. That might have been manageable in normal circumstances—the wage growth rate had been 6.5 percent over the previous ten years, but not with all other costs rising.[6]

G.M.'s new car would have to be produced on the cheap, with smaller amounts of cheaper materials, less distinctiveness in design, more sharing of designs and parts with other cars, and more efficiency rather than greater care in assembly. The Vega was praised on introduction for its looks, functionality, and handling, winning *Motor Trend*'s Car of the Year award. Before long, however, the compromises showed. There were massive recalls to fix unreliable throttles, defective axles, backfiring engines, and other problems. The car's aluminum engine was known to leak and buckle. The body rusted. Together with the AMC Gremlin and Ford Pinto, the Vega held imports below a 20 percent market share through the early and mid-1970s but it did not drive them back as the Corvair had done. The impression that G.M. cars were not what they used to be, a sentiment that arose in 1966 and 1967 with little to back it, was now becoming demonstrable.[7]

All of the factors that conspired against G.M.'s new small car affected its other lines, as well. The company doubled down on savings and took fewer risks in styling and technological innovation. Pontiacs became difficult to distinguish from Chevrolets because they were, by the start of the 1970s, increasingly similar in design and component parts. The quality of all cars suffered as G.M. counted pennies in hopes of restoring profits. Cole, as president, was under constant pressure to standardize G.M.'s automobiles. He complained publicly about financial executives "meddling in production decisions about which they knew nothing." His reluctance to move as aggressively as his board wished on standardization was one reason he did not succeed the retiring James Roche as chairman in 1971 (the position went to the financier Richard Gerstenberg). Roche, too, was frustrated. In one of his final speeches, he complained that the company had been pushing up its prices and working hard to find efficiencies yet still was unable to improve its profitability. All of this happened before 1973.[8]

Another contributing factor to the sameness of G.M. vehicles was antitrust pressure. The du Pont family had sold its last block of General Motors shares by 1965 as directed by the courts. The cry of "break up G.M." nevertheless reverberated into the 1970s, and joined with cost pressures to undermine a sacred principle of the Sloan-era corporation: divisional autonomy. In its first half century, General Motors had famously allowed its divisional leaders to independently develop new cars, revamp existing models, and develop new processes and technology. This friendly competition had ensured the long-admired diversity of G.M. product, keeping Pontiacs distinct from Buicks or Oldsmobiles, and keeping all of them a step ahead of Ford and Chrysler. Donner, however, had centralized the corporation's assembly functions to forestall Washington from forcing him to divest of Chevrolet. His move probably helped to keep the corporation whole but a cornerstone of G.M.'s business strategy was sacrificed to ward off the enemies of scale.[9]

The enemies of scale were not imaginary. They had been a constant headache for G.M. throughout the postwar period, occasionally with good reason, and they were not about to let up because the company was flailing and imports were returning. In October 1967, *The Wall Street Journal* reported the existence of a live "antitrust bomb" in the files of the Justice Department, a 104-page suit attacking the acquisitions made by G.M. prior to 1921, allowing it to monopolize the manufacture, sale, and distribution of automobiles in violation of the Sherman and Clayton antitrust acts.

The suit wanted to see G.M. undo more than forty acquisitions and "reconstitute itself into a sufficiently large number of companies" to restore competitive conditions. The bomb was held over the corporation's head at least until 1975, by which time its market share was below 40 percent and its dominance, supposed for so long to be eternal, was crumbling. The federal government, more than Detroit, underestimated the competition domestic automakers would meet from foreign entries.[10]

As it turned out, the courts had done the du Ponts a favor by forcing their exit at the top of the market, but the loss of its lead investor was yet another blow to General Motors. Shrewd managers of capital, the du Ponts encouraged a long-term view of the automobile business, riding out minor and sometimes major declines in share price with equanimity, always investing in future growth. Their departure left executives at G.M. beholden to the Wall Street crowd with its notorious fixation on short-term results. Predictably, G.M. now struggled to commit to a long-term strategy for fixing the core business.

Slimmer profits. A depressed share price. Cost pressures. Product problems. Reputational problems. These would be recurring themes at General Motors for the rest of the twentieth century, which is how long it took for the company's share price to recover its 1966 level. There were occasional years of strong sales but more of weak sales. Years of brilliant new car designs but more of lemons. Years when the company, led by Ed Cole, overcame resistance from some of its own engineers and oil companies to introduce the catalytic converter, revolutionizing the internal combustion engine, reducing emissions at the expense of performance. Years when the rebates and discounts required to move cars off dealer lots meant that G.M. lost thousands of dollars on each unit sold. Years of employee work stoppages and long strikes triggered by the need to reduce costs and goose productivity. Years of desperate investment in supposedly futuristic data systems and assembly technologies that usually brought more trouble than they were worth.[11]

After 1966, General Motors was like an automobile back on the road after a severe crash. It looked fine from the outside but never ran properly again. It never regained the stability and confidence and consistent growth it had enjoyed over the previous half century.

Because G.M. was roughly half of the domestic auto industry, and usually the leading half, Detroit was never the same, either. Its problems multiplied. U.S. manufacturers were always headed toward a reckoning with rapidly improving foreign automakers whose plant and operating systems, born later, were by the late 1970s a generation more advanced. Pressures to improve the industry's fuel efficiency and environmental record intensified. Once all of America's two-car garages were filled, the mature domestic industry had less room to grow. The lack of improvement in middle-class incomes post-1960s presented yet another obstacle. All this might have been insurmountable for the healthiest companies. After being whomped with a chain mace in 1966, General Motors and Detroit met these challenges on their knees. (Of the Big Three, only Ford, able to take some advantage of G.M.'s relative weakness, had managed to increase its share price by the time the oil price shock hit.)

The saddest development post-1966 was that G.M.'s goal of becoming a truly global corporation, dominating the world automobile markets, went nowhere. Its investment in new plant and equipment tells the story. After growing at a ferocious pace in the first half of the 1960s, peaking at $1.3 billion in 1965, it averaged $874.5 million for the rest of the decade. It was still down at $1.16 million in 1973 despite years of inflation and respectable top-line growth. Not only was less capital being spent but by 1973 less than 15 percent of it was headed overseas compared to 25 percent in the earlier era. Expressed as a percentage of gross revenue, overseas capital spending was off by two thirds. This effectively took G.M. out of competition with Germany and Japan in foreign markets, and sunk its bid to acquire "the latest and best in plant layout, tools, equipment, and methods" throughout its operations, as Donner had aspired to do in 1965. It reduced G.M.'s exposure to foreign markets where, as another G.M. executive said in 1967, it had been learning to adapt its vehicles to shorter travel distances and higher fuel costs, and consumer preferences for smaller cars with smaller engines.[12]

Given its problems on the domestic front, it is reasonable to wonder if General Motors made a mistake by curtailing its global ambitions. Notwithstanding its share price, the company was still rich enough to have funded major international acquisitions or expansions. More exposure to fast-growing foreign markets might have been the tonic G.M. needed. The decision was not entirely Detroit's, however.

The Kennedy administration had been modestly interested in promoting U.S. investment abroad, securing reductions in tariff rates imposed by its trading partners, as requested by General Motors and other multinationals. The Johnson administration was another matter. Its first trade measure affecting automobiles was accidental: the infamous "chicken war" with the European community in late 1963.* Two years later, President Johnson, anxious to reduce the U.S. foreign trade deficit, imposed voluntary guidelines to limit the ability of corporations to engage in foreign investment. The guidelines were briefly effective but a rising inflation rate and the high costs of the Vietnam War reduced dollar receipts while increasing dollar outflows, prompting more drastic action from President Johnson. He signed an executive order prohibiting U.S. investors from acquiring more than 10 percent of foreign business ventures, and requiring them to repatriate liquid foreign assets.[13]

Prior to the imposition of these restrictions, James Roche had stated that G.M. intended to spend 25 percent of its capital allotment overseas. Post-restrictions, that did not happen. The government's disapproval of overseas investment may have played as large a role in the decline of G.M.'s foreign capital spending as the company's financial predicament. The company was still able to purchase stakes and enter into various production and sales agreements with foreign automakers in the years to follow but these moves were later and less significant than they might have been.[14]

Washington did help the auto industry in various ways over the last half century, from Nixon's import surcharges, intended to

---

* Several nations had slapped tariffs on U.S. exports of inexpensive frozen poultry. Washington retaliated by imposing "temporary" 25 percent tariffs on Danish hams, Dutch cheese, and French cognac. Needing to include the Germans, it extended the tariff to imports of Volkswagen vans, reducing their sales by several thousand units, an inconsequential number at the time. The temporary "chicken tax" on imported trucks has never been rescinded. In recent decades, its protections have been an important factor in Detroit's reliance upon and dominance of truck sales in the United States.

level the playing field with imports, to later quotas on foreign-made vehicles, and the 2009 bailout. None of that changes the many ways in which government, deliberately or inadvertently, made business more difficult for Detroit or circumscribed the options of its managers. They could not even raise prices, one of the simpler ways to improve profitability, without looking to Washington. The Consumer Price Index had risen by 19 percent from 1959 to 1968 as the new car component of the index declined by 3 percent, meaning that automobiles were a bargain. Yet when Detroit announced a modest price increase in 1968, mentioning the new safety standards as well as rising material and labor costs as contributing factors, it found itself under fire from Warren Magnuson and the Senate Commerce Committee. Indifferent to the financial impact of the safety program when the legislation was passed, the Senate now implausibly expected automakers to eat the costs of its new standards rather than pass them along to consumers. In the late Johnson years, General Motors resorted to clearing its annual price increases with the White House. For three years during the Nixon administration, Detroit was subject to legislated anti-inflationary price controls.[15]

There were many differences between the auto industries in America and Japan. In some elements of its business systems, assembly practices, and automotive technology, the Japanese were superior by the late 1970s. It was not a contest between communal state-guided capitalism and dog-eat-dog capitalism, however. It was a contest between the United States and a Japanese system in which government took an active role in nurturing and protecting a domestic industry with tariff and nontariff barriers to automobile imports, and an aggressive trade policy designed to expand exports. The first priority of Japan's national industrial policy was the creation of a world-leading automotive industry. The U.S. government, by contrast, had gone to war with its auto industry. Jimmy Carter's Department of Transportation admitted that government had fostered "an adversarial relationship" with Detroit, investing too much energy in "fruitless and bitter regulatory battles," and undermining the health of the industry.

By the time the oil crisis hit, the automobile was the most regulated product in America, more so than pharmaceuticals, and the demands from Washington kept coming. Between 1974 and 1979, when it desperately needed to be building better cars, G.M. spent $8 billion on regulatory compliance. In 1979 alone, it spent $2 billion, or 40 percent of its capital budget, and had 26,000 full-time employees working on compliance. Some of the environmental regulation was advisable. All of the automotive regulation, at once, was punitive. It added substantially to the price of an America car and made foreign competitors that much more affordable.[16]

There is a school of thought that the economic benefits of the American automobile were exhausted by 1970 with the domestic market for cars near its peak, making the industry's decline inevitable. But there was still plenty of growth to be had. While the domestic market slowed, it still managed to absorb fourteen to eighteen million new vehicles annually after 1980, many more than the nine million of 1970. The problem was less that the U.S. market was mature than that almost all of the growth was captured by imports. What's more, the annual global market for automobiles exploded from just over 26.5 million in 1971 to 56 million by 2013. At the beginning of that time period, America's global market share was 32.5 percent; by the end it was 7.7 percent. Germany increased its market share by almost a third and Japan's more than doubled. Its leading automobile companies had seen the opportunity for global growth coming in the early 1960s but America whiffed. It remains one of the great missed opportunities in the history of American industry.[17]

Ed Cole retired from General Motors at age sixty-five in 1974. He worked hard until the end, arriving at 7:30 a.m. each day with a briefcase full of work completed the night before. His last years at the company had not been fulfilling. He had proposed in 1970 that G.M. aggressively reduce the size of all of its cars, only to get shot down in committee. He had led the development of a rotary engine, which appealed to him as something smaller, lighter, less expensive, and easier to build (with fewer moving parts) than conventional reciprocating piston engines. Ultra-efficient, the G.M. rotary promised to run for half a million miles with minimal wear. Twice a week, Cole made the trek to Warren to check on its progress, which was complicated by ever-shifting federal emissions and fuel economy standards. Weeks before his retirement, unable to get his board to buy in, he announced that the rotary engine had been sidelined. Soon after it was canceled entirely.[*18]

Cole had also embraced the cause of safety as president of G.M., committing the company to meet or exceed all federal standards and to lead the field regardless of what the government required. For a time, he was practically the only man in Detroit who thought air bags could be made to work in the short run. After many experiments and trials, he admitted that the technology was not ready and (as yet) too expensive for mass production.

On his way out the door, Cole said in an interview, "If I knew all that I know today, I would have some reservations about going into the business." What had attracted him to the automobile industry as a young man was the chance to build better cars. By the end of his career, most of his time had been spent on government, regulation, and cost discipline. At some level, he understood the necessity of these efforts but they grated. "For the type of guy I am," he said, "I don't see enough coming along that is challenging." He was celebrated on retirement as "the spirit of engineering innovation at G.M., the rebel who broke most of the rules but always stayed on the team," yet it was also said that there was now less room for freewheeling spirits at the company and that some were glad to see him go.[19]

A quiet retirement was never in the cards for Cole. In October 1974 he met Ralph Nader for a two-hour face-to-face debate on *The Phil Donahue Show*. It turned out to be more a friendly conversation about automotive issues than a debate, although the columnist Joe Callahan, who gave it comprehensive coverage, divided the program into sixteen segments and scored it nine for Cole, three for Nader, and three draws. Cole's restless engineering mind was working on an idea for an automobile engine that would run on a fuel made from

---

* In 1966, Cole had worked on an electric version of the Corvair in an effort to rehabilitate the brand and showcase his company's engineering prowess. Powered by a Tesla-style AC induction motor using silver-zinc batteries, it had a range of forty to eighty miles and a top speed of eighty miles per hour. Weighing eight hundred pounds more than a regular Corvair, largely because of its batteries, which cost $15,000 and could only be charged about one hundred times, it was never a candidate for production. *New York Times*, October 29, 1966.

water and air instead of gasoline. In addition to kicking the tires on the Oakland Athletics (owner Charles O. Finley was considering a sale), he set up an air freight business and with several other investors purchased control of the nation's smallest automaker, Checker Motors of Kalamazoo, Michigan. It built taxicabs and a single passenger car, and ran taxi fleets and airport limousine and bus services. Cole intended to make Checker's vehicles smaller, lighter, and more fuel efficient. He never got the chance.[20]

An experienced pilot, he commuted daily from the suburbs north of Detroit to Checker's Kalamazoo headquarters in a red-white-and-blue British-made Beagle aircraft. At around 9:30 a.m. on May 2, 1977, he radioed that he was making his last turn for final approach to the Kalamazoo airport. He was flying alone in heavy rain with poor visibility. Eyewitnesses said he circled for about fifteen minutes with his engines sputtering before the twin-engine Beagle nose-dived into a freshly plowed cornfield.[21]

Cole was remembered for his magnificent V8 engines, his eighteen major patents, his support for catalytic converters, rotary engines, and air bags, and, of course, the Corvair. *Chevy Hardcore* magazine placed him behind only Billy Durant as the most important Chevrolet person of all time.[22]

CHAPTER 17

AVOIDABLE DEATHS

There is no arguing with Ralph Nader, Abraham Ribicoff, Alabama's Kenneth Roberts, and every other safety crusader that the 49,163 fatalities on American roads in 1965, the last year before passage of Lyndon Johnson's landmark traffic safety legislation, were a public health catastrophe. An alarm needed to be rung. Progress was imperative. The transportation system, said President Johnson, "is not good enough when it builds super-highways for super-charged automobiles—and yet cannot find a way to prevent 50,000 highway deaths this year." The auto industry did not contradict him. "When 50,000 a people a year are killed on the roads of the United States," said Henry Ford II, "this is a bad situation." Reducing the death toll was a perfectly legitimate goal of public policy. The question remains, did the safety crusaders solve the problem, or at least save more lives than would have been saved without their intervention?[1]

A half century down the road, the Center for Auto Safety, founded by Nader, together with *The Nation* magazine announced that the 1966 federal laws and their creation, the National Highway Traffic Safety Administration, had averted 3.5 million driving deaths. The assertion was based on the difference between the number of fatalities that would have occurred if the death rate had stayed at 5.50 per hundred million vehicle miles (the 1966 level) instead of falling to 1.07 by 2014.[2]

Author Michael Lemov in his book *Car Safety Wars* credits the legislation with a 77 percent drop in the fatality rate. His data is based on the NHTSA's estimations of the total effects of improvements in automobile design, which show that all safety technologies introduced to American vehicles from 1960 to 2010 resulted in 610,566 lives saved.[3]

On its own website, the NHTSA claims that the 1966 laws "led to one of the most effective public health and safety efforts of the past century."[4]

The magazine and NHTSA celebrations occurred in 2016, a year after the fiftieth anniversary of the publication of *Unsafe at Any Speed*. Nader marked the occasion by issuing a press release that credited his book with prompting the 1966 safety legislation. As in times past, he insisted that the Corvair had "a faulty rear suspension system," the product of "corporation negligence" and "industrial irresponsibility," that could cause it to "skid violently and roll over." The media played along. Nader, said *Time*, "has kept American drivers safe for fifty years." The magazine placed the book at No. 21 on its list of a hundred all-time greatest nonfiction books, ahead of John Hersey's *Hiroshima*, Jane Jacobs's *The Death and Life of Great American Cities*, and Rachel Carson's *Silent Spring*. The Detroit-friendly *Automotive News* gave Nader space to repeat his claims. Even the website GM Authority, run by General Motors enthusiasts, gave Nader most of the credit for a half century's improvements in traffic safety.[5]

While traffic safety outcomes have certainly improved since 1966, the proffered statistics do not prove the effectiveness of the safety crusade or the federal legislation.* If the gross improvement

---

* It is important to keep in mind that even with another half century of experience, analyzing traffic fatalities and their causes remains an inexact science. We now know much more about how age, gender, driving experience, driver personality, geography, road conditions, time of day, time of year, speed, volume and patterns of traffic, traffic controls, vehicle equipment, substance abuse, the availability of emergency services, and many other factors affect rates of injury and death in crashes. We still have much to learn, however, and driving environments, human behavior, and vehicle technologies are in constant flux. Comparisons over time are perilous. This demands caution in any approach to the data.

in lifesaving after 1966 is to be the standard by which effectiveness is measured, the legislation failed: the pace of improvement in the fatality rate per 100 million vehicle miles slowed slightly in the half century after its passage compared to the half century before. The disparaged Triple-E gang did the better job.[6]

Even then, the post-legislation results are misused. The claim that all reductions in the fatality rate since 1966, a total of 3.5 million lives, are due to the safety laws gives the crusaders and Congress credit due to subsequent improvements in local road design and maintenance, new lifesaving medical technologies, and changes in driver behavior. What the safety crusade and the 1966 laws added to existing safety measures was a heavy emphasis on the crashworthy vehicle.

The claim of Lemov and the NHTSA that more than 600,000 lives were saved by vehicle safety technologies—the second-collision project—is also misleading. Former NHTSA expert Charles J. Kahane attributed lives saved to particular technologies for the years 1960–2012, during which 610,566 automobile occupants were killed. More than half of the improvement (329,715 lives) is credited to seat belts, which automakers, under pressure from state legislatures, had adopted as standard equipment before Ribicoff began his hearings and before Nader published his book.[7]

The second most effective safety technology of the last half century, the energy-absorbing steering column (79,989 lives), was in development a decade prior to 1966 and was made standard equipment at the instigation of the General Services Administration before the new federal laws were enacted. Other crucial improvements to instrument panels, windshield glass, and door locks (to which a total of 86,465 lives are credited) also predated the legislation. They, too, were introduced by the General Services Administration, an effective and relatively light-touch regulatory precedent that should have been built upon.

The number of lives saved as a direct result of the Nader-Ribicoff crusade, the Johnson legislation, and the NHTSA is a small fraction of the 610,566 total. And to give the crusade, the legislation, and the NHTSA credit for even these one needs to believe that, in the absence of the 1966 laws, the auto industry would not have made improvements of its own, the GSA would not have imposed similar (or better) standards, and the states would not have acted when, in fact, they had demonstrated real effectiveness in the decade leading up to federal legislation.

What is clear from the available data is that the two greatest safety measures introduced since 1966 have nothing to do with the crashworthiness of vehicles. They addressed driver behavior. The first was the mandatory seat-belt-usage law. When worn, according to NHTSA data, seat belts reduce fatality risk in a crash by 45 percent. Before the law required vehicle occupants to buckle up, less than 20 percent of Americans did so. Present usage hovers around 90 percent. Again, more than half of lives saved in crashes over the last century are attributable to seat-belt use. The second most effective tactic has been sobriety legislation. Campaigns against drunk driving began to gain traction in the 1970s. Stricter laws were passed at the state level. Between 1982 and 2018, the rate of alcohol-related driving fatalities per 100,000 population declined by 65 percent. The absolute number of impaired-driving fatalities fell from 21,113 in 1982 to 10,497 in 2016, for a total of more than 200,000 lives saved in the period.[8]

Seat belts and drunk drivers were largely ignored in the crusade that produced the 1966 legislation. Like other elements of driver behavior, they were irrelevant to a campaign to hold Detroit accountable for fifty thousand annual deaths. Once front and back seat belts had been installed in automobiles, Congress had the opportunity to make their usage mandatory. All that was required was a law. But Moynihan, Nader, Ribicoff, and others argued that attempting to convince the public to buckle up was futile. Drivers and passengers were incorrigible, they said, a thesis that gave federal politicians an excuse not to impose on people who voted.

In the early 1970s, when Congress considered making the states do its dirty work by attaching a 25 percent bonus in highway funding to states that adopted compulsory seat-belt laws, Nader, still stuck on a Detroit-oriented solution, refused his support. In 1977, after twenty-three countries and territories around the world had made seat belts mandatory to real effect, the issue arose again in Congress. Joan Claybrook, formerly Nader's chief lobbyist and now head of the NHTSA, took the same stand as her former boss.

As late as 1983, when even Detroit was beseeching the NHTSA to make seat belts mandatory, Nader was insisting the effort would fail. People would not comply with "behavior control laws," he said. "We learned that in prohibition." He accused Detroit of pushing seat belts to avoid requirements for passive safety equipment such as air bags. A year later, as New York was passing its mandatory seat-belt measures, Claybrook said they were a waste of time; the public would recoil from the discomfort and inconvenience of wearing them.[9]

Nader and Claybrook viewed automakers as dilatory for their failure to make air bags work and they were not alone in that position. "Somebody's got to prove to me it cannot be done," said Nixon's secretary of transportation, John Volpe. "Those auto companies are so big and powerful that they can do anything they want." While it is true that Chrysler and some foreign automakers opposed air bag technology as impractical and a diversion from more useful lines of safety research, Ford and G.M. took up the challenge and raced to bring the purely passive restraint to market, coming up against such obstacles as unreliable air bag sensors, inadvertent activations, a serious danger to children and the frail, hearing damage, and the inability of the technology to protect occupants who were not properly positioned in the car (likely unbelted) or who were involved in side or rear collisions. It was a difficult assignment. A Ford air bag failed to discharge in a demonstration on national television. Legions of baboons and pigs were injured or killed standing in for small humans in endless air bag tests.[10]

Largely because Ed Cole was an air bag enthusiast, General Motors took an early lead in their development. When its progress became apparent, Ford changed tack, asking the NHTSA to delay the air bag program and instead allow alternative technological solutions: for instance, that cars be equipped with buzzers that would not stop buzzing, or ignitions that would not catch until occupants fastened their safety belts. Although not entirely consistent with the emphasis on passive safety, these alternatives were permitted in 1974. They sparked a revolt among drivers indignant at being scolded by their cars to wear seat belts. Congress killed the buzzers and locks in a matter of months. The buzzer fiasco confirmed to federal regulators and politicians that further advances in safety must demand nothing of the public toward its self-protection. Air bags regained the contentious center of the safety debate.[11]

G.M. spent $60 million installing air bags in 100,000 automobiles from 1975 to 1976 but sold only 10,000, notwithstanding a substantial amount of publicity and marketing. The NHTSA blamed the low sales on a lack of commitment among General Motors dealers to selling the new technology. Others said that some car buyers considered air bags nonessential, or were frightened by the idea of driving with what was essentially an unproven explosive device in their car. Further complicating matters were cost-benefit studies that cast doubt on the practicality of air bags, and the fact that their first sixty deployments brought fourteen lawsuits.[12]

After these failures, the industry came out hard in favor of mandatory seat-belt laws as an alternative to the passive restraint. The NHTSA would not budge, insisting that air bags would reduce fatalities by 40 percent, a number the industry said was absurd. Joan Claybrook began training tort lawyers on how to bring suit against automakers for failing to install air bags.

It fell to Ronald Reagan's transportation secretary, Elizabeth Dole, to break the stalemate in 1984. She did not take a stand for one technology or the other but ordered automakers to install air bags or other automatic passenger protections in cars by 1989, with the proviso that the regulation would be voided if states imposed mandatory seat-belt laws in the interim. By 1988, behind a massive industry-funded seat-belt advocacy campaign, thirty-two states representing three quarters of the population had made seat belts compulsory. In three more years, a solid majority of Americans were buckling up and, eventually, every state but New Hampshire would adopt mandatory usage. Credit for the most effective safety measure of all time thus falls to Elizabeth Dole, the states, and the auto industry, not the NHTSA.[*13]

That the states would deliver most of the progress on traf-

---

* Dole never needed to waive the air bag requirement. By 1989, Detroit had figured out how to make and market air bags as supplements to seat belts, a practice that lessened the load on the new technology and eased manufacturers' concerns of liability. The NHTSA wisely blessed the practice and both seat-belt usage and passive restraints became commonplace in American vehicles.

fic safety over the last fifty years makes sense. They were largely responsible for the significant gains in the fifty years before federal involvement. It had always been productive to have fifty largely independent legislatures apply themselves to saving lives on the road. The success of one, in any area, tended to spread quickly to others. Nor did the states find it difficult to coordinate their efforts, especially with the federal government quite legitimately incentivizing them to do so.

The denigration of state efforts by safety crusaders, indeed, the denigration of the entire safety establishment that had made driving in the United States safer than any country in the world, is one of the tragedies of postwar American policy. One cannot help but wonder how much safer U.S. roads would have been had Johnson's government contented itself with supporting the states and the safety establishment with a comprehensive approach to traffic safety, considering the road, policing, and especially the driver, in addition to the crashworthiness of automobiles, rather than insisting on its own blinkered leadership.

It is no coincidence that America lost its position as the safest driving nation in the world, never to regain it, in the wake of *Unsafe at Any Speed* and the passage of the 1966 legislation. The slide became noticeable in the mid-1970s and by the end of the decade the United States had been overtaken. Between 1979 and 2002, America reduced its annual fatality count by 16 percent while Canada, Australia, and Great Britain, with their similar driving populations and automotive fleets, posted drops of 49.9 percent, 51.1 percent, and 46.0 percent respectively. Canada and Australia both made wearing seat belts mandatory in the mid-1970s. Great Britain and Canada reduced impaired driving using breathalyzer tests and firm blood-alcohol limits in the 1960s. (Norway was specifying legal amounts of blood alcohol in the 1930s.)[14]

All countries that turned sooner than the United States to mandatory seat-belt and anti-drunk-driving laws reaped the benefits. Between 1979 and 2011, twenty-five other developed nations reduced their gross fatality counts from peak levels (the States topped out at 54,589 road deaths in 1972) further and faster than America. Over that same period, the United States sank from first to nineteenth in deaths per 1,000 vehicles registered, and first to thirteenth among the nineteen nations that tracked fatalities per billion kilometers traveled.* The United States had almost fallen off the map in traffic safety leadership even as its officials were claiming one of the most effective public health and safety efforts of the past century.[15]

In a 2014 issue of the *American Journal of Public Health*, safety scientist and author Leonard Evans argued that there is more than enough research available to declare a fundamental traffic safety law: vehicles are important, but less so than roads, and far less so than road users. This has been the case since the 1920s. It is essentially what Howard Pyle of the National Safety Council told the Ribicoff committee in 1966. Two studies from the early 1970s, one at Indiana University and another from the U.K., both concluded that the driver was at least 93 percent responsible for crashes, the automobile 2 percent (usually due to worn tires or brakes or other maintenance issues). Yet the NHTSA continued to place great emphasis on vehicle recalls, crash test results, new safety technology, and bullying Detroit instead of leading the public.[16]

The 1966 safety legislation and the NHTSA's activities undoubtedly raised the profile of traffic safety issues generally and some of the administration's efforts have paid dividends. Frontal air bags are estimated to have saved 43,856 lives between 1960 and 2012, and side-impact air bags another 32,288. That is progress, but it is more than offset by the number of lives lost by the federal government's insistence on passive, Detroit-targeted responses to safety concerns and the active opposition of the crusaders to measures aimed at humans. The fact is that Ralph Nader and the federal government harmed the cause of traffic safety. If, in 1966, Congress had told the driving public to sober up, buckle up, and drive right, rather than scourging Detroit for its failure to protect people from their own recklessness, the fatality rate would have fallen significantly faster and further.[17]

---

* A study using 2011 data found that if the United States had been able to remain among the top seven leading nations in traffic safety, twenty thousand additional lives would have been saved that year. An update using 2018 data showed that if the United States had been among the top twenty-one leading nations, twenty thousand additional lives would have been saved.

Epilogue

THE END OF AMERICAN ENTERPRISE

In 1606, King James of England, for a variety of economic and geopolitical reasons, gave investors in a joint-stock venture known as the Virginia Company exclusive rights to establish a permanent agricultural settlement and extract timber, fur, and whatever else might be found on the eastern coast of North America between latitudes 34° and 41° N around Chesapeake Bay. Which is to say that government has been integrally involved in American business from the outset. At the Constitutional Convention of 1787, Congress was assigned powers to borrow money and collect taxes, regulate interstate and international commerce, build infrastructure, promote science and the useful arts, and protect intellectual property, all crucial elements of a stable, flourishing business environment. The promotion of enterprise, wrote Alexander Hamilton, was a central purpose of the union: "The prosperity of commerce is now perceived and acknowledged by all enlightened statesmen to be the most useful as well as the most productive source of national wealth."[1]

Import tariffs protected America's nascent manufacturing. Trade policy fueled the tobacco industry and the South's cotton boom. The military secured new territories, which were given over to private development. Publicly financed roads, canals, and harbors reduced the cost of moving goods and promoted inland trade. Lands were distributed to encourage railroads and money was granted for the development of the telegraph. Banks were chartered. Laws were enacted to extend the privileges of incorporation. Public officials at the state and national levels did all they could to grease the wheels of commerce and protect the rights of property.

Government interest in commerce was a function of popular values. As a whole, the American people in the eighteenth and nineteenth centuries were quick to see the benefits of economic development, especially as they pertained to standards of living. Restless, individualistic, and enterprising, they equated market-driven change with progress and measured their welfare by material abundance. "I perceive clearly," wrote Walt Whitman in 1871, "that the extreme business energy, and this almost maniacal appetite for wealth prevalent in the United States, are parts of amelioration and progress."[2]

Here was an oft-remarked distinction between American and European culture. The French traveler Alexis de Tocqueville found the "feverish ardor" with which Americans pursued their personal welfare, and their embrace of moneymaking as a means to social advance, alien to his experience. There were Americans who shared Europe's relative veneration of sacred and aristocratic values, courtly and martial behavior, and who disdained their countrymen's obsessions with material success and the accumulation of capital, but they were a minority and they posed no serious obstacle to commercial expansion. Status and power in America accrued to the capable, prosperous man of property and economic imagination.[3]

It was not until the late nineteenth century, by which time America was extraordinarily rich, that a critical mass of public officials, having encouraged the proliferation of giant industrial enterprises through the development of nation-spanning infrastructure, became alarmed at the ruthlessness with which those enterprises fulfilled their roles as nation builders. Absent external restraints on their growth and business practices, some of the corporate monsters were subjecting employees to miserable working conditions, crushing smaller companies with anticompetitive business practices, and exploiting consumers with inferior goods and high prices. Of course, smaller companies were ruthless, too: the blindness of capitalists to the public welfare, their unique ability to "esteem [their] immediate interests . . . to be the common Measure of Good and

Evil," was a truism remarked by economist Dudley North a century before the American Revolution. But seeing these practices at scale was disturbing, never mind that they had reached scale as a natural and foreseeable consequence of the nation's unbridled pursuit of economic development. The monsters would be regulated. Railroads first.[4]

With its abundance of geography, scattered peoples, and economic ambition, nineteenth-century America could not lay tracks quickly enough. Railway building was accelerated by government engineering expertise, land grants, land acquisition policies, and government bonds, and railway companies grew huge by supplying the public want and taking advantage of a wide-open business environment. As the only viable way to travel or ship goods by land in many parts of the country, the railways were often in position to set their own rates, an opportunity they exploited to the fullest. Their predictable price-gouging outraged farmers and small businessmen (i.e., voters), as well as the policymakers who had helped create the mess. A number of states began investigating railway pricing practices in the 1870s and some eventually prescribed rates and established agencies to oversee the industry in the public interest. This prompted Congress to belatedly assert its dominion over interstate commerce, passing the Interstate Commerce Act of 1887, and creating the Interstate Commerce Commission to regulate transportation between states.

More wariness of large corporations led to the Sherman Antitrust Act of 1890, which, among other measures, made it a criminal offense to monopolize or attempt to monopolize any part of trade or commerce. In the early years of the twentieth century, President Theodore Roosevelt and his successor, William Howard Taft, used the Sherman Act to prosecute and break up Standard Oil and the American Tobacco Trust. This was the era of Progressivism, which sought by disciplining large businesses to enhance their contributions to amelioration and progress in American life. Among other reforms, Progressivism brought the 1906 Pure Food and Drug Act and, in 1914, the Federal Trade Commission, dedicated to enforcing competition policy.

Reformers of capitalism were by the early twentieth century many and well organized, and the sins of large corporations were

ever better enumerated and declaimed. The motives of the reformers were not uniform. Some wanted to hold bad actors to account
and smooth the rough edges of corporate capitalism. Others had a
sincere preference (or nostalgia) for the Jeffersonian ideal of a nation
of farmers and small businessmen; they saw massive industrial corporations as a corruption of the American way. Whether pragmatic
or in some way ideological or moralistic, all of the reformers, born
of an enterprising people, were a mix of good intentions and opportunism. Politicians exposed corporate depredations and monopolistic behavior and raked in votes. Newspapers and magazines (some
of them enormous businesses in their own right) assailed predatory
wealth on behalf of their subscribers. The muckrakers made careers
and found lasting fame.

   Like everything else in American political and legal life, reform
was noisy and adversarial. This was by design. The authors of the
American Constitution believed the way to avoid one faction of the
nation from exercising tyranny over another was, in James Madison's
famous phrase, to make "ambition counteract ambition." Competing interests would fight it out at the polls, in the legislatures, and
in courtrooms where, faith had it, optimal policies would triumph.[5]

Theodore Roosevelt, idol of the Progressives, was an uncommon
American. Born to a large and distinguished family, he was raised by
a socialite mother and a wealthy father devoted to culture and phi-
lanthropy. Captivated as a youth by Viking and Germanic tales of
conquest and discovery, Teddy inherited a small fortune, gave rare
thought to money, and sought glory instead as military hero and
leader of men. His mania for reform mingled a lust for power with
strongly held Progressive ideals and aristocratic paternalism. He
addressed the growing tensions between America and its business
community in a 1907 speech at Pilgrim's Memorial, complaining
of "malefactors of great wealth," and the "ignoble character" of the
"mere money-getting American" who was insensible to duty, putting his fortune to the base use of personal pleasure. Roosevelt also
located the "genesis" of the nation in the quest for freedom of conscience and personal liberty symbolized by Plymouth Rock, sidelin-
ing the essential contributions of commercial enterprise to the early

colonies. He described interstate commerce as a nasty by-product of modern life, one unimagined by the drafters of the Constitution, rather than one explicitly encouraged by them.[6]

Despite his denigration of the importance of business to American life, Roosevelt sought not to impede the nation's commerce but to temper capitalism and punish those who broke rules. He called for care in regulation. Not only the legislatures but the courts and the people needed "to be educated so that they may see what the real dangers are and what the real remedies." He had no tolerance for reckless or vindictive behavior:

> It is idle to ask me not to prosecute criminals, rich or poor. But I desire no less emphatically to have it understood that we have sanctioned and will sanction no action of a vindictive type, and above all no action which shall inflict great and unmerited suffering upon innocent stockholders or upon the public as a whole. Our purpose is to act with the minimum of harshness compatible with attaining our ends. . . . In any great movement, such as that in which we are engaged, nothing is more necessary than sanity, than the refusal to be led into extremes by the advocates of the ultra course on either side. . . . The rich man who with hard arrogance declines to consider the rights and the needs of those who are less well off, and the poor man who excites or indulges in envy and hatred of those who are better off, are alike alien to the spirit of our national life.[7]

The economy advanced rapidly in the decade after the Great War, and large firms were generated in utilities, communications, finance, retail, oil, and transportation. Concerns about monopolistic capitalism and the depredations of business were muted by the relief of peace and the enjoyment of plenty. The next great regulatory spasm was occasioned by the Great Depression and the election of Franklin Roosevelt in 1932.

With a family fortune and social outlook similar to that of his distant cousin Theodore, Franklin Roosevelt used the Depression to insert the federal government directly into huge swaths of business and to establish the federal state as the fount of amelioration

and progress in American society. Many agreed with him that security, protecting individuals and communities from the vicissitudes
of life, was more important than growth in personal and national
wealth. FDR was not out to dismantle or replace capitalism. In fact,
he believed that more consumption would dig America out of its
economic hole. But he did seek in important ways to subordinate
capitalism to government. To that end, he outstripped Cousin Theodore with a 1936 speech recasting two centuries of U.S. history as a
plot by business against the people. The revolution had been fought
to win freedom from European tyranny, he said, only to give way to
a new domestic tyranny of "economic royalists." They had built new
kingdoms "upon concentration of control over material things. . . .
The whole structure of modern life was impressed into this royal
service." With his calculated attacks on economic royalists, FDR
violated TR's decree against the harsh and the vindictive.[8]

Franklin Roosevelt being a complex character, there was also a
constructive moral impulse behind his bid to subordinate commerce
to governance. As he said in his first inaugural:

> Happiness lies not in the mere possession of money; it lies
> in the joy of achievement, in the thrill of creative effort. The
> joy and moral stimulation of work no longer must be forgot-
> ten in the mad chase of evanescent profits. These dark days
> will be worth all they cost us if they teach us that our true
> destiny is not to be ministered unto but to minister to our-
> selves and to our fellow men.[9]

In his second inaugural, he added that the test of progress "is not
whether we add more to the abundance of those who have much; it
is whether we provide enough for those who have too little."[10]

It was a combination of these nobler sentiments, animus toward
business, and political ambition that inspired the likes of Galbraith
and Schlesinger after the Second World War to attempt to rally the
Democratic Party with a new agenda exalting public over private
pursuits. When society reverted to its commercial enthusiasms in
the postwar years, which were for many people a welcome respite

from war and depression, these disappointed New Dealers and reform-minded intellectuals declared the nation to be backsliding. Their ongoing campaigns for less materialism and more public purpose in American life led directly to Johnson's Great Society and Apollo 11. They also made a target of Detroit, capital of American capitalism.

The experience of the auto industry in the twentieth century can be seen as the history of American business in microcosm. The automobile was a product of American commercial genius, wholeheartedly embraced by the American people as a tool for the advancement of personal, social, and economic welfare. Automobile culture was American culture, and it remade the nation top to bottom without any involvement by the federal government beyond cheerleading and roadbuilding. This continued until the wonders of automobiling grew familiar, automakers became huge and powerful, and the adverse consequences of car culture and the larger commercial economy to which it was central became more apparent. Critics of the automobile grew in number and eventually focused their criticisms not on the driving public or the national government that had funded the highways and refused the role of regulator, but the greedy corporate entities purportedly enslaving the people in a profit-spewing project, and killing them by the tens of thousands with unsafe vehicles. Decisive federal action was required before the automobile wiped out a third or a half or, in Nader's mind, the whole of the population.

Notwithstanding the historical antecedents for the treatment of the automobile, the third spasm of regulatory expansion that hit America in the 1960s was different in kind and scale from what passed before. It was still ambition counteracting ambition, but whereas the Progressives had intervened in the economy tentatively and largely in response to popular agitation, and the New Deal was instigated by a determined president and like-minded reformers in response to economic catastrophe, this onslaught occurred in the midst of unprecedented economic growth and was overtly entrepreneurial in nature. It represented the combined efforts of intellectual entrepreneurs advancing their own ideas about how to run America; congressional entrepreneurs who improved their electoral chances by championing consumers against corporate interests; legal entrepreneurs who expanded torts to better hold businesses to account and keep themselves busy; and public interest entrepreneurs who built careers on exposing corporate abuses and rallying consumers, politicians, and media to effect change. Together these new entrepreneurs represented a shift of a large portion of America's energies from the almost maniacal pursuit of capital to an almost maniacal pursuit of reform and, in some cases, capitalists.

The old notion that economic growth was the engine of amelioration and progress gave way to new conventional wisdom. Economic growth was the enemy of amelioration and progress. Its pursuit was wrongheaded. The economy was likely to expand on its own in perpetuity and, besides, America was already rich enough. It could afford unlimited social improvements. Better that the private economy, rigged in favor of a powerful elite, be subordinated to and supervised by the national government, where the best minds, eager and equipped to solve America's greatest social problems, were now gathered. The plausibility of these ideas was enhanced by a strong economy that made all change seem affordable, a generational turnover that broke logjams in Congress, the legislative ambition of the White House, and the antiauthoritarian temper of the times.

As ever, the motives of the reformers were mixed. All professed to be working in the public interest. Many were genuinely concerned for the social implications of America's rampant materialism, outraged at real and perceived injustices against unwitting consumers, convinced of the rightness of their ideas and actions, and optimistic that a more just society was achievable. And, to be sure, there were wrongs to be righted. It can't be said often enough that forty thousand or more people dying on American highways every year was a tragedy and a colossal waste of human potential.

Even with honest disagreement over the state of automotive technology and the best approach to traffic safety, critics were correct to identify a regulatory opportunity. Regulators step in where markets fail, and markets were failing on auto safety. Consumers did not want to pay for more safety in their vehicles and it was not in the interests of automakers to force unwanted safety on car buyers. With so many people dying on the roads, calls for the federal government to take an interest were legitimate and, to a point, they were answered sensibly, even boldly, before Nader and Ribicoff came along. The combined use of federal purchasing power and state-level regulation was sufficient to enact the full slate of second-collision safety standards requested by the American Medical Association, notwithstanding what the experts at Cornell said was a lack of evidence that the standards would save lives.

Still, these federal measures were insufficient to satiate the entrepreneurial reformers. A reasonable, deliberate approach to improving traffic safety—what TR called real remedies to real dangers—was never going to satisfy them because most had goals that extended well beyond the problem at hand. A reduction in the number of traffic fatalities was not going to convince Americans to stop caring so much about their damned automobiles, or turn their attention to higher purposes than getting and spending, or undermine their veneration of business leaders and the gigantic enterprises they had built. It was not going to change minds about how far government should intervene in the economy, or convince everyone that government, not commerce, was the fount of amelioration and progress in American life. Nor would it further the electoral prospects of challenged congressmen or the legislative record of the Great Society, or build the businesses of personal injury attorneys or make the reputation of public interest advocates. Like earlier generations of reformers, this one, too, was born of an enterprising people. But here, to a greater extent than in earlier instances, the problem at hand was the start rather than the end of ambition.

What would satiate these reformers was bringing the hammer down on General Motors, Detroit, its products, and the business sector in general. Rather than the minimum of harshness recommended by the first Roosevelt, what befell Detroit in the 1960s was a maximum of harshness that inflicted great and largely unmerited suffering on an industry, its employees, its investors, a lot of effective and well-intentioned people in the so-called traffic safety establishment, and the public at large.

Second-collision theory was a perfect weapon for such a mission. It was a grand theoretical approach that supposedly "solved" the problem of traffic deaths for good. Every question of road safety was reduced to the role of the automobile and the culpability of the automaker. The hard-won, incremental progress of the Triple-E crowd was rendered risible. The expertise of automakers, engineers, public officials, safety advocates, and others who favored a broader, systemic (and correct) approach to protecting motorists was delegitimized. Second-collision theory had all the answers. Better still, it did not require that politicians and public interest advocates impose on the public (voters and supporters) to change its behavior and take some responsibility for road carnage.

That the goal of the 1966 reformers was a sack of Detroit was never well disguised. "I intend to be a crusader," said Ribicoff. His hearings bore no resemblance to the careful investigation into possible answers to traffic fatalities run by his predecessor, Kenneth Roberts of Alabama. Ribicoff was out for blood. His agenda was to damage the reputation of automakers, brand them as killers, and bring them under the thumb of the federal government. His panel's crude ambush of G.M.'s executives had all the earmarks of a show trial. Ribicoff's cavalier treatment of experts with opinions inconvenient to his personal mission was intellectually dishonest. Rather than congratulate the Post Office for lifesaving safety advances it had achieved on its G.M. trucks, he berated it for working with the enemy. His presentation of Nader as an independent witness and a lone actor rather than an agent of his subcommittee was shameful.

Ribicoff was hardly alone. The American Trial Lawyers Association, an array of congressmen and staffers, and President Johnson all participated in the association's disgraceful Stop Murder by Motor campaign with its plain implication that Detroit was intentionally killing people with its vehicle designs. None held Nader accountable for his rhetorical excesses. It served their interests to have him allege corruption in the auto safety establishment, smear safety researchers, accuse General Motors of building cars as safe as "a roomful of knives" and suppressing evidence and engaging in a "massive lie" and a "massive conspiracy" and being "an authoritarian pocket" immune from prosecution. They fought alongside him as he misrepresented facts and arguments to suit his purposes, and joined him in pretending that the automobile industry was "outside the law," as though states were nullities and Congress had a monopoly on legislation. The legend of Ralph Nader, a solitary man representing a personal conception of the public interest, was their joint fabrication.

Scholars admiring of the consumer movement argue that there was nothing radical about it, that its adherents never questioned the fundamentals of capitalism or "the beneficial fruits of mass production and mass consumption." Rather, they wanted only to smooth rough edges in the public interest. This is not the case. Nader testified that he wanted Americans to throw off the chains of capitalism. John Kenneth Galbraith called for "a major wrench in our attitudes" toward economic production and growth. Daniel Patrick Moynihan rejoiced in 1967 that "the central concerns of American society are no longer in the hands of free enterprise, and that free enterprise is no longer in the hands of men who expect to lead society." Moynihan was wrong in two ways: business was never so independent and domineering as he supposed, and it had not been pushed as far to the sidelines as he suggests. But Moynihan's statement reveals his objectives, which are consistent with many of his fellow crusaders.[11]

In their assault on Detroit, the reformers, as a class, proved themselves susceptible to many of the human frailties they attributed, often correctly, to their capitalist opponents: the inclination, noted by Dudley North, to measure right and wrong by selfish advantage; blindness to inconvenient facts and arguments; a paternalistic disdain for ordinary citizens; a remorseless ability to harm the public good. There is no more reason to take at face value the altruism of crusaders and reformers than there is to assume altruism in capitalists. They are all born of an enterprising people.

Robert Kennedy, whom the writer Elizabeth Drew credited with putting "the auto industry on a one-way street to federal regulation" with his treatment of G.M.'s executives, blithely changed his tune when broadening his base in pursuit of the presidency in mid-1967. America now had an overabundance of federal administrative agencies, he said, and these had not "achieved the high degree of fundamental fairness to which business concerns are entitled." Many federal agencies, he continued, operated in unfair and untimely manners, prejudging cases, and acting with partiality or bias against business.[12]

Around the same time, Moynihan, nursing political ambitions of his own, appeared before the House Committee on Interstate and Foreign Commerce to say: "As with the harassment of the driver in the first era of traffic safety, it seems we are now entering a period of indicting the businessmen involved. The need to impose guilt in this field is obviously deep seated, and we may very well be over-correcting."[13]

None of this is to excuse General Motors' conduct. The company had a history of bullying, predatory behavior. Its definition of the public good, while broader than recognized at the time, was too narrow for its own good. It could have done more for automobile safety. Management guru Peter Drucker had warned as early as 1946 that G.M. needed to be more aware of the world around it and the externalities of its business. Some of Nader's claims may be sketchy (for instance, a half century later, we still have no evidence to support the sensational stories of women being used to entrap him, or a child decapitated by a glovebox), but G.M.'s demonstrated actions against him were nevertheless reprehensible. It deserved to get slapped around in the public sphere for using private investigators to seek personal dirt on Nader. His subsequent lawsuit was fair game. Although G.M. was not the aggressor in this particular battle, some indeterminable portion of the damage it suffered was self-inflicted.

What made no sense at all was Congress voting unanimously to approve a hasty, sweeping, and counterproductive regulation of America's most important industry because General Motors had been ambushed by a Senate subcommittee, or because it was looking for dirt on Nader. Any decision on federal involvement in the auto industry should have been made on the merits of the regulatory proposal. The legislators displayed minimal curiosity about the safety issues they were putatively addressing, and no concern for the costs of their measures borne by General Motors, the rest of Detroit, or consumers. They were primarily interested in the severity of the regulation they could impose and the fight for legislative credit. They were as reckless in their treatment of Detroit as Nader and

Ribicoff imagined Detroit to be in its management of vehicle safety. Finally, and unfortunately, congressional action was seen by many as proof that General Motors and Detroit were building death traps, and that drivers were absolved of responsibility for traffic fatalities.[14]

Not only did the safety crusade kill the Corvair and cripple General Motors and the American auto industry, it contributed, as we have seen, to a lasting change in industry's relations with government and the American public. The safety crusade opened the door to a flood of consumer regulation and consumer agencies in Washington, as well as larger budgets and more vigilance in existing agencies. What has been called by the historian David Vogel a kind of "Great Society for the private economy" enabled "a fundamental transformation of both the politics and administration of government regulation of corporate social conduct." Nader's success, writes Lizabeth Cohen, the leading historian of consumer activism, was "just the spark needed" to produce a "major conflagration for greater legislative and regulatory protection."[15]

Hordes of Naderites were inspired to take up shop in Washington. By 1977, there were eighty-three public interest groups with offices in the capital, more than half of them arriving after 1968. Eighty-six public law firms were active in D.C. by the mid-1970s, more than 80 percent of them formed since 1968. Of the 165 organizations to attend the first major conference of public interest activists in 1976, nearly all were less than a decade old. Their leadership and staffs were overwhelmingly well-educated middle-class young adults. They were aided in their campaigns by the receptiveness of courts to their presentation of themselves as aggrieved parties, and legal recognition of the right of private citizens to participate in the decision-making of administrative agencies. Before long, they were as capable as business had ever been of infiltrating and capturing government agencies, and using them to pursue a narrow conception of the public good.[16]

The rise of the public interest movement triggered an arms race with business. Prior to 1968, the hundred-odd American corporations with a permanent presence in D.C. were primarily concerned, like General Motors, with landing government contracts and other aspects of procurement. Between 1968 and 1978, their ranks were swollen to 500. There were 175 firms with federally registered lobbyists in 1971 and 650 by 1979. By 1981, a survey of 400 large and medium-sized firms found 361 of them had an active presence on Capitol Hill. The role of the public affairs specialist in corporations was aggrandized and chief executives gave increasing amounts of attention to relations with government and external stakeholders.[17]

Business also sought strength in numbers. Existing lobbies such as the U.S. Chamber of Commerce and National Federation of Independent Business sharpened their defense of the rights of capital, and were joined on the barricades by dozens of industry-specific groups and right-leaning think tanks, including the new Heritage Foundation and the revived American Enterprise Institute. Author-activists George Gilder, Michael Novak, and Irving Kristol sought to counter the influence of Nader and company. (The fighting response of the corporate sector has not been one-dimensional or uniform. Many business leaders have used mounting public hostility and the denigration of their contributions to society as an alibi to more aggressively outsource, offshore, avoid taxes, and otherwise follow their natural inclinations to mistake their financial welfare for the public good.)

In addition to fighting door-to-door with public interest advocates in Washington, the business lobby looked to shore up faltering public support for business as a whole. In 1964, the historian Richard Hofstadter had written that "the existence and workings of the corporations are largely accepted, and in the main they are assumed to be fundamentally benign." That approval of business peaked in 1966 when 55 percent of Americans expressed "a great deal of confidence" in the leaders of major corporations, and 96 percent agreed that free enterprise had made America great. By 1971, only 27 percent of Americans expressed a great deal of confidence in business leadership, and by 1974 only 16 percent. Other contemporaneous surveys found big business the least trustworthy of twenty-four major social groups tested, and 82 percent of Americans attested that corporations had too much power.[18]

The young were especially disaffected from the corporate sector by the late 1960s. One poll found 94 percent of young adults believed business "was too profit-blinded and not concerned with public welfare." A *Newsweek* survey found only 12 percent of college graduates considered a career in business their first choice, a sentiment reflected in business school enrollment, which grew at one third the rate of total college enrollment. The more elite the college, the greater the resistance to corporate life. Only 63 of Harvard's 1,091 graduates in 1966 went to work in the for-profit sector, and at Princeton the percentage of seniors looking for immediate employment in business fell by half between 1961 and 1966. Many of the best and brightest now sought to work against rather than for business interests, fulfilling the hopes of an earlier generation of liberal intellectuals. The historic preference of ambitious young people to start their own firms fell by the wayside. The number of start-ups per 100,000 working-age people has fallen by more than half since the 1970s, and the proportion of new firms to old firms has been shrinking steadily since that time.[*][19]

This shift in energies from making private goods to the pursuit of public goods contributed to what we now recognize as aggravated levels of polarization. Ambition countering ambition at epic scale. Take your pick: the safety controversy was a demand by an increasingly well-educated citizenry for a minimum of public responsibility from corporate reprobates, or an attack of coastal elites on an unworthy bourgeois status symbol manufactured in a flyover state.

The growing conflict between American business and the champions of the public interest, of which General Motors versus the safety crusaders was symptom and catalyst, has since spilled into every corner of business, political, and legal life. Here, and not within the corporate sector itself, is dog eat dog.

The fights are ostensibly over statutes, agencies, and regulations, over the rights of property against the common good, over the size and budgets of governments, over redistricting and election finance, judicial appointments and tort reform, legal formalism versus legal reformism, but, at bottom, each is about who will define the central concerns of American life. What cannot be won in a legislature is pursued in a court, and vice versa. Politics has

---

[*] While substantial numbers of graduates from elite schools still go into not-for-profit sectors, the pendulum has since swung back in favor of finance and consulting, in no small part because of the disproportionately high rewards.

become unprecedentedly legalistic and the law is unprecedentedly politicized.* Everybody is under attack. Everybody has lawyered up. "In a world of constant litigation by friend and foe," writes Thomas Keck, "any decision not to litigate would amount to an act of unilateral disarmament, leaving the field to ideological opponents." In 1960, there was one lawyer for every 627 Americans. By 1995, there was one for every 307. Annual legal billing increased from $9 billion to $54 billion (in constant dollars) between 1960 and 1987. In addition to lawyers, each side raises funds and develops political action committees and organizes the grass roots, all with the aim of bending the law to their values, ideologies, and financial interests, hammering at the other side with every available club, and never conceding an inch.[20]

This form of conflict, as the famed prosecutor and academic Milton Wessel once said, is "a medieval solution to modern problems." It is an intellectual adaptation of the ancient common law practice of trial by combat wherein plaintiff and defendant hammer away at each other with every weapon and trick at their disposal, and the last man standing is declared in the right. Today the weapons are not fists or clubs but lawsuits, lobbying, legislation, and public rhetoric. No other advanced industrialized nation has anywhere near so legalistic, belligerent, and costly a system of managing its differences. Americans seem to believe that such devices as administrative guidance and negotiation, voluntary agreements, financial inducements, and cost sharing represent craven forms of private sector appeasement. Among the results of the hammer-and-tong approach are deeper enmities, fewer compromises, reduced public regard for lawyers, legislatures, and businesspeople, suboptimal policy, and economic stagnation.

The exact degree to which the new regulatory agenda, the rise of public interest activists, the growth of torts, and the alienation of a substantial portion of the public from business activity have com-

---

* The battle lines aren't always clear. Some public interest advocates, like Nader, mistrusted bureaucrats almost as much as capitalists, and federal indictments of public officials have skyrocketed.

bined to affect American productivity and its standard of living is impossible to determine with precision.

The direct costs of torts are easiest to calculate. They reached $429 billion by 2016, which means that Americans annually spend 70 percent of their world-leading national defense budget warring with one another in the courts over injuries, real and perceived. Compared to today's tort industry, G.M. is a small business. And the $429 billion includes only direct costs. The total economic effect of the expansion of tort liability, including product design expenses, lost sales of targeted products and services, the impact on innovation and new product introduction, is far higher. American defenders of the tort system tend not to dispute the costs but to argue for its efficacy, a perspective scholars outside the country tend to view as insane.*[21]

Estimates of the cost of regulation are fraught. Regulation is a manifold and exceedingly complex phenomenon involving several levels of government and courts, a tangle of statutes and rules that vary from state to state, and inconsistent enforcement and compliance. As with torts, cost estimates tend to focus on the observable cost of compliance, the dollars spent by the regulated firm on meeting new standards, while ignoring the indirect and intangible costs, the reputational damage, the demoralization, the uncertainty created in the business environment, the increased risks of innovation, the deterrence to new business start-ups, and the opportunity costs of shifting corporate attention from innovation and competitiveness to regulatory affairs. The case of General Motors suggests that these additional costs can be enormous and lasting, and are largely untracked.

The most recent (2016) estimates of the cumulative cost of regulation from the Mercatus Center at George Mason University identified 1.1 million federal regulatory restrictions and probabilistically matched them to industries and estimated the impact on GDP, small

---

* "Our review of the empirical evidence leads us to a relatively bleak judgment about the properties of the tort system as a deterrent mechanism and an even bleaker evaluation of the tort system as a compensatory mechanism," write Don Dewees and Michael J. Trebilcock, "The Efficacy of the Tort System and Its Alternatives," *Osgoode Hall Law Journal* 30, no. 1 (Spring 1992). They find far better social insurance systems in other nations.

business, and prices. Regulations were found to have reduced the annual rate of U.S. growth by 0.8 percent between 1977 and 2012. If the number of regulations had been frozen at 1980 levels, the U.S. economy would be roughly 25 percent larger today.[22]

It would be rash to suggest that all of the new regulations were undesirable and/or inefficient. Defenders of regulation point to untold numbers of lives saved by higher standards for baby cribs, the requirement for childproof caps on pill bottles, and warning labels on cigarette packages. Emission controls on automobiles are also cited as a positive, even if implemented in a disorderly and costly manner.

Defenders admit that they load heavy costs on business, generate economic uncertainty, alienate business from government and the public, reduce aggregate economic efficiency, yet claim the social benefits "massively outweigh those costs." They tend to rely on the regulators themselves for estimates of both benefits and costs, which permits the regulators to mark their own homework, and most follow the NHTSA example on traffic fatalities, crediting their agencies and programs for all improvements regardless of whether they could have occurred without intervention, or could have been achieved in a more efficient manner. These calculations are designed to justify the existence and the budget of the agency rather than to rigorously analyze its effectiveness. And that's if the homework gets done at all. "Do the safety benefits of the program justify its costs? Curiously, no one knows," stated NHTSA's advisory council in 1976, and the answer had not changed as late as 2009.[23]

Given that cost-benefit analyses are weaponized by their authors and political partisans in the United States, external sources might be preferred to measure the net impact of government regulation of business. In 2005, the World Bank found that a 10 percent increase in a country's regulatory burden slows the annual growth rate of GDP by half a percentage point annually; between 1975 and 2016, the number of rules in the U.S. Code of Federal Regulations increased 107 percent and the amount of federal spending on regulation rose similarly. The Organization for Economic Cooperation and Development estimates the cost of regulation in the States between 4 percent and 10 percent of GDP and maintains that it could be substantially reduced without impacting social welfare. In short, the costs of fifty years of regulatory onslaught appear to be immense, greater than necessary, and a net drag on America's productivity and standard of living.[24]

The high cost of America's approach to regulation matters more as its economic growth slows. As mentioned in the Prologue, U.S. national output per person has fallen by a third in the half century since 1970 compared to the half century before. Total factor productivity, a metric favored by economists to isolate innovation and technical progress in an economy, has risen in the past fifty years at one third the rate of the previous fifty years. That the real income of the average American climbed at an annual rate of 2.58 percent between 1948 and 1972, and by only 0.48 percent since, is not unrelated. In their recent history of American capitalism, Alan Greenspan and Adrian Wooldridge load the blame for these declines on the growth of federal regulation and entitlement programs. This shortchanges the effects of America's aging population, income inequality, and the increase in foreign economic competition, among other factors, but regulation does play a significant role.[25]

The consequences of the alienation of a large portion of Americans from business activity are best approached from a historical perspective. The sack of Detroit was the point at which the old consensus that wealth-building and profit-seeking were the means to amelioration and progress in American life was permanently ruptured at both the individual and collective levels. The consensus had been tested before, most notably in the Great Depression, but it had survived intact into the presidency of John F. Kennedy, who had no higher domestic priority than 5 percent annual economic growth. It was shortly after his death in 1963 that torrents of entrepreneurial energy shifted from producing growth to identifying and combating growth and its consequences or, as Robert Gordon puts it, from creating goods to fighting bads. That spelled the end of American enterprise as it was known for the first two hundred years of national history. The United States now employs more people in its not-for-profit sector than in its manufacturing sector. Of course, many people in the not-for-profit sector do noble work, but the diversion of energies is significant, as is the anti-corporate animus.[26]

The last great economic expansion in American history collapsed simultaneously with the consensus that economic growth was the first priority of the American people, the one thing from which all public blessings—the rise in middle-class living standards, the alleviation of poverty, the security of the nation—flowed. It was not cause and effect; nor was it coincidence. The redeployment of many intelligent, motivated, and well-positioned people to managing, curbing, or combating commercial enterprise in what remains, by world standards, a ridiculously adversarial system of laws and governance was bound to harm growth. Like all large organizations, nations lose momentum when their priorities become confused. A country permanently at war with itself over whether a growing commercial economy is the answer or the problem is unlikely to flourish.

A perverse dynamic is now entrenched in American life. An invention or advance, through the united efforts of entrepreneurs, policymakers, and the public, is accepted as a tool of amelioration and progress until the major benefits have been wrung from it or its associated costs, previously unknown or unacknowledged, begin piling up. The nation then turns to heap responsibility for all of those costs entirely on business and seeks to collect.

Opioids, man-made chemical compounds with morphine-like properties, were a huge twentieth-century breakthrough in the management of intractable pain. Scientists created them, the Food and Drug Administration approved them, doctors prescribed them, and patients took them, gratefully, because they were central to their treatment. Today, America is the hot center of an epidemic of opioid abuse. It is an appalling public health problem responsible for tens of thousands of unnecessary deaths annually. Following the example of tobacco lawsuits from the 1990s, state attorneys general are lining up to sue for huge sums the pharmaceutical firms that make and market opioids. The "logic" of the suits is simple: the drug companies manufactured the opioids that caused the health crisis; they should pay for it. The states point to first responders who cannot keep up with the pace of overdoses and coroner's offices unable to store all the dead bodies as evidence of a financial drain and the need for pharmaceutical firms to pay up.

Few would disagree that drug companies should be held

accountable for any misleading claims about the addictive nature of their product, or irresponsible marketing practices, just as tobacco companies were earlier deemed responsible for denying or muddying the link between cigarettes and cancer. But the pharmaceutical firms were not alone in this public health crisis. The FDA approved the drugs and some of the controversial claims for them, as well as the allegedly inadequate warnings they carried. The FDA also failed to demand restrictions on the use of more powerful opioids on their release. The aggressive opioid marketing campaigns were aimed at medical professionals who should have known better, not benighted consumers. Those same professionals relied upon third-party research from other experts who said opioids were safe and nonaddictive. It was physicians, not pharma companies, who wrote excessive opioid prescriptions and did little to prevent doctor-shopping. Even when states were reporting more prescriptions for opioids than they had residents, the Drug Enforcement Administration, which was supposedly tracking the distribution of the drugs, neither disrupted their illicit flow nor placed production quotas on manufacturers. Many individual Americans, for their part, did not use opioids as prescribed, or obtained them illegally on the black market, or otherwise abused the drugs.[27]

The opioid crisis is a general social failure yet the costs are being attributed to capital in an aggressive, punitive manner that, to the extent it succeeds, will harm the employees and shareholders of the companies and their insurers, and decrease the industry's ability and willingness to innovate and provide new and better drugs in the future. Worse, if the tobacco experience is any guide,* what money escapes the lawyers' pockets will go into general state revenues rather than toward public health and combating the opioid epidemic. A tiny percentage of the money received from the massive tobacco settlements (and tobacco taxes) has gone to tobacco prevention. The number of smokers in the United States fell by a third in the twenty years before the tobacco settlement and by a third in the

---

* Tobacco was another general social failure blamed entirely on corporations. Federal and state governments protected and nurtured the tobacco industry throughout the twentieth century, and then were a decade behind the United Kingdom and other nations in calling out the link between cigarettes and cancer.

twenty years after. Nothing changed. Why should we expect anything different with opioids?[28]

The pursuit of corporate malefactors is not always about solving
public problems, reducing public squalor, or making them pay for
the costs of harm associated with their product. Often it is about
assigning blame and sacking rich targets. It is true that some moneys
will find their way to the public but it is hard to see how the public
comes out ahead. In the opioid instance, pharmaceutical companies,
which continue to make these useful drugs, will take the blame while
public health officials, the FDA and DEA, the medical community,
and drug abusers will absolve themselves of responsibility for a crisis
they helped to create, one that still promises to waste many more
lives in the years to come. Sacking companies is a proxy for actually
dealing with problems.*

Technology companies are now in the dock. Silicon Valley grew
from a unique combination of American entrepreneurial genius and
massive subsidies from the nation's defense establishment. Congress, responding to public enthusiasm for the possibilities of global
interconnectedness and an endless flow of easily accessible information, decreed that online platforms would have no liability for third-
party content that flowed through their pipes. The Internet, as the
next tool of progress and amelioration, would be free.[29]

Tech companies harnessed the massive energy of billions of people eager to gain a presence online, to share, to learn, to be enter-
tained, to work, to shop. The web remade the nation physically,
economically, and socially with encouragement and a minimum of
interference from the federal government. Web culture became
American culture.

By the time the wonders of the Internet grew familiar and tech
companies became huge and powerful, the adverse consequences of
connecting *everyone* without adequate supervision became glaringly
apparent. The Internet was used for pornography, sex trafficking,
terrorist recruiting, an infinite variety of scams, the evasion of laws

---

* Studies show that U.S. regulations, despite being more prescriptive and punitive, are less effective in making progress against environmental ills than regulatory
regimes encouraging a collaborative relationship between business and government. Kagan, *Adversarial Legalism*, p. 226.

and regulations, the invasion of privacy, harassment and defamation, foreign propaganda, and fake news. Once more, blame falls not to the public officials who refused a regulatory role, or a public complicit in every facet of the Internet, but the greedy corporate entities that have purportedly enslaved the people in their profit-spewing projects, debasing the culture and threatening democracy.[30]

The tech giants have much to answer for. They have been arrogant and reckless, single-mindedly pursuing growth and profits and ignoring, if not encouraging, the regrettable purposes to which their platforms and services are inevitably put. Willful blindness is nothing new in business; nor is social damage from commercial activity. Again, careful and constructive intervention is warranted. Is that what awaits tech?

The dynamic observed with automobiles and opioids is not inevitable. The financial crisis of 2007–08 brought a relatively constructive response from government in the form of the Dodd-Frank Wall Street Reform and Consumer Protection Act. And Microsoft's anticompetitive practices were reined in at the turn of the century without undo harm to the company. The particulars of those precedents are important, however. The financial sector was in mortal peril at the time government intervened; nobody was mistaking it for a rich, sackable target. Microsoft, meanwhile, involved the Department of Justice fighting one tech company on behalf of other tech companies; opportunities to play to the gallery were relatively limited.

Big Tech is not in peril today. Quite the opposite: its leading companies have the same appearance of invincibility and immortality once attributed to General Motors. And the ways in which their behavior affects ordinary people are many and direct. It is no surprise that hordes of reformers wielding class-action lawsuits, antitrust investigations, and regulatory proposals are already pounding at the gates, displaying the usual mix of good intentions and opportunism. The scale, wealth, and unpopularity of the major tech firms do not bode well for them.

It may seem unlikely today that a tech company could be crippled by regulatory attack to the same extent that G.M. was in 1966, in part because governments are more sophisticated in their regulatory approaches, and corporations are better equipped to defend themselves. But the old playbook is still available. All it would take is one skilled entrepreneur to stoke public outrage with a revelation of harm, and a boneheaded move by one company or another (there are always boneheaded moves). Congress would be roused to punish the sector. "Crowds look for scapegoats for their own sins," said an executive of the Newsom group trying to account for the virulence of attacks on General Motors in the 1960s.[31]

Constant warfare between the bringers of private goods and the champions of public goods wastes the nation's resources and energies. It is self-defeating for America. It is self-defeating for liberalism. Galbraith, Schlesinger, and other leaders of the "public goods" movement in the 1960s recognized that improvements in social welfare needed to be affordable. It was on the basis of material plenty, the observable fact that the United States had achieved an unprecedented level of affluence, liberating many from scarcity and insecurity, that they saw opportunity to redistribute wealth and spend on schools, public health, the environment, culture, and urban redevelopment. Their major miscalculation was to think that America was wealthy enough and that further growth could be de-prioritized. The American economy has been stagnant for fifty years and so, in terms of delivering social goods to people, has liberalism.

It is not enough for a nation to be rich relative to other nations, writes Benjamin Friedman in *The Moral Consequences of Economic Growth*. The nation must grow. The sense of security and well-being that comes from steadily increasing wealth and rising standards of living is a necessary precondition for constructive social change. Growth produces opportunity and social mobility. Growth convinces citizens that they can afford openness, fairness and civility, the toleration of diversity, and a commitment to democratic values. "Only with sustained economic growth," says Friedman, "and the sense of confident progress that follows from the advance of living standards for most of its citizens, can even a great nation find the energy, the wherewithal, and most importantly the human attitudes that together sustain an open, tolerant, and democratic society."*[32]

---

* That is a liberal attitude, yet it has often been shared by enlightened American conservatives. That label is seldom applied to Calvin Coolidge, whose best-known

This is more than an American project. Historically, America's outstanding economic growth has been liberal democracy's best advertisement to the nations of the world. In recent decades, illiberal countries, most notably China, have discovered for themselves that the prosperity of commerce is the most useful and productive source of national wealth, and the route to amelioration and progress. Their outstanding growth and America's relative decline are fueling a democratic crisis around the world. Authoritarian states and parties are gaining traction; twenty-five fewer democracies exist on the planet than at the start of the century.[34]

While there is no going back to the 1950s and Cold War Consensus, nor is there a route to reestablishing America as an admirable, functional liberal democracy without reestablishing its economic dynamism. This does not require the elimination of conflict between regulators and capitalists, or for Americans to overlook corporate abuses, problems of monopoly and inequality, and environmental concerns. It does demand a far more intelligent and efficient approach to the management of competing interests, and an admission that business and America are on the same team, meaning that the success of one is impossible without the success of the other.

---

quote might be "the chief business of the American people is business," but few read through to the next part of his quote:

> In all experience, the accumulation of wealth means the multiplication of schools, the encouragement of science, the increase of knowledge, the dissemination of intelligence, the broadening of outlook, the expansion of liberties, the widening of culture. Of course, the accumulation of wealth cannot be justified as the chief end of existence. But we are compelled to recognize it as a means to well-nigh every desirable achievement.[33]

ACKNOWLEDGMENTS

I want to thank my agent, Andrew Wylie, for encouraging this project, and my fine editor at Knopf, Andrew Miller, for helping me to realize it. Also thanks to Leonard Evans, David Cole, and David Paterson, who read drafts of the manuscript and gave me direction; Javier Miranda of U.S. Census Bureau and Jason Faberman of the Federal Reserve Bank of Chicago, who helped me with particular data; Pascale Craan, who helped with my research at the Library of Congress; Christo Datini at the General Motors Heritage Center; and Maris Dyer at Knopf. As always, my deepest gratitude to Tina Leino-Whyte and Thea Whyte for their love and support.

NOTES

PROLOGUE AMERICAN BERSERKS

1. Robert Weisbrot and G. Calvin Mackenzie, *The Liberal House: Washington and the Politics of Change in the 1960s* (New York: Penguin, 2008), p. 272; James T. Patterson, *Grand Expectations: The United States, 1945–1974* (New York: Oxford University Press, 1996).
2. Jill Lepore, *These Truths* (New York: W. W. Norton, 2018).
3. Robert Gordon, *The Rise and Fall of American Growth* (Princeton: Princeton University Press, 2016), p. 16.
4. Ibid., p. 377; United States Congress, *Technology Assessment of Changes in the Future Use and Characteristics of the Automobile Transportation System, Vol. 3* (Washington: U.S. Government Printing Office, 1979), p. 4; *Commentary*, June 1966, p. 88.
5. https://theatlas.com/charts/BJ9rQT7-E; Social Research Inc. and Gallup surveys, 1957–1967, Earl Newsom Papers, Wisconsin Historical Society (ENP WHS); United States Congress, Senate, *Hearings Before the Committee on Armed Services* (Washington: U.S. Government Printing Office, 1953), Jan. 15–23, 1953.
6. Ralph Nader, *Unsafe at Any Speed* (New York: Grossman, 1965), p. 1; *New York Times*, March 6, 1966, p. 94.
7. *Detroit Free Press*, March 25, 1966, p. 52.
8. Philip Roth, *American Pastoral* (New York: Vintage, 1997).

CHAPTER 1 ALL ROADS LEAD TO DETROIT

1. Denise F. Su, "The Earliest Hominins: *Sahelanthropus, Orrorin,* and *Ardipithecus,*" *Nature Education Knowledge* 4(4):11, 2013; "What Does It Mean to Be Human?," *Smithsonian*, http://humanorigins.si.edu/evidence/human-fossils/species/homo-erectus; Clive Gamble, *Settling the Earth: The Archaeology of Deep Human History* (Cambridge: Cambridge University Press, 2013), pp. 118, 136, 224.
2. Geoffrey Chaucer, *The Canterbury Tales* (New York: Penguin, 2003).
3. John B. Rae, *The American Automobile Industry* (Boston: Twayne, 1984), pp. 11, 37; Tom Lewis, *Divided Highways: Building the Interstate Highways, Transforming American Life* (Ithaca: Cornell Uni-

versity Press, 2013), p. 33; Research Committee on Social Trends, *Recent Social Trends in the United States*, Vol. 1 (New York: McGraw-Hill, 1933), p. 177.

4. Gordon, Robert, *The Rise and Fall of American Growth* (Princeton: Princeton University Press, 2016), p. 377.

5. Ed Cray, *Chrome Colossus: General Motors and Its Times* (New York: McGraw-Hill, 1980), p. 45.

6. Brian Ladd, *Autophobia: Love and Hate in the Automotive Age* (Chicago: University of Chicago Press, 2008), pp. 24–27.

7. Three of the best books on the impact of the automobile on the United States are James Flink, *The Automobile Age* (Cambridge: MIT Press, 1990); Dan Albert, *Are We There Yet: The American Automobile Past, Present, and Driverless* (New York: W. W. Norton, 2019); and John Heitmann, *The Automobile and American Life* (Jefferson, NC: McFarland, 2009).

8. Nathan Miller, *New World Coming* (New York: Scribner, 2003), p. 191.

9. Sinclair Lewis, *Babbitt* (New York: Modern Library, 2002), pp. 22, 35.

10. James Truslow Adams, *Big Business in a Democracy* (New York: Charles Scribner's Sons, 1945), p. 85.

11. Research Committee on Social Trends, pp. 177–80; Kathleen Franz, *Tinkering: Consumers Reinvent the Early Automobile* (Philadelphia: University of Pennsylvania Press, 2005).

12. Miller, p. 179.

13. Ibid., p. 180.

14. Cray, p. 294.

15. F. Scott Fitzgerald, *The Great Gatsby* (New York: Scribner, 1925), pp. 34, 63.

16. Leah Graysmith, "Sex and Gender in the Equine in Literature," master's thesis, Iowa State University, 2008.

17. Cray, p. 314.

18. Rae, p. 181; Edwin D. Goldfield, *Statistical Abstract of the United States, 1955* (Washington: U.S. Government Printing Office, 1955), p. 49.

19. Robert Gordon, p. 377; National Tourism Resources Review Commission, *Destination USA: Domestic Tourism*, Vol. 2 (Washington: National Tourism Resources Review Commission, 1973), p. 89; Cray, p. 434.

20. Cray, p. 247; Ladd, p. 34.

21. Daniel Horowitz, *The Anxieties of Affluence* (Amherst: University of Massachusetts Press, 2005), p. 41.

22. Heitmann, pp. 162, 216; Vladimir Nabokov, *Lolita* (New York: Vin-

tage, 1997); Robert Penn Warren, *All The King's Men* (New York: Harcourt, 1946); Jack Kerouac, *On the Road* (New York: Penguin, 1976).

23. 1910, 1940, and 1950 Censuses, United States Census Bureau, https://www.census.gov/; U.S. Bureau of Economic Analysis, Gross National Product series, https://fred.stlouisfed.org/series/GNPA.

24. *New York Times*, March 3, 1958, March 28, 1958; *Time*, Jan. 6, 1958.

25. *Time*, Aug. 3, 1953; *New York Times*, April 28, 1958.

26. *Sacramento Bee*, Dec. 7, 1957.

27. *New York Times*, Dec. 7, 1957, Dec. 9, 1957, April 2, 1958, April 14, 1958, April 23, 1958, April 24, 1958, March 2, 1958, March 9, 1958, March 12, 1958, Oct. 3, 1982; U.S. Bureau of Economic Analysis, fred.stlouis.org/series/gdp; U.S. Bureau of Labor Statistics, fred.stlouis.org/series/unrate; "Dow Jones Industrial Average 100 Year Historical Chart," https://www.macrotrends.net/1319/dow-jones-100-year-historical-chart; Jean Edward Smith, *Eisenhower in War and Peace* (New York: Random House, 2013); William I. Hitchcock, *The Age of Eisenhower: America and the World in the 1950s* (New York: Simon & Schuster, 2019).

28. *Detroit Free Press*, May 5, 1958; Dwight D. Eisenhower, *Public Papers of the Presidents of the United States: Dwight D. Eisenhower, 1958* (Washington: U.S. Government Printing Office, 1959), p. 303.

29. *Honolulu Star-Bulletin*, April 16, 1958.

30. *New York Times*, May 18, 1958; *Detroit Free Press*, April 13, 1958, May 14, 1958, Sept. 7, 1958.

31. Eisenhower, *Public Papers of the Presidents, 1958*, p. 303.

32. Ronald R. Krebs, "Tracking the Cold War Consensus," in Krebs, *Narrative and the Making of U.S. National Security* (Cambridge: Cambridge University Press, 2015); Lawrence B. Glickman, *Buying Power: A History of Consumer Activism in America* (Chicago: University of Chicago Press, 2009), p. 263.

33. Fortune 500, 1958, https://money.cnn.com/magazines/fortune/fortune500_archive/full/1958/; *Fortune*, Oct. 1959; Cray, p. 7; *New York Times*, May 4, 1958.

34. *Lansing State Journal*, April 8, 1958; *New York Times*, May 4, 1958.

35. *Fortune*, March 1958, March 1969; *Detroit Free Press*, April 17, 1958, 35 27, 1958; *New York Times*, June 13, 1957, May 4, 1958, Feb. 19, 1959.

36. *Fortune*, Aug. 1957, May 1958; *Detroit Free Press*, May 22, 1958, Dec. 17, 1958, March 12, 1959; *New York Times*, Jan. 16, 1958.

37. *New York Times*, April 6, 1958, July 12, 1959; *Detroit Free Press*, April 6, 1958, May 22, 1958; *Fortune*, Aug. 1957.

38. *Detroit Free Press*, May 19, 1958, July 8, 1958; *New York Times*,

May 4, 1958, April 6, 1958; Jack Mingo, *How the Cadillac Got Its Fins* (New York: HarperCollins, 1995), p. 218; *Fortune*, Aug. 1957, March 1969.

39. *New York Times*, April 6, 1958; *Fortune*, Aug. 1957, May 1958, March 1969.

40. *Detroit Free Press*, March 4, 1958, Nov. 1, 1959; *Fortune*, Aug. 1957, May 1958, March 1969; *New York Times*, June 21, 1957, April 6, 1958, April 5, 1959, June 14, 1959.

41. *Fortune*, March 1958.

42. *New York Times*, May 4, 1958.

CHAPTER 2 BURSTS OF UNTAMED IDEALISM

1. While much has been written about Ralph Nader, the most reliable biography for the facts of his life is Justin Martin, *Nader: Crusader, Spoiler, Icon* (Cambridge, MA: Perseus, 2002), written with the cooperation of the Nader family; for a more critical perspective, see Charles McCarry, *Citizen Nader* (London: Jonathan Cape, 1972). *New York Times*, July 9, 1991; Martin, p. 1.

2. Martin, pp. 1, 6, 9.

3. Ibid., pp. 5, 10.

4. Ibid., p. 8.

5. Ibid., p. 8; McCarry, pp. 36–37.

6. Martin, p. 7; *New Yorker*, Oct. 15, 1973; McCarry, pp. 35–36.

7. McCarry, pp. 34–35.

8. Ibid., p. 40; Martin, pp. 14–15.

9. McCarry, pp. 33, 41.

10. Martin, pp. 16–17; McCarry, p. 43.

11. McCarry, p. 46.

12. *Princeton Alumni Weekly*, July 11, 1977.

13. *New York Times*, Aug. 17, 1977.

14. *The Nation*, March 18, 2009; Daniel Geary, *Radical Ambition: C. Wright Mills, the Left, and American Social Thought* (Oakland: University of California Press, 2009), pp. 1, 3, 182; C. Wright Mills, *The Power Elite* (New York: Oxford University Press, 1956); C. Wright Mills, Kathryn Mills, et al., *C. Wright Mills: Letters and Autobiographical Writings* (Oakland: University of California Press, 2001).

15. Mills, *The Power Elite*, pp. 28, 29, 70.

16. Ibid., pp. 281, 283, 9, 99–100.

17. Ibid., pp. 29, 326.

18. Ibid., pp. 46, 129, 136–37, *passim*; Alan Wolfe, "Gonzo Sociology," *New Republic*, Oct. 8, 2008.

19. Vance Packard, *The Hidden Persuaders* (New York: Ig Publishing, 2007), p. 31.
20. Ibid., pp. 97–98.
21. Ibid., p. 34; Vance Packard, *The Waste Makers* (New York: David McKay, 1960), p. 186.
22. *New York Times*, June 2, 1957, Aug. 4, 1957, June 22, 1958; John Kenneth Galbraith, *The Affluent Society* (New York: Mariner Books, 1998); Richard Parker, *John Kenneth Galbraith: His Life, His Politics, His Economics* (New York: Farrar, Straus & Giroux, 2005).
23. Galbraith, p. 8.
24. Ibid., pp. 223, 129.
25. Ibid., pp. 1, 115.
26. Ibid., pp. 56, 143, 208.
27. Ibid., pp. 52, 85.
28. Ibid., pp. 191, 187–88.
29. Horowitz, p. 50.
30. Martin, p. 21.
31. McCarry, p. 49.
32. Ibid., pp. 49, 50; Martin, p. 23.
33. Martin, p. 26.
34. Ibid., p. 29.

CHAPTER 3   THE PLAGUE OF THE TWENTIETH CENTURY

1. Martin, p. 21.
2. McCarry, p. 56; Harold A. Katz, "Liability of Automobile Manufacturers for Unsafe Design of Passenger Cars," *Harvard Law Review* 69, no. 5 (March 1956): 863–73.
3. "Harold A. Katz, 1921–2012," *The Bar News*, Illinois State Bar Association, https://www.isba.org/barnews/2013/01/03/harold-katz-1921-2012; Michael R. Lemov, *Car Safety Wars: One Hundred Years of Technology, Politics, and Death* (Madison, NJ: Fairleigh Dickinson University Press, 2015), pp. 24–26.
4. *New York Times*, June 23, 1896, Sept. 14, 1899, Sept. 15, 1899.
5. Ibid., Sept. 14, 1902.
6. Ibid., March 17, 1918.
7. Ibid., March 17, 1918, Oct., 7, 1922.
8. David Von Drehle, *Triangle: The Fire That Changed America* (New York: Grove, 2004); *New York Times*, Jan. 3, 1912.
9. "Motor Vehicle Traffic Fatalities, 1900–2007," Department of Transportation, https://www.fhwa.dot.gov/policyinformation/statistics/2007/pdf/fi200.pdf; https://www.accessmagazine.org/wp-content/uploads/sites/7/2016/07/Access-30-02-Horse-Power.pdf;

E. S. Clowes, "Street-Accidents—New York City," *Publications of the American Statistical Association,* June 1913; *Detroit News,* April 26, 2015; *New York Times,* Jan. 3, 1914, June 9, 2008; Harold Bolce, "The Horse vs. Health," *Appleton's Magazine,* May 1908.

10. "Motor Vehicle Traffic Fatalities"; Fanis Grammenos and G. R. Lovegrove, *Remaking the City Street Grid* (Jefferson, NC: McFarland, 2015), p. 193; William Richard Black, *Sustainable Transportation* (New York: Guilford Press, 2010), p. 55; Irving Fisher, *National Vitality: Its Wastes and Conservation* (Washington: U.S. Government Printing Office, 1910), p. 659; *New York Times,* June 29, 1914.

11. "Mortality Trends in the United States, 1900–2018," National Center for Health Statistics, https://www.cdc.gov/nchs/data-visualization/mortality-trends/index.htm; "Motor Vehicle Traffic Fatalities and Fatality Rates, 1899–2018," National Highway Traffic Safety Administration, https://cdan.nhtsa.gov/tsftables/Fatalities%20and%20Fatality%20Rates.pdf; "Leading Causes of Death, 1900–1998," Centers for Disease Control and Prevention, https://www.cdc.gov/nchs/data/dvs/lead1900_98.pdf; Anne Leland, "American War and Military Operations Casualties," Congressional Research Service, Feb. 26, 2010, p. 2; "1918 Pandemic," Centers for Disease Control and Prevention, https://www.cdc.gov/flu/pandemic-resources/1918-pandemic-h1n1.html.

12. William W. Hamilton, "Rights and Liabilities of Gratuitous Automobile Passengers," *Chicago-Kent Law Review* 10, no. 1 (Dec. 1931); Xenophon P. Huddy, "The Motor Car's Status," *Yale Law Journal* 15, no. 2 (Dec. 1905).

13. Peter D. Norton, *Fighting Traffic: The Dawn of the Motor Age in the American City* (Cambridge: MIT Press, 2008), p. 26.

14. *New York Times,* Nov. 25, 1924.

15. Ibid., Aug. 12, 1928, June 21, 1929.

16. "Car Crash Deaths and Rates," National Safety Council, https://injuryfacts.nsc.org/motor-vehicle/historical-fatality-trends/deaths-and-rates/.

17. "Licensed Drivers, Population, and Motor Vehicles," Federal Highway Administration, U.S. Department of Transportation, https://www.fhwa.dot.gov/ohim/onh00/line5.htm; "Vital Statistics of the United States," 1958, Vol. 2.

18. *New York Times,* Feb. 2, 1958.

19. Ibid., Jan. 13, 1955, Sept. 9, 1951, Aug. 26, 1956.

20. Ibid., Oct. 24, 1926, Jan. 21, 1936, Nov. 11, 1938, April 25, 1937, Jan. 23, 1938.

21. Ibid., Dec. 4, 1955.

22. Ibid., Sept. 15, 1958.

23. Lemov, p. 17; John D. Graham, *Auto Safety: Assessing America's Performance* (Dover, MA: Auburn House, 1989).

24. S. H. Woolf and H. Schoomaker, "Life Expectancy and Mortality Rates in the United States, 1959–2017," *Journal of the American Medical Association* 322, no. 20 (Nov. 26, 2019).

25. Department of the Navy, Bureau of Medicine and Surgery, *United States Naval Medical Bulletin* 45, no. 1 (July 1945); C. Hunter Shelden, "Prevention, the Only Cure for Head Injuries Resulting from Automobile Accidents," *The Journal of the American Medical Association* 159, no. 10 (1955).

26. Shelden, "Prevention, the Only Cure for Head Injuries Resulting from Automobile Accidents."

27. Ibid.

28. Ibid.

29. Ibid.

30. Katz, "Liability of Automobile Manufacturers for Unsafe Design of Passenger Cars."

31. Ibid.

32. G. Edward White, *Tort Law in America: An Intellectual History* (New York: Oxford University Press, 2003); Stephen S. Walters, "Product Liability and the Problem of Proof," *Stanford Law Review* 21, no. 6 (June 1969); Stephen D. Sugarman, "A Century of Change in Personal Injury Law," *California Law Review* 88, no. 6 (Dec. 2000).

33. White, pp. 120, 125–27; Katz, "Liability of Automobile Manufacturers for Unsafe Design of Passenger Cars."

34. Katz, "Liability of Automobile Manufacturers for Unsafe Design of Passenger Cars."

35. Ibid.; Lemov, pp. 24–26; Martin, p. 30.

36. Ralph Nader, "The Safe Car You Can't Buy," *The Nation*, April 11, 1959; Martin, p. 30.

37. Nader, "The Safe Car You Can't Buy."

38. Ibid.

39. Martin, pp. 31–32.

40. Ibid., p. 32; Ralph Nader and David F. Binder, "Cuban Report," *Harvard Law Record* 28, no. 3 (Feb. 19, 1959); C. Wright Mills, *Listen, Yankee: The Revolution in Cuba* (New York: Ballantine, 1960).

41. Martin, pp. 33–35.

42. Ibid., p. 37; McCarry, p. 59.

CHAPTER 4   THE RISE OF THE HONKERS

1. *Washington Post*, March 2, 1954; Lemov, p. 37.

2. Lemov, pp. 35, 36–37.

3. United States Congress, *Hearings Before a Subcommittee of the Committee on Interstate and Foreign Commerce, Eighty-fourth Congress, Second Session on Investigation of Highway Traffic Accidents* (Washington: U.S. Government Printing Office, 1957).

4. *New York Times*, Aug. 19, 1956.

5. Graham, p. 22; Lemov, p. 36.

6. *The Nation*, April 11, 1959.

7. *San Francisco Examiner*, Oct. 3 1958; Lemov, p. 53.

8. Lemov, pp. 43–44.

9. *New York Times*, July 31, 1960.

10. Espen Moe, *Governance, Growth and Global Leadership: The Role of the State in Technological Progress, 1750–2000* (Burlington, VT: Ashgate, 2007), p. 187; Gordon, p. 389; Miller, p. 190.

11. Lemov, pp. 8, 9.

12. Franklin D. Roosevelt, "Columbus, Ohio Campaign Speech," Aug. 20, 1932, http://www.fdrlibrary.marist.edu/_resources/images/msf/msf00502, p. 16; "New York City, Madison Square Garden Address," Oct. 31, 1936, http://www.fdrlibrary.marist.edu/_resources/images/msf/msf01033, p. 6; "Acceptance Speech for the Re-nomination for the Presidency," June 27, 1936, https://www.presidency.ucsb.edu/documents/acceptance-speech-for-the-renomination-for-the-presidency-philadelphia-pa.

13. David Cannadine, *Mellon: An American Life* (New York: Vintage, 2008), pp. 506, 546–47. Roosevelt's pursuit of Mellon is treated at length in Cannadine.

14. Cray, pp. 265, 283; David M. Kennedy, *Freedom from Fear: The American People in Depression and War, 1929–1945* (New York: Oxford University Press, 1999), pp. 87, 151, 308–14.

15. Cray, pp. 288, 290.

16. Kennedy, *Freedom from Fear*, pp. 308–14; Cray, pp. 286–308.

17. Cray, pp. 315, 318.

18. Cray, pp. 339–40; *New York Times*, Jan. 15, 1946, Jan. 16, 1946, Jan. 17, 1946.

19. *New York Times*, Dec. 7 1950, Dec. 22, 1950, Aug. 15, 1951.

20. *Pittsburgh Press*, Dec. 5, 1953.

21. Cray, pp. 354–55, 358–59.

22. *New York Times*, March 31, 1954.

23. *New York Times*, Oct. 4 1954, April 25, 1956.

24. Cray, pp. 388–98, 401.

25. Ibid., pp. 385–88; *New York Times*, June 4, 1957.

26. *Detroit Free Press*, Sept. 9, 1945.

27. Arthur M. Schlesinger Jr., "The Future of Liberalism: The Challenge of Abundance," *Saturday Review*, Vol. 40, No. 8 (June 1957); James A. Nuechterlein, "Arthur M. Schlesinger, Jr., and the Discon-

tents of Postwar American Liberalism," *Review of Politics*, Vol. 39, No. 1 (Jan. 1977); Richard Aldous, *Schlesinger: The Imperial Historian* (New York: W. W. Norton, 2017).

28. Aldous, p. 388.

29. Arthur M. Schlesinger, Jr., *A Thousand Days: John F. Kennedy in the White House* (Boston: Houghton Mifflin, 1965), pp. 211, 214.

30. Ibid., pp. 60, 210, 620; Nuechterlein, "Arthur M. Schlesinger, Jr., and the Discontents of Postwar American Liberalism."

31. Schlesinger, *A Thousand Days*, pp. 99, 657; *New York Times*, May 26, 1960.

32. Schlesinger, *A Thousand Days*, pp. 68, 645.

33. Ibid., p. 677.

34. John F. Kennedy, *Public Papers of the Presidents of the United States: John F. Kennedy, 1961* (Washington: U.S. Government Printing Office, 1962), pp. 19, 336.

35. Richard Reeves, *President Kennedy: Profile of Power* (New York: Simon & Schuster, 1993), pp. 26, 27, 37, 54.

36. Ibid., p. 100; James T. Patterson, *Grand Expectations: The United States, 1945–1974* (New York: Oxford University Press, 1996), p. 465.

37. Reeves, *President Kennedy*, pp. 123–24, 357.

38. Ibid., pp. 295, 313, 317.

39. Ibid., pp. 275, 295

40. Ibid., p. 294.

41. Ibid., p. 296.

42. Ibid., pp. 296–97.

43. Ibid.

44. Ibid.

45. Ibid., pp. 299–302.

46. Ibid., p. 300.

47. Ibid.

48. Schlesinger, *A Thousand Days*, p. 638; Reeves, pp. 303, 316.

49. Bruce Buchanan, *The Presidential Experience: What the Office Does to the Man* (Upper Saddle River, NJ: Prentice-Hall, 1978), p. 38.

50. Reeves, p. 303; Schlesinger, *A Thousand Days*.

51. Galbraith, *The Affluent Society*, pp. 210, 256; Schlesinger, *A Thousand Days*, p. 214.

52. David Vogel, *Fluctuating Fortunes: The Political Power of Business in America* (New York: Basic Books, 1989), p. 34.

53. Rudy Abramson, *Spanning the Century: The Life of W. Averell Harriman, 1891–1986* (New York: William Morrow, 1992); Godfrey Hodgson, *The Gentleman from New York: Daniel Patrick Moynihan* (Boston: Houghton Mifflin, 2000), p. 54.

54. Hodgson, *The Gentleman from New York*, pp. 25–52.

55. Ibid., pp. 60–62; *New York Times*, Dec. 20, 1964; W. Haddon et al., *Accident Research: Methods and Approaches* (New York: Harper & Row, 1964).

56. Daniel Patrick Moynihan, "Epidemic on the Highways," *The Reporter*, April 30, 1959.

57. Ibid.

58. Ibid.

59. Ibid.

60. McCarry, p. 72; Steven R. Weisman, *Daniel Patrick Moynihan: A Portrait in Letters of an American Visionary* (New York: PublicAffairs, 2010), p. 36.

61. Daniel P. Moynihan to Henry Robbins, May 14, 1959, Daniel P. Moynihan Papers, Library of Congress.

CHAPTER 5 SAVIOR SANS TAILFINS

1. *Time*, Oct. 5, 1959; *New York Times*, Oct. 31, 1967; *Hemmings Classic Car*, May 2007; National Academy of Engineering, *Memorial Tributes: National Academy of Engineering*, Vol. 1 (Washington: The National Academies, 1979), p. 38; *New York Times*, Sept. 29, 2011.

2. *Detroit Free Press*, Nov. 7, 1961.

3. Brock Yates, *The Decline and Fall of the American Automobile Industry* (New York: Empire Books, 1983), pp. 78, 80.

4. *Time*, Oct. 5, 1959.

5. *U.S. News & World Report*, Vol. 32, 1952, p. 61; *New York Times*, Oct. 31, 1967.

6. *Automotive News*, Aug. 26, 2014; *New York Times*, Oct. 31, 1967; Yates, p. 85.

7. *Time*, Oct. 5, 1959.

8. Ibid.; David E. Cole, "An Historical Overview of the Development of the Chevrolet Small-Block V-8 Engine," *Proceedings of the ASME Internal Combustion Engine Division 2013 Fall Technical Conference*, Columbus, IN, 2014.

9. *New York Times*, May 13, 1956; Louise A. Mozingo, *Pastoral Capitalism: A History of Suburban Corporate Landscapes* (Cambridge: MIT Press, 2011), p. 83.

10. Mozingo, p. 83; *New York Times*, Nov. 8, 1967.

11. *Time*, Oct. 5, 1959.

12. Ibid.

13. Ibid.

14. Ibid.

15. *Detroit Free Press*, March 4, 1958.

16. Ibid., March 4, 1958, April 22, 1958; *Newsweek*, March 10, 1958.

17. Ibid., March 5, 1959; Aug. 21, 1959; *New York Times*, April 5, 1959.

18. *Detroit Free Press*, Jan. 15, 1958, Nov. 26, 1958, Jan. 21, 1959.

19. Ibid., Jan. 15, 1958, Jan. 30, 1958, May 19, 1958, Nov. 26, 1958, Dec. 14, 1958, Jan. 21, 1959, Jan. 27, 1959; Feb. 5, 1959, Feb. 24, 1959, Nov. 1, 1959.

20. *BusinessWeek*, Oct. 8, 1960; *Fortune*, Nov. 1958; *Detroit Free Press*, Feb. 19, 1959; *New York Times*, Nov. 1, 1959.

21. Cray, p. 371; *Fortune*, Nov. 1958; *Detroit Free Press*, Feb. 19, 1959; *New York Times*, Feb. 19, 1959.

22. *Detroit Free Press*, March 27, 1958, June 17, 1959, July 24, 1958.

23. Ibid., March 17, 1959, July 2, 1959; *New York Times*, July 3, 1959.

24. *Detroit Free Press*, Sept. 28, 1959; *Time*, Oct. 5, 1959.

25. *Time*, Oct. 5, 1959; *Detroit Free Press*, Jan. 14, 1959, June 30, 1959, July 5, 1959, Sept. 28, 1959; *New York Times*, Aug. 16, 1959.

26. *Detroit Free Press*, July 19, 1959; *New York Times*, Aug. 16, 1959.

27. *New York Times*, Sept. 14, 1959.

28. *New York Times*, Sept. 15, 1959, Oct. 16, 1959, Oct. 18, 1959, Oct. 20, 1959; *Detroit Free Press*, Sept. 11, 1959.

29. *Detroit Free Press*, Sept. 11, 1959.

30. Ibid., Sept. 28, 1959; General Motors, "Car Report: An Authoritative Edition of Corvair Facts," 1959, General Motors Heritage Center Reference Collection.

31. "Target for Corvair," General Motors Corporation, https://www.youtube.com/watch?v=IS-btlJOfnA.

32. Chevrolet Corvair Commercial, General Motors Corporation, https://www.youtube.com/watch?v=m313FamUhdQ; Chevrolet Corvair Commercial, General Motors Corporation, https://www.youtube.com/watch?v=1UX1Q2gF1e4.

33. Cray, p. 367; General Motors Heritage Center Reference Collection, Chevrolet Corvair Advertisements, 1960.

34. "The Corvair in Action," General Motors Corporation, https://www.youtube.com/watch?v=WmPpry8JiKo.

35. "No Contest," Ford Motor Company, https://www.youtube.com/watch?v=ShBoZt71pbs.

36. "Economy Plus," Chrysler Corporation, https://www.youtube.com/watch?v=CgVJjzSeBgE.

37. *New York Times*, Aug. 29, 1948, Jan. 28, 1951, March 17, 1957.

38. Ibid., Oct. 18, 1959.

39. *Sports Illustrated*, Oct. 12, 1959.

40. General Motors Heritage Center Reference Collection, Chevrolet Corvair Articles, 1960; *Detroit Free Press*, Feb. 18, 1960.

41. *Motor Trend*, April 1960; *Detroit Free Press*, Jan. 5, 1962.

42. *Fortune*, June 1959.

43. *Detroit Free Press*, March 12, 1959, July 19, 1959, Aug. 21, 1959, Nov. 1, 1959.

44. Ibid., Dec. 23, 1959.
45. *New York Times*, Oct. 15, 1960.
46. *Detroit Free Press*, Feb. 21, 1961; *New York Times*, Nov. 16, 1960, Jan. 9, 1961, Feb. 21, 1961, April 2, 1961.
47. *Detroit Free Press*, Feb. 21, 1961.
48. Robert Sobel, *Car Wars: The Untold Story* (New York: Truman Talley Books, 1984), p. 79; *New York Times*, April 25, 1960; General Motors Annual Report, 1961.
49. *Detroit Free Press*, Feb. 21, 1961; *New York Times*, March 14, 1960; "Poor Man's Porsche," *Classic Auto Restorer*, June 1993.
50. *Detroit Free Press*, April 1, 1959, April 30, 1959, May 17, 1959, Nov. 10, 1959, Feb. 14, 1960; *New York Times*, March 14, 1960; *Popular Science*, July 1959.
51. Cray, pp. 374–75; *New York Times*, Oct. 16, 1960.
52. Yates, pp. 34, 41; *New York Times*, April 22, 1962.
53. *Detroit Free Press*, Feb. 24, 1959; *New York Times*, April 18, 1960, Jan. 9, 1961.
54. *New York Times*, May 27, 1962; United States Department of Commerce, *The U.S. Market for Imported Automobiles* (Washington: U.S. Government Printing Office, 1969), p. 12.
55. *New York Times*, Nov. 27, 1960, March 22, 1961.
56. Ibid., Feb. 19, 1963, April 22, 1963.
57. Ibid., Nov. 27, 1960.
58. Ibid., Oct. 2, 1963, Nov. 21, 1965; General Motors Annual Reports, 1963, 1964.
59. *New York Times*, Nov. 21, 1965.

CHAPTER 6 "THIS MEANS TAKING ON DETROIT"

1. Weisman, pp. 52, 122; Hodgson, pp. 68, 70.
2. McCarry, p. 72; Weisman, p. 56.
3. Martin, pp. 36, 39–41, 44, 65–66; McCarry, pp. 128–37.
4. McCarry, pp. 73–74; Leo R. Werts to Daniel P. Moynihan, Feb. 27, 1967, Daniel P. Moynihan Papers, Library of Congress.
5. McCarry, pp. 73–74.
6. Ibid.
7. Martin, p. 40; McCarry, p. 6.
8. Martin, p. 40; McCarry, p. 75; Hodgson, pp. 63–64.
9. McCarry, pp. 6-7; Martin, pp. 40–41.
10. *Bridgeport Post*, Nov. 7, 1962; *New York Times*, May 13, 1979, Feb. 23, 1998; United States Congress, "Proceedings and Debates of the 87th Congress, Vol. 107, Pt. 1," *Congressional Record*, 1961, p. 1040.
11. UPI Archives, April 6, 1983; Joseph M. Siracusa, *Encyclopedia of the Kennedys*, Vol. 1 (Santa Barbara: ABC-CLIO, 2012), p. 669;

Schlesinger, *A Thousand Days*, pp. 130, 141–42; "The Month in Washington," *Journal of the Iowa State Medical Society* 57 (1961).

12. *New York Times*, March 13, 1960.
13. John F. Kennedy, *Public Papers of the Presidents of the United States, John F. Kennedy, 1962* (Washington: U.S. Government Printing Office, 1963), p. 235; Lizabeth Cohen, *A Consumer's Republic: The Politics of Mass Consumption in Postwar America* (New York: Vintage, 2004), pp. 21, 24, 28–30, 345, 351.
14. Kennedy, *Public Papers of the President*, 1962, p. 235.
15. Cohen, p. 343; Packard, *The Waste Makers;* Jessica Mitford, *The American Way of Death* (London: Hutchinson, 1963); Rachel Carson, *Silent Spring* (New York: Houghton Mifflin, 1962).
16. Wallace R. Blischke and D. N. Prabhakar Murthy, *Product Warranty Handbook* (Boca Raton: CRC Press, 1995), p. 735.
17. Carson, pp. 2, 3.
18. "Use of Pesticides," A Report of the President's Science Advisory Committee, May 15, 1963; Carson, pp. 3, 12; Linda Lear, *Rachel Carson: Witness for Nature* (Boston: Mariner Books, 1997), p. 334.
19. Horowitz, pp. 153, 157, 170.
20. Lear, pp. 453–54; *New York Times*, June 5, 1963, April 16, 1964.
21. Haddon et al., *Accident Research;* McCarry, p. 89.
22. *New York Times*, Jan. 29, 1956, April 22, 1956, June 24, 1956, Nov. 4, 1956.
23. McCarry, p. 89.
24. Martin, p. 44.
25. Abraham Ribicoff Papers, Library of Congress, Correspondence, 1963, 1964; McCarry, p. 107.
26. Martin, p. 44.

CHAPTER 7   HEAD OF THE CLAN, AT SEA

1. *Time*, Jan. 2, 1956, April 27, 1959.
2. *New York Times*, March 1, 1987; *Automotive News*, Sept. 14, 2008; Yates, p. 99.
3. General Motors Annual Report, 1965.
4. *Fortune*, July 15, 1966.
5. Benjamin C. Waterhouse, *The Land of Enterprise: A Business History of the United States* (New York: Simon & Schuster, 2017), pp. 170–72.
6. Frederic Donner, "Competing for Tomorrow's World Markets," ENP WHS, 1964.
7. General Motors Annual Reports, 1964, 1965.
8. Ibid.
9. Frederic Donner, "The World-Wide Corporation in a Modern

Economy," and "Competing for Tomorrow's World Markets," ENP WHS, 1962, 1964.

10. The Social Research Inc., "Big Business and General Motors: A Study of Public Attitudes," ENP WHS, 1964.

11. Ibid.

12. Ibid.

13. *Wall Street Journal*, June 7, 1965; Cray, pp. 406–407; Robert F. Freeland, *The Struggle for Control of the Modern Corporation: Organizational Change at General Motors, 1924–1970* (Cambridge: Cambridge University Press, 2000).

14. James Bush, Alan Binder, and Ferris Deebe, *General Motors in the 20th Century* (Southfield, MI: Ward's Communications, 2000), p. 266; Heon Stevenson, *American Automobile Advertising, 1930–80: An Illustrated History* (Jefferson, NC: McFarland, 2008); "General Motors Automotive Innovations," June 1967, ENP WHS; Joel Eastman, *Styling vs. Safety* (Lanham, MD: University Press of America, 1984), p. 6.

15. John Horsch, David Viano, and James DeCou, "History of Safety Research and Development on the General Motors Energy-Absorbing Steering System," *Journal of Passenger Cars* (1991), pp. 1818–63; *New York Times*, Jan. 23, 1994; General Motors, "Tested Value—The GM Concept," General Motors Heritage Center Reference Collection, 1963; Leonard Evans, *Traffic Safety* (Bloomfield Hills, MI: Science Serving Society, 2004), p. 381.

16. *New York Times*, Jan. 8, 1950.

17. Stevenson, pp. 107, 189; "Automobile Safety," Smithsonian, https://americanhistory.si.edu/america-on-the-move/essays/automobile-safety.

18. Stevenson, *American Automobile Advertising*, pp. 189–95.

19. *Tampa Tribune*, Sept. 19, 1992; Rae, pp. 101–2; Lemov, p. 10; Richard M. Langworth, *Kaiser-Frazer: The Last Onslaught on Detroit* (Kutztown, PA: Automobile Quarterly Publications, 1975); Eastman, pp. 186–88.

20. *Automotive News*, June 26, 1996; Daniel Strohl, "Spitting in the Wind," Hemmings.com, May 27, 2016; *New York Times*, Sept. 8, 1955, Dec. 4, 1955, March 11, 1956; Stevenson, pp. 192–94; Eastman, pp. 222–32.

21. James Ciment, ed., *Social Issues in America: An Encyclopedia* (New York: Routledge, 2006), p. 207; Graham, p. 27; Lemov, pp. 58, 60.

22. Eastman, p. 243; Lemov, pp. 43–44.

23. "G.M. Information Handbook"; Frederic Donner, "Remarks, 40th Anniversary of the GM Proving Ground," May 14, 1964, General Motors Heritage Center Reference Collection.

24. *Morning Post* (Camden, NJ), June 2, 1896; *New York Times*, Dec. 22, 1899.

25. *New York Times*, Sept. 29, 1927, March 10, 1929.

26. Ibid., May 22, 1927.

27. Ibid., Oct 26, 1927.

28. Ibid., Sept. 29, 1927, March 10, 1929; American Bar Association, *ABA Compendium of Professional Responsibility Rules and Standards* (Chicago: American Bar Association, 2004), p. 357.

29. Alexander Schwab, "In Defense of Ambulance Chasing: A Critique of Model Rule of Professional Conduct 7.3," *Yale Law & Policy Review* 29, no. 2 (2010).

30. *St. Louis Post Dispatch*, Aug. 21 1954; *New York Times*, July 29, 1954; *New York Daily News*, Feb. 15, 1950.

31. *New York Times*, Jan. 19, 1954.

32. *Courier-Post* (Camden, NJ), Aug. 10, 1956; *Fortune*, Oct. 1960.

33. Byrne A. Bowman, "An Inspection of a Personal Injury Law Firm," *American Bar Association Journal*, Oct. 1965, p. 929.

34. Ibid., pp. 929–31.

35. Ibid., p. 931; Stuart M. Speiser, *Lawsuit* (New York: Horizon Press, 1980), p. 24.

36. *New York Times*, April 12, 1973; Scott M. Cutlip, *The Unseen Power: Public Relations, A History* (Hillsdale, NJ: LEA Publishers, 1994), chapters 20–22.

37. Earl Newsom, Personal Notes, Jan. 3, 1964, ENP WHS.

38. Earl Newsom to Frederic Donner, March 19, 1965, ENP WHS; Betty Friedan, *The Feminine Mystique* (New York: W. W. Norton, 1963).

39. Newsom Memorandum for Discussion, "Earl Newsom & Company's Role for General Motors," 1965, ENP WHS; Earl Newsom, Personal Notes, Jan. 3, 1964, ENP WHS.

40. Newsom & Co. Internal Memo, July 5, 1966; Earl Newsom to Frederic Donner, April 8, 1965, ENP WHS; Confidential Discussion Memorandum, "Broadening the Base of Management Interests," undated, ENP WHS.

41. Earl Newsom to Frederic Donner, April 8, 1965, ENP WHS.

42. "Gallup Polls: 1949–1962," ENP WHS, 1965; Newsom Memorandum for Discussion: "Earl Newsom & Company's Role for General Motors," 1965, ENP WHS.

CHAPTER 8 "I INTEND TO BE A CRUSADER"

1. *New York Times*, Jan. 3, 1965.

2. *New York Times*, Oct. 18, 1965; "Résumé of Congressional Activity,"

Congressional Record, Oct. 22, 1966, https://www.senate.gov/legisla
tive/ResumesofCongressionalActivity1947present.htm.

3. "Résumé of Congressional Activity," *Congressional Record.*

4. United States Congress, *Hearings Before the Subcommittee on Executive Reorganization of the Committee on Government Operations, United States Senate, Eighty-Ninth Congress, First Session: Traffic Safety: Examination and Review of Efficiency, Economy, and Coordination of Public and Private Agencies Activities and the Role of the Federal Government, March 22, 25, and 26, 1965, Part 1* (Washington: U.S. Government Printing Office, 1965), p. 1.

5. Ibid.

6. Ibid., p. 2.

7. Ibid.

8. Ibid., pp. 2–4, 6.

9. Ibid., pp. 10–12.

10. Ibid., p. 41.

11. Ibid., p. 49; "Gov. Milward L. Simpson," National Governors Association, https://www.nga.org/governor/milward-l-simpson/.

12. *Hearings Before the Subcommittee on Executive Reorganization, Part 1,* pp. 85–86, 87, 88, 89.

13. Ibid., pp. 89, 153; *New York Times,* May 31, 1983.

14. *Hearings Before the Subcommittee on Executive Reorganization, Part 1,* p. 187ff.

15. Ibid., pp. 203, 205, 210.

16. Ibid., pp. 208–9.

17. Ibid., pp. 214, 221.

18. Ibid., pp. 215–16.

19. Ibid., 241–43.

20. Ibid., p. 243.

21. Ibid., p. 443.

22. Ibid., pp. 462, 463, 486.

23. Ibid., p. 438.

24. Ibid., pp. 278, 292, 307, 315; *The Reporter,* Dec. 31, 1964.

25. *Hearings Before the Subcommittee on Executive Reorganization, Part 1,* p. 321.

26. Ibid., pp. 282, 283, 304.

27. Ibid., pp. 283, 326.

28. Ibid., pp. 274, 282.

29. Ibid., pp. 308, 309.

30. Notes to Annual Report, 1967, WHS ENP.

31. *New York Times,* July 8, 1965.

32. Wendell Pigman to Jerome Sonosky, and Robert F. Kennedy to Abraham Ribicoff et al., Correspondence Subject File, 1965, Robert F. Kennedy Papers, John F. Kennedy Library; "When Win-

ning Becomes Everything," *Car & Driver,* Nov. 1974; McCarry, pp. 18–19.

33. United States Congress. Senate. "Federal Role in Traffic Safety: Hearings Before the Subcommittee on Executive Reorganization of the Committee on Government Operations, United States Senate, Eighty-Ninth Congress, First Session, July 13, 14, 15, and 21, 1965, Part 2," Washington: U.S. Government Printing Office, 1966, p. 648.

34. Ibid.; *Car & Driver,* Nov. 1974.

35. *Hearings Before the Subcommittee on Executive Reorganization, Part 2,* p. 657.

36. Ibid., p. 671.

37. Ibid., pp. 681–82.

38. Ibid. p. 682.

39. Ibid., p. 683ff.

40. Ibid., p. 724.

41. Ibid.

42. Ibid., p. 725.

43. Ibid.

44. Ibid., pp. 725–26.

45. Ibid., p. 770.

46. Ibid., pp. 772, 773–74.

47. Ibid., pp. 775–75.

48. Ibid., pp. 777–78.

49. Ibid., p. 778.

50. Ibid., pp. 780–81.

51. Ibid., p. 781.

52. Ibid., p. 791; *Detroit Free Press,* July 14, 1965; Yates, p. 257.

53. McCarry, p. 19.

54. Martin, pp. 44–45; McCarry, p. 7.

55. Michael Harrington, *The Other America: Poverty in the United States* (New York: Macmillan, 1963); Jane Jacobs, *The Death and Life of Great American Cities* (New York: Random House, 1961).

56. Patterson, pp. 452–53.

57. Ibid., pp. 442–57.

58. Wilmeth O. Evitts to Miss Kotellow, Subject File: Traffic Safety, Daniel P. Moynihan Papers, Library of Congress.

59. Nader, *Unsafe at Any Speed,* p. 4.

60. Ibid., pp. 1, 17, 32, 36.

61. Ibid., p. 9.

62. Ibid., pp. 41, 3, 233.

63. Ibid., p. viii.

64. Ibid., pp. ix, x.

65. Ibid., p. 170.

66. "Report on the Context, Condition, and Recommended Direction of Federal Activity in Highway Safety," Advisory Committee on Traffic Safety file, Moynihan Papers, Library of Congress.
67. Ibid., p. 35.
68. Ralph Nader to Barry King, Aug. 2, 1964, Moynihan Papers.
69. Ibid. Also Daniel P. Moynihan to Leo R. Werts, Feb. 27, 1967, Moynihan Papers.
70. Martin, p. 45.

CHAPTER 9   SOMETHING STUPID

1. *Wall Street Journal,* July 20, 1965.
2. Newsom & Co. Memo, "Car Safety Hearings," Aug. 6, 1965, ENP WHS; Newsom & Co., Internal Memo, July 14 1965, ENP WHS.
3. *Hearings Before the Subcommittee on Executive Reorganization, Part 2,* p. 816ff.
4. Ibid., pp. 825–26.
5. Ibid., pp. 829–30, 854, 879.
6. Ibid., p. 870; Subcommittee Staff to Robert F. Kennedy, July 15, 1965, Correspondence Subject File, RFK Papers.
7. *Hearings Before the Subcommittee on Executive Reorganization, Part 2,* pp. 857, 871.
8. Ibid., p. 907.
9. Ibid., p. 916.
10. Ibid., pp. 790, 684.
11. Ibid., p. 685.
12. United States Congress, *Hearings Before the Committee on Armed Services,* Jan. 15–23, 1953; David Strohl, "Fact Check: Did a GM President Really Tell Congress 'What's Good for GM Is Good for America'?," *Hemmings,* Sept. 5, 2019, https://www.hemmings.com/blog/2019/09/05/fact-check-did-a-gm-president-really-tell-congress-whats-good-for-gm-is-good-for-america/.
13. Anthony DeLorenzo to Ed Cole, Jan. 25, 1966, ENP WHS; *Hearings Before the Subcommittee on Executive Reorganization, Part 2,* p. 889.
14. J. Newsom to Earl Newsom, March 25, 1966, ENP WHS.
15. Earl Newsom & Co. Memo, Aug. 11, 1965, ENP WHS.
16. Ibid.; William Lydgate to Anthony DeLorenzo, Nov. 22, 1965, ENP WHS.
17. Anthony DeLorenzo to Newsom Group, Nov. 24 1965, ENP WHS.
18. "Anthony G. DeLorenzo," biography, March 5, 1965, ENP WHS.
19. James M. Roche Address, Jan. 17, 1966; Newsom Memo, Dec. 22, 1965, ENP WHS; *Wall Street Journal,* Jan. 13, 1965.

20. Lydgate Memo, Newsom Group, Nov. 15, 1965, ENP WHS; University of Michigan Announcement, Dec. 17, 1965, ENP WHS; *Battle Creek Enquirer*, July 22, 1965.
21. James M. Roche Address, Jan. 17, 1966, ENP WHS.
22. Robert E. Lane, *The Regulation of Businessmen* (Hamden, CT: Archon Books, 1966), p. 19.
23. Cray, p. 436.
24. Robert F. Kennedy, "Why Can't We Make Cars Safer?," *Popular Science*, Nov. 1965; Joint Statement, Senators Ribicoff and Kennedy, Dec. 31, 1965, RFK Papers.
25. Harry Philo, "Accident Reconstruction Problems in Corvair Cases," Speech to the American Trial Lawyers, Miami, July 25, 1965, RFK Papers.
26. Ibid.
27. *San Francisco Chronicle*, Oct. 8, 1965; *New York Times*, Nov. 30, 1965; *Science*, Nov. 26, 1965.
28. Ralph Nader interview, Channel 2 News, WCBS-TV, New York, Jan. 27, 1966, ENP WHS.
29. *Midnight*, Aug. 23, 1965, Dec. 20, 1965; United States Congress. Senate. "Federal Role in Traffic Safety: Hearings Before the Subcommittee on Executive Reorganization of the Committee on Government Operations, United States Senate, Eighty-Ninth Congress, Second Session, February 2, 3, and 16, 1966, Part 3," Washington: U.S. Government Printing Office, 1966, pp. 1408–9; FBI Files on Vincent Gillen Investigation of Ralph Nader, March 8, 1969, Vincent W. Gillen Papers, Baker Library Special Collections, Harvard Business School.
30. United States Congress. Senate. "Federal Role in Traffic Safety: Hearings Before the Subcommittee on Executive Reorganization of the Committee on Government Operations, United States Senate, Eighty-Ninth Congress, Second Session, March 22, 1966, Part 4," Washington: U.S. Government Printing Office, 1966, p. 1413; FBI File, Gillen Papers.
31. Ralph Nader, "Automobile Design Hazards," *American Jurisprudence Proof of Facts* (San Francisco: Bancroft-Whitney, 1965); *Trial*, Jan. 1965.
32. Thomas Whiteside, *The Investigation of Ralph Nader* (New York, Arbor House, 1972), p. 163.
33. *Hearings Before the Subcommittee on Executive Reorganization, Part 4*, pp. 1438–39.
34. O'Neill Investigation of Ralph Nader, Nov. 21, 1965, Gillen Papers.
35. Whiteside, p. 170.
36. *Hearings Before the Subcommittee on Executive Reorganization, Part 4*, p. 1515.

37. *Detroit Free Press*, Jan. 7, 1966.

38. *Sioux City Journal*, Jan. 12, 1966; *The Greene Recorder* (Iowa), Feb. 2, 1966; Thomas Whiteside, *The Investigation of Ralph Nader* (New York: Arbor House, 1972), pp. 21–22.

39. *Detroit Free Press*, Jan. 11, 1966; *Hearings Before the Subcommittee on Executive Reorganization, Part 4*, p. 1412; *Consumer Reports*, Vol. 31, 1966, p. 195.

40. *Hearings Before the Subcommittee on Executive Reorganization, Part 4*, pp. 1412–13.

41. Ibid., pp. 1440, 1442; Eileen Murphy instructions to Richard G. Danner, Gillen Papers.

42. Whiteside, p. 85; *Hearings Before the Subcommittee on Executive Reorganization, Part 4*, p. 1517; FBI File, March 11, 1968, Gillen Papers.

43. *Hearings Before the Subcommittee on Executive Reorganization, Part 4*, p. 1523; United Press International, June 15, 1966; Gillen Speech, June 6, 1966, Gillen Papers.

44. FBI File, Gillen Papers; Gillen Notes of Jan. 15, 1966, Gillen Papers; *Time*, April 1, 1966.

45. Gillen Memo, Jan. 19, 1966, Gillen Papers.

46. Robert F. Kennedy correspondence, July 9 to Aug. 16, 1965, Jan. 5, 1966, Correspondence Subject File, RFK Papers.

47. American Trial Lawyers Association to Robert F. Kennedy, Aug. 31, 1965; Kennedy statement, Feb. 2, 1966, RFK Papers; Lemov, p. 29.

48. FBI File, Gillen Papers.

CHAPTER 10   ANARCHY ON WHEELS

1. Joshua Zeitz, *Building the Great Society: Inside Lyndon Johnson's White House* (New York: Penguin, 2019); Robert Dallek, *Lyndon B. Johnson: Portrait of a President* (New York: Oxford University Press, 2005); Joseph A. Califano Jr., *The Triumph and Tragedy of Lyndon Johnson: The White House Years* (New York: Atria, 2015).

2. *Time*, April 10, 1964.

3. Ibid.; *The Georgetowner*, Dec. 20, 2017.

4. *Time*, April 10, 1964; Michael R. Beschloss, *Taking Charge: The Johnson White House Tapes, 1963–1964* (New York: Simon & Schuster, 1967), p. 307n.

5. *Pittsburgh Press*, March 31, 1964.

6. *Des Moines Register*, April 8, 1964; *Los Angeles Times*, April 9, 1964; *Boston Globe*, April 12, 1964; *Time*, April 10, 1964.

7. "Annual Message to the Congress: The Economic Report of the President," Jan. 27, 1966, *Public Papers of the Presidents of the United States: Lyndon B. Johnson* (Washington: U.S. Government Printing Office, 1967), pp. 96–97.

8. "Annual Message to the Congress of the State of the Union," Jan. 12, 1966, ibid., pp. 6–7; *Car & Driver,* Nov. 1974.

9. "Special Message to the Congress on Transportation," March 2, 1966, *Public Papers of the Presidents of the United States: Lyndon B. Johnson,* pp. 251, 253.

10. "Remarks Upon Signing the Budget Message," Jan. 24, 1966, p. 61; "Economic Report," p. 106; "Special Message on Transportation," p. 256; "Message to the American Trial Lawyers Association Meeting in New York City," Feb. 2, 1966, p. 137, *Public Papers of the Presidents of the United States: Lyndon B. Johnson.*

11. "Special Message on Transportation," p. 257.

12. Ibid.

13. Ibid., pp. 257, 258.

14. "Message to the American Trial Lawyers Association Meeting In New York City," Johnson, *Public Papers of the President,* 1966.

15. *Hearings Before the Subcommittee on Executive Reorganization, Part 4,* p. 1503.

16. Ibid., pp. 1524–26.

17. "Joe Vale, Publisher," undated, Gillen Papers.

18. *Hearings Before the Subcommittee on Executive Reorganization, Part 4,* p. 1535.

19. Ibid., p. 1534; Gillen to Danner, March 3, 1966, Gillen Papers.

20. Interview of Frank McElroy, Gillen Papers; *Hearings Before the Subcommittee on Executive Reorganization, Part 4,* p. 1535.

21. Interview of Robert Gidel, Gillen Papers; Leo R. Werts to Daniel P. Moynihan, Feb. 27, 1967, Moynihan Papers; https://www2.census .gov/prod2/popscan/p60-049.pdf.

22. Gillen to Danner, undated, "Suggested areas of continued investigation," March 3, 1966, Gillen Papers; Charles Kale Interview, Gillen Papers; *Hearings Before the Subcommittee on Executive Reorganization, Part 4,* p. 1442.

23. Surveillance Reports, Feb. 7, 1966, Gillen Papers.

24. *Hearings Before the Subcommittee on Executive Reorganization, Part 4,* p. 1527.

25. Surveillance Report, May 5, 1966, Gillen Papers; Whiteside, p. 172.

26. Richard Danner to Vincent Gillen, Feb. 28, 1966, Gillen Papers; Eileen Murphy to Richard Danner, Feb. 25, 1966, Gillen Papers.

27. Murphy to Danner, Feb. 25, 1966, Gillen Papers.

28. Whiteside, pp. 182–87.

29. *Hearings Before the Subcommittee on Executive Reorganization, Part 4,* p. 1416.

30. Ibid., pp. 1422–27.

31. *Car & Driver,* Nov. 1974.

32. Lemov, p. 81.

33. Ibid., pp. 81–82.
34. Whiteside, p. 35.
35. *Playboy*, Oct. 1968; Norman Podhoretz, "The Old New Republic," *New York Review of Books*, April 8, 1965.

CHAPTER 11 EXPOSED

1. *Hearings Before the Subcommittee on Executive Reorganization, Part 3*, p. 1266.
2. Ibid.
3. Ibid.
4. Ibid.
5. Ibid., pp. 1266–67.
6. Ibid., p. 1267.
7. Ibid., pp. 1267–68.
8. Ibid., p. 1271.
9. Ibid., pp. 1272–73.
10. Ibid., p. 1274.
11. Ibid.
12. Ibid.
13. Ibid.
14. Ibid., p. 1275.
15. Ibid.; *Playboy*, Oct. 1968.
16. *Hearings Before the Subcommittee on Executive Reorganization, Part 3*, p. 1275.
17. Ibid.
18. Ibid., p. 1276.
19. Ibid., p. 1277.
20. Ibid., p. 1288ff.
21. Ibid., pp. 1324–25; Nader, *Unsafe at Any Speed*, p. 211.
22. *Hearings Before the Subcommittee on Executive Reorganization, Part 3*, p. 1325.
23. Ibid., pp. 1333–35.
24. Ibid., p. 1336.
25. Ibid.
26. Ibid., pp. 1336–37.
27. Ibid., p. 1337.
28. Ibid., pp. 1337–38.
29. Ibid., p. 1339.
30. Ibid.
31. Ibid., p. 1340.
32. Ibid., pp. 1342–43.
33. Transcript of David Sanford interview of V. Gillen, Feb. 28, 1966, Gillen Papers.

34. R. Danner to V. Gillen, Feb. 28, 1966, Gillen Papers.

35. V. Gillen to R. Danner, March 3, 1966, Gillen Papers.

36. Ibid.

37. James Ridgeway, "The Dick," *New Republic*, March 12 1966.

38. Ibid.

39. Ibid.

40. Ibid.

41. *New York Times*, March 6, 1966.

42. Ibid.

43. *Lansing State Journal*, March 9, 1966.

44. *Hearings Before the Subcommittee on Executive Reorganization, Part 4,* p. 1389.

45. Ribicoff Statement, March 10, 1966, ENP WHS.

46. *Spokesman-Review* (Spokane), March 12, 1966; *Detroit Free Press,* March 11, 1966.

47. *Hartford Courant*, March 12, 1966.

CHAPTER 12   PLAYING A LOSING HAND

1. *Hearings Before the Subcommittee on Executive Reorganization, Part 3,* p. 1278.

2. Ibid., p. 1078ff.

3. Ibid., p. 1105.

4. Ibid., pp. 1105–9.

5. Ibid., pp. 1105–9, 1175.

6. Ibid., pp. 1119, 1134.

7. Ibid., p. 1109ff.

8. Ibid., pp. 1141–42.

9. Ibid., p. 1157.

10. Ibid., p. 1158.

11. Ibid., pp. 1155–62.

12. Ibid., p. 1155.

13. Ibid., p. 1156.

14. Ibid., p. 1144.

15. Ibid., pp. 1144–45.

16. Ibid., pp. 1145–50.

17. Ibid., p. 1175ff.

18. Ibid., pp. 1296, 1326; Nader, *Unsafe at Any Speed,* pp. 214, 262, 263, 269.

19. Nader, *Unsafe at Any Speed,* p. 300; *Hearings Before the Subcommittee on Executive Reorganization, Part 4,* p. 1590.

20. *Hearings Before the Subcommittee on Executive Reorganization, Part 3,* p. 1348; *Hearings Before the Subcommittee on Executive Reorganization, Part 4,* p. 1590.

21. *Hearings Before the Subcommittee on Executive Reorganization, Part 1,* p. 210.

22. Cornell Aeronautical Laboratory Inc. to Jerome Sonosky, Sept. 20, 1965, RFK Papers.

23. Cornell Aeronautical Laboratory Inc.'s response to Ralph Nader's *Unsafe at Any Speed,* RFK Papers.

24. McCarry, p. 69.

25. U.S. Department of Health, Education, and Welfare, *Proceedings of the White House Conference On Health, Nov. 3 and 4, 1965* (Washington: U.S. Government Printing Office, 1965), pp. 469, 471.

26. *Los Angeles Times,* June 8, 2004; *Time,* May 20, 1966; James Roche biography, ENP WHS.

27. *Wall Street Journal,* March 16, 1971; Cray, p. 425.

28. *Hearings of the Subcommittee on Executive Reorganization, Part 4,* p. 1380.

29. *Ibid.,* p. 1381; *Detroit Free Press,* March 22 1966.

30. *Hearings of the Subcommittee on Executive Reorganization, Part 4,* p. 1381

31. *Ibid.,* pp. 1381–85.

32. *Ibid.*

33. *Ibid.,* p. 1396.

34. *Ibid.,* p. 1403.

35. *Ibid.,* p. 1405.

36. *Ibid.,* pp. 1406, 1408–9.

37. *Ibid.,* pp. 1416–20, 1438–39.

38. *The Nation,* Nov. 1, 1965.

39. *Hearings Before the Subcommittee on Executive Reorganization, Part 4,* p. 1449.

40. *Ibid.,* p. 1465ff.

41. *Ibid.*

42. *Ibid.,* pp. 1508–9.

43. *Ibid.,* pp. 1507–11.

44. *Ibid.,* pp. 1523–24.

45. *Ibid.,* p. 1530.

46. *Ibid.,* p. 1531; *Detroit Free Press,* March 23, 1966.

47. *Hearings Before the Subcommittee on Executive Reorganization, Part 4,* p. 1531.

48. *Ibid.,* p. 1540.

49. *Ibid.,* p. 1541.

50. *Ibid.,* p. 1532.

51. *Ibid.*

52. *Ibid.,* p. 1538.

53. *Ibid.,* pp. 1538–39.

54. John Newsom to Earl Newsom, March 29, 1966, ENP WHS; *Detroit Free Press*, March 23 1966.

CHAPTER 13   KILL SHOT

1. Shelby Scates, *Warren G. Magnuson and the Shaping of Twentieth-Century America* (Seattle: University of Washington Press, 1997).
2. *Washington Post*, Nov. 23, 1980.
3. United States Congress, *National Traffic and Motor Vehicle Safety Act of 1966: Legislative History* (Washington: U.S. Department of Transportation, 1985), p. 22.
4. United States Congress, *Traffic Safety: Hearings Before the Committee on Commerce* (Washington: U.S. Government Printing Office, 1966), p. 1.
5. United States Congress. Senate. "Federal Role in Traffic Safety: Hearings Before the Subcommittee on Executive Reorganization of the Committee on Government Operations, United States Senate, Eighty-Ninth Congress, Second Session, December 1966, Appendix," Washington: U.S. Government Printing Office, 1967, pp. 1, 78.
6. Ibid., p. 78.
7. *New York Times*, May 7, 1966.
8. Ibid.
9. Ibid., June 12, 1966.
10. "Highway Safety Act of 1966," 89th Congress, Second Session, House of Representatives, *House Reports* (Washington: Government Printing Office, 1966).
11. *Car & Driver*, Nov. 1974.
12. Elizabeth Brenner Drew, "The Politics of Auto Safety," *Atlantic Monthly*, Oct. 1966.
13. Ibid.; *Fortune*, Aug. 1966; Cray, p. 427.
14. Lemov, p. 103.
15. Haddon to Robert F. Kennedy, Dec. 20, 1967, RFK Papers; McCarry, pp. 90–91, 96; *Detroit Free Press*, Sept. 10, 1966.
16. Graham, p. 32.
17. Lemov, p. 103.
18. Jerry L. Mashaw and David L. Harfst, "Regulation and Legal Culture: The Case of Motor Vehicle Safety," *Yale Journal on Regulation* 4, no. 2 (1987); Cohen, pp. 346, 357, 359; Stan Lugar, *Corporate Power, American Democracy, and the Automobile Industry* (Cambridge: Cambridge University Press, 2000), p. 77; Graham, p. 17.
19. United States Congress, *Consumer Protection: Hearings Before the Committee on Commerce, United States Senate, Ninety-first Congress* (Washington: U.S. Government Printing Office, 1969), p. 340;

Cohen, p. 349; John A. Andrew III, *Lyndon Johnson and the Great Society* (Chicago: Ivan R. Dee, 1999), p. 168.

20. *Time*, Dec. 12, 1969.
21. F. H. Buckley, ed., *The American Illness: Essays on the Rule of Law* (New Haven: Yale University Press, 2013).
22. *Barron's*, Jan.12, 1970.
23. "U.S. Tort Cost Trends, 2011 Update," Towers Watson, https://www.casact.org/library/studynotes/Towers-Watson-Tort-Cost-Trends.pdf.
24. Rick Swedloff, "Uncompensated Torts," *Georgia State University Law Review* 28, no. 3 (Spring 2012); A. Mitchell Polinsky and Steven Shavell, "The Uneasy Case for Product Liability," *Harvard Law Review* 123, no. 6 (April 2010); Michael Trebilcock and Paul-Erik Veel, "A Tamer Tort Law," in Buckley, ed., *The American Illness;* Robert A. Kagan, *Adversarial Legalism: The American Way of Law* (Cambridge: Harvard University Press, 2009); Sugarman, "A Century of Change in Personal Injury Law."
25. Cohen, pp. 354, 359, 363.

CHAPTER 14   NO DEFECTS, NO NEGLIGENCE

1. *Detroit Free Press*, March 27, 1966, Jan. 29, 1966, Jan. 30, 1966.
2. Transcripts, *Meet the Press*, May 29, 1966, and *CBS Special Report*, May 13, 1966, ENP WHS; *Detroit Free Press*, May 13, 1966.
3. *Detroit Free Press*, May 18, 1966, May 21, 1966.
4. Ibid., May 21, 1966.
5. Ibid., May 29, 1966.
6. Ibid.
7. Ibid., June 15, 1966, July 3, 1966, Jan. 5, 1967.
8. General Motors Owner Satisfaction Study, 1967, ENP WHS.
9. Memorandum of Decision, *Drummond and Lyford v. General Motors Corporation*, Superior Court of the State of California, July 29, 1966.
10. Ibid. p. 10.
11. Ibid., p. 70.
12. *Chicago Tribune*, July 30, 1966, p. 9; *Boston Globe*, July 30, 1966, p. 4; *Arizona Republic*, July 30, 1966, p. 68; *New York Times*, July 30, 1966, p. 17, Jan. 12, 1967.
13. *Detroit Free Press*, July 4, 1967; *New York Times*, Oct. 31, 1967, May 13, 1969, Jan. 18, 1970, April 5, 1970; Cray, pp. 427–28.
14. *New York Times*, Dec. 12, 1968; *Palm Beach Post*, Dec. 13, 1968.
15. *New York Times*, May 13, 1969, Jan. 18, 1970.
16. United States Congress, Senate, *Auto Safety Oversight Hearings Before the Committee on Commerce* (Washington: U.S. Government Printing Office, 1972), p. 323; *New York Times*, Sept. 4, 1970.

17. *New York Times*, Sept. 9, 1970, March 16, 1973, May 3, 1977.

18. *Hearings Before the Subcommittee on Executive Reorganization, Part 4*, p. 1510.

19. E. L. Resler, P. H. Wright, and R. W. Caldwell, "Panel Evaluation of the NHTSA Approach to the 1960–1963 Corvair Handling and Stability" (Springfield, VA: General Testing Labs, 1972); *Auto Safety Oversight Hearings*, p. 313.

20. *Auto Safety Oversight Hearings*, pp. 38, 311, 313; *New York Times*, April 23, 1972, July 21, 1972, July 26, 1972.

21. *New York Times*, July 21, 1972, Feb. 4, 1973.

22. Ibid., Oct. 30, 1971.

23. Speiser, p. 24.

24. Ibid., p. 101.

25. Ibid., p. 24.

26. David Sanford, *Me & Ralph* (New York: Simon & Schuster, 1976); *Forbes*, Sept. 17, 1990; Darren K. Carlson, "Gallup Brain: Public Perceptions of Ralph Nader," Gallup, March 2, 2004, https://news .gallup.com/poll/10828/gallup-brain-public-perceptions-ralph -nader.aspx.

CHAPTER 15   THE DEATH OF ALFRED P. SLOAN

1. Social Research Inc., Jan. 1964; "A Study of College Students' Attitudes Towards Business," Gallup, 1966, ENP WHS.

2. "Gallup Polls: 1949–1962," ENP WHS, 1965.

3. Alfred P. Sloan, *My Years with General Motors* (New York: Doubleday,1963); *Fortune*, April 23, 1990.

4. *New York Times*, Feb. 18, 1966.

5. *Detroit Free Press*, Feb. 15, 1966.

6. *New York Times*, Feb. 18, 1966, Feb. 19, 1966.

7. Ibid., Feb. 18, 1966.

8. *Detroit Free Press*, May 4, 1966, July 7, 1966.

9. New York Stock Exchange (NYSE), 1966; *Time*, May 20, 1966.

10. *Detroit Free Press*, April 29, 1966, May 11, 1966; *Time*, May 20, 1966; Dow Jones Industrial Average (DJIA), 1966; NYSE, 1966.

11. "Federal Funds Rate—62 Year Historical Chart," *Macrotrends*, https://www.macrotrends.net/2015/fed-funds-rate-historical-chart; DJIA, 1966.

12. General Motors Annual Report, 1966; NYSE, 1966–1967; DJIA, 1966–1967.

13. "A Study of Public Attitudes Toward Consumer Protection and Big Business," Ira O. Glick & Assoc., June 1967, ENP WHS.

14. Ibid.

15. Ibid.

16. Ibid.; "1967 Owner Loyalty Report," Feb. 1967, ENP WHS.

17. Ira O. Glick & Assoc., Sept. 28, 1967.

18. G.M. Safety Memo, June 2 1967; G.M. Public Affairs Committee meeting, March 7, 1967; DeLorenzo to Newsom Group, Sept. 29, 1967; John Newsom memo, June 19, 1967; all in ENP WHS.

19. *Wall Street Journal*, Nov. 3, 1966; Ira O. Glick & Assoc., April 10, 1967.

20. G.M. Divisional PR Conference, March 9–10, 1967, ENP WHS.

21. Ibid.

22. Ibid.

23. DeLorenzo to Newsom Group, Sept. 29, 1967, ENP WHS; Earl Newsom, "Notes on Donner with Mr. Roche at the Detroit Club," June 28, 1967; ENP WHS.

24. General Motors Annual Reports, 1965–1970; DJIA, NYSE, 1965–1970.

25. Lane, p. 19.

26. *Wall Street Journal*, March 26, 1971; *New York Times*, March 26, 1971.

27. *Wall Street Journal*, May 21, 1971, March 26, 1971.

CHAPTER 16   THE END OF DETROIT

1. Department of Transportation, "The U.S. Automobile Industry, 1980," Washington, 1981; David Halberstam, *The Reckoning* (New York: William Morrow, 1986), pp. 12, 41, 504.

2. Halberstam, *The Reckoning*, p. 13.

3. See ibid.; Alex Taylor, *Sixty to Zero* (New Haven: Yale University Press, 2010); Yates, *The Decline and Fall of the American Automobile Industry*; Bob Lutz, *Car Guys vs. Bean Counters* (New York: Portfolio/Penguin, 2011); *Roger & Me* (1989), director, Michael Moore; Department of Transportation, "The U.S. Automobile Industry, 1980"; Flink, *The Automobile Age*.

4. *New York Times*, Jan. 18, 1971; "Automotive Trade Statistics, 1964–1980," United States International Trade Commission, December 1981, https://www.usitc.gov/publications/332/pub1203.pdf.

5. Cray, p. 435.

6. "U.S. Inflation Rate, 1960–2020," *Macrotrends*, https://www.macrotrends.net/countries/USA/united-states/inflation-rate-cpi; James Roche Speech, May 7, 1968, ENP WHS; General Motors Annual Reports, 1966–1973.

7. "Past Car of the Year Winners," *MotorTrend*, Nov. 16, 2015, https://www.motortrend.ca/en/news/car-of-the-year-winners/; "Automotive Trade Statistics, 1964–80," United States International Trade Commission.

8. Cray, pp. 451, 479.
9. Ibid., pp. 387–97; Freeland, *The Struggle for Control of the Modern Corporation.*
10. *Wall Street Journal,* Oct. 31, 1967; *New York Times,* Jan. 8, 1976.
11. NYSE, 1966–2000.
12. General Motors Annual Reports, 1965–1973; G.M. speeches, Nov. 18, 1964, Nov. 13, 1967, ENP WHS.
13. Michael Smitka, "Foreign Policy and the US Automotive Industry," *Business & Economic History* 28, no. 2 (Winter 1999).
14. William W. Lancaster, "The Foreign Direct Investment Regulations: A Look at Ad Hoc Rulemaking," *Virginia Law Review* 55, no. 1 (Feb. 1969); James Roche to Indiana News Media, April 22, 1968, ENP WHS.
15. James Roche Press Conference, Sept. 23, 1968, ENP WHS; Cray, p. 463; *Detroit Free Press,* Sept. 19, 1968.
16. N. P. Kannan, Kathy K. Rebibo, and Donna L. Ellis, *Downsizing Detroit* (New York: Praeger, 1982), p. 99.
17. Gordon, pp. 374–75; "Automotive Trade Statistics, 1964–80," United States International Trade Commission; "World Motor Vehicle Production, Selected Countries," Bureau of Transportation Statistics, https://www.bts.gov/content/world-motor-vehicle-production-selected-countries; "Total Vehicle Sales," U.S. Bureau of Economic Analysis, https://fred.stlouisfed.org/series/TOTALSA.
18. *Detroit Free Press,* Jan. 11, 1974, Sept. 27, 1964.
19. *New York Times,* May 3, 1977.
20. *Detroit Free Press,* May 3, 1977; *Hillsdale Daily News* (Michigan), Dec. 31, 1974.
21. *Detroit Free Press,* May 3, 1977; *Chicago Tribune,* May 3, 1977.
22. Bobby Kimbrough, "Top 5 Chevy People of All Time," *Chevy Hardcore,* April 9, 2015, https://www.chevyhardcore.com/news/top-5-chevy-people-of-all-time-2-edward-n-cole/.

CHAPTER 17   AVOIDABLE DEATHS

1. *Emporia Gazette* (Kansas), July 4, 1966; Lyndon B. Johnson, *Public Papers of the Presidents: 1966,* Book 1 (Washington: U.S. Government Printing Office, 1967), pp. 251–52; Lemov, p. 53.
2. "On 50th Anniversary of Ralph Nader's Unsafe at Any Speed," Center for Auto Safety, https://www.autosafety.org/on-50th-anniversary-of-ralph-naders-unsafe-at-any-speed-safety-group-reports-declining-death-rates-have-saved-3-5-million-lives/.
3. Lemov, p. 201.
4. "Understanding the National Highway Traffic Safety Administration," U.S. Department of Transportation, https://www

.transportation.gov/transition/understanding-national-highway
-traffic-safety-administration-nhtsa.

5. *"Unsafe at Any Speed*—Fiftieth Anniversary," Nader.org, https://
nader.org/2015/11/30/unsafe-at-any-speed-fiftieth-anniversary/;
Time, Aug. 30, 2011, Nov. 30, 2015; *Automotive News*, April 27,
2015; "Ralph Nader's *Unsafe at Any Speed* Turns 50 Years Old," *GM
Authority*, Dec. 1, 2015, https://gmauthority.com/blog/2015/12
/ralph-nadars-unsafe-at-any-speed-turns-50-years-old/.

6. "Motor Vehicle Traffic Fatalities, 1900–2007," https://www.fhwa.dot
.gov/policyinformation/statistics/2007/pdf/fi200.pdf; https://cdan
.nhtsa.gov/tsftables/Fatalities%20and%20Fatality%20Rates.pdf.

7. Charles J. Kahane, "Lives Saved by Vehicle Safety Technologies
and Associated Federal Motor Vehicle Safety Standards, 1960 to
2012," Paper Number 15-0291, https://www-esv.nhtsa.dot.gov
/Proceedings/24/files/24ESV-000291.PDF.

8. "Fatality Reduction by Safety Belts for Front-Seat Occupants of
Cars and Light Trucks," National Highway Traffic Safety Admin-
istration, Dec. 2000, https://crashstats.nhtsa.dot.gov/Api/Public
/ViewPublication/809199; "Primary Enforcement of Seat Belt
Laws," Centers for Disease Control and Prevention, https://www
.cdc.gov/motorvehiclesafety/calculator/factsheet/seatbelt.html;
"Alcohol-Impaired Driving," National Highway Traffic Safety
Administration, Oct. 2017, https://crashstats.nhtsa.dot.gov/Api
/Public/ViewPublication/812450.

9. Graham, pp. 76, 231; United Press International, Dec. 6, 1983; *New
York Times*, May 11, 1984.

10. Graham, pp. 38–43, 48–49; *New York Times*, Jan. 14, 1968.

11. *National Motor Vehicle Safety Advisory Council Annual Report*, 1974
(Washington: Highway Safety Research Institute, 1975), pp. 31–33.

12. Graham, pp. 89, 90; Yates, p. 264.

13. Graham, pp. 157, 220.

14. Leonard Evans, "Traffic Fatality Reductions: United States Compared with 25 Other Countries," *American Journal of Public Health*,
Aug. 2014; Evans, *Traffic Safety*, p. 383.

15. Evans, *Traffic Safety*, p. 381ff; Evans, "Traffic Fatality Reductions."

16. Evans, *Traffic Safety*, pp. 336–37; Evans, "Traffic Fatality Reductions."

17. Kahane, "Lives Saved by Vehicle Safety Technologies and Associated Federal Motor Vehicle Safety Standards, 1960 to 2012."

EPILOGUE   THE END OF AMERICAN ENTERPRISE

1. Waterhouse, pp. 14, 22, 23; Stanley Buder, *Capitalizing on Change: A
Social History of American Business* (Chapel Hill: University of North
Carolina Press, 2009), pp. 28–31.

2. Buder, p. 1.

3. Richard J. Payne, *The Clash with Distant Cultures* (New York: State University of New York Press, 1995), p. 90.

4. Buder, p. 59.

5. James Q. Wilson, ed., *The Politics of Regulation* (New York: Basic Books, 1980).

6. Theodore Roosevelt, *Address of President Roosevelt on the Occasion of the Laying of the Corner Stone of the Pilgrim Memorial Monument* (Washington: U.S. Government Printing Office, 1907).

7. Ibid.

8. Franklin D. Roosevelt, "Acceptance Speech for the Re-Nomination."

9. Franklin D. Roosevelt, "Inaugural Address," March 4, 1933, https://www.presidency.ucsb.edu/documents/inaugural-address-8.

10. Franklin D. Roosevelt, "Inaugural Address," Jan. 30, 1937, https://www.presidency.ucsb.edu/documents/inaugural-address-7.

11. Cohen, p. 358; Galbraith, p. 210; Daniel Patrick Moynihan, *Traffic Safety and the Health of the Body Politic* (Middletown, CT: Wesleyan University Press, 1966), p. 12; Weisman, p. 34.

12. Drew, "The Politics of Auto Safety"; "Robert Kennedy on Government Injustice to Business," *Congressional Record*, Vol. 113, Part 15 (July 1967), pp. 20, 132.

13. Moynihan, *Traffic Safety and the Health of the Body Politic*, p. 12.

14. Cray, p. 436.

15. David Vogel, *Fluctuating Fortunes*, p. 59; Cohen, pp. 354–55.

16. David Vogel, *Fluctuating Fortunes*, p. 94.

17. Ibid., pp. 195, 197.

18. Ibid., pp. 33, 114.

19. Ibid., pp. 54, 55; *Washington Post*, Feb. 12, 2015.

20. Thomas M. Keck, *Judicial Politics in Polarized Times* (Chicago: University of Chicago Press, 2014), Lepore, p. 15; Kagan, p. 44.

21. Amanda Bronstad, "U.S. Tort System Costs $429B," Law.com, Oct. 25, 2018.

22. Dustin Chambers, "The Regressive Effects of Federal Regulation and a Roadmap for Reform," Senate Committee on Homeland Security and Governmental Affairs, Subcommittee on Regulatory Affairs and Federal Management, Sept. 27, 2018.

23. Richard Vietor, "Government Regulation of Business," *The Cambridge Economic History of the United States*, Vol. 3 (New York: Cambridge University Press, 2001); Kagan, pp. 228–34; *New York Times*, July 22, 2009.

24. Patrick McLaughlin and Robert Greene, "The Unintended Consequences of Federal Regulatory Accumulation," Mercatus Center, May 8, 2014, https://www.mercatus.org/publications/regulation/unintended-consequences-federal-regulatory-accumulation; "The

Growth Potential of Deregulation," Council of Economic Advisors, Oct. 2, 2017, https://www.whitehouse.gov/sites/whitehouse .gov/files/documents/The%20Growth%20Potential%20of%20 Deregulation_1.pdf; https://www.oecd.org/regreform/regulatory -policy/2478900.pdf; https://upfina.com/wp-content/uploads/2017 /07/Budgetary-Costs-Of-Regulations.jpg.

25. Gordon, p. 609; Alan Greenspan and Adrian Wooldridge, *Capitalism in America: A History* (New York: Penguin, 2018).

26. Gordon, p. 590.

27. Alana Samuels, "Are Pharmaceutical Companies to Blame for the Opioid Epidemic," *The Atlantic*, June 2, 2017; Zachary Siegel, "The Opioid Crisis Is About More Than Corporate Greed," *New Republic*, July 30, 2019; Ronald Hirsch, "The Opioid Epidemic: It's Time to Place Blame Where It Belongs," *Missouri Medicine*, March–April 2017; Joyce Frieden, "Don't Just Blame the Drug Companies for the Opioid Crisis," *MedPage Today*, April 14, 2019, https://www .medpagetoday.com/meetingcoverage/acp/79220.

28. Sarah Milov, *The Cigarette: A Political History* (Cambridge: Harvard University Press, 2019); "In US, Smoking Rate Hits New Low at 16%," Gallup.com, July 24 2018; "The Health Consequences of Smoking—50 Years of Progress," U.S. Department of Health and Human Services, 2014, https://www.ncbi.nlm.nih.gov/books /NBK179276/pdf/Bookshelf_NBK179276.pdf.

29. Jeff Kosseff, *The Twenty-Six Words That Created the Internet* (Ithaca: Cornell University Press, 2019).

30. Ibid.

31. Newsom Memo, undated, ENP WHS.

32. Benjamin Friedman, *The Moral Consequences of Economic Growth* (New York: Vintage, 2006), p. 436.

33. Calvin Coolidge, "Address to the American Society of Newspaper Editors," Washington, D.C., January 17, 1925.

SELECTED BIBLIOGRAPHY

ARCHIVES

General Motors Heritage Center Reference Collection
Vincent W. Gillen Papers, Baker Library Special Collections, Harvard
    Business School (Gillen Papers)
Robert F. Kennedy Papers, John F. Kennedy Library (RFK Papers)
Daniel P. Moynihan Papers, Library of Congress (Moynihan Papers)
Earl Newsom Papers, Wisconsin History Society (ENP WHS)
Abraham Ribicoff Papers, Library of Congress

ARTICLES, REPORTS, AND GOVERNMENT DOCUMENTS

American Bar Association. "ABA Compendium of Professional Responsi-
    bility Rules and Standards." Chicago: American Bar Association, 2004.
Bostdorff, Denise M., and Daniel J. O'Rourke. "The Presidency and the
    Promotion of Domestic Crisis: John Kennedy's Management of the
    1962 Steel Crisis." *Presidential Studies Quarterly* 27, no. 2 (Spring 1997).
Bowman, Byrne A. "An Inspection of a Personal Injury Law Firm." *Ameri-
    can Bar Association Journal*, Oct. 1965.
Chambers, Dustin. "The Regressive Effects of Federal Regulation and a
    Roadmap for Reform." Senate Committee on Homeland Security and
    Governmental Affairs, Subcommittee on Regulatory Affairs and Fed-
    eral Management, Sept. 27, 2018.
Drew, Elizabeth Brenner. "The Politics of Auto Safety." *Atlantic Monthly*,
    Oct. 1966.
Evans, Leonard. "Traffic Fatality Reductions: United States Compared
    with 25 Other Countries." *American Journal of Public Health*, Aug.
    2014.
Gannett, Henry. *Report of the National Conservation Commission*, Vol. 3.
    Washington: U.S. Government Printing Office, 1909.
Graysmith, Leah. "Sex and Gender in the Equine in Literature." Master's
    thesis, Iowa State University, Ames, Iowa, 2008.
Hamilton, William W. "Rights and Liabilities of Gratuitous Automobile
    Passengers." *Chicago-Kent Law Review* 10, no. 1 (Dec. 1931).

Highway Safety Research Institute. *National Motor Vehicle Safety Advisory Council Annual Report, 1974*. Washington, 1975.

Hirsch, Ronald. "The Opioid Epidemic: It's Time to Place Blame Where It Belongs." *Missouri Medicine*, March–April 2017.

Horsch, John, David Viano, and James DeCou. "History of Safety Research and Development on the General Motors Energy-Absorbing Steering System." *Journal of Passenger Cars* (1991).

Huddy, Xenophon P. "The Motor Car's Status." *Yale Law Journal* 15, no. 2 (Dec. 1905).

Katz, Harold A. "Liability of Automobile Manufacturers for Unsafe Design of Passenger Cars." *Harvard Law Review* 69, no. 5 (March 1956).

Lancaster, William W. "The Foreign Direct Investment Regulations: A Look at Ad Hoc Rulemaking." *Virginia Law Review* 55, no. 1 (Feb. 1969).

Leland, Anne. "American War and Military Operations Casualties." Congressional Research Service, Feb. 26, 2010.

Mashaw, Jerry L., and David L. Harfst. "Regulation and Legal Culture: The Case of Motor Vehicle Safety." *Yale Journal on Regulation* 4, no. 2 (1987).

Moynihan, Daniel Patrick. "Epidemic on the Highways." *The Reporter*, April 30, 1959.

———. "The War Against the Automobile." *The Public Interest*, Spring 1966.

Nader, Ralph, "Automobile Design Hazards." *American Jurisprudence Proof of Facts*. San Francisco: Bancroft-Whitney, 1965.

———. "The Safe Car You Can't Buy." *The Nation*, April 11, 1959.

Nader, Ralph, and David F. Binder. *Harvard Law Record* 28, no. 3 (Feb. 19, 1959).

National Tourism Resources Review Commission. *Destination USA: Domestic Tourism*, Vol. 2. Washington, 1973.

Nuechterlein, James A. "Arthur M. Schlesinger, Jr., and the Discontents of Postwar American Liberalism." *Review of Politics* 39, no. 1 (Jan. 1977).

Podhoretz, Norman. "The Old New Republic." *New York Review of Books*, April 8, 1965.

Polinsky, A. Mitchell, and Steven Shavell. "The Uneasy Case for Product Liability." *Harvard Law Review* 123, no. 6 (April 2010).

Resler, E. L., P. H. Wright, and R. W. Caldwell. "Panel Evaluation of the NHTSA Approach to the 1960–1963 Corvair Handling and Stability." Springfield, Virginia, General Testing Labs, 1972.

Ridgeway, James. "The Dick." *New Republic*, March 12, 1966.

Samuels, Alana. "Are Pharmaceutical Companies to Blame for the Opioid Epidemic?" *The Atlantic*, June 2, 2017.

Schlesinger, Arthur M., Jr. "The Future of Liberalism: The Challenge of Abundance." *Saturday Review* 40, no. 8 (June 1957).

Schwab, Alexander. "In Defense of Ambulance Chasing: A Critique of Model Rule of Professional Conduct 7.3." *Yale Law & Policy Review* 29, no. 2 (2010).

Shelden, C. Hunter. "Prevention, The Only Cure for Head Injuries Resulting from Automobile Accidents." *Journal of the American Medical Association* 159, no. 10 (1955).

Siegel, Zachary. "The Opioid Crisis Is About More Than Corporate Greed." *New Republic*, July 30 2019.

Smitka, Michael. "Foreign Policy and the US Automotive Industry." *Business & Economic History* 28, no. 2 (Winter 1999).

Sugarman, Stephen D. "A Century of Change in Personal Injury Law." *California Law Review* 88, no. 6 (Dec. 2000).

Superior Court of the State of California. Memorandum of Decision, *Drummond & Lyford v. General Motors Corporation*, July 29, 1966.

Swedloff, Rick. "Uncompensated Torts." *Georgia State University Law Review* 28, no. 3 (Spring 2012).

United States Congress. House of Representatives. *Hearings Before a Subcommittee of the Committee on Interstate and Foreign Commerce, Eighty-fourth Congress, Second Session on Investigation of Highway Traffic Accidents.* Washington: U.S. Government Printing Office, 1957.

United States Congress. *National Traffic and Motor Vehicle Safety Act of 1966: Legislative History.* Washington: U.S. Department of Transportation, 1985.

United States Congress. "Proceedings and Debates of the 87th Congress, Vol. 107, Pt. 1." *Congressional Record*, 1961.

United States Congress. "Résumé of Congressional Activity." *Congressional Record*, 1966.

United States Congress. Senate. *Auto Safety Oversight Hearings Before the Committee on Commerce.* Washington: U.S. Government Printing Office, 1972.

United States Congress. Senate. "Federal Role in Traffic Safety: Hearings Before the Subcommittee on Executive Reorganization of the Committee on Government Operations, United States Senate, Eighty-Ninth Congress, First Session, March 22, 25, and 26, 1965, Part 1," Washington: U.S. Government Printing Office, 1965.

United States Congress. Senate. "Federal Role in Traffic Safety: Hearings Before the Subcommittee on Executive Reorganization of the Committee on Government Operations, United States Senate, Eighty-Ninth Congress, First Session, July 13, 14, 15, and 21, 1965, Part 2," Washington: U.S. Government Printing Office, 1966.

United States Congress. Senate. "Federal Role in Traffic Safety: Hearings

Before the Subcommittee on Executive Reorganization of the Committee on Government Operations, United States Senate, Eighty-Ninth Congress, Second Session, February 2, 3, and 16, 1966, Part 3," Washington: U.S. Government Printing Office, 1966.

United States Congress. Senate. "Federal Role in Traffic Safety: Hearings Before the Subcommittee on Executive Reorganization of the Committee on Government Operations, United States Senate, Eighty-Ninth Congress, Second Session, March 22, 1966, Part 4," Washington: U.S. Government Printing Office, 1966.

United States Congress. Senate. "Federal Role in Traffic Safety: Hearings Before the Subcommittee on Executive Reorganization of the Committee on Government Operations, United States Senate, Eighty-Ninth Congress, Second Session, December 1966, Appendix," Washington: U.S. Government Printing Office, 1967.

United States Congress. Senate. *Consumer Protection: Hearings Before the Committee on Commerce, United States Senate, Ninety-first Congress.* Washington: U.S. Government Printing Office, 1969.

United States Congress. Senate. *Hearings Before the Committee on Armed Services.* Washington: U.S. Government Printing Office, 1953.

United States Congress. *Technology Assessment of Changes in the Future Use and Characteristics of the Automobile Transportation System,* Vol. 3. Washington: U.S. Government Printing Office, 1979.

United States Department of Commerce. *The U.S. Market for Imported Automobiles.* Washington: U.S. Government Printing Office, 1969.

United States Department of Health, Education, and Welfare. *Proceedings of the White House Conference on Health, Nov. 3 & 4, 1965.* Washington: U.S. Government Printing Office, 1965.

United States Department of the Navy, Bureau of Medicine and Surgery. *United States Naval Medical Bulletin* 45, no. 1 (July 1945).

United States Department of Transportation, *The U.S. Automobile Industry, 1980.* Washington, 1981.

Vietor, Richard. "Government Regulation of Business." *The Cambridge Economic History of the United States,* Vol. 3. New York: Cambridge University Press, 2001.

Viscusi, W. Kip. "Does Product Liability Make Us Safer?" *Regulation,* Spring 2012.

Walters, Stephen S. "Product Liability and the Problem of Proof." *Stanford Law Review* 21, no. 6 (June 1969).

Vogel, David. "The Public Interest Movement and the American Reform Tradition." *Political Science Quarterly* 95 (Winter 1980–81).

Wolfe, Alan. "Gonzo Sociology." *New Republic,* Oct. 8, 2008.

Woolf, S. H., and H. Schoomaker. "Life Expectancy and Mortality Rates in the United States, 1959–2017." *Journal of the American Medical Association* 322, no. 20 (Nov. 26, 2019).

BOOKS

Abramson, Rudy. *Spanning the Century: The Life of W. Averell Harriman, 1891–1986.* New York: William Morrow, 1992.

Adams, James Truslow. *Big Business in a Democracy.* New York: Charles Scribner's Sons, 1945.

Albert, Dan. *Are We There Yet: The American Automobile Past, Present, and Driverless.* New York: W. W. Norton, 2019.

Aldous, Richard. *Schlesinger: The Imperial Historian.* New York: W. W. Norton, 2017.

Anderson, Terry H. *The Movement and the Sixties.* New York: Oxford University Press, 1996.

Andrew, John A., III. *Lyndon Johnson and the Great Society.* Chicago: Ivan R. Dee, 1999.

Berger, Michael. *The Devil Wagon in God's Country.* Brooklyn: Shoe String Press, 1980.

Beschloss, Michael R. *Taking Charge: The Johnson White House Tapes, 1963–1964.* New York: Simon & Schuster, 1967.

Black, William Richard. *Sustainable Transportation.* New York: Guilford Press, 2010.

Blanke, David. *Hell on Wheels: The Promise and Peril of America's Car Culture, 1900-1940.* Lawrence: University Press of Kansas, 2007.

Blischke, Wallace R., and D. N. Prabhakar Murthy. *Product Warranty Handbook.* Boca Raton: CRC Press, 1995.

Blum, John Morton. *Years of Discord.* New York: W. W. Norton, 1992.

Brands, H. W. *American Dreams: The United States Since 1945.* New York: Penguin, 2010.

Buchanan, Bruce. *The Presidential Experience: What the Office Does to the Man.* Upper Saddle River, NJ: Prentice-Hall, 1978.

Buckley, F. H., ed. *The American Illness: Essays on the Rule of Law.* New Haven: Yale University Press, 2013.

Buder, Stanley. *Capitalizing on Change: A Social History of American Business.* Chapel Hill: University of North Carolina Press, 2009.

Burns, James MacGregor. *Roosevelt: The Lion and the Fox.* New York: Konecky & Konecky, 1956.

Burt, Dan M. *Abuse of Trust: A Report on Ralph Nader's Network.* Chicago: Regnery, 1982.

Bush, James, Alan Binder, and Ferris Deebe. *General Motors in the 20th Century.* Ward's Communications, 2000.

Califano, Joseph A., Jr. *The Triumph and Tragedy of Lyndon Johnson: The White House Years.* New York: Atria, 2015.

Cannadine, David. *Mellon: An American Life.* New York: Vintage, 2008.

Carson, Rachel. *Silent Spring.* New York: Houghton Mifflin, 1962.

Chaucer, Geoffrey. *The Canterbury Tales.* New York: Penguin, 2003.

Ciment, James, ed. *Social Issues in America: An Encyclopedia*. New York: Routledge, 2006.

Coffee, John C. *Entrepreneurial Litigation: Its Rise, Fall and Future*. Cambridge: Harvard University Press, 2015.

Cohen, Lizabeth. *A Consumer's Republic: The Politics of Mass Consumption in Postwar America*. New York: Vintage, 2004.

Collins, Robert M. *More: The Politics of Economic Growth in Postwar America*. New York: Oxford University Press, 2000.

Crandall, Robert. *Regulating the Automobile*. Washington: Brookings, 1976.

Cray, Ed. *Chrome Colossus: General Motors and Its Times*. New York: McGraw-Hill, 1980.

Cross, Gary. *An All-Consuming Century*. New York: Columbia University Press, 2000.

Cutlip, Scott M. *The Unseen Power: Public Relations, A History*. Hillsdale: LEA Publishers, 1994.

Dallek, Robert. *Lyndon B. Johnson: Portrait of a President*. New York: Oxford, 2005.

———. *An Unfinished Life: John F. Kennedy, 1917–1963*. New York: Back Bay Books, 2003.

Dickstein, Morris. *Gates of Eden: American Culture in the Sixties*. New York: Basic Books, 1977.

Donner, Frederic. *The World-Wide Industrial Enterprise*. New York: McGraw-Hill, 1967.

Eastman, Joel, W. *Styling vs. Safety: The American Automobile Industry and the Development of Automotive Safety, 1900–1966*. Lanham, MD: University Press of America, 1984.

Eisenhower, Dwight D. *Public Papers of the Presidents of the United States: Dwight D. Eisenhower, 1958*. Washington: U.S. Government Printing Office, 1959.

Engerman, Stanley L., and Robert E. Gallman. *The Cambridge Economic History of the United States*, Vol. 3. New York: Cambridge University Press, 2000.

Evans, Leonard. *Traffic Safety*. Bloomfield Hills, MI: Science Serving Society, 2004.

Farber, David R. *Sloan Rules: Alfred P. Sloan and the Triumph of General Motors*. Chicago: University of Chicago Press, 2005.

Fitzgerald, F. Scott. *The Great Gatsby*. New York: Scribner, 1925.

Flink, James. *The Automobile Age*. Cambridge: MIT Press, 1990.

Foer, Franklin, ed. *Insurrections of the Mind*. New York: Harper, 2014.

Franz, Kathleen. *Tinkering: Consumers Reinvent the Early Automobile*. Philadelphia: University of Pennsylvania Press, 2005.

Freeland, Robert F. *The Struggle for Control of the Modern Corporation: Organizational Change at General Motors, 1924–1970*. Cambridge: Cambridge University Press, 2000.

Friedan, Betty. *The Feminine Mystique*. New York: W. W. Norton, 1963.

Friedman, Benjamin. *The Moral Consequences of Economic Growth*. New York: Vintage, 2006.

Friedman, Lawrence M. *Law in America*. New York: Modern Library, 2004.

———. *Total Justice*. New York: Russell Sage Foundation, 1994.

Galbraith, John Kenneth. *The Affluent Society*. New York: Mariner Books, 1998.

Gamble, Clive. *Settling the Earth: The Archaeology of Deep Human History*. Cambridge: Cambridge University Press, 2013.

Geary, Daniel. *Radical Ambition: C. Wright Mills, the Left, and American Social Thought*. Oakland: University of California Press, 2009.

Glickman, Lawrence B. *Buying Power: A History of Consumer Activism in America*. Chicago: University of Chicago Press, 2009.

Goldfield, Edwin D. *Statistical Abstract of the United States, 1955*. Washington: U.S. Government Printing Office, 1955.

Gordon, John Steele. *An Empire of Wealth: The Epic History of American Economic Power*. New York: Harper, 2004.

Gordon, Robert. *The Rise and Fall of American Growth*. Princeton: Princeton University Press, 2016.

Graham John D. *Auto Safety: Assessing America's Performance*. Dover: Auburn House, 1989.

Greene, Robert John. *America in the Sixties*. Syracuse: Syracuse University Press, 2010.

Greenspan, Alan, and Adrian Wooldridge. *Capitalism in America: A History*. New York: Penguin, 2018.

Haddon, W., et al. *Accident Research: Methods and Approaches*. New York: Harper & Row, 1964.

Halberstam, David. *The Fifties*. New York: Random House, 1993.

———. *The Reckoning*. New York: William Morrow, 1986.

Harrington, Michael. *The Other America: Poverty in the United States*. New York: Macmillan, 1963.

Heitmann, John. *The Automobile and American Life*. Jefferson, NC: McFarland, 2009.

Hitchcock, William I. *The Age of Eisenhower: America and the World in the 1950s*. New York: Simon & Schuster, 2019.

Hodgson, Godfrey. *The Gentleman from New York: Daniel Patrick Moynihan*. Boston: Houghton Mifflin, 2000.

Horowitz, Daniel. *The Anxieties of Affluence*. Amherst: University of Massachusetts Press, 2005.

Ingrassia, Paul. *Crash Course*. New York: Random House, 2010.

———. *Comeback: The Fall and Rise of the American Automobile Industry*. New York: Simon & Schuster, 1994.

Irwin, Alan. *Risk and the Control of Technology*. Manchester: Manchester University Press, 1985.

Jacobs, Jane. *The Death and Life of Great American Cities*. New York: Random House, 1961.

Johnson, Lyndon B. *Public Papers of the Presidents of the United States: Lyndon B. Johnson, 1966*. Washington: U.S. Government Printing Office, 1967.

———. *Public Papers of the Presidents of the United States: Lyndon B. Johnson, 1967*. Washington: U.S. Government Printing Office, 1968.

Kagan, Robert A. *Adversarial Legalism: The American Way of Law*. Cambridge: Harvard University Press, 2009.

Kannan, N. P., Kathy K. Rebibo, and Donna L. Ellis. *Downsizing Detroit*. New York: Praeger, 1982.

Keck, Thomas M. *Judicial Politics in Polarized Times*. Chicago: University of Chicago Press, 2014.

Keller, Maryann. *Rude Awakening: The Rise, Fall, and Struggle for Recovery of General Motors*. New York: HarperCollins, 1990.

Kennedy, David M. *Freedom from Fear: The American People in Depression and War, 1929–1945*. New York: Oxford University Press, 1999.

Kennedy, John F. *Public Papers of the Presidents of the United States: John F. Kennedy, 1961*. Washington: U.S. Government Printing Office, 1962.

———. *Public Papers of the Presidents of the United States, John F. Kennedy, 1962*. Washington: U.S. Government Printing Office, 1963.

Kerouac, Jack. *On the Road*. New York: Penguin, 1976.

Kosseff, Jeff. *The Twenty-Six Words That Created the Internet*. Ithaca: Cornell University Press, 2019.

Krebs, Ronald R. *Narrative and the Making of U.S. National Security*. Cambridge: Cambridge University Press, 2015.

Ladd, Brian, *Autophobia: Love and Hate in the Automotive Age* (Chicago: University of Chicago Press, 2008).

Lane, Robert E. *The Regulation of Businessmen*. Hamden, CT: Archon Books, 1966.

Langworth, Richard M. *Kaiser-Frazer: The Last Onslaught on Detroit*. Kutztown, PA: Automobile Quarterly Publications, 1975.

Lear, Linda. *Rachel Carson: Witness for Nature*. Boston: Mariner Books, 1997.

Lemov, Michael R. *Car Safety Wars: One Hundred Years of Technology, Politics, and Death*. Madison, NJ: Fairleigh Dickinson University Press, 2015.

Lepore, Jill. *These Truths*. New York: W. W. Norton, 2018.

Lewis, Sinclair. *Babbitt*. New York: Modern Library, 2002.

Lewis, Tom. *Divided Highways: Building the Interstate Highways, Transforming American Life*. Ithaca: Cornell University Press, 2013.

Lichtenstein, Nelson, ed. *American Capitalism*. Philadelphia: University of Pennsylvania Press, 2006.

Lovegrove, G. R. *Remaking the City Street Grid*. Jefferson, NC: McFarland, 2015.

Lugar, Stan. *Corporate Power, American Democracy, and the Automobile Industry.* Cambridge: Cambridge University Press, 2000.

Lutz, Bob. *Car Guys vs. Bean Counters.* New York: Portfolio/Penguin, 2011.

MacAvoy, Paul W. *Industry Regulation and the Performance of the American Economy.* New York: W. W. Norton, 1992.

Mackenzie, G. Calvin, and Robert Weisbrot. *The Liberal Hour.* New York: Penguin, 2009.

Maranis, David. *Once in a Great City: A Detroit Story.* New York: Simon & Schuster, 2015.

Martin, Justin. *Nader: Crusader, Spoiler, Icon.* Cambridge, MA: Perseus, 2002.

Matusow, Alan J. *The Unraveling of America: A History of Liberalism in the 1960s.* Athens: University of Georgia Press, 2009.

Maynard, Micheline. *Collision Course: Inside the Battle for General Motors.* New York: Birch Lane, 1995.

McCarry, Charles. *Citizen Nader.* London: Jonathan Cape, 1972.

McCraw, Thomas K., and William R. Childs. *American Business Since 1920.* Hoboken: John Wiley & Sons, 2018.

Miller, Nathan. *New World Coming.* New York: Scribner, 2003.

Mills, C. Wright. *Listen, Yankee: The Revolution in Cuba.* New York: Ballantine, 1960.

———. *The Power Elite.* New York: Oxford University Press, 1956.

Mills, C. Wright, Kathryn Mills, et al. *C. Wright Mills: Letters and Autobiographical Writings.* Oakland: University of California Press, 2001.

Milov, Sarah. *The Cigarette: A Political History.* Cambridge: Harvard University Press, 2019.

Mingo, Jack. *How the Cadillac Got Its Fins.* New York: HarperCollins, 1995.

Mitford, Jessica. *The American Way of Death.* London: Hutchinson, 1963.

Moe, Espen. *Governance, Growth and Global Leadership: The Role of the State in Technological Progress, 1750–2000.* Burlington, VT: Ashgate, 2007.

Moynihan, Daniel Patrick. *Traffic Safety and the Health of the Body Politic.* Middletown, CT: Wesleyan University Press, 1966.

Mozingo, Louise A. *Pastoral Capitalism: A History of Suburban Corporate Landscapes.* Cambridge: MIT Press, 2011.

Nabokov, Vladimir. *Lolita.* New York: Vintage, 1997.

Nader, Ralph. *Unsafe at Any Speed: The Designed-In Dangers of the American Automobile.* New York: Grossman, 1965.

Norton, Peter D. *Fighting Traffic: The Dawn of the Motor Age in the American City.* Cambridge: MIT Press, 2008.

O'Neill, William. *American High: The Years of Confidence, 1945–1960.* New York: Free Press, 1986.

Packard, Vance. *The Hidden Persuaders.* New York: Ig Publishing, 2007.

———. *The Waste Makers.* New York: David McKay, 1960.

Packer, Jeremy. *Mobility Without Mayhem*. Durham, NC: Duke University Press, 2008.

Parker, Richard. *John Kenneth Galbraith: His Life, His Politics, His Economics*. New York: Farrar, Straus & Giroux, 2005.

Patterson, James T. *The Eve of Destruction: How 1965 Transformed America*. New York: Basic Books, 2012.

———. *Grand Expectations: The United States, 1945–1974*. New York: Oxford University Press, 1996.

Payne, Richard J. *The Clash with Distant Cultures*. New York: State University of New York Press, 1995.

Pertschuk, Michael. *Revolt Against Regulation*. Berkeley: University of California Press, 1982.

Rae, John B. *The American Automobile Industry*. Boston: Twayne, 1984.

Research Committee on Social Trends. *Recent Social Trends in the United States*, Vol. 1. New York: McGraw-Hill, 1933.

Reeves, Richard. *President Kennedy: Profile of Power*. New York: Simon & Schuster, 1993.

Roosevelt, Theodore. *Address of President Roosevelt on the Occasion of the Laying of the Corner Stone of the Pilgrim Memorial Monument*. Washington: U.S. Government Printing Office, 1907.

Roth, Philip. *American Pastoral*. New York: Vintage, 1997.

Samuelson, Robert J. *The Good Life and Its Discontents*. New York: Times Books, 1995.

Sanford, David. *Me & Ralph*. New York: Simon & Schuster, 1976.

Scates, Shelby. *Warren G. Magnuson and the Shaping of Twentieth-Century America*. Seattle: University of Washington Press, 1997.

Schlesinger, Arthur M., Jr. *A Thousand Days: John F. Kennedy in the White House*. Boston: Houghton Mifflin, 1965.

Schulman, Bruce K. *The Seventies: The Great Shift in American Culture, Society, and Politics*. Boston: Da Capo, 2002.

Siracusa, Joseph M. *Encyclopedia of the Kennedys*, Vol. 1. Santa Barbara: ABC-CLIO, 2012.

Sloan, Alfred P. *My Years with General Motors*. New York: Doubleday, 1963.

Smith, Jean Edward. *Eisenhower in War and Peace*. New York: Random House, 2013.

———. *FDR*. New York: Random House, 2008.

Smith, Mark A. *American Business and Political Power*. Chicago: University of Chicago Press, 2000.

Sobel, Robert. *Car Wars: The Untold Story*. New York: Truman Talley Books, 1984.

Speiser, Stuart M. *Lawsuit*. New York: Horizon Press, 1980.

Srinivasan, Bhu. *Americana: A 400-Year History of American Capitalism*. New York: Penguin, 2017.

Stevenson, Heon. *American Automobile Advertising, 1930–1980.* Jefferson, NC: McFarland, 2008.

Taylor, Alex. *Sixty to Zero.* New Haven: Yale University Press, 2010.

Tye, Larry. *Bobby Kennedy: The Making of a Liberal Icon.* New York: Random House, 2016.

Unger, Irwin. *The Best of Intentions: The Triumph and Failure of the Great Society Under Kennedy, Johnson and Nixon.* New York: Doubleday, 1996.

Vanderbilt, Tom. *Traffic.* New York: Alfred A. Knopf, 2010.

Vogel, David. *Fluctuating Fortunes: The Political Power of Business in America.* New York: Basic Books, 1989.

Vogel, Steven K. *Freer Markets, More Rules: Regulatory Reform in Advanced Industrial Countries.* Ithaca: Cornell University Press, 1996.

Von Drehle, David. *Triangle: The Fire That Changed America.* New York: Grove, 2004.

Warren, Robert Penn. *All the King's Men.* New York: Harcourt, 1946.

Waterhouse, Benjamin C. *The Land of Enterprise: A Business History of the United States.* New York: Simon & Schuster, 2017.

Weiner, Greg. *American Burke: The Uncommon Liberalism of Daniel Patrick Moynihan.* Lawrence: University Press of Kansas, 2015.

Weisbrot, Robert, and G. Calvin Mackenzie. *The Liberal House: Washington and the Politics of Change in the 1960s.* New York: Penguin, 2008.

Weisman, Steven R. *Daniel Patrick Moynihan: A Portrait in Letters of an American Visionary.* New York: PublicAffairs, 2010.

White, Andrew J. *The Assassination of the Corvair.* New Haven: Reader's Press, 1969.

White, G. Edward. *Tort Law in America: An Intellectual History.* New York: Oxford University Press, 2003.

White, Lawrence J. *The Automobile Industry Since 1945.* Cambridge: Harvard University Press, 1971.

Whiteside, Thomas. *The Investigation of Ralph Nader.* New York: Arbor House, 1972.

Wilson, James Q., ed. *The Politics of Regulation.* New York: Basic Books, 1980.

Winston, Clifford. *Blind Intersection? Policy and the Automobile Industry.* Washington: Brookings Institute, 1987.

Wolfe, Alan. *America's Impasse: The Rise and Fall of the Politics of Growth.* New York: Pantheon, 1981.

Wright, J. Patrick. *On a Clear Day You Can See General Motors.* Grosse Point, MI: Wright Enterprises, 1979.

Yates, Brock. *The Decline and Fall of the American Automobile Industry.* New York: Empire Books, 1983.

Zeitz, Joshua. *Building the Great Society: Inside Lyndon Johnson's White House.* New York: Penguin, 2019.

INDEX

Kenneth Whyte is the author of *Hoover: An Extraordinary Life in Extraordinary Times*, which was a finalist for the NBCC Award, and *The Uncrowned King: The Sensational Rise of William Randolph Hearst*, a *Washington Post* and *Toronto Globe and Mail* Book of the Year, and a nominee for the Los Angeles Times Book Award. He is publisher of Sutherland House Books, author of the *SHuSH* newsletter, and retired chairman of the Donner Canadian Foundation. A former telecommunications executive, he was editor in chief of *Maclean's* magazine, editor of *Saturday Night* magazine, and founding editor of the *National Post*. He lives in Toronto.

A NOTE ON THE TYPE

This book was set in Janson, a typeface long thought to have been made by the Dutchman Anton Janson, who was a practicing typefounder in Leipzig during the years 1668–1687. However, it has been conclusively demonstrated that these types are actually the work of Nicholas Kis (1650–1702), a Hungarian, who most probably learned his trade from the master Dutch typefounder Dirk Voskens. The type is an excellent example of the influential and sturdy Dutch types that prevailed in England up to the time William Caslon (1692–1766) developed his own incomparable designs from them.

Composed by North Market Street Graphics,
Lancaster, Pennsylvania

Printed and bound by Berryville Graphics,
Berryville, Virginia

Designed by Soonyoung Kwon